Dear Paul,

Well, as promised here it is, my cure to insomnia!

I am really delighted to send you a copy of the book I have co-authored and very much hope you find it interesting and useful. I'd like to think some of the concepts will help you through some of your future challenges.

I am proud to be able to call you a friend and have thoroughly enjoyed the discussions we have had on many Business issues.

Enjoy the read and utilise those that will help resolve issues you may have today.

All the very best

Lloyd

Praise for *Supercharged Supply Chains*

"As president over two separate turnaround situations, I fully implemented Business Excellence Planning, as described in the book, across both opportunities, which gave us the ability to focus, prioritize and ultimately execute the long-term vision of each company.

With a single set of integrated financials, utilized across every aspect of the business, we were also able to generate significant behavioral change that impacted consistent top and bottom-line performance while positively impacting employee engagement and company moral. The entire business operated on a rolling 36-month forecast which ultimately allowed customer service levels to improve from 73% to 99%, total inventory decreased by 31%, financial projections were consistently within forecasted levels and most importantly our business relationships with our customers improved significantly.

I fully endorse the 'Unparalleled Business Planning and Execution Practices' explained in this book."

Douglas Strohmeier, President, Covidien Ltd. TE Connectivity Ltd.

"*Supercharged Supply Chains* is a clear route to hyper-conductivity in your supply chain. This book details real life scenarios of extremely common business hazards. More important are the step-by-step, detailed maps to resolution. With this book and great leadership an organization can plan better those resources most critical to them."

Charlie Aspden, Head of S&OP, Hunter Boots

"*Supercharged Supply Chains* is a great read, especially for senior managers/leaders who generally need to do a much better job of sharing the vision of a well-run company. It is complete with real life examples to support the technical aspects of supply chain management. I will reference this book in future APICS courses and professional meetings and at the colleges I occasionally lecture or teach at."

Hank Barr, APICS Recognized Master Instructor, CPIM-F, CSCP, CLTD, AIPICS

"I have used the practices described in this book while VP of Finance at three totally different companies: (industrial), (consumer packaged goods), and (medical device manufacturing). We had incredible results following the recommendations in each case. I particularly like the chapter in the book that describes the role of finance throughout organization. The 'bottom line' for any company is whether they make a profit and generate positive cash flow. By following a fully integrated process outlined in this book, all companies can improve their profits and cash flow. This is a must read for the financial organization of a business to understand the benefits to be gained from being fully integrated."

John Frisco, VP Finance, Tyco Flow Control, Covidien (Retail Group), TE Connectivity (Medical Products).

SUPERCHARGED
SUPPLY CHAINS

OLIVER WIGHT

SUPERCHARGED
SUPPLY CHAINS

DISCOVER UNPARALLELED

BUSINESS PLANNING

AND EXECUTION PRACTICES

JAMES G. CORRELL | LLOYD C. SNOWDEN | JAMES BENTZLEY

WILEY

Published by John Wiley & Sons, Inc., Hoboken, New Jersey.

Published simultaneously in Canada.

For general information on our other products and services or for technical support, please contact our Customer Care Department within the United States at (800) 762-2974, outside the United States at (317) 572-3993 or fax (317) 572-4002.

Wiley publishes in a variety of print and electronic formats and by print-on-demand. Some material included with standard print versions of this book may not be included in e-books or in print-on-demand. If this book refers to media such as a CD or DVD that is not included in the version you purchased, you may download this material at http://booksupport.wiley.com. For more information about Wiley products, visit www.wiley.com.

Library of Congress Cataloging-in-Publication Data is Available:

ISBN 9781119782414 (Hardcover)
ISBN 9781119782438 (ePDF)
ISBN 9781119782421 (ePub)

COVER DESIGN: PAUL MCCARTHY
COVER ART: © ANUCHA SIRIVISANSUWAN | GETTY IMAGES

SKY10025345_030521

We dedicate this book to like-minded Leaders who are determined to make a difference and who are motivated to create the right environment for people, processes, and technology to be successful and sustainable. Leaders who, from this foundation, will continue the application of Unparalleled Business Planning and Execution Practices as their Maturity improves to establish a competitive and progressive Business and Business Model.

We would also like to reflect on Ollie Wight and remember his Thought Leadership, which has enabled so many managers and rising stars to become leaders in their own right.

Finally, we dedicate this book to all those Transformation Leaders as a tool to support their journeys to Business Planning Excellence.

Contents

Foreword

Why You Should Read This Book

This book is about what works – what works now, and what will work in the future.

It assumes you want to manage your business effectively: to get both tangible financial benefits and intangible benefits like improved control of the business.

At Oliver Wight, we keep a sharp eye out for advances to improve planning and execution systems. The new technologies such as blockchain, machine learning, image recognition, natural language processing, 3D printing, drones, and advances in autonomous vehicles have had enormous impact. But planning and execution systems are not high on the list of applications disrupted by these technologies.

Why is that?

Planning and execution systems work because they are a valid simulation of the real world. They are a model of the business inside a computer. In more recent terminology, they are a "digital twin."

Those things that represent a valid simulation of reality tend to be stable over time.

For example, the laws of thermodynamics were formulated in the nineteenth century. These laws were not the invention of a single person. Rather, they were the result of extensive experimentation and work by many leading scientists. The laws have not changed since. This is because the equations are a valid representation of the physical world – how heat behaves. The behavior of heat has not changed in the last century and a half, and it's not likely to change in the future.

Double-entry bookkeeping is another example. Franciscan friar Luca Pacioli published the first book on double-entry accounting in 1494. While Luca published the first book, many others contributed to the development. Five hundred years later, we're still using that system of debits and credits because it represents a valid simulation of a company's finances.

The systems and approaches described in this book are not fads or fashion. They are the bedrock of planning. That bedrock has not changed fundamentally because the underlying reality has not changed. We need to know what we are going to sell, what we have, what it takes to make it, and what we have to get in terms of material, equipment, and people.

Vince Lombardi, the renowned football coach of the Green Bay Packers in the 1960s, explained the bedrock idea succinctly: "Football is two things. It is blocking and tackling. I do not care about formations or new offenses or tricks on defense. You block and tackle better than the team you're playing, you win." Similarly, the approaches explained in this book are the "blocking and tackling." If you use them more effectively than your competitors, you will win.

Having a valid simulation of reality is not a magic bullet. As you will see in this book, a valid simulation of reality gives you a picture of the future. It is up to you to use that picture. If that picture, for example, shows a gap between your company's financial goals and what's likely to happen, it is up to you to figure out how to close that gap. Greater visibility gives you more time to make that happen. It does not automatically fix it.

Similarly, work continues to make a better picture of the future. How do we better anticipate the needs of our customers? How do we better anticipate the delays in our supplier network or within our own manufacturing facilities? All of these are worthwhile areas of experimentation with the goal of incrementally improving our simulation of reality.

I have worked directly with Oliver Wight for seven years before his death, and with two of the authors as part of the Oliver Wight organization. The authors have been where you are. They have done what you want to do.

Hopefully, I have some credibility with readers as I make this endorsement. I have been on the bleeding edge of these systems and the use of these systems for almost 50 years. Early on, I wrote the generally accepted software standard. Subsequently, my clients were the first in their industries to use the approaches explained in this book including pharmaceuticals, distribution, remanufacturing, textiles, shipbuilding, and retail.

You can have no better guides or advisors. I have great admiration for the authors. I hope you enjoy and benefit from their book.

Mr. Darryl Landvater

Introduction

Another book on turning supply chain processes into competitive advantage? Is that really needed?

Yes.

Because most companies today have the tools, but they are not using them well.

Ollie often used a golf analogy. You can have the best clubs money can buy, but if you cannot hit the ball, they are not going to do you much good. Similarly, you can have the best or most expensive software (they are not the same), but if people do not understand and know how to use the approaches explained in this book, it will not do you much good.

This is not unique to companies. The best safety device in aviation is a proficient crew at the controls.

It is now recognized that "Hard (numbers, plans) is Soft. Soft (people, relationships) is Hard."

For these reasons, one of the recurring themes throughout this book is the "soft" or people side of what it takes for you and your people to understand how to apply these approaches to your business.

Second only to people in importance is the accuracy of your information; specifically inventory records, bills of material, routings, and item information. While less exciting than a new algorithm, good accurate data is the bedrock. So, you'll see this as another recurring theme.

Another theme that runs through the book is the need for integration; stand-alone processes, functions, and people will never deliver their full potential until they are fully integrated and working together to achieve the desired direction and goals.

Businesses change, and when that happens, people have to understand how to revise what they have to do to take advantage of that change. This requires big-picture understanding like a pilot, not "more of the same" training. Unfortunately, in many companies, new people never really see the big picture and just do what the previous person in their job did.

Management is always looking for the silver bullet that will solve all of their problems. A new software feature or features that promise to solve a problem is more appealing than behavior change and data accuracy.

As Oliver Wight said many times, people and their behaviors are first, processes and accuracy are second, and tools such as software are third because you need to know what to specify before authorizing often huge investments.

Prelude: The Awakening

A major manufacturer's expert supply chain planning coach,[1] a long-time friend of the company President, was attending a meeting with his leadership team and plant managers through video conferencing. The purpose was to review the status of a project to improve company performance. As was the norm, the meeting degenerated into a detailed discussion of how to manage the master schedule to make it "valid" (accurate and achievable). The coach, there to observe and give guidance to the President, leaned over and whispered that they were "down in the weeds" again. The President immediately interjected and returned to the agenda. He said "clearly, the project will have more success when the education and workshops program has been delivered to Leadership, Middle Management, and Department Operating Teams; for now, the task at hand is to determine the required resources."

The coach, in despair, realized he was 10 years older than anyone else in the room and 30 years older than most. The resistance to change exhibited by the younger executives was amazing and disheartening to him. They were all protecting their areas and not thinking about how to make the company better – not a new observation for the coach. Most people initially resisted change, because as a young man he and others had to fight for improvements against people of a similar age and especially those more senior. Those memories and the successes he experienced, despite the initial resistance, made him smile. There was hope for this team.

The President was a believer because he and the coach had previously worked together in another company, years before, and experienced dramatic results. He was adamant that the company's planning and execution capabilities must be improved. The team had already come a long way but there was still resistance. Age is touted as an obstacle to change, but the coach knows it shares and applies knowledge, so education and its shared application is the key to successful and sustained change.

Studying the people, he realized that none of them had any formal education about how a company's planning and execution systems should work. His evidence, lack of effective planning, was causing missed customer deliveries due to shortages; excessive inventories; poor productivity in offices and the factories; new products not released on schedule; and, worst of all, poor morale everywhere. The coach smiled, as the reason was obvious to him. Typical of most companies, management had been promoted based on the "make it happen" philosophy – the best firefighter gets the job done and is rewarded. Their motto is, "Get it done NOW and maybe fix it later." Later never comes because emergencies occupy their attention. Success was not fueled by understanding how the company could be effective, but by their tenacious drive to get the job done and "put out the fire of the day . . . or hour." Put that drive and energy together with an understanding of the supply chain . . . then, you have a real winning company!

Shaking his head again, he wondered, why isn't there extensive education programs initiated to run businesses correctly? Would you go to a general practitioner doctor for brain surgery? Of course not; you would go to a doctor with a degree in brain surgery. Why would you delegate a company, employing thousands of people, to a team that has not been formally educated on using Unparalleled Business Planning and Execution Practices?[2]

The coach had experienced, in over 100 companies, the success of these Unparalleled Business Planning and Execution Practices in transforming companies, eliminating all these disruptive and costly issues. But some companies fail because their leadership just do not have the commitment or knowledge to implement these Practices.

So, what is missing in most companies that experience churn?

- Education and training on data integrity (inventory, bill of material accuracy, etc.)
- Education and training on Unparalleled Business Planning and Execution Practices (Integrated Business Planning, master scheduling, Material Requirements Planning (MRP), capacity planning, etc.)
- Commitment by Leadership to implement the learnings from the education.
- A focus on business as opposed to functional area optimization.

Reflecting on his nine years in industry with three different companies who implemented Unparalleled Business Planning and Execution Practices and his

33 years as a coach, he recognized that his clients did not understand or practice planning basics. When he started Consulting, he thought he might have 10–20 years of providing education and coaching before these business practices would become the norm, yet here he sat, 33 years later, with an even greater need for his skills.

Companies still did not understand or practice the basics and had often have less desire to learn. The attitude is either "just get it done" (at a huge cost in materials, operating cost, productivity, and the impact caused by stress), or "do the best you can" (a sure indicator of mediocrity, at best, for a company's future). Neither approach works. What happened to the companies that were successful? Some continue, but invariably a new leader who refuses to be educated immediately heads back to the "get it done mode" and things start to fall apart.

The coach reflected about how much more this company, or any company, could achieve with a solid understanding of Unparalleled Business Planning and Execution Practices and the commitment of leadership to drive the implementation. He sighed with relief, knowing that with his friend's leadership as President, this company would experience a successful transformation.

Jotting down some key thoughts for the education, the coach leaned over to the President whispering, "We have some work to do!" The President said, "Now you know why I called you."

Notes

1. We are firm believers that *coach* is the correct term because we don't want to do your work for you but coach you to do it. The practices stay in place even after the outside help leaves.
2. Since the inauguration of the Oliver Wight Companies in 1969 and through its global expansion, Ollie and his associates transferred knowledge and capabilities to companies that resulted in a published set of documented "Practices." During the past 50 years, these "Practices" have been continually enhanced and were captured originally in a series of Oliver Wight Class A Checklists, which evolved into today's globally recognized *The Oliver Wight Class A Standard for Business Excellence,* seventh edition. This Standard is a world-class benchmark of Unparalleled Business Planning and Execution Practices that can be applied in all industries, both manufacturing and service industries. It will continue to be enhanced as we work with the world's best companies.

List of Figures

CHAPTER 1

Churn: The Cause of Disruption

We hear more and more complaints about working in End-to-End Supply Chains,[1] and, even worse, we see more and more young people leaving and saying they are glad to have escaped. Throughout this book we will ex-

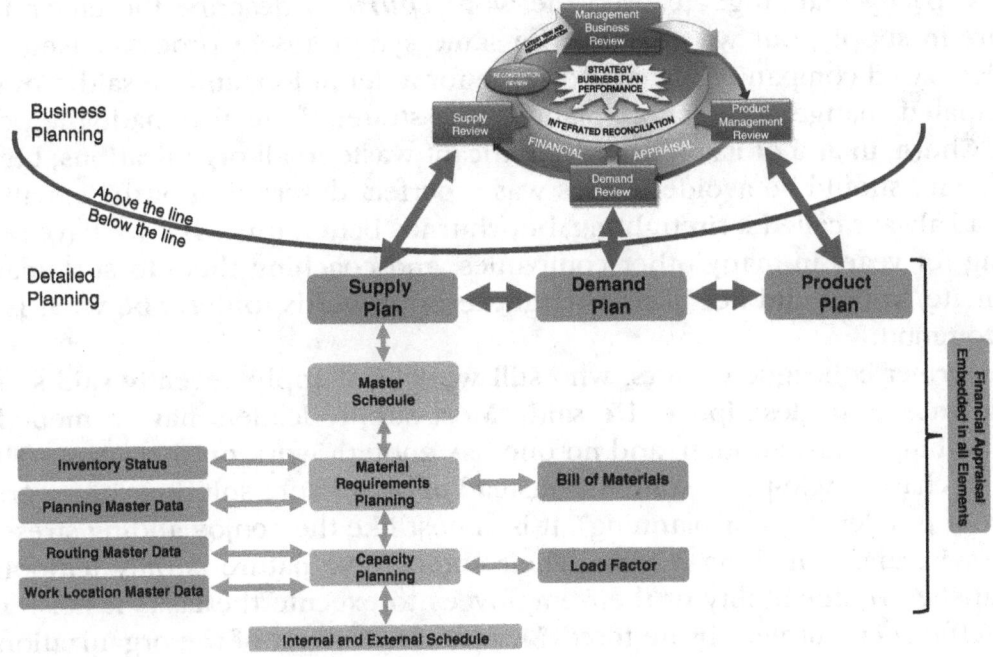

FIGURE 1.1 Business Excellence Planning

plore and identify the need to implement and use consistently Business Excellence Planning, Figure 1.1, through committed and engaged Leadership driving business processes with a team-based culture.

The youngest daughter of one of the authors recently said, after leaving a manufacturing company to start her own company, "I'm glad to be out of there! I do not mind working hard, but constantly scrambling because of poor planning and poor Leadership has caused me to be demotivated, tired, and frustrated. Instead of feeling any success I feel deflated and undervalued." What in the world is happening in companies? As one person told us, "You can never plan on anything because shortly after you arrive at work somebody drops a bomb in your planned daily schedule, and then you spend the rest of the day chasing your tail." All of the authors have experienced this, starting their careers many years ago, expecting things to get better over time, but, instead, seeing the disruption maintained or even getting worse.

A good term of reference to describe this constant disruption was not available until we met Wade Sheffer, the Managing Director at GM Ventures. As Oliver Wight coaches, we were doing an assessment at General Motors when we first met Wade, who at the time was the project leader for improving supplier capacity planning. He used the word *churn* to describe the chaos that occurs in supply, but we also see the same symptoms in process-based and service-based companies. We asked Wade for a definition, and he said, "An unanticipated change in direction, plan, and/or strategy." He also made the point that "Churn, in and of itself, drives significant waste in all organizations, big or small, and should be avoided." This was a perfect description of the situation. We had always called it firefighting, but churn is better. It is what we have been seeing for years in many other companies, and coaching them to sustainably eliminate, but we did not have the right term or words to describe what is all too common.

A former colleague of ours, who still works in Supply, recently said something even more descriptive. He said, "Most supply leaders have a mentality that nothing is fast enough, and no one has enough work on their plate. They tend to chase single-point solutions instead of big-picture solutions uncovering the root problems (poor planning). It is almost like they enjoy adding stress to the environment, making it toxic. Their competitive nature is only temporarily satisfied by the ability of their employees to execute the tasks faster – not with efficiency but with brute force. Meanwhile, the rest of the organization is operating less efficiently because of the churn." That is a brutal statement, but certainly describes the situation in too many companies.

Companies need an excellent planning process to thrive. Planning processes can only operate when they have accurate data, good information, and are managed properly. When someone does not do their job correctly and makes changes in isolation, their failure, lack of knowledge, and integration causes the plan to change, and the churn begins. When multiple people/departments drive errors into the planning process, the churn causes job dissatisfaction, consumes everyone, including customers, and erodes bottom-line results.

How does churn cause job dissatisfaction? Let us count the ways:

1. **Increases frustration:** not being able to do a quality job, few daily successes, and always dealing with issues.
2. **Undermines job satisfaction:** feeling bad at the end of the day; we all need some success.
3. **Lack of recognition:** even when you do something right, it is overwhelmed by the bad things that have happened.
4. **Constant belittling and bullying:** because you seem to be blamed for all the things that go wrong, being tired increases the possibility for more human error.
5. **Being overworked:** spending long hours trying to make things right in the middle of churn.
6. **Unacceptable attitude:** giving up trying to make things right and just getting through the day; not feeling valued.
7. **Lack of understanding and listening:** up and down the organization.
8. **Tell and do:** an environment with no empowerment or delegated authority; we're just a number.
9. **Eroding teamwork:** driving people to be individualistic and not team members often results in blame.

Many readers will have experienced at least some of these during their career. Jim Correll distinctly remembers one of the worst periods of his career:

I had just moved from Quality Control Manager to Machine Shop Manager. My new boss said that the General Manager had forced him to take me, and told me that I would not survive three months. I was told the reason the job was vacant was because the previous manager did not have a "sense of

FIGURE 1.2 Supply Chain Personnel – Frustration

urgency." Every day started with prepping with the Scheduler, for the 1½ hour shortage meeting. The Machine Shop had between 100 and 200 shortages every day and we were expected to give dates for resolution of each of the shortages with delivery within a day or two. I struggled with my Scheduler because he certainly did not have a "sense of urgency," but he was not the one being dragged over the coals during the meeting because the dates were never good enough. Name calling and anger occurred every day, and I bore the brunt of most of it. My machine shop made a lot of gears for the assemblies; many of these gears had 10-plus operations, meaning long Supply Lead Times. Being on the receiving end of the anger and name calling was not fun! [Recognize the "Face of Churn" in Figure 1.2.] One morning the Scheduler did not show up until I was already en route to the shortage meeting. At the shortage meeting the usual berating started and, since I did not have dates for many of the items, it was even worse. At this point, I had had enough and responded with a "will advise" for all the shortage items, even those for which I had dates. It was clear that I was upset and was not to be messed with that morning. The bullied person suddenly turned into the bully. My boss looked at me and said, "Well, it looks like you might make it after all." I was just praised for my bad behavior.

This story has a happy ending. Six months later, the company had installed an excellent planning system, as we describe in the following chapters, and we implemented them in the Machine Shop. Unfortunately, the other production managers had not implemented the Unparalleled Business Planning and Execution Practices. One morning, instead of showing up early to the shortage meeting, I hid out of sight until it started. When my boss said, "Where's Correll?" I stepped in and said, "I have no reason to attend today." Before my boss could explode, I said, "I do not have any shortages." He looked at the rest of the people in the meeting and said, "If the rest of you performed like Correll, we would not have to have this meeting!" Not exactly his words, because I have removed his expletives. Did we have shortage meetings after the rest of the production department implemented the Unparalleled Business Planning and Execution Practices? Yes – but they were 10 minutes with no "bull," belittling, and name calling; just action plans to handle the few potential delays. These new shortage sessions became the norm.

A different type of churn was demonstrated one Christmas at a well-known frozen food confectionery. The last production before the Christmas shutdown was a chocolate torte with a thick layer of cream on top. This was a top seller, produced every 10 days or so. During the manufacturing run, the operation ran out of cream. Upon investigation, it was discovered that cream was not in the system's torte recipe. The last recipe change recorded was 18 months earlier. How could this be the case? The torte was made every 10 days. As it turned out, every 10 days there was insufficient cream. Every 10 days production chased the warehouse and the warehouse chased purchasing and purchasing chased the supplier. Every 10 days the supplier reacted, pulling forward the next day's cream delivery. Consequently, the day after torte production, there was a shortage of cream, and the same churn re-occurred. The cream scheduler was provided a message from the system to purchase more cream and obliged. At the end of the month a variance was reported. Everyone blamed everyone else, but it was "just the way it is here" and the root cause was hidden by many other causes of churn. No one had the time to find the cause, because they were consumed by coping with it and other shortages.

At another company, the shortage meeting was referred to as the "daily prayer meeting." It got its name because those who had to attend prayed for a suitable answer.

At yet another company, the leader of the shortage meeting had a fantastic solution: "Let's get it automated!" When we suggested that the right solution would be to eliminate the shortages, he said, "Never been done in my time and never will be!" Maybe his experience drove him to think he was right; however, once he understood the solution, he realized that spending less than 15 minutes to be sure everything was integrated drove his shortages down. This has been done in many companies that followed the Unparalleled Business Planning/Execution Practices.

So, how can we solve churn? To fix churn, Leadership must recognize the problem, have a vision of life without churn, and be committed to eliminating it. Oliver Wight illustrated commitment by explaining the difference in participation between a chicken and a pig for breakfast. He said the chicken was involved and the pig was committed! Knowledgeable commitment is what is required by Leadership to achieve the required behavior changes because so many areas must perform well in order to achieve Class A. What gets measured gets done and can be managed more effectively; the Class A Standard provides the recommended measures.

The term *Class A* has been mentioned several times. This is a good time to provide a definition to understand Class A and its relationship to Business Maturity. The concept of Business Maturity has been around since the early 1990s, when the Oliver Wight organization was invited by Harvard Business School to commercialize a theoretical study they had completed on Beretta, the Italian gun company, that had won an order to supply the United States Army with weapons, in preference to Smith & Wesson.

This resulted in the Four Phases of Business Maturity (see Figure 1.3), which Oliver Wight continues to use to benchmark companies, following an Oliver Wight assessment of their processes, procedures, culture, and performance:

Phase 1: As a company progresses from the bottom to the top of Phase 1, behaviors, processes, and tools are improved sufficiently to gain control and eliminate unplanned events, thus delivering a minimum performance level of 95% for schedules that are completed on time within agreed time and quantity tolerances.

FIGURE 1.3 Business Maturity – Four Phases

Source: © Oliver Wight International.

Phase 2: Once Phase 1 has been achieved and can be sustained, the next step on the journey is simplification and removal of process waste, while increasing customer service levels. At the top of Phase 2, companies operate at a Six Sigma 250 parts per million defect opportunities.

Phase 3: Phase 3 focuses on taking knowledge-based business processes and, where appropriate (based on the required investment and market needs), automates them to further increase velocity and reduce the need for manual intervention. This results in a further step change in performance. Phase 3 maturity must be defined and agreed for each company, according to their strategy, business plan, and strategic business objectives.

Phase 4: Finally, in Phase 4, automated business processes are fully integrated with technology; this is often characterized by "lights-out factories," where robots have replaced traditional blue-collar teams. Again, this change in maturity must be based on competitive advantage as well as a cost-effective response to customer needs and a real understanding of the value they require.

Business Maturity has also "matured" since the Beretta case study and has seen many of the attributes of Phases 3 and 4 collapse into Phases 1 and 2. As the world moves on with ever-increasing technological advances, Maturity must reflect this progress. Consequently, Phases 1 and 2 today include, within their scope, automation and integration, effectively meaning that Phases 3 and

4 have become more of a focus on market and technology disruptors, especially those that a company must focus on to support their strategic goals. The Oliver Wight organization, as the Thought Leaders of Business Maturity, are constantly reviewing Business Maturity and the associated Maturity Transitions, as is done with all the material, so they are often updated to reflect current trends and thinking.

Oliver Wight's message over the years has evolved to enable a focus in the first two Phases of Business Maturity to drive KPI performance levels to near-perfection at the top of Phase 2. At this maturity level, use of percentages at 98% is not beneficial. Therefore, performance is discussed in terms of Six Sigma and the use of Statistical Process Control techniques.

Oliver Wight is a learning organization and through this approach has been thought leaders in the development and implementation of Detailed and Business Planning approaches. For 50 years the Detailed Planning hierarchy shown in Figure 1.1 has been refined and optimized with all the elements displayed playing a key role. MRPI and MRPII (Manufacturing Resource Planning), from their original conception in the early 1970s, were the basis for this evolution, and the resulting structures for detailed planning work best when they are all used as shown.

A more detailed and general description of business maturity from the bottom of Phase 1 to the top of Phase 2 are outlined in Figure 1.4.

Churn is the state of being in an organization that is operating at the bottom of Phase 1.

So, if you are a company somewhere toward the bottom of Phase 1, you have significant opportunities for improvement. Often companies have Phase 1 Business Maturity but still generate significant profit. This is often due to the market accepting very high prices that cover the inefficiencies of the processes delivering the customers' products. Oliver Wight's position is that profitability is often an enemy of excellence.

From Figure 1.4, improvement is effectively a journey, and companies need to transition from one level of maturity to the next. For a journey from the bottom of Phase 1 to the top of Phase 2, a company will travel through five transitions, which are shown in Figure 1.5. Understanding transitions is very important, as a company cannot just jump from Transition 1 (the bottom of Phase 1) to Transition 3 (the top of Phase 1) as it will not be sustainable because the foundations provided by Transition 2 have not been established and achieved. Figure 1.4 shows a general picture for the journey; however, Oliver

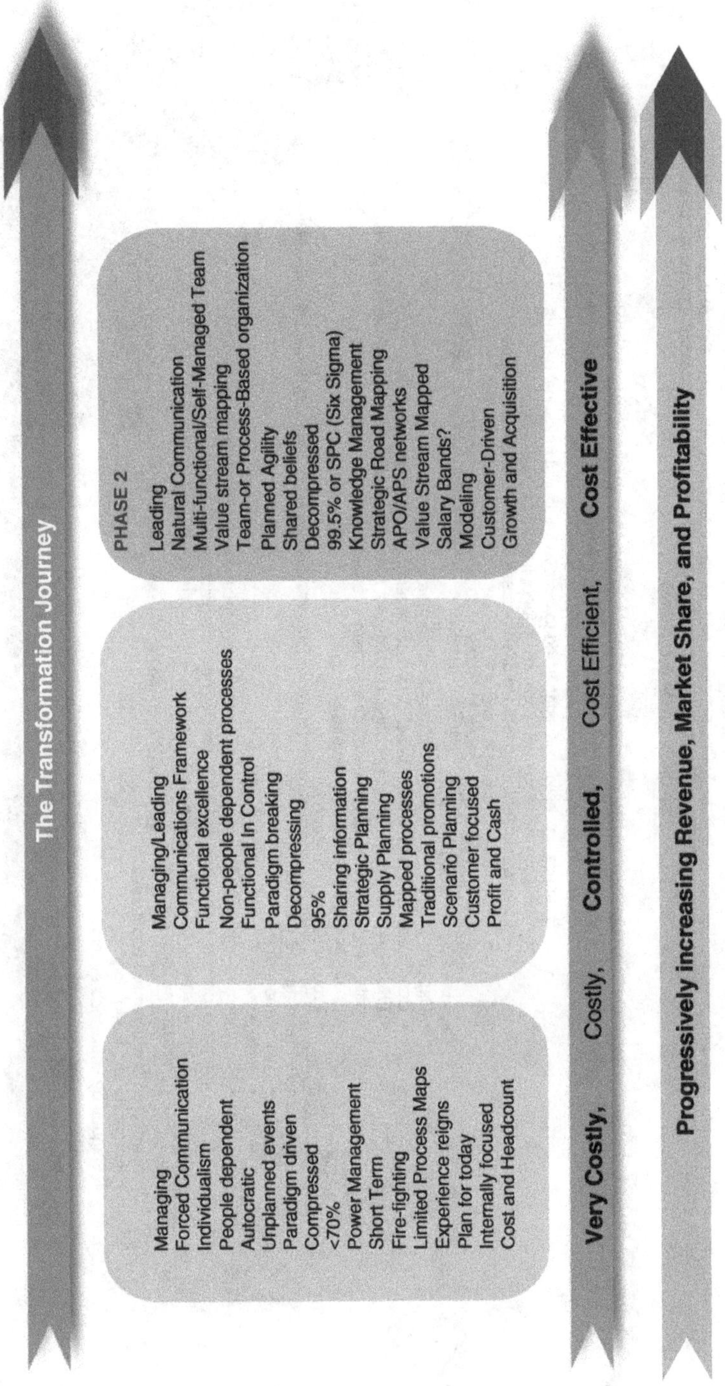

The Transformation Journey

Managing
Forced Communication
Individualism
People dependent
Autocratic
Unplanned events
Paradigm driven
Compressed
<70%
Power Management
Short Term
Fire-fighting
Limited Process Maps
Experience reigns
Plan for today
Internally focused
Cost and Headcount

Managing/Leading
Communications Framework
Functional excellence
Non-people dependent processes
Functional In Control
Paradigm breaking
Decompressing
95%
Sharing information
Strategic Planning
Supply Planning
Mapped processes
Traditional promotions
Scenario Planning
Customer focused
Profit and Cash

PHASE 2

Leading
Natural Communication
Multi-functional/Self-Managed Team
Value stream mapping
Team-or Process-Based organization
Planned Agility
Shared beliefs
Decompressed
99.5% or SPC (Six Sigma)
Knowledge Management
Strategic Road Mapping
APO/APS networks
Value Stream Mapped
Salary Bands?
Modeling
Customer-Driven
Growth and Acquisition

Very Costly,   Costly,   Controlled,   Cost Efficient,   Cost Effective

Progressively increasing Revenue, Market Share, and Profitability

FIGURE 1.4 General Descriptions of Phase 1 to Phase 2 Business Maturity

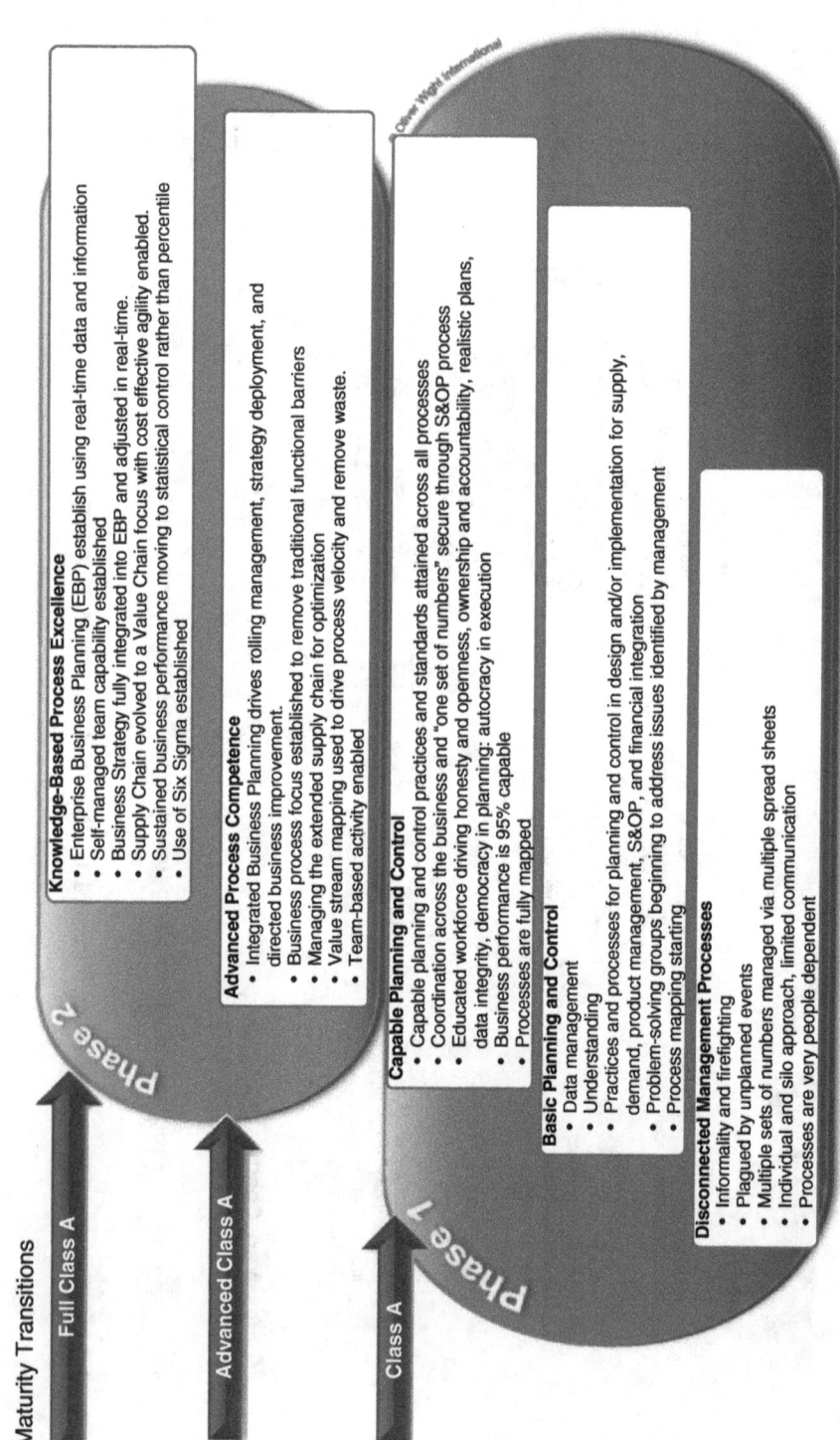

Maturity Transitions

Full Class A

Advanced Class A

Class A

Phase 2

Phase 1

Oliver Wight International

Knowledge-Based Process Excellence
- Enterprise Business Planning (EBP) establish using real-time data and information
- Self-managed team capability established
- Business Strategy fully integrated into EBP and adjusted in real-time.
- Supply Chain evolved to a Value Chain focus with cost effective agility enabled.
- Sustained business performance moving to statistical control rather than percentile
- Use of Six Sigma established

Advanced Process Competence
- Integrated Business Planning drives rolling management, strategy deployment, and directed business improvement.
- Business process focus established to remove traditional functional barriers
- Managing the extended supply chain for optimization
- Value stream mapping used to drive process velocity and remove waste.
- Team-based activity enabled

Capable Planning and Control
- Capable planning and control practices and standards attained across all processes
- Coordination across the business and "one set of numbers" secure through S&OP process
- Educated workforce driving honesty and openness, ownership and accountability, realistic plans, data integrity, democracy in planning: autocracy in execution
- Business performance is 95% capable
- Processes are fully mapped

Basic Planning and Control
- Data management
- Understanding
- Practices and processes for planning and control in design and/or implementation for supply, demand, product management, S&OP, and financial integration
- Problem-solving groups beginning to address issues identified by management
- Process mapping starting

Disconnected Management Processes
- Informality and firefighting
- Plagued by unplanned events
- Multiple sets of numbers managed via multiple spread sheets
- Individual and silo approach, limited communication
- Processes are very people dependent

FIGURE 1.5 The Journey – Through Phases 1 and 2

Wight has developed Maturity Transitions for some 35 to 40 key business processes that are used to support an improvement or transformation journey in more detail for specific business requirements. Figure 1.5 shows one example.

From the early 1970s, clients frequently asked Oliver Wight himself, "How well are we doing?" That question became the catalyst for developing the first Checklist. In its initial version it was a single piece of paper listing 20 questions to be answered "yes" or "no" by the client. If all questions were answered "yes," the client was confirmed as being in "good shape."

Since that initial version of the Checklist, there have been six further evolutions, bringing us up to date with *The Oliver Wight Standard for Business Excellence*, seventh edition (Figure 1.6).

FIGURE 1.6 The Oliver Wight Class A Standard for Business Excellence

In contrast to the first version's 20 questions, the seventh edition has nine chapters, which include approximately 750 Business Maturity definitions and descriptions that are positioned at the top of Phase 2.

The Standard today is too expansive to be implemented in a single improvement initiative. To enable a laser-like focus on business processes that are in the greatest need of improvement, the Class A Standard has been organized into Class A Milestones; these are explained in more detail in Chapter 19, Implementation.

Now, let us go back to the topic of churn and consider some of its fundamental causes.

Inventory Accuracy: When an item quantity of 10 is received but the transaction incorrectly records 100 (see Figure 1.7), the planning system believes that 100 have been received and does not recommend reordering until it calculates that the 100 in inventory will be depleted. However, when the 11th unit is needed, churn begins in earnest. The Material Planner must break their daily routine to expedite an emergency order for the item. If it is an externally sourced item and there is a material shortage, Purchasing must jump through hoops to get the material delivered. When Production gets the material, they will suboptimize their schedule to make the part while under constant pressure from their internal customer, the assembly area. The result is that the build schedule will not be completed on time and Customer Service will miss a customer shipment. Churn has started!

FIGURE 1.7 The Need for Trusted Data Accuracy

Bill of Material Accuracy: Consider the same part. The Bill of Material states usage of one part per assembly, but the assembly requires two. Because the part is normally ordered in large quantities, the incorrect Bill of Material is not usually a problem; Assembly knows of the error and keeps extra parts at the assembly line. But when there is a large assembly order and the part inventory is low, churn begins. Like the inventory accuracy example, everyone blames everyone else, but the real issue, Bill of Material accuracy, is never addressed. Churn spreads geometrically! Churn can be even worse when companies use an engineering design bill instead of Bills of Material structured for Supply, owned by Supply and constantly updated to reflect reality.

Material Planner: A Material Planner who is not properly educated, trained, or managed simply react to individual planning system messages and not consider the bigger picture. This frequently leads to changes in safety stock settings, on all items, because of a shortage; add to this Leadership pressure to reduce material inventory, then churn never ends. Because of the churn, the Material Planner receives thousands of planning system messages daily, in this case to "reschedule in," which causes the Planner to expedite these parts. At the same time, the Planner could also receive thousands of messages to "reschedule out," which the Planner ignores. John Proud, a highly regarded manufacturing process educator and Oliver Wight Principal, emphases that "reschedule out" messages should be prioritized. Why? Because this provides the capacity to successfully execute the reschedule-in messages. Since they cannot possibly respond to 2,000-plus messages, Planners do the 'best they can' which is usually to react only to the reschedule-in messages and leave the other messages uncleared in the system. Because the planners are only maintaining part of the planning system this leads to ever increasing 'Churn'. Without the time to correctly analyze the re-schedule in messages it is only a matter of time before some of this become a shortage, then Leadership becomes involved causing everybody to scramble around even more, hence 'Churn' accelerates.

Master Scheduler: If a Master Scheduler position exists[3] but the individual does not fully understand the primary purpose of Master Scheduling (i.e., matching supply to demand), then churn will explode. Matching supply to demand means the Master Scheduler takes control away from the planning system for all orders (planned, firm planned, and released) out through the cumulative lead time. How does the

Master Scheduler demonstrate they are in control? By decoupling supply from demand. When a demand requirement suddenly appears inside the agreed-upon lead time, the Master Scheduler should investigate whether it can be accepted as requested through discussions with Internal Supply and/or External Sourcing to see if the new requirement can be achieved. Every time the Master Scheduler releases an order inside lead time without first ensuring availability from Internal Supply and/or External Sourcing, churn begins. Sometimes it affects only a few items, but when exploded through the Bill of Material it could affect thousands of items and result in countless reschedule-in and reschedule-out action/exception messages that overwhelm Material Planners. Churn explodes!

Integrated Business Planning: Where there is an Integrated Business Planning (IBP)[4] process in place, it must be owned and driven by Leadership with a focus on decision-making extending out into the future, far enough to enable long-range decisions, such as equipment acquisition or physical facility changes – typically the horizon is 4 to 24 or 36 months. When required decisions out through this time frame are not identified, resolved, and implemented with adequate lead time, they become near-term crises. This leads to churn of the greatest volume and business impact. It is like a set of gears with one large gear (IBP), a medium size gear (Master Schedule), and a small gear (MRP). One half revolution of the large gear sends the smallest gear flying. The large gear represents Leaderships decisions, and the smallest gear represents Material Planning, External Sourcing, and Internal Supply. Living in a reactive company culture, instead of a proactive change culture, is the norm when Leadership does not understand the impact of its decisions to change aggregate plans without adequately planning lead time. The old mindset of just "do your best to make it happen" just does not work anymore. Changes without understanding the impact causes unmanageable churn!

Demand Planning: The Demand Plan starts off as an Unconstrained Demand Plan (see the Demand Planning chapter) that Sales and Marketing bring to Integrated Business Planning monthly. When the Supply Chain confirms it can support the unconstrained plan, and it is approved by the owner of the IBP process, the President, it becomes the new, approved Demand Plan.

The process of Demand Management starts with understanding market assumptions, including prices and volumes, and the development of an Aggregate Demand Plan by product family, by month over the full planning horizon of 4 to 24 or 36 months before worrying about the detail of end items and their resulting financials. Next, following plan approval, is the detailed demand for the end items. There is now a focus on options by week, by ship point, and on the near term, normally three to four months, in both volume and financial terms.

One of our clients demonstrated accuracy within ±0.5% in dollars every month but only 76% accuracy by mix of end items.[5] Accurate Demand Planning, especially planning the mix, is one of the most difficult tasks to perform in any company, but it drives all supporting plans. Nobody gets a perfect forecast except by sheer luck, but good, reliable, and useful forecasts are achievable. Companies that use only algorithms to predict the future based on past results never achieve good forecasts at the end item level and are also seldom successful at aggregate levels. Algorithms provide a useful starting point for a Demand Plan, but incorporating input from Product Managers, Sales Representatives, Marketing, Customers, and any other sources that can provide insight to the cause of demand, will result in the best Aggregate Demand Plans and detailed end item forecasts and schedules.

By formally identifying and tracking assumptions, risks, and opportunities for each product family, the entire demand picture can be seen, the best decisions can be made resulting in the most accurate forecasts possible. With clear knowledge and understanding around the assumptions that have been incorporated, documented, and communicated, the Supply Chain can appropriately prepare to support the Demand Plan. Inaccurate and disjointed Demand Plans drive churn into Integrated Business Planning and throughout the End-to-End Supply Chain. As stated earlier, there are no perfect forecasts, but improving accuracy and having a good understanding of what has been factored in gives Leadership, Master Schedulers, and MRP Planners an opportunity to provide the safety stocks and safety capacities required to protect against any demand and supply variation.

In brief, the Demand Plan needs to be a clear statement of what is believed will happen in the marketplace over the planning horizon and the plan has been developed based on "truth as we know it." Then churn will be reduced significantly (Figure 1.8).

FIGURE 1.8 Reduce Churn

As you read this you might think that Wade Sheffer, who was quoted earlier, and others mentioned, along with the authors, do not like Supply Chain organizations or people. That is not true at all. In fact, we love helping companies with the challenges they face. There are solutions, all of them proven time and again, for every problem. You can never eliminate churn completely but resolving the underlying issues that you can control will ensure that the amount of churn is reduced to a fraction of what it was. This will ensure that there is a stable and manageable environment. As you read the remaining chapters, you will find solutions to all the churn and problems identified earlier, and many more. The solutions often require a change in the culture of the company and always require good discipline. That kind of change must be led and driven by Leadership. Education to understand the "why" and training to understand the "how" are required to sustainably reduce churn to a minimal level, if not eliminate it.

Summary

To get people to want to stay in End-to-End Supply Chains, there must be a change in how they operate. Being bullied to perform better is not acceptable, and making money is a requirement of all businesses. The rest of the chapters explain how to create a workplace that performs at an extremely high level with an environment that allows people to perform at their highest levels and to go home with a feeling of satisfaction and of a job well done.

For additional but more specific reading please visit the Oliver Wight Website and gain access to the extensive library of White Papers.

Notes

1. The End-to-End Supply Chain includes Customers, Sales, Marketing, Engineering, Planning, Production, Purchasing, Suppliers, Warehousing, and Distribution; see Chapter 14.
2. "Doing the best you can" is for Little League. In business and manufacturing it is not acceptable. Ask your customer when the shipment shows up late if "We did the best we could" is an acceptable response. Successful companies discover the problem, find a solution, and then implement it (too many companies are still not as successful as they should be).
3. All companies need a Master Scheduler, and, in many companies, there is a need for multiple Master Schedulers. Master Scheduling is not a clerical job; a Master Scheduler's most important skill is the ability to communicate with all the functional resource managers the reasons (such as requirements driven by IBP, resource limitations identified by RCCP, etc.) supporting or justifying the what, when, and how much product is required per period in the Master Schedule.
4. All companies need a properly operating Integrated Business Planning (Advanced Sales and Operations Planning) process.
5. 76% forecast accuracy by Master Scheduled item is close to world class according to Institute of Business Forecasting benchmarking. This high level of accuracy was achieved because the client followed the Unparalleled Business Planning and Execution Practices recommendations.

CHAPTER 2

Get the Basics Right: Eliminate the Churn

A constant and common complaint about planning systems is that the information is not accurate, not realistic, and the planning system is overly nervous (it sends so many exception messages that planners cannot work

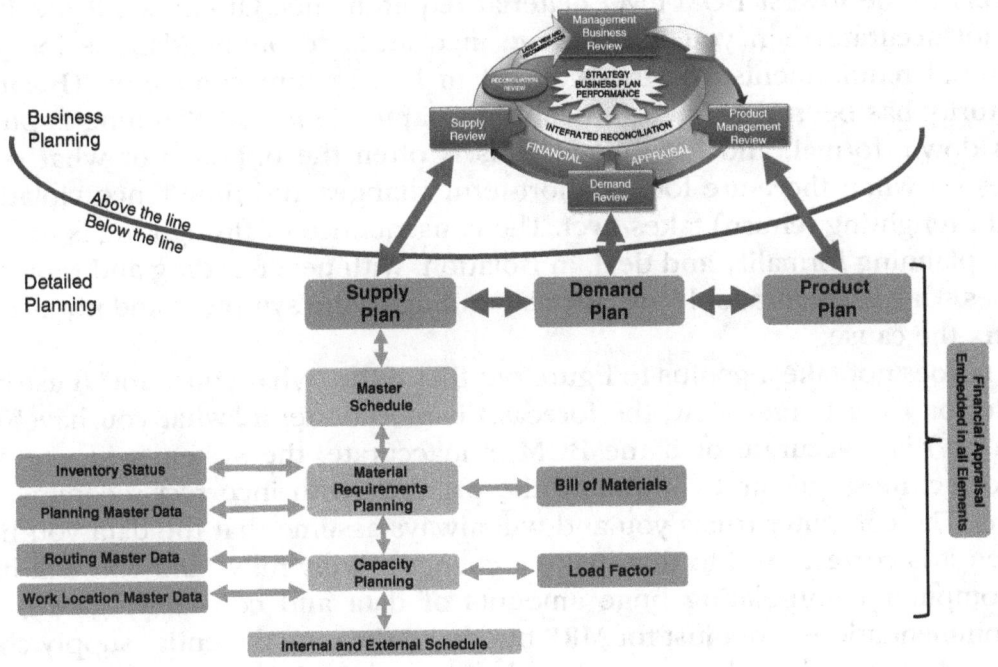

FIGURE 2.1 Business Excellence Planning

with them all). That is ironic since the first Material Requirement Planning (MRP) system was built on the very simple and sound logic of exploding dependent demand down through the bill of material into material requirements. Dr. Joseph Orlicky was the guru of the original system implemented in 1961 at the J. I. Case Company. Oliver Wight made it famous by simplifying the explanation of the process so Leadership and Middle Management could understand its power, how it works, and how it should be used. For instance, Ollie would say that the basic logic of MRP is simple: "Tell me what you want, what you have, and I will tell you what to get." The actual calculation is simple, perfectly accurate, and the outcome will not change no matter how many times you run the computer through recalculations of the plan. Planning in this manner is formal and top down, as depicted by Figure 2.1, Business Excellence Planning.

But change the "what you want" or "what you have" and the system will recalculate what you need to get. If the data in the system is not accurate, you will get an incorrect recommendation. What Ollie did not include in his basic logic, but knew, was that if you have a multi-level Bill of Material (BOM), the system will calculate the need for all items very accurately, level by level, until it gets to the lowest BOM-level material requirements. Of course, if the BOM is not accurate then you will receive inaccurate recommendations for your material requirements. Another conflict in less mature companies (Business Maturity has been described in detail in Chapter 1) is that Planning is purely top down, formal, and disciplined. This is often the opposite of what really goes on when there are lots of short-term changes and time fence violations and firefighting (churn) takes over. The consequence of firefighting is to override planning formality and deal, in isolation, with never-ending and repeating crises. This is when people are just responding to the symptom and not driving to fix the cause.

It does not take a genius to figure out that if the "what you want" (customer order or, for a longer view, the forecast) is inaccurate; if "what you have" (inventory) is inaccurate or if the BOM is inaccurate, the system will give you incorrect messages and compound the problem with incorrect recommendations. The computer trusts you and will always assume that the data you have given it is correct. Add to that making changes "willy-nilly" and you will have a computer manipulating huge amounts of data and constantly giving bad recommendations – not just for MRP but down through the entire supply chain network. Remember, the system is only as good as the way you use it. If the data is wrong, the system cannot correct it. Ultimately, a planning system is needed because there are thousands of transactions processed continuously; the system is effectively a huge calculator that will simply "multiply" errors if inputs to the system are inaccurate. The bottom line is there are two basic requirements: first, the data in the system must be accurate, and second, leadership and management must understand how the system is to be used and hold people accountable for doing just that. Listed next are the subsets of each of these.

Data Accuracy (see chart at end of this chapter for measurement requirements)
- **Inventory**
- **Bills of Material** (Recipe, Formula, Ingredients, depending on your business)
- **Planning Item Master**
- **Work Location Master Data**, process line Item Masters
- **Routing Master Data**

Planning and Scheduling Management
- **Integrated Business Planning (IBP)**
- **Demand Planning**
- **Product and Portfolio Planning**
- **Master Scheduling**
- **Material Requirements Planning**
- **Capacity Planning**
- **Internal and External Schedules** (factory and suppliers)
- **Financials** (involved at every level)

Additional Business Excellence Planning Information

As shown in Figure 2.1, Business Excellence Planning is divided into two sections: Business Planning and Detailed Planning. We often call it "above the line" and "below the line," as indicated. Above the line is primarily the responsibility of Leadership and Senior Management and below the line is the responsibility of Middle Management. The MBR is the Management Business Review, the culmination of each month's Integrated Business Planning (IBP) process in which high-level decisions are made (based on trusted recommendations) to ensure that the company is aligned and stays aligned to its communicated Business and Strategic Plans; see Chapter 8.

Figure 2.1 shows all the elements necessary to make formal planning operate properly and how data and information must be used to make the End-to-End Supply Chain perform effectively and efficiently. Later in the book, we discuss each element to describe *what* must be done and *how* to do it.

There should be no surprises in the above discussion. It makes complete sense, yet our estimate is that 98% of companies do not address all of these processes and, therefore, have Planning and Scheduling systems that are not performing to the level they are capable of and are not providing the benefits expected when purchased. Because of the shortages (and overages and wasted money and effort) that occur as a result of underperforming MRP computer systems, leadership is often pulled in to assist with the firefighting and, more often than not, actually drive it, doing the work that middle managers are paid to do! This is a very common situation referred to as "eyes down and look in." The company needs to gain the control needed to enable eyes to "look up and look out." With eyes down and looking in, companies do not address the cause of data issues that drive the churn because they do not understand the following:

- **Importance:** How important accurate data is.
- **Cost-effective methods:** To achieve and maintain minimum accuracy levels.
- **Shared knowledge:** How much is required by the people using the processes
- **Formality and Discipline:** How to maintain and leverage the system.
- **Integration** How to ensure integrated plans are developed and used.
- **How to manage:** Using a valid (accurate and achievable) plan and planning system.

We have observed, many times, companies that started with low data accuracy and followed our advice reached extremely high levels of accuracy quickly and sustainably, and then provided more trusted information to support decisions. In addition, they went on to enable operating areas to run with fewer people than originally required with much lower cost levels, resulting in the progressive elimination of firefighting.

The management of data accuracy and planning will be covered in detail in later chapters describing how to implement the required process improvements and the required measures, and how to calculate performance to drive improvement.

Data Is the Foundation

Data is the foundation of the pyramid, with the next level being Information based on the data. The next level is Knowledge enabled by the information, with the top level being Wisdom, enabled by the wise use of the knowledge to make good decisions.

Where to Start Improving Data Accuracy

The easy answer is everywhere. This is not as absurd as it might sound. In most cases the resources that work on the each of the elements of Business Excellence Planning are different. The resources required to resolve inventory accuracy issues are different from those required to improve accuracy of BOMs, routings, Planning Master Data, Work Location Master Data, and so on, making it indeed possible to address these simultaneously. The education and training covering each of these areas is acquired separately, except for a general overview, which ensures that all employees have the same understanding as to why their specific data element is so important in reducing churn. This, in turn, will drive a standard approach to achieving and maintaining data accuracy.

But every improvement initiative is as different as the people involved, because at lower levels of maturity the company is people dependent, not

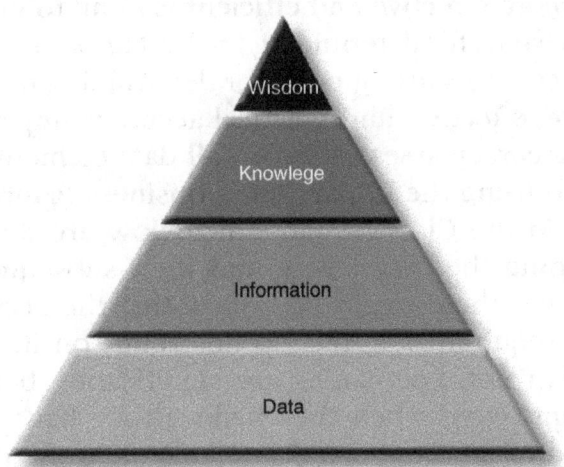

FIGURE 2.2 Data Accuracy Is the Foundation for Information, Knowledge, and Wisdom

FIGURE 2.3 Data Accuracy – Focus and Ownership Are Essential

process enabled. As companies mature and people across various functions become more integrated and informed, then knowledge tends to be ingrained within processes, and the company becomes less people (personality, individual knowledge, and power management) dependent. We have experienced divisions of the same large company right down the street from each other requiring different process improvement approaches. However, a standard data accuracy approach facilitates learning and knowledge transfer as people move between divisions. Organizing data accuracy improvement initiatives, keeping this in mind, is far more effective and efficient leading to greater benefits.

Following are the steps for determining the best approach for your company:

Scope the project: The starting point for determining the best approach for developing complete, effective, and practical accuracy improvement initiatives is a thorough data accuracy assessment, for all data elements. This assessment should be conducted using the Unparalleled Business Planning and Execution Practices identified in the Class A Standard. Below are the four elements to consider when scoping the assessment and then subsequently defining the projects. In some areas there might be a view that the accuracy is above the minimum accuracy requirements, but do not count on it. Our experience is that, more often than not, companies are significantly below the minimum accuracy requirements even when they believe they have good accuracy, so they incorrectly tend to ignore those data elements in the project plan scope, a big mistake.

1. **Measurements:** The evaluation begins with accuracy audits to measure the status of each of the data elements. These measurements are quite simple; for instance, inventory accuracy is determined by checking a specific location to see if the part number is correct, the quantity is correct, the location is correct, and any other required data elements are correct. If even one of those elements is incorrect, that location is recorded as inaccurate. An essential assumption is that the auditors do not correct the record to influence a higher accuracy result.
   As an example:
   Consider inventory accuracy; the final calculation for the inventory record accuracy (IRA) audit is:

   $$\text{Inventory accuracy} = \frac{\text{Number of correct locations}\,(\text{quantity and location})}{\text{Number of locations checked}}$$

   If that number is greater than 95% (see the chart at end of this chapter) or 100% for finished product locations, then the *minimum accuracy requirement* is achieved, and the planning system will operate effectively regarding this data element. You may not need to audit many locations. If after 20 locations you are at 50% accuracy, you know you have a significant accuracy issue. Accuracy audits and measures for other data elements are discussed later in this book.

2. **Staffing:** Once you know the accuracy level of all data elements in an operating area, you can determine the magnitude of the problem. Some areas can address their accuracy gaps with current staffing, but often, for those data elements with very low accuracy, additional resources are required to "get over the hump." Remembering the previous statement that fewer people are needed to run the business as churn is eliminated, how you staff the improvement "resource hump" is important. To manage each piece of the data accuracy improvement project, you must select the very best people. The question then is how to replace that person or persons in running the day-to-day business. To resolve the issues quickly and sustainably, select the best person (probably the area supervisor) to lead the improvement project. To replace the leader, elevate the next best person in the hierarchy until you get to the bottom level of the hierarchy. If additional resources are needed, hire temporary employees to do the simplest and most redundant

required activities. There are lots of reasons for this approach, but the most important is that the change in general is about developing new processes which people typically resist. Their involvement/commitment in designing new processes is the best way to ensure success. These changes are as much culture changes as they are process changes. Culture changes must start with Leadership and progressively flow throughout the organization. If the additional staffing requirements are more than you can absorb immediately, simply focus first on the data elements with the worst audit accuracy results and then move to the next. This prioritization is also an element of Leadership that is missing; in many companies they simply try to do everything all at once.

We conducted an evaluation at a division of a very large heavy equipment company. This division's data accuracy was worse than terrible and the division was losing huge sums of money because of its inability to deliver products on time. At the end of the evaluation, we prepared a plan with key members of the Leadership Team. Part of that plan included six temporary employees for six months. When we presented the plan to the President, he said it was a really good plan, but he didn't know how he could get the money for the temps even though the site employed more than 2,000 people, and even though the return on investment was staggering. When the President said no, we were stunned. There is no question about why this company continues to be in so much trouble today.

3. **Do it yourself:** Some companies try to improve data accuracy and planning system management by hiring outsiders to do the work. This approach has many problems:

   - **Expensive:** It is very expensive, and you do not know what you do not know!
   - **Experience:** The outside team will probably have one senior consultant with a team of young college graduates who are learning at your expense.
   - **Ownership and understanding:** Finally, and by far the most serious, it will result in a lack of internal understanding and ownership.

This kind of improvement initiative requires a change in how you operate and, as mentioned above, company culture which must be driven by Leadership. Occasionally, there will be someone who refuses to change; that must be dealt with directly and quickly. Consistently, when people currently in the company are educated and trained so that they understand why and how to accomplish the improvement objective, the newly implemented processes will then take hold and deliver the improved results. But, if outside people do the hands-on work of design and implementation, the new process will disappear as soon as they leave because the people in the company do not have working knowledge or ownership of the process. Therefore, we strongly recommend the use of internal resources supported by coaches with hands-on experience of this type of transformation. Like a sports coach, they do not play the game, but coach players to achieve significant improvement quickly, avoiding bad habits and false starts. Detailed planning can be implemented much faster with minimum expense using the coaching approach.

4. **Artificial intelligence (AI):** AI is getting lots of attention now and may help improve business results, but people, processes, and culture will remain central in improving, achieving, and sustaining desired business results. (See Chapter 17, Technology Enhancement, for more information about technology enhancements, including AI.)

Understanding Your Domains

It is important to expand your thinking at this point as data can be examined in three domains.

Information Domain

The information domain is all about the ease with which people can access and use information, especially without the need to sit in redundant and inefficient meetings to gain information. Trust in the information is based on the relevance and accuracy of the data, the reason this has been discussed earlier in this chapter. Relevance of the data means that emphasis is often placed on data that is not critical in determining data accuracy for planning purposes. For instance, the inventory quantity in a location is critical, but the item spelling or the vendor phone number is not.

Making information visible is very useful, such as through the use of Team Boards/Displays (see Chapter 18), on which a team openly displays all the things they are working on and the results being achieved compared to their performance objectives. This enables managers to be better informed and have positive dialogue with members of the team as they walk about.

Enabling access to information through other visual displays is also practiced in many companies using electronic scrolling bars with messages, TV screens, and so forth. For business information, that data can be displayed on all monitors positioned in communal areas, such as break rooms, to enable easy access, especially for shop floor teams if they do not have ready access to monitors in production areas.

There is also the question of capturing information that individual employees develop during their day-to-day work. How can it be made easy for them to capture that information? For example, people may be working on a process when they develop a better way to carry out that process or activity. This improvement must be immediately captured so it becomes imbedded, once approved, for others to share and use.

Physical/Material Domain

This is very much more about collecting data and information by being out there and physically seeing and sensing the situation, often referred to as management by walking around (MBWA). There is so much information and knowledge to be gained by walking through facilities. You may hear in a meeting that a certain facility is working very well and meeting all scheduled due dates. However, when you visit the site, you see just what a mess is being endured, with huge levels of work in progress (WIP) and overfilled storage areas adjacent to the work areas. Sure, they might be meeting their schedules, but at what cost? Physically witnessing the work areas, offices, or shop floor rather than just looking at numbers provides a much more accurate and in-depth assessment of the reality of what you see and how this may challenge or correct your data, enabling better and more informed decisions.

Value/Cost Domain

What does all this mean in terms of delivered value or earned revenue and spent costs? Very often there is a huge focus on cost reduction. Many companies have major projects to identify savings opportunities. But sometimes it makes far more sense to concentrate on increasing revenue than on reducing costs!

Too often, because there is not the right focus or understanding, companies are forced to reduce costs simply through headcount reduction. This certainly and quickly reduces cost, but it does nothing to fix the underlying problems, nor does it eliminate work required. Overtime increases, production defects increase, and customer service is impacted. By the way, just having fewer people is not a definition of Lean.

Lean, as a methodology, is about eliminating waste in all processes and improving process velocity. Velocity is defined as the total value-adding time in a process or part process divided by the total elapsed time that the materials are under control of the company and then expressed as a percentage. Generally, this is an extremely low percentage. The higher the percentage, the more waste has been removed, and the process speed from material receipt to product shipment increases.

A documented suite of "Mapped Processes" will enable you to bring down costs significantly. This approach represents a true application of Lean; see Chapter 16.

To understand just where a process has value-adding activity, you need to convert Mapped Processes to Value Stream Maps. To do this, you will need to understand value differently. All too often, when employees have been working for several years, they start to believe that everything they do is value-adding. Consequently, people need to view value as something the customer would pay for. So, with the application of Lean we need to identify value adding, non-value adding, and essential but non-value adding activities:

- **Value adding:** Actual work required to build a product or item, or perform a service.
- **Non-value adding:** Waste such as inventory, excess movement, scrap, and so forth.
- **Essential but non-value adding:** A customer inspection point: essential, but it does not add value. Often, some of these can be included in the value-adding category due to the customer having little trust in your capabilities, another improvement opportunity.

So, these domains intertwine like a triple helix, as shown in Figure 2.4. Information developed from data determines the physical situation, which, in turn, confirms the consequence of what you are doing financially as value and cost. If the base (your data) is incorrect, then the consequence will be reduced or delayed value (revenue) and higher cost.

It is recommended that you look at these through the entire End-to-End Supply Chain.

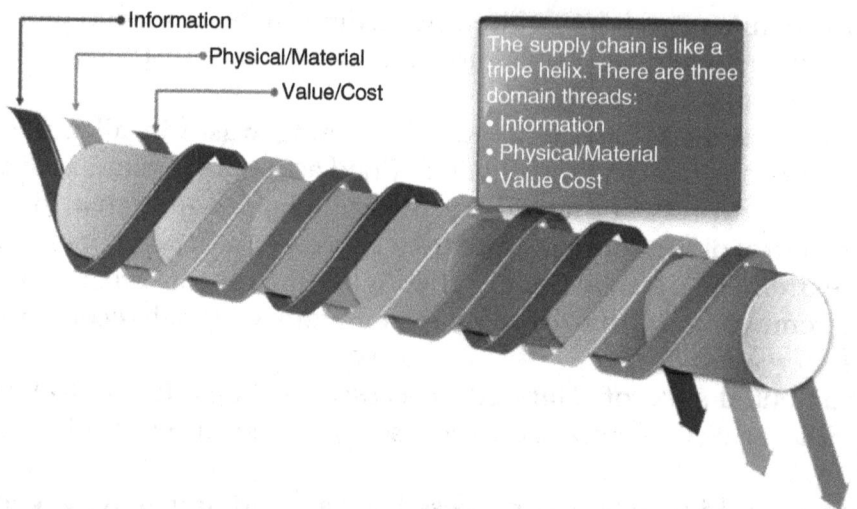

FIGURE 2.4 The Three Domains – Intertwine Like a Triple Helix

Summary

This chapter is about accurate data. What has not been addressed is what data must be accurate and just how accurate it must be. The following chart provides the answers. More detail on how to measure and improve these data elements is included in following chapters.

How accurate is accurate?

Requirement minimums for a Class A Capable Milestone:

Item Master Records	95%+
Bill of Material Records	98%+
Inventory Records	95%+
Routings	95%+
Work Center Master Records	95%+
Valid Price and Cost Data	95%+
Master Schedule Item Master	95%+
MRP Item Master	95%+
Logistics Master Records	95%+

For additional but more specific reading please visit the Oliver Wight Website and gain access to the extensive library of White Papers.

CHAPTER 3

Inventory: Essential to Know What You Have

A primary input to MRP is inventory. For the MRP system to create an accurate plan it must have accurate inventory data.

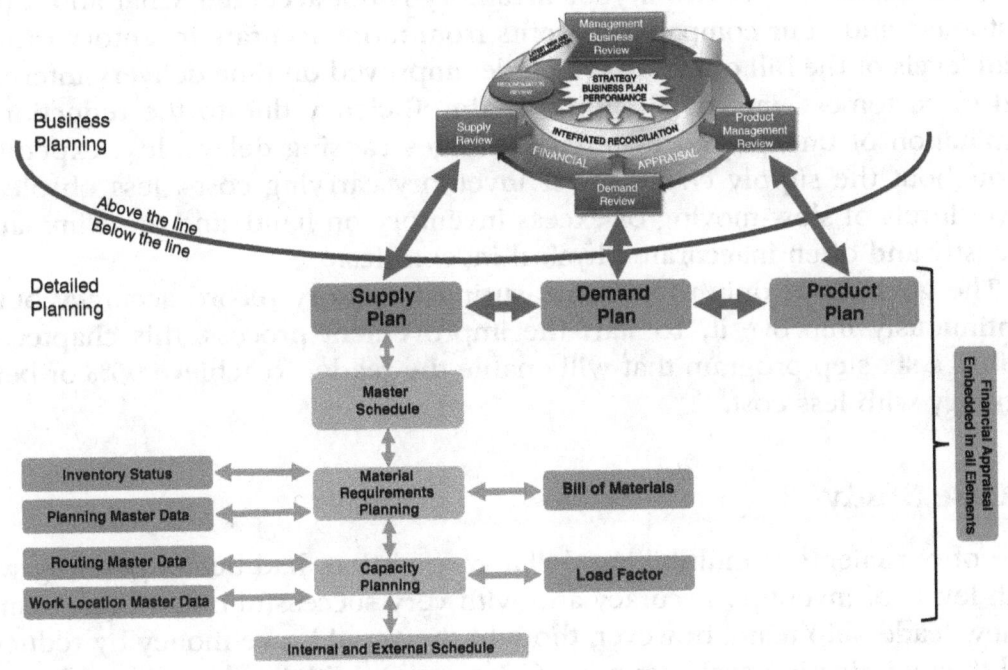

FIGURE 3.1 Business Excellence Planning

The world-class standard for inventory record accuracy today stands at 99.5%. Very few organizations can claim they are performing at or above this standard. Many achieve good accuracy in automated warehouse locations but fall short in more informal storage, transport, and supply chain areas. The harsh reality is that most companies are still struggling with very inaccurate inventory records.

Oliver Wight himself, during a class that he taught in 1975, asked the class what industry has better than 99.9% inventory accuracy, recognizing that there lots of those locations nearby. No one could answer the question. His response was, "Banks." They count the money when it goes in and when it goes out. That simply is the basis for inventory accuracy.

In this chapter we focus on the Inventory Status box of Business Excellence Planning, Figure 3.1, and its relationships with the other disciplines.

Imagine if Amazon.com had only 90% inventory accuracy. Would customers accept that 10% of their orders would be shipped later than the delivery promise that comes with their Prime membership? Also consider traceability, which is becoming required at more and more companies. How can you have good traceability processes if your inventory is not accurate? What about your customers and your company? Benefits from more accurate inventory records at all levels of the bill of material include: improved on-time delivery internally and to customers, improved supply chain efficiency due to the reduction or elimination of unexpected material shortages causing delays, less expediting throughout the supply chain, lower inventory carrying costs, less obsolesce, lower levels of slow-moving or excess inventory on hand, and the elimination of costly and often inaccurate physical inventories.

The goal is not only to start measuring inventory record accuracy but to continuously improve it. To start the improvement process, this chapter describes a six-step program that will enable the reader to achieve 95% or better accuracy with less cost.

A Case Study

One of our clients, a multibillion-dollar corporation, had been operating with high levels of inventory accuracy and with very successful bottom-line results. A new leadership team, however, thought they could save money by reducing and then eliminating cycle counting (12 people). Initially, they did achieve the savings, and the Six Sigma Team was well rewarded. But then they began to miss deliveries due to shortages caused by inventory inaccuracies. To compensate for the shortages, 40 expeditors were hired to improve customer service. Even with the additional expeditors the situation continued to get worse.

Our client called us back for assistance. When we started to work with them on improving inventory record accuracy, our goal was not only to restore the accuracy quickly, but to ensure that it was sustainable over time. Together, we defined sustainable as:

- **Documented:** systems (processes and software) that are designed to operate at the lowest possible cost;
- **Measurements:** that identify the root causes of inventory discrepancies and address any lack of discipline in the systems;
- **Shared knowledge:** a documented education and training program that cascades throughout all levels of the organization.

Measuring Inventory Record Accuracy

We also had to bring back the inventory record accuracy definition. This measurement requires that the item number, quantity, and location all be accurate for each location checked. If any one of the three is incorrect, the inventory record for that location is inaccurate (a "miss" rather than a "hit"). In organizations requiring traceability, the addition of lot code or other unique identification code is a fourth element that must be correct in the audit.

The calculation for inventory accuracy is:

$$\text{Inventory accuracy} = \frac{\text{Number of correct locations (quantity and location)}}{\text{Number of locations checked}}$$

The finance department was pleased with this measurement because it was absolute (pluses and minuses did not cancel each other). From a financial perspective, whenever the defined measurement was at 95% (100% for finished goods) or better, the accuracy of the inventory from a financial standpoint was above 99%.

The business's initial goal was to achieve a minimum of 95% inventory record accuracy. Their longer-term objective (beyond the first year) was to increase their minimum acceptable level to 99.5%, which is world class.

Six Steps to Better Inventory Record Accuracy

In the future, when radio-frequency identification (RFID) or similar technology is universally implemented, physically counting inventory will no longer be required (see Chapter 17). Of course that assumes that everyone will always follow the process using RFID. People have an extraordinary ability to bypass processes, and automated systems can fail.

Until that time, we recommend six straightforward steps to achieve inventory accuracy target levels. The process is relatively simple, but the implementation is another story. The new process is a disciplined approach, one in which individual and company behavior requires significant change – the real issue.

The six steps to improving inventory accuracy include:

Step 1: Education and Training: Education is the first and most critical step. If people do not understand why they are doing something, they will not embrace it. Recall that this is a culture change for the company; so, education must start at the very top of the organization and flow down to the rank and file. Commitment without understanding is a liability. So, Leadership and Middle Management as the "leaders" must understand in order to give the proper direction, and the rank and file must understand why, because they are the "doers." Next is training. Training is the "how" to accomplish the task. Steps 2 through 6 describe the how. Providing a good education and training program addressing the responsibilities and needs of each organizational level is the best way to quickly achieve your inventory accuracy goal. It must address the question, "What's in it for me?" at every level. When that connection is established, the culture change will begin.

Step 2: Assign Accountability: Inventory accuracy improvement begins with recognition of its importance by people at all levels of the business. That means that all employees must live in that culture. For example, when you go to a bank, there is no doubt about accuracy; it is part of their culture! In a bank there is a culture that expects the *cause* of an inaccuracy to be fixed immediately – locked down until it is found!

That same culture must exist in your company. It begins with a business policy stating the importance of inventory accuracy, affirming that it is the foundation of all planning and execution processes. The policy must also clearly state that disciplinary action will result if the policy is not adhered to. Finally, the policy statement must be signed by leadership, who must "walk the talk."

An important lesson to remember: A basic principle of good management is to *hold people accountable for only the things they can and do control*. This means that the manager of a function, such as supply, must be held accountable for the accuracy of the inventory in their areas because only they can exert both direct and indirect influence over the personnel in those areas. To reinforce its importance, inventory accuracy must be included in their roles and responsibilities and be included in the reward system.

Step 3: Identify Inventory Areas: Clearly identify every area in the facility that contains inventory and assign an "owner" to it. This is often done for stockrooms but must be expanded to all areas. That includes, for example, supply, quality, in-transit, and staging areas. All locations in which inventory resides must be included throughout the End-to-End Supply Chain. Even the owners of areas that should not have inventory should be held accountable if they allow inventory to be stored in those areas.

An easy test to determine if this step has been taken is to walk through the facility. Where inventory is present, determine the location's identity and who owns the inventory. Who should you ask? Not management, but the employees working in the area. If they say they do not know, that area fails the test.

As a part of the identification step, the owner of the area must be held accountable for its cleanliness and orderliness (5S). Additionally, it should have Team Boards/Displays showing the current inventory accuracy performance for the area and at least the previous three months' results. This type of visual management must be encouraged (see Chapter 18), expected, and owned by the teams that work in those areas, not only for inventory storage areas but throughout the company. It must be part of the company's overall communications to help drive and sustain culture change efforts. One of our clients hang pictures of the people who own an area, along with a posting of the area's inventory accuracy. The company produces small electronic parts, but their inventory accuracy results are regularly above 99.8%.

FIGURE 3.2 Team Boards with Current Team Performance and Actions

To emphasize culture and ownership, we are reminded of when we worked for a heavy equipment manufacturer. Initially, saying that getting employees to adopt this new culture was a challenge is an understatement. We wanted to fence off an outside area where welding department components were stored. The General Manager was against our request because the area was between two buildings and fencing it off would make movement between them difficult. We gave in even though following policy was certainly not a company strong suit, but we did get the GM to sign off on a policy (noted in Step 2) that clearly stated that disciplinary action would be taken if the inventory accuracy policy was violated. The stock keepers told us it would never work without a fence – we were doubtful also. We spent the weekend arranging a third of the area and putting parts away while double-checking accuracy and clearly marking the area as a "controlled stores area." The stock keepers encouraged us to come to the area first thing the following Monday morning because one of the supervisors declared he was not going to follow the policy. On Monday morning, the welding supervisor walked out, waved to us, and then took a part (one that he could lift without a forklift or trolley) and carried it into the welding shop. We raced to the GM's office to report the violation. The Plant Manager was in the GM's office when we arrived. The GM said that he would take disciplinary action, but the Plant Manager interrupted, saying that the supervisor was the only employee who knew how to weld the frames so they would fall within required tolerances. The GM told the Plant Manager to start training several people on how to weld the frames and then told his assistant to go get the supervisor. Everyone was watching. When the supervisor arrived, the GM informed him that this was a verbal warning that would be recorded in his file but would be removed it if there were no additional offenses. When other employees questioned the supervisor on why he took the part, he said he was just testing the resolve and would never take anything again. We never had a problem with people taking parts after that. There must be serious consequences for people who deliberately violate policy, process, or instructions. By taking disciplinary steps, management demonstrates walking the talk, showing commitment to their communications and demonstrating that if others do it, they can expect the same consequence. This incident was not about the supervisor but about whether the GM would enforce his policy. Hopefully much less severe disciplinary action is required to ensure that policies and procedures are followed in your company.

Methods of gaining and maintaining inventory accuracy can be much less authoritarian. In the middle of a factory we worked with, there was an open store that was staffed only on the day shift but accessed by operators on two shifts. Accuracy was poor and was causing problems completing planned assemblies. The solution was simply to educate operators and to ask them how the situation could be improved. The improvements accepted included an increased focus on kitting accuracy for assemblies scheduled on the shifts, and a clipboard at each storeroom entry area for people to log what they took on the occasions they still had to serve themselves after hours. People felt involved in both the problem and the solution, accuracy increased to well above the minimum level, and barriers between production, stores, and planning were reduced.

Another good example occurred at a very large manufacturer of branded consumer foods. The warehouse employees began to own the Inventory Record Accuracy program to the point they changed the sign on the stores office door to read "Inventory Record Accuracy Team." At the time of their Class A assessment, they were achieving IRA accuracy of 99.9%.

Step 4: Design "Simple" Systems: A "simple system" (process/software) is one that a computer-literate person can learn and operate effectively with a reasonable amount of training.

For example, one company we worked with initially implemented a system with 27 different inventory transactions. The result: due to the system's complexity, the people recording the transactions were constantly making mistakes. The number of transactions was reduced to five (issue, receive, stock to stock, scrap, hold), after which inventory accuracy skyrocketed. Once again, educate the individuals first, get them to then apply their new knowledge to the process design, ensure the software reflects this new process, and then train them on the processes and the software transactions.

Automation can have a huge impact on inventory accuracy if movement of material can be automatically logged. The six steps to improved Inventory Record Accuracy must be followed up and supported by whatever technology is currently available. As investment is made, automatic transaction recording should be incorporated when possible. Although this is not necessarily simple technology, it leads to a simple process to operate accurately. See Chapter 17, Technology Enhancements.

Step 5: Be Easy to Count: For inventory to be accurate, it must be counted with some frequency to confirm that inventory processes are being followed and that the planning system contains valid data. For people to count inventory accurately, inventory must be made easy to count. Take eggs as an example. How long would it take to count a case full of eggs if they were randomly put into a large container? Then consider how long it would take to count them as a store receives them – 12 to a carton, 20 cartons to a case, or 240 eggs. If an internal or external supplier has packaged its product so that it is easy to count and has historically demonstrated 99.5% accuracy, only a spot or random audit is required.

Typically, the first answer to the challenge of making inventory easy to count is to have the packaging specialists define the packing requirements for each item. This is absolutely the right starting point for items requiring special packaging for protection but is absolutely the wrong answer for most items. It transfers a simple process into a bureaucracy with all the delays that go with it. This is not a "Six Sigma" project; it is a "One Sigma" project. Anyone who handles inventory can make it easy to count with a little education and training.

One excuse for not addressing the easy-to-count requirement is that it will cost more. Our experience is exactly the opposite. When people

FIGURE 3.3 Inventory, with Improved Accuracy Spot or Random Audits Used

understand what is required and do it right the first time, it costs less. Significant costs can be saved throughout the supply chain when the inventory is easy to count.

Step 6: Adopt Cycle Counting: A bank teller balances to the penny their "inventory" at the end of each day. This is not possible in a supply chain environment because each SKU would have to be balanced at the end of every day or even every shift and would interrupt supply.

Consequently, some type of cycle-counting process must be used and has been proved to be both effective and efficient. However, be forewarned that cycle counting itself does not improve inventory record accuracy. The reason for cycle counting is to locate, identify, and eliminate the root cause of inventory errors. Resolving the root causes of errors is what drives significant and rapid inventory record accuracy improvement.

There are numerous cycle-counting processes. Considering that 99% of the reason for cycle counting is to identify errors, drive root cause analysis/resolution, and be cost effective, only one cycle-counting process meets all criteria: Process Control Cycle Counting. This methodology gets its efficiency from counting what is in contiguous locations and comparing the results with what is recorded in the planning system. Process Control Cycle Counting allows the cycle counter to spend time efficiently counting and not moving from one location to another. Process Control Cycle Counting, combined with Step 5 (be easy to count), allows a cycle counter to perform more than 300 counts per day. As inventory accuracy levels approach and exceed 95% over a sustained period of, for example, three months, a large number of counts are required to find enough errors to do a root cause analysis.

Next is a simple example of Process Control Cycle Counting. The process starts with a printout by location, as shown in Figure 3.4, with room to record the result. Note that cycle counters become owners of the cycle counting process and storage area personnel become protective of the validity of Inventory Record Accuracy (IRA) results to the point that they are provided the system inventory information before they begin their cycle counts each day.

Submitted By: Date:

Location	Item Number	On Hand	Count	Hit	Miss	Audit
A100	12497	2				
A101	10921	403				
A102	11273	229				
A103	10314	1168				

FIGURE 3.4 Process Control Cycle Counting Template

Principles:

- **Easy** to count – count it
- **Obvious** error – count it
- **Not obvious** error/hard to count – audit

Methodology:

- **Location A100** is easy to count so counting is quick and efficient.
- **Location A101** is easy to count because it is in boxes of 100 – four boxes of 100 and three loose – so count it.
- **Location A102** items are just loose in the bin, but it is obvious that there are nowhere near 229 in the bin – so count it (when counting, consider placing some into packaging so next time it will be easy to count and request purchasing or factory to package the items properly in the future).
- **Location A103** is not easy to count because items dumped into the bin, but it looks reasonably accurate so will be recorded as a completed count but not included in the accuracy count. When the bin gets down to a reasonable level it is then counted and packaging occurs. If properly educated the cycle counters can do an incredible job of estimating.
- **Non-storage location**, a traffic aisle, should not have any inventory stored in it, and is not on the cycle count audit list, but has two pallets of product sitting in the aisle. Count the items, record the count as a miss, and add it to the cycle count results for the day.

Many people object to the count being available to the cycle counter because they might just take the count and not do their job. Without the count, Process Control Cycle Counting can't be done. This whole book is about training, engaging, and trusting your employees to their job if properly educated (why) and trained (how); see Chapter 18.

Inventory counts need not be performed only by Cycle Counters. With appropriate education and training there are times that others can contribute to the cycle counting process. Following are a couple of examples.

1. When an item is pulled from stock creating a zero balance at that location, there should be a verification of that zero balance that can be included in cycle count results. The system says that we should now be at zero balance and the warehouse/delivery person can easily verify and report that the actual balance in this location is or is not zero.
2. When inventory is being put away (a standard amount at a standard location), a balance verification is relatively easy and can be performed by the person transacting that move.

Whenever errors are found, root cause analysis and problem resolution must follow quickly. Cycle counting and root cause analysis are a waste of time if the problem is not resolved. Therefore, going back to Step 2 (assign accountability), the person who is responsible for the area's inventory accuracy must have cycle counter(s) report directly to them.

Below are some tips regarding cycle counting:

- **Root cause** error analysis should be performed immediately upon discovery of an error, not just during the cycle counting process.
- **Designated person** – most often, a designated person/team (such as a Cycle Counting Team) performs the analysis, especially if it is a complex issue.
- **Metrics** must be calculated and tracked not just of the accuracy percentage, but of the frequency of error root causes. This analysis will point to system problems, even if you believe the processes and systems are operating as designed.
- **Systems** (processes/software), including documentation, should be fully reviewed and verified/validated during the root cause/corrective action process and periodically for continuous improvement.

When the system (process/software) is validated, errors are almost always due to lack of process discipline. Lack of discipline must be addressed by the area owner. Timeliness of transaction recording is one of the most important factors in inventory accuracy. When you use a debit card on a day of shopping, your bank doesn't wait until the end of the day to deduct your expenses, it does it immediately as you shop!

Another key organizational consideration and the reason to have storage area employees conduct cycle counts is that it is much faster and efficient to take corrective action when direct reports are exposing accuracy problems rather than have another outside department exposing and reporting them. Defensiveness is automatically eliminated.

Audits

The objective of cycle counting is to achieve an unbiased measure of inventory accuracy trusted by everyone. While our experience is that qualified cycle counters can be relied upon without question, it still makes sense to conduct occasional audits of the results conducted by knowledgeable and trained people. While similar, an audit is different from a cycle count. As stated before, an area inventory process owner has the Cycle Counters as direct reports but, being human, will have a vested interest in meeting accuracy objectives and may possibly bias the results. To avoid this, we encourage audits to be conducted by people with no vested interest, such as Finance or Quality. The auditor's job is simply to verify the accuracy of the cycle count. Should errors be discovered, understanding and root cause analysis remain the responsibility of the inventory owner, who would then adjust the figures accordingly. If this were to be carried out for the inventory owner by the auditors, there will be no learning or ownership of the required actions. This is the second objective of the audit. It should be noted that any inventory record errors discovered by the auditor are not changed in the system without verification by the inventory owner of the inventory. The auditor should not have the ability to change counts.

Technology Enhancements

Chapter 17 is devoted to technology enhancements, with some that will facilitate inventory accuracy procedures. In an effort to collect more information about technology enhancements being used today, we checked in with a huge distribution warehouse. There was some resistance to share what could be a competitive advantage, but we were provided some helpful information. First, we learned that warehousing is highly automated. While that is interesting, automation is not the subject of this chapter. This chapter is focused on maintaining accurate inventory. The following is what we discovered at this distribution warehouse:

- **Suppliers:** They do not count the inventory when it comes in the door but simply take the suppliers' counts.
- **Cycle Counting:** They do perform cycle counts. The Process Control Cycle Counting methodology described does not work in quite the same way because of the automation. Cycle Counters cannot walk down the aisles to count contiguous locations. Instead, they select the items/locations and have the computer and automated system deliver the contents to their cycle counting station.
- **Ownership:** As we suggest above, cycle counters and auditors are not authorized to change the count in the system but must have the inventory owner approve the adjustment.
- **Accuracy:** The inventory accuracy level is very high (but they would not share their percentage or their calculation method).

We could not understand how this company has such reportedly high accuracy when they don't count or even audit supplier counts when received. They explained that if a supplier provides an incorrect count, it knows it is in big trouble and their contract will be terminated quickly. They know their counts must be accurate. They could not have given us a better answer.

Summary

Customer expectations for high on-time delivery performance and low prices have increased, and scrutiny of corporate bottom lines has never been more intense. With these added pressures, there is no excuse for having inventory accuracy less than 95% using our earlier definition, knowing that the norm for your competitors is much higher. The six steps described previously provide a perfect way to begin your journey to best practice Inventory Record Accuracy results.

Far beyond 95% accuracy, Six Sigma inventory record accuracy levels are an achievable goal, if the process is designed correctly, people are adequately educated and trained on the process and held accountable. Specific training on cycle counting, root cause analysis, and empowerment to resolve problems is essential for this performance level.

A closing comment: Inventory management is not rocket science. It is simply common sense based on an understanding of how an accurate inventory enables you to better manage your business. The simple truth is that people must realize that if they need inventory, they must formally request it, and if they add inventory, they must formally transact that receipt.

For more information about improving inventory record accuracy, we recommend *Inventory Record Accuracy: Unleashing the Power of Cycle Counting*, second edition, by Roger B. Brooks and Larry W. Wilson (John Wiley & Sons, 2007).

For additional but more specific reading please visit the Oliver Wight Website and gain access to the extensive library of White Papers.

CHAPTER 4

Bill of Material: A Solid Foundation

The Bill of Material is another critical input to Material Requirements Planning as shown in Business Excellence Planning, Figure 4.1. Our focus in this chapter is the accuracy required to create a valid (accurate and achievable) plan.

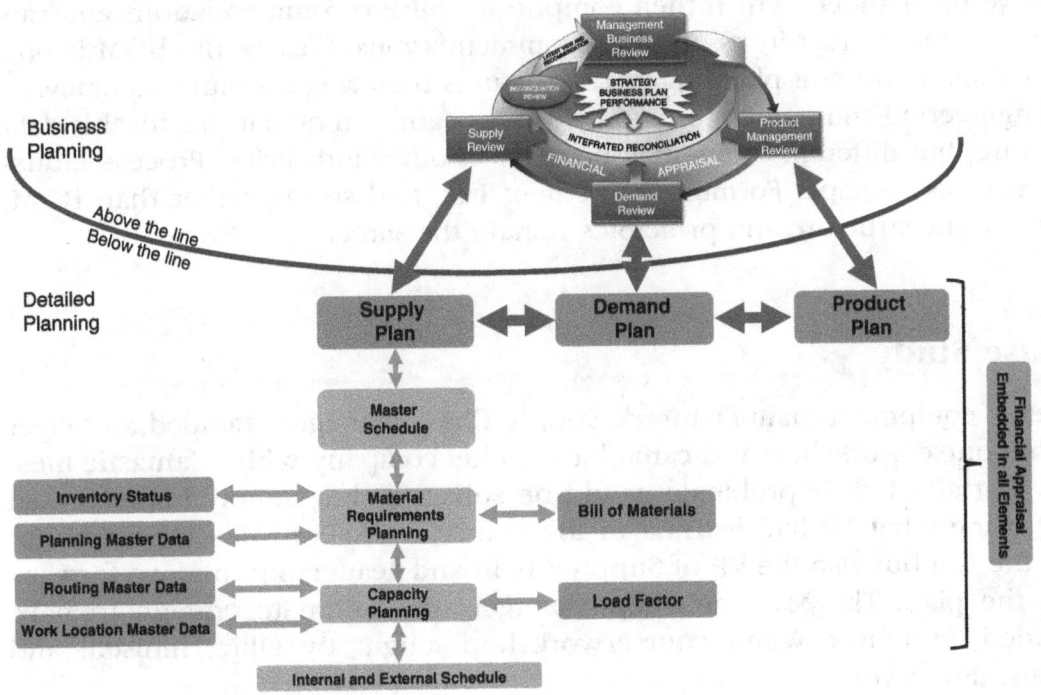

FIGURE 4.1 Business Excellence Planning

Dr. Joseph Orlicky introduced Material Requirements Planning (MRP) at J. I. Case in 1961, based upon the concept of Dependent Demand, which would lead to "matched sets" of components using a Bill of Material (BOM). With an accurate BOM, regardless of how many parent-component levels are within that BOM, the planning system's MRP function calculates how many units of each component are needed to produce the number of end items scheduled, resulting in matched sets of components to produce that product. For instance, if you wanted to build a car, the bill of material would include four tire assemblies, which would drive down to the next BOM level showing four tires, four wheels, and 20 lug nuts. Since a car has only one engine, the BOM would drive down from one engine to the next level showing one machine block, eight pistons (assuming eight cylinders), eight rods, two heads, and so forth. From there it would drive down from the machine block to the next level showing a block casting, eight rod forgings, and so forth. Most cars have thousands of parts and some aircraft have over a million. MRP calculates that information in a manner that is absolutely 100% correct in the number of components required if the system data is accurate and the use of modifiers, such as lot size quantities, is minimized. Unfortunately, in many companies too many unnecessary modifiers have been added, which then complicates MRP recommendations and can even undermine trust in its output recommendations. Clearly, the BOM is one of the most important planning data structures requiring absolute accuracy.

Engineering companies commonly use the term Bill of Material for this data structure, but different terms may be used in other industries. Process industries may use Recipe, Formula, Ingredient List, and so on, rather than BOM; however, the structure and principles remain the same.

A Case Study

A heavy equipment manufacturer's Supply Chain manager attended an Oliver Wight course/workshop and came back to his company with a fantastic message that all of their problems would be solved if they simply implemented MRP using what he had learned in the course/workshop. He convinced not only the GM but also the VP of Supply Chain and Leadership to move forward with the plan. The Machine Shop Manager was fortunate enough to have attended an Oliver Wight course/workshop taught by Ollie, himself, and became a believer.

Clearly, the need for data accuracy was important, and the BOM was foremost in the Machine Shop Manager's mind. If it was not accurate, his company would make or buy too much of some items and not enough of others. His first problem was that he had no resources that could identify BOM errors, although Engineering committed to correcting any errors found. Initially, he was not sure how best to tackle the problem, but he was quite certain, based on comments he had overheard on the shop floor, that the people in the shop had a good idea of what the BOM errors were. He began to put together an improvement plan that got all the people involved in finalizing the approach and process described later in this chapter. As it turned out, the shop floor employees made improving BOM accuracy for their items very easy because it made their work easier, and the results were extraordinary. Of course, whenever you get something working well in your area of responsibility you find yourself being promoted or moved to another position in the company. This time the Machine Shop Manager became the Final Assembly Manager. BOM accuracy there was an even greater challenge given the extremely large number of assemblies. However, the new Final Assembly Manager applied the same process (explained later) he had used in the machine shop and it worked even better in final assembly, as we find it has for every client we have coached.

In the process industry, most companies swear that their BOM accuracy must be 100% because of their being heavily governed by bodies such as the Food and Drug Administration (FDA), only to find their BOM accuracy to be 0.0% (zero) when they properly measured it. We encourage our new clients to write down the estimate of accuracy for all master data areas during the initial master data workshop. We then bet them that their estimate is higher than our actual audit of their accuracy. Without fail, Oliver Wight wins that bet every time. The result of the client's loss is that task teams must be established to resolve the inaccuracy root causes. In one example, a division of a leading pharmaceutical company, the initial audit result was 0.0%, but they tried to justify the outcome by saying they already knew all the reasons why the BOMs were inaccurate, so they concluded that the audit outcome was not really an issue. Really?

At another company, a food manufacturer, R&D was responsible for establishing and documenting all BOMs. They did so based upon the laboratory recipe, down to the last decimal point, and swore it had to be correct. When they audited the BOMs for one of their product lines, they noted that the amount of sugar per batch was stated as 14.50 kg, but sugar was received in

16 kg bags. How much do you think went into every batch? You are right – one bag. This company had many more issues than just BOM accuracy!

At a large Internet retail company, the specific box in which an item is shipped to the customer is included in the BOM. There is a large selection of shipping boxes available to the shipping associates. Which box size do you think the shipping associates use? Of course, the box closest to the person doing the packing! The people who order boxes based on BOM projections continuously run out of the boxes staged closest to the shipping clerks and have too much inventory of the boxes that are stored furthest away from the shipping clerks. Accountability?

Measuring Bill of Material Accuracy

Before auditing BOM accuracy, what's included in the accuracy audit must be determined and documented. When determining what to include, include everything that could affect the material plan but nothing that would not, such as a misspelled word. Of course, misspelled words and other related errors must be corrected, but are not the priority in measuring BOM accuracy.

BOM accuracy results are based upon single-level Bills of Material. Each single-level parent-component relationship within a multi-level BOM is assessed separately for its accuracy.

The BOM must include the following elements:

- **Correct Structure** – components making up the parent must be correct (nothing additional or missing)
- **Item Numbers** – must be correct.
- **Quantity Per** – component quantities must be accurate.
- **Unit of Measure** – must be correct.
- **Integration** – each level in the BOM must have the proper components linked to the parent (parent–child relationship) in the MRP planning system.

All of these must be correct to have an accurate BOM. Some companies add additional information to this list, but those additions must be necessary in creating a valid plan. If even one of these BOM elements is missing or wrong, the single-level BOM is inaccurate.

$$\text{BOM accuracy} = \frac{\text{Number of correct single-level bills}}{\text{Number of single-level bills checked}}$$

The minimum acceptable accuracy to effectively operate an MRP planning system is 98% using the formula above. If back-flushing is used to decrement component quantities when the finished item batch is reported complete, then the minimum acceptable is much higher depending on the items that are being back-flushed. BOM minimum acceptable accuracy for back-flushed items is 99.5%. The BOM accuracy goal is 100%. How to achieve this level is explained below.

When measuring BOM accuracy, there must be a three-way match comparing:

1. **Drawing/formula** – the official, approved document defining what must be included in the product.
2. **Computer file** – components, quantities, and so on, in the planning system's BOM file used for planning component quantities and the time the components are required.
3. **Floor** – what the production operators put in the product.

For a process industry company, it would be:

- Specification
- Computer file – what is included in the planning system's MPS/MRP files.
- Floor – what component quantities are being used in production.

Five Steps to Improved Bill of Material Accuracy

The five steps to improving Bill of Material Accuracy include:

Step 1: Education and Training: Everyone from leadership down through all who use the BOM must be educated on why BOM accuracy is critical in operating the company. Specific roles and their reliance on the BOM include, for example:
- **Engineers/Designers/Chemists:** Define what the product is and how it is manufactured.
- **MRP Planners:** Determine what components to order, when to order and receive them, and how much to order.
- **Production:** Follows the BOM in manufacturing products.
- **Finance:** Establishes product cost.
- **Quality:** Ensures that the product is built as designed.

- **Service:** Determines what replacement parts are needed to support customers.

  Education and training on BOM accuracy improvement processes for each person currently in or moving into a role that uses BOMs must include why each of these steps is required, the importance of each, and how to ensure BOM accuracy is sustained at required levels. After that, accuracy can be maintained through the ownership and change management commitment resulting from these education and training activities. Without this understanding, BOM accuracy improvement will be just another project with no meaning or commitment from the majority of managers and employees.

Step 2: Assign Accountability: BOM accuracy falls under the accountability of:

- Engineering/Designers/Chemists: Create and maintain.
- Supply: Feedback errors discovered in production.
- Everyone: Feedback errors discovered:
  Product Development
  Marketing
  R&D
  Operations
  Supply Chain
  Procurement

Step 3: Design the BOM Change Process: This is a much-overlooked step in BOM process management. Many companies design one process that ensures that all changes go through a complex series of authorization steps. However, many changes are straightforward and don't require all the authorizations that other more complex changes require. For instance, a change from three to four bolts in assembly is straightforward, while a modification of the material content of a bolt requires an engineering review to ensure that the content change has not degraded the bolt's strength. Class A companies develop three or four different paths a change request can follow depending upon the type of change proposed. This saves time and resources, allows a simple change to be approved immediately, and appropriately focuses authorization resources on more complex changes. Regardless of the authorization path, authorization or rejection must be accomplished quickly.

Step 4: Establish the Feedback and Accountability Process: A Machine Shop Manager, mentioned earlier in this chapter, needed a way to keep track of BOM shop floor feedback for Engineering. There was immediate resistance from supervisors and machinists who said that the idea was a waste of time. At one time in the past they reported errors regularly, but no one did anything about the errors. The same error occurred again and again, but when it was reported, Engineering never responded. To get past the resistance, the Machine Shop Manager designed a three-part form (see Figure 4.2) that included a header, the Bill of Material in question, and the Routing, which will be addressed in Chapter 5. The supervisors worked with the machinists to fill out the forms, keeping one copy and sending the other copy to Engineering. If there was no reply within 48 hours, the Machine Shop Manager

Date:			
Work Order#:			
Item #:			
Description:			
This form should be filled out and submitted to report any error on either the Bill of Material or Routing for the parent item number being manufactured on this plant floor.			
BILL OF MATERIAL			
Item#	Qty Per	U / M	Other
ROUTING			
Operation Seq. #	Department	W / C	Other
Submit The Completed Form To:			
Location / Mail Stop:			
Submitted By:			
Location / Mail stop:			
All Submitted Forms Will Be Acted Upon With 48 Hours			

FIGURE 4.2 BOM/Routing Error Notification and Correction Template

would meet with Engineering to resolve the issue. Since the problem and the new approach was reviewed and approved in advance by the GM, there was no issue in beginning this culture change; the new improvement procedure worked. When the manager later implemented the procedure in assembly, there was initially more resistance from Engineering just because of the sheer volume of errors reported, but Engineering came through and made the requested corrections in a timely manner.

It is important to emphasize the need for timely BOM error resolution. We have come across companies with convoluted and unnecessarily bureaucratic processes for fixing master data errors. One company, for example, carefully recorded the time taken to respond to each change request, but the average time to correct the error exceeded 180 days, with some requests still not corrected after 12 months. That same company required Finance to sign off on all requests for BOM changes. Finance just sat on them, especially if the change meant increasing standard costing!

Step 5: Audits: BOM audits are performed in different ways. If there are different BOMs, such as an Engineering BOM and a Planning BOM, maintained in the MRP planning system but not automatically synchronized, there must be an automated computer program to flag the differences. Those differences must be compared and corrected regularly. Most planning software today has only one BOM, which is designed to allow multiple bills to be recognized.

In the example shown in Figure 4.3, we show two different bills – a Planning BOM and an Engineering BOM. The auditor is checking to see if the Planning BOM matches what is being done on the production floor. If the operator says that the Planning BOM is incorrect, the Planning BOM is a miss. Now the auditor must check to see if the Planning BOM and Engineering BOM are synchronized. According to the BOMs shown, they are. It is now the responsibility of the Industrial Engineer to determine, through a discussion with the operator, which BOM is correct. Then either the BOM must be changed or the operator must be retrained. "Who is right, the engineer or the operator?" Want to bet who wins?

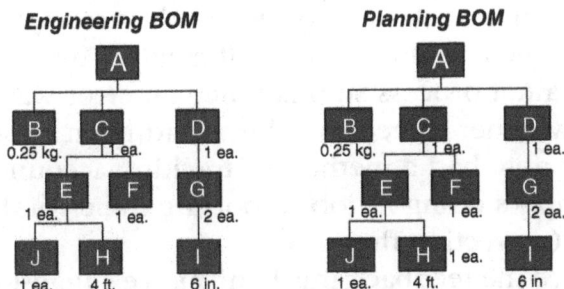

FIGURE 4.3 The Engineering BOM to the Planning BOM; It *Must* Be Right

Now comes a very important step in the process. What does the auditor do with this error? It would seem correct to have the auditor ask the engineer to correct it (see Figure 4.4). This would represent a significant process breakdown if Step 4, Establish the Feedback and Accountability Process, is in place. It is the responsibility of the operator, not the auditor, to report the error. Unfortunately, in too many environments operators are rewarded for "operating" or plowing ahead instead of correcting process issues.

FIGURE 4.4 Audit Finds the Fault; Working Together Is Essential

A Business Process Improvement Project Manager in a large electronic instrument company added an auditor to the staff. He started hearing that the auditor was finding and correcting BOM errors he found. The Project Manager explained to the auditor that initiating the corrective action caused operators and their supervisors to depend on the auditor to find, report. and correct them. The Project Manager also explained that since the auditor started correcting the errors, the number of feed-back forms turned in dropped significantly. The Project Manager also modified the audit process so that when an error was found, the auditor would note whether a feedback form had been submitted. With those changes they now had a method of tracking accountability and perfor-mance of Supply's doing its job (reporting the errors) and Engineering's doing its job (correcting the errors).

To reinforce the feedback mechanism, we suggest that when an error is documented and submitted by Manufacturing, and Engineering cor-rects the error by the time the auditor checks the file again (the end of the day), it should not be counted as an error. If the process is working exceptionally well, errors will all be corrected quickly and BOM accu-racy will be 100%. When the process is working well, and feedback has become part of the culture, we have seen companies eliminate the need to complete a feedback form and simply rely on phone calls or emails to get faster responses and very close to 100% BOM accuracy.

When these changes were completed, the auditor's job became re-porting BOM accuracy. Tracking the effectiveness of the feedback mech-anism and performing root cause analysis is the responsibility of the engineers.

Selecting the right auditor(s) for the position is important. They must be independent of Engineering and Production. A great deal of product knowledge is not required. Often auditors come from Finance or Qual-ity. The auditor simply asks the person doing the job and takes their word for it. If Engineering disagrees, Engineering must investigate and resolve the problem. An additional benefit if Finance is the auditor is that a great deal of real-life knowledge and real-life experience is gained in the manufacturing side of the business. This is typically not a full-time job. If done right this is often a one- or two-days-a-month job.

Step 6: Leadership: We have used the preceding steps with great success in many companies in which we were employed and, later in our ca-reers, with clients whom we coached. All were successful in meeting their BOM accuracy objectives. But here is a given: to work, there must be Leadership commitment and leadership. When we say commitment and direction, we mean that Leadership supports the process with their words and their actions – holding themselves and their people account-able for following the formal process.

There is an excellent story regarding leadership in a division of a large aerospace company. As coaches, we helped them design and implement the first five steps except for reporting how the feedback system was working. We were due for a coaching visit. Quality was performing the audit but had not remembered to perform the audit until the Project Manager sent out a note reminding them that we were coming to review progress. They then immediately performed the audit. The results were the same as with the first audit: 85% BOM accuracy. The GM was beside himself because no improvement had been seen in a month. He began looking for someone to blame, but everyone pointed a finger at someone else. Oliver Wight used to call this finger-pointing exercise the Supply Chain Coat of Arms, with an individual standing with arms crossed and index fingers pointed in any direction except back at himself. It was at that point with this client that we suggested during the audit to identify whether the feedback mechanism was working. It was simple enough. The auditor asked if a feedback form had been initiated. The GM quickly agreed to this addition to the BOM accuracy process.

The following month, like the previous month, Quality had forgotten to do the audit so scrambled the day before we arrived and had just put the charts together when we started the review with the GM and his staff. The audit numbers were the same. We could see the GM's irritation. The numbers displayed the number of feedback forms that had been submitted by production. It was "0%." To say that the GM was angry would not do his response justice! The GM got the full attention of the Production VP when he announced that there would be no more pay increases for Production management until BOM accuracy reached the required target level to enable effective use of the planning system. This company granted pay increases once a year and the annual review cycle was to begin in four months. Based upon the reaction of the Production VP, I thought he might actually have a heart attack. But to his credit he told all his production managers that they were to meet immediately after the GM's meeting. Later that day the production managers rolled out their gap-closing plan to their supervisors and then to all production employees on all three shifts to ensure that feedback forms were completed as required.

It worked. When we visited in the following month, Quality had performed the audits on time. When we got to the GM meeting's BOM accuracy agenda item, we noticed the Production VP's smug look and the Engineering VP's bored demeanor. When Quality displayed the accuracy number, there was still no improvement, but the measure of feedback from Production was 100%. To the shock of the Engineering VP and the dismay of the Production VP, the GM announced that there would be no pay raises for Engineering or Production until BOM accuracy reached 98%. With completion of that last agenda item, the GM got up and left the conference room.

The result: Engineering and Production VPs began working together, and over the next three months improved BOM accuracy to over 98%. Raises resumed.

That is a real example of GM leadership. We had developed a great relationship, the culture continued to change, and that division went on to deliver some extraordinary results using their new Unparalleled Business Planning and Execution Practices and leveraging the capabilities of their planning and control system. They were awarded Oliver Wight Class A credentials.

Summary

The importance of BOM accuracy in effectively operating a planning system is typically a gap of understanding for most leadership and management teams. Perhaps some of the lack of awareness is because they do not understand that there is a realistic and proven method of improving and sustaining BOM accuracy. The six steps described earlier provide the "how-to" roadmap to economically achieve and sustain BOM accuracy. The primary challenges are to develop Leadership's understanding and commitment and then to take the time for the required education and training.

Education is essential in providing employees at all levels the understanding of why the change is required. Until this is complete, many will understand that there are errors, but will not necessarily appreciate the importance of accurate data in running the business. Having that knowledge provides the understanding and motivation required to execute the six improvement steps, achieving required BOM accuracy levels, and in sustaining those results over time.

For additional but more specific reading please visit the Oliver Wight Website and gain access to the extensive library of White Papers.

CHAPTER 5

Routings: Accuracy Required for Valid Plans

Companies with many Supply Chain Nodes (Supply Points) and/or multiple steps in the manufacture of their products typically need some very important additional data or information and system capabilities beyond just

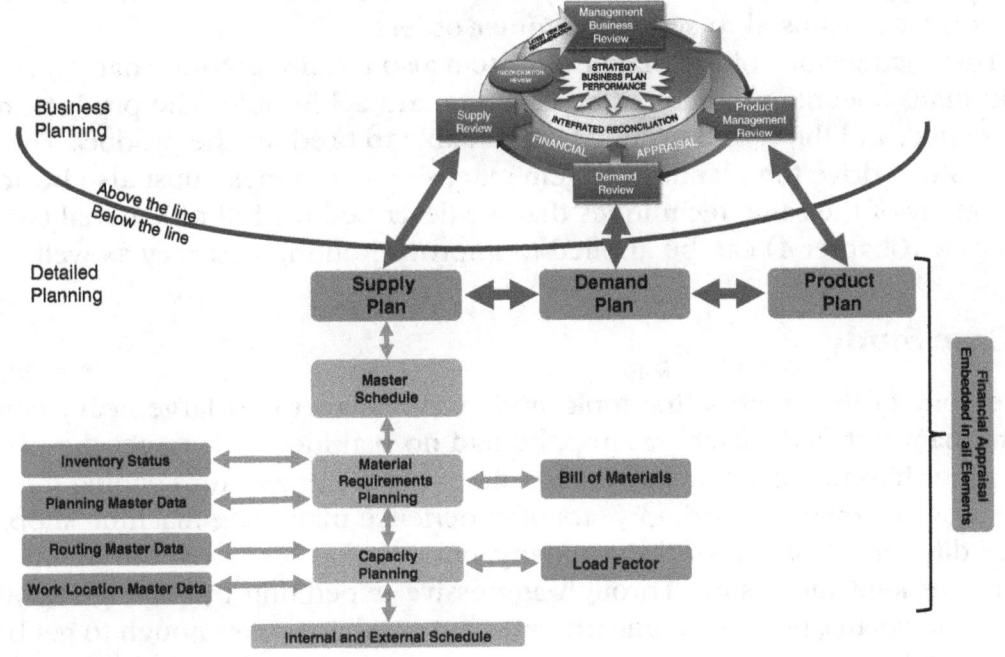

FIGURE 5.1 Business Excellence Planning

materials requirements. Those capabilities and related data/information within the planning system include, for example:

- **Detailed Capacity Planning:** by work location (rated and/or demonstrated capacity)
- **Scheduling:** by Supply Chain
- **Appraisal:** Financial appraisal, such as cost optimization
- **Evaluation:** Financial evaluation by operation
- **Performance:** Performance reporting and improvement activities

This chapter focuses on Routing Master Data, which support these capabilities as shown in Business Excellence Planning (BEP), Figure 5.1. To successfully utilize Detail Capacity Planning and/or the internal scheduling step and much of the financial information in the system, the basic data must be accurate. The Routing contains the production steps (there could be only one) required to produce the product. The work location (often referred to as a work center) identifies where the work is performed and provides information about the machine, group of machines, and/or skill sets required to perform the operation. For a process industry, this would be the production line or production facilities used to satisfy customer orders.

These extensions of the planning system also require accurate data to create valid plans, meaning they must be accurate and achievable. The product must be needed, and the resources must be available to produce the product. The databases that drive the planning system extensions, Routings, must also be accurate. Many of the same techniques that we described for Bill of Material (BOM) accuracy (Chapter 4) can be applied to improve Routing accuracy as well.

A Case Study

When one of the authors first took the job as manager of a large heavy equipment manufacturer's machine shop, he had no real idea how to get the plant's machine shop to meet and stay on schedule, a requirement for keeping the job. The previous manager had 43 years of experience managing machine shops in three different divisions of the company, but even on his watch the number of shortages kept increasing. Through aggressive expediting by paying attention to minute details, he made some progress but nowhere near enough to get back on schedule. Another eye-opening experience came from the supply chain guru and consultant Oliver Wight himself, at the week-long education session (this entire book is about what was presented in that session). What he learned was such common sense that he began to see light at the end of the tunnel. He walked away from the class with countless ideas about what to tackle first, but most prominent in his thinking was the need for BOM and Routing accuracy. He had taken on the bill of material but now needed to address routing accuracy because it was required for capacity planning and operations scheduling, and there was a desperate need for both in his machine shop.

It did not take him long to develop a plan to improve BOM accuracy, but improving Routings was a different story. Getting work locations (machines, groups of machines, or skill sets) and their sequence accurate (see Figure 5.2) was not a problem; production operators were happy to provide that information. But when it came to setup and run times, the challenge became daunting. He needed honest input, but Engineering wanted to tighten times to reduce product costs, while the operators and supervisors wanted to loosen the times to improve productivity metrics compared to standards. Neither side wanted to budge. Big Eddie, Finance VP, one of the most knowledgeable and nicest guys you could ever meet, solved the problem. He said he simply wanted them to be accurate.

8052			Arm		
Part Number			**Part Description**		
Operation No.	Department	Work Location	Operation	Setup Standard Hours	Run-Time Standard Hours
			Pull		
05	S	14	Saw	.05	.10
10	M	40	Drill	.50	.25
			Stock		

FIGURE 5.2 Simple Example of a Routing

An education and training program was developed to explain the need for accurate information so that accurate capacity plans and priorities by operation could be developed, and so that production operations could stay on schedule. This education and training program included what was in it for the operators, such as being able to predict overtime and unplanned schedule disruptions, for supervisors so that they could stop constantly looking over their shoulders, and for everyone, just being able to feel good about a job well done. In creating the new procedures there was also a need to change how feedback to the production floor would be managed. The biggest culture change from the production side was the elimination of the need to browbeat operators about low productivity. If a standard time was not realistic, management and production employees would work together to achieve the time. If that was not achievable we would get the Engineers to help us by redesigning the required operations or production equipment. While there were some limited number of instances in which standards were loosened, in most cases process/equipment improvements were made. To our shock, operators reported that some time standards were too loose. With a great deal of pride, he began seeing Engineering and Production personnel beginning to work together, reducing schedule misses and product costs. Simply building trust was the answer.

Measuring Routing Accuracy

Determining Routing accuracy starts with deciding what to measure. When deciding what to measure, it is necessary to identify everything related to Routings that could affect the planning system while keeping the measurements simple. Misspelled words, for example, which should be corrected but are not critical, should not be included in the measurement criteria. The recommendation with all measures is to document clear, unambiguous definitions and measurement procedures that everyone accepts, understands, and follows.

Above all, Routings must reflect the agreed way a product or service will be produced or provided. Remember, others, such as Finance and Sales, for example, will use the same Routings to develop prices. Should the optimal Routing not be possible when it comes to scheduling or production, then the resulting product cost will be different from the planned cost, a very important understanding.

Routing elements that must be accurate (see Figure 5.2):

- **Operation Number:** Operation numbers must be sequenced in the way the product is built, starting with the lowest number first and increasing with numerical increments of 5 to 10, as shown in the example, to allow later the addition of extra operations, should they be required, without having to renumber all other operations.

- **Department/Work Location (Work Center) Number:** In Figure 5.2, there are department numbers and work location numbers, which is very common and acceptable, provided they are unique numbers. A work location number should not be confused with a machine number since machines are often grouped into one work location, a good practice as it cuts down on planning complexity. Also, if there is a Lean initiative underway, there may be "flow cells" made up of multiple machines through which work flows continuously, not in discrete batches. A flow cell made up of multiple machines would have a singular work location number, further simplifying planning.

- **Operation Description:** This description explains the purpose of the operation. Some companies include significant Routing detail that includes tooling, fixtures, setup procedures, and so forth. Other companies opt to use ancillary systems that include that detail. Either approach is acceptable, but this information is not typically part of a Routing audit. Separate audit procedures and measures should be used to identify the accuracy of this information.

- **Setup Standard Hours:** This allows documentation of how long it takes to set up the machine for an operation. In a cell with multiple machines this number may be dependent upon how many people are performing the setup. If one person performs the setup for all included machines, setup time is simply the total for all the machines in that work location.

- **Run-Time Standard Hours:** This data element is the time required to run a single piece. Run times in a cell do not total the time required for a piece to go through the entire cell (i.e., it is not the addition of each machine's run time in the cell, but a measure of the time between pieces coming out of that cell). In effect, it is the measure of the cell's constraint, or pacing step, to determine run time.

For each operation, all the elements must be accurate to have an accurate Routing. Some companies include additional information in this list but must be sure that the addition is necessary (keep it simple). If one element of an operation is missing or incorrect, the Routing is considered inaccurate. The measure is of the accuracy of each operation within the Routing. Trying to audit the entire Routing would be next to impossible.

Measuring Routing Accuracy

The formula for calculating Routing accuracy is:

$$\text{Routing accuracy} = \frac{\text{Number of accurate routing operations}}{\text{Number of routing operations audited}}$$

The minimum acceptable Routing accuracy for operating the planning system is 95% using the formula above. The goal is 100%; achievement of this is explained shortly.

Another related and important measure is feedback adherence. Feedback adherence is the time elapsed from when an error is found until the record is changed, or the error report is rejected. This can vary by the type of error but should generally be about one day.

In addition to Routing accuracy, work location accuracy is equally important and is covered in Chapter 12, Capacity Planning.

Five Steps to Improved Routing Accuracy

The five steps to improving both Routing accuracy include:

Step 1: Education and Training: Committed Leadership and those who use Routing data must be educated on why Routing accuracy is so important in creating valid plans and how to achieve the required accuracy. Examples of employees to be educated and their interest in accuracy include:

- **Manufacturing Engineers:** Responsible for determining how and where to manufacture the product and its alternatives.
- **MRP Planners:** Responsible for determining and documenting in the planning system the lead and processing times to manufacture the product.
- **Supply:** Responsible for meeting operation due dates and managing capacity requirements of each work center.
- **Finance:** Uses Routing data to establish product cost and financial performance measures.
- **Quality:** Documents require inspection time to release products so that start and finish times for that operation can be established.

- **Committed Leadership:** Holds those accountable for their roles in creating and maintaining Routing accuracy; ensures that Routings are properly used in creating valid schedules.

Process education and training must include how necessary corrections are to be made to achieve and maintain required Routing data accuracy. Without understanding, improving Routing accuracy will be just another project on a long list of projects with no meaning for many of the employees. To ensure that Routings remain accurate, their accuracy must be measured each week or, at a minimum, monthly. Each month, inventory, BOM, Routing, and accuracy must be reported to leadership, normally included in the Integrated Business Planning Management Business Review's results agenda item. A result less than the minimum required accuracy presented to leadership must be accompanied by a plan to bring it back above the minimum, with progress presented each month.

To maintain data integrity, there must be clear, specific ownership (remember that if everyone is accountable, no one is accountable) and a change control process to ensure that changes are made to Routings only when proven in practice and authorized. If ownership is not defined, changes can be made by anyone, which leads to even less accuracy over time. This need for clear accountability is vital in maintaining accuracy.

Step 2: Assign Accountability: Accountability must be clearly defined and documented, with clear performance expectations. For instance, accountability for Routing accuracy means to that process leader that he or she will achieve and maintain the minimum required or above level of accuracy if they want to keep their job. Merit raises are sometimes made contingent on how much above the minimum level is achieved.

Accountability for Routing Accuracy

- **Manufacturing Engineering:** Create and maintain Routings.
- **Supply:** Feedback errors/deviations (an alternative Routing may be agreed if, for example, a machine has broken down. In that case, review by Finance is required to determine product cost).
- **Everyone:** Feedback errors/deviations.

Step 3: Establish a Feedback Process: Like the example presented in Chapter 4, a way to keep track of Routing error feedback for Engineering, Figure 5.3, had to be developed. The immediate pushback on this requirement from supervisors and machinists was based on prior failed attempts to provide feedback to correct BOM errors; they viewed this effort as another waste of time. In the past, they regularly reported errors to Engineering, but no one did anything to correct the errors. The same errors occurred again and again, but when direct labor personnel questioned the lack of response, Engineering just did not respond. To solve the problem, the three-part form shown in Figure 5.3 was introduced. The form was designed for both BOM and Routing accuracy (its BOM use was explained in Chapter 4). Despite the history of no response, supervisors began working with machinists to fill out the new form, keeping one copy in the Production Department. If there was no reply within a few days of submitting a completed form, they would meet with the Engineering Manager to resolve the issue. As explained previously, most of the errors or changes submitted involved setup and run times.

Date:			
Work Order#:			
Item #:			
Description:			
This form should be filled out and submitted to report any error on either the Bill of Material or Routing for the parent item number being manufactured on this plant floor.			
BILL OF MATERIAL			
Item#	Qty Per	U / M	Other
ROUTING			
Operation Seq. #	Department	W / C	Other
Submit The Completed Form To:			
Location / Mail Stop:			
Submitted By:			
Location / Mail stop:			
All Submitted Forms Will Be Acted Upon With 48 Hours			

FIGURE 5.3 Bill of Material and Routing Change Request

Step 4: Audits: Routing audits: Routing auditing is relatively simple. Go to the floor and ask the operator if the step on the Routing they performing is correct (see Figure 5.4). If any of the data for that operation is incorrect, then that step on the Routing is recorded as a miss. In many companies the Routing audit is performed simultaneously with the BOM audit.

Typical types of Routing errors:

- **Incorrect Operations Sequence:** Is the operations sequence correct?
- **Incorrect Work Location:** Is this the correct work location for this operation?
- **Setup Time/Run Time:** Are the actual setup times and run times within tolerance? (A starting point for setup and run times is +/- 20% with continuous improvement techniques applied thereafter to tighten those tolerances.)

8052			Arm		
Part Number			**Part Description**		
Operation No.	Department	Work Location	Operation	Setup Standard Hours	Run-Time Standard Hours
			Pull		
05	S	14	Saw	.05	.10
10	M	40	Drill	.50	.25
			Stock		

FIGURE 5.4 Auditing: Work with the People Who Know

- **Missing/Unnecessary Operation:** Are there any missing or unnecessary operations in the Routing?
- **Feedback:** There have been no feedback forms turned in for a known issue/error.

Auditing the Routing requires some guidelines. The primary objective of a Routing audit is to determine whether the Routing represents the way the product should be made. There are times when actual production must deviate from the Routing, but when the audit is performed, the focus is whether the Routing correctly represents the way Engineering intends for the product to be produced.

The following are some examples of when deviations from the Routing are legitimate, so long as the Routing represents the best way to manufacture the product.

- **Sequence:** Is the operation out of sequence? The answer could simply be the previous machine has broken down and Engineering has approved performing this operation on another machine to maintain the schedule, thus allowing time for the scheduled machine to be repaired. Some companies document alternative Routings to allow for this flexibility.
- **Work Location:** Sometimes an alternate work location is used for any number of reasons. If this is the case, as with an incorrect sequence, the auditor must verify that the proper work location is reflected on the Routing. At times, the number of variations can become unmanageably high. At one company, the General Manager (GM) was concerned that productivity was very low. The auditor told us that there was an excessive number of alternative work locations in the Routings. We asked the auditor to start keeping track of the number of work location alternatives as a separate measure. When the official numbers were published after the audit, 50% of the Routings audited were using alternative work locations. We worked with Supply and Engineering on implementing a process change stipulating that supervisors and machinists were not allowed to randomly substitute work location changes without Engineering approval. Productivity quickly increased to a level above what anyone had ever seen.
- **Setup Time:** If setup time is required, it must be included in the Routing. It cannot be averaged in with the run time because of

varying lot sizes. Of course, whatever the setup time, there should be a continuous improvement initiative to reduce that time, which consumes valuable capacity. Setup time can be addressed through Lean practices or through technology changes. For example, one aerospace company eliminated setup time by buying a piece of equipment with a tool holder that could produce all parts produced in that work location and could simultaneously load a pallet with different part numbers while the machine was still running the currently scheduled part. In this case, the setup time was reduced to zero. Setup times will almost always vary from the standard because the previously produced item number could have a setup similar to the one for the next item to be produced. This means the setup time will be less because of the similarity. The setup time should represent the time it takes to tear down the previous setup and until the first quality piece of the next item is produced.

- **Run Time:** This can vary in practice. For example, a machining resource area might be working with a material that is harder than normal and so takes more time to process, or an assembly area may experience a shortage of some materials due to higher than normal scrap. Again, the audit objective is to determine whether the time in the Routing reflects reality. The "harder than normal" material and material shortage issues mentioned earlier are further described in the "Load Factor" discussion in Chapter 12, Capacity Planning.
- **Missing/Unnecessary Operations:** The Routing auditor must always ask about missing or unnecessary operations in a Routing. If either is reported, the Routing is recorded as a miss; in other words, incorrect.

As with the BOM audit process, this step is critical. The auditor's job is to perform the audit and record the results. Auditors do not correct the errors because that action is the responsibility of Supply and Engineering. Auditors cannot inspect "in" the accuracy any more than quality inspectors can inspect "in" the quality. The process must drive the accuracy.

Step 5: Leadership: During a break in an education workshop we were conducting for a client, the President said privately to us that he was really enjoying the content and approach. He asked, "What is the biggest accuracy improvement initiative implementation obstacle?" We stepped into the hallway with him, so that no one could hear our response, and said, "You." He looked at us dumbfoundedly and asked why. We told him that his company lacked discipline (like most companies we have worked with) and that the accuracy improvement process is all about discipline. Will leadership insist on the new process being followed and hold their team accountable? Success is easy to measure, as shown earlier. Holding people accountable to following the process is the real challenge, and it starts with Leadership. If you want managers, peers, and subordinates to know what is important, you cannot just tell them you must show them! Make sure they see you spending your time and energy measuring and improving what you say is important. When leadership buys in, they must address the next big obstacle: middle management commitment. If the President responds properly, an organization will almost always be successful. This President did, and the company delivered incredible results, including a Class A certification.

Summary

The importance of Routing accuracy is often underestimated either because the support systems stated before are not being used or there is simply a lack of leadership knowledge regarding the importance of Routing accuracy in running the business. If you are not utilizing these support systems, you are missing out on the information that will help your company realize significant top- and bottom-line improvement. We have made the case through all these chapters that education is the starting place for improving your planning system. When that is in place and has increased understanding and commitment, the way forward is much easier.

For more detailed descriptions of Routing, work location, and item master accuracy, please see *Gaining Control: Managing Capacity & Priorities* by James G. Correll, and Kevin Herbert (John Wiley & Sons, 2007).

For additional but more specific reading please visit the Oliver Wight Website and gain access to the extensive library of White Papers.

CHAPTER 6

Manage MRP: Do Not Let MRP Manage You (Do Not Let the Tail Wag the Dog)

In Chapter 2, Get the Basics Right: Eliminate the Churn, there was discussion about the constant complaints associated with computerized planning and control systems. Supply Chain guru Oliver Wight had a simple planning logic:

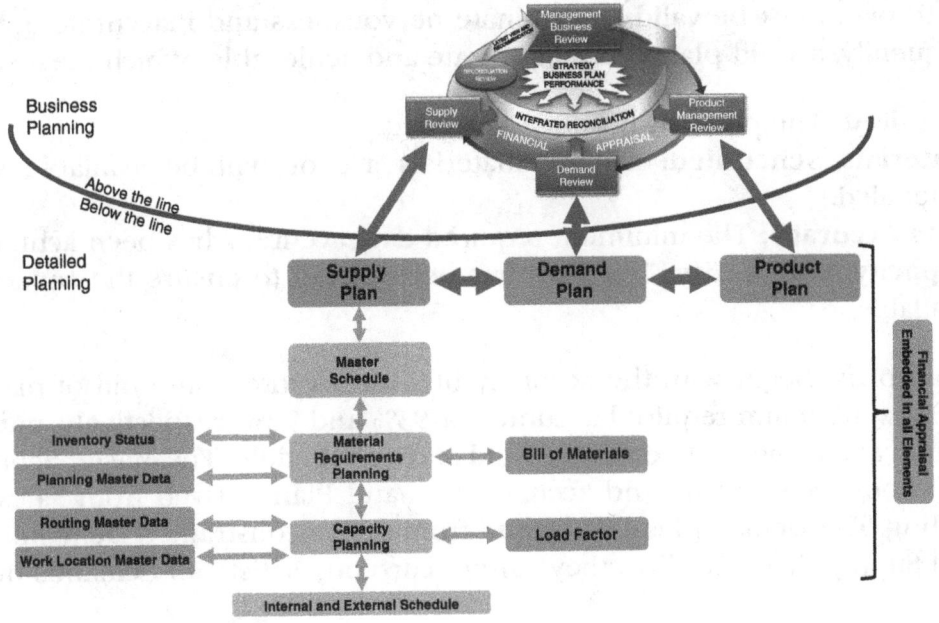

FIGURE 6.1 Business Excellence Planning

"Tell me what you want, what you already have, and I will tell you what to get" is perfectly stated and the answer will never change unless you change or mismanage the data in the planning system.

Previous chapters (Inventory: Essential to Know What You Have, Bill of Material: A Solid Foundation, and Routings: Accuracy Required for Valid Plans), have described how to achieve and sustain the minimum required accuracy thresholds necessary for planning systems to recommend valid plans (accurate and achievable). This chapter introduces the basics of Material Requirements Planning (MRP) planning systems and how to best utilize their capabilities. Future chapters will present the drivers of MRP – Integrated Business Planning (IBP) and Master Scheduling. Also presented are chapters covering critical MRP inputs (Demand Planning) and outputs (Capacity Planning, Internal and External Scheduling (i.e. Supplier Scheduling), and Financials), which address all the elements in Business Excellence Planning, Figure 6.1. In Chapter 18 the importance of people and their behavior is explored to ensure that the right knowledge and capabilities are available to support and utilize all the Planning Methodologies identified.

Valid MRP

An MRP plan must be valid to eliminate nervousness and inaccurate outputs; consequently, a valid plan is both accurate and achievable, which means:

- **Required:** The planned product is needed.
- **Materials Scheduled:** All the materials are or will be available when scheduled.
- **Data Accuracy:** The minimum required data accuracy has been achieved.
- **Capacity Availability:** The plan has been tested to ensure the capacity is available.

Valid plans begin with the accuracy of your inventory and bill of material (BOM) – a minimum required accuracy of 95% and 98%, respectively, must be measured and achieved to enable a valid Master Schedule. The Master Schedule is based on a realistically and accurate Demand Plan derived from Sales and Marketing. The Demand Plan is derived from the Unconstrained Demand Plan, should Supply Chain confirm they cannot currently satisfy all demands due to

Supply Chain constraints. These Supply Chain constraints must have been agreed upon through the Integrated Business Planning process. It is Supplies' responsibility to explain all constraints and recommendations to resolve, which are supported by current demonstrated capacities, their improvement and alternative sources of supply designed to achieve the Demand Plan volumes in the near- and longer-term horizons. In this chapter we will assume that all these inputs are valid. Later chapters address the Master Schedule, Chapter 7, and Demand Plan, Chapter 10.

Achievable means there is a capacity planning process in which the required capacities and all resources are matched against current and future requirements to ensure they are available to meet the operations schedules, which will be described later in Chapters 11 and 12.

With a valid Master Schedule, the MRP Planner's job is to align material due dates at all BOM levels with the Master Schedule required dates until there is a valid plan from top to bottom. It is common knowledge that things change continuously in a manufacturing environment, so the MRP Planner's next job is to determine how often to recheck the plan. Logically, this is based on knowing how often the plan changes. In our experience, something changes every day, so MRP Planners should also reside within the location for which they are planning. In a mature company most changes are relatively minor, but in an immature company changes can be extremely disruptive. These changes could be because of damaged inventory, BOM yield changes, scrap, rework, unplanned customer requirements, . . . the list goes on. To determine how often to rerun the MRP planning system, first determine how often the plan is updated top to bottom. In a mature company with a valid schedule, this is done at least daily, so changes are quickly communicated. That means MRP Planners must work the planning system output every day, where "working" means the MRP Planner reviews all system action/exception messages and decides the most appropriate response. If the MRP Planner works the messages and there are no further changes, there will be no actionable messages from the next system update. If the MRP Planner does not work all the messages, the messages not worked will be generated by the planning system after its next update. In an immature company, one that does not have a valid schedule, updating the planning system every day simply overwhelms the MRP Planner with action/exception messages, the number of "unworked" messages increases nearly exponentially, and MRP Planners quickly return to their trusted spreadsheets to plan the business. Companies normally spend $500 million and as much as $1 billion to implement planning systems that are no longer used for planning.

Working within several divisions of a large aerospace company, helping them to improve their Business Excellence Planning, it should be no surprise that our initial focus was data accuracy and measurement. However, for the first time in the company's history they were not "flying the planes over the fence on time" (i.e. they were not making their promised delivery dates), so suddenly we were asked to focus on schedule attainment. The stated major cause of the missed delivery dates was shortages. Customer pressure was so intense that the company President was visiting his internal component supply sites to make sure they had a plan to recover and get back on schedule. The worst offender was the plant that machined large components, called, not surprisingly, Large Machining. They consistently had 300 shortages; 100 of them were satisfied each day, but then 100 new shortages were added each day. We were asked to help them develop a plan to get that site back on schedule quickly. We knew their data accuracy was not at minimum levels required to develop valid plans, but we also knew that accuracy was improving and getting close. In response, we developed an MRP Education and Training session, covering Unparalleled Business Planning and Execution Practices, and then coached all of them specifically on how to apply and implement those Practices to create valid plans using their current software.

After the education and training had been completed the MRP Planners that planned end items were redesignated Master Schedulers. As Master Schedulers they put firm planned orders on all end items through to the emergency time fence (this is known as the firm zone) and planned orders from the emergency time fence to the cumulative lead time (this is known as the trading zone); see Chapter 7. Large Machining then took an MRP feed from the assembly plants' planning systems. They then shut off that feed (decoupled supply from demand), and the Master Schedulers and MRP Planners worked together, as a team, until all of the items at that BOM level until they were confident that they had a valid plan. Still, with no new feed from the assembly plants, they then ran MRP and worked all the second-level components until they were confident that they had a valid plan at that BOM level, and then moved on to the next level. They proceeded down through all BOM levels (some items had as many as 18 levels because of subassemblies) until all items had valid plans, all the while never taking new feeds from the assembly plants. When that was complete after four days in total, two of which were weekend days, and running MRP 18 times, they ran the capacity plan (see Chapter 12). They discovered their plans presented two capacity constraints, each of which they quickly resolved through subcontracting. Concurrently, all work locations began following the operations schedule (see Chapter 11) religiously, thanks to the strong commitment, support, and ownership of the Plant Manager. Meanwhile, MRP Planners accepted an updated feed from the assembly plants and began the "valid plan" process again. Within two weeks they could go through the entire process every two days. More than one day was required because of the poor planning coming from the assembly plants, largely because they had such terrible inventory accuracy – they could not find items that were there.

Shortly after we began putting together this plan with the Plant Manager and Materials Manager, the Director for MRP and Lean implementation for all the component plants (seven in total) asked how much we could reduce the part shortages; of course, he needed the information immediately. Quickly, off the top of our head and based upon our experience, we provided an estimate but asked for more time to think about it. He just grabbed our graph about the plan and our estimate and disappeared. Later, we learned he took our plan directly to the Division VP, who was extremely pleased. Our original prediction was that they would get down from 300 to 100 shortages a day within three months, but that they would not get below 100 because that is how many shortages they experienced every day. Our prediction underestimated by quite a bit. In less than a month, Large Machining was down to 100 shortages but continued to improve over the next month until shortages were down to single digits. We knew the improved process would work but had never seen it be that successful that fast. We underestimated their ability to reduce the shortages into the single digits because we did not realize that they allowed five days' travel time to the two assembly plants when, in reality, the duration was just two hours. As they had no capacity constraints and were following the internal operations schedule (dispatch list), now driven by a valid plan from the planning system, they were delivering five days early to the assembly plants' requirements. The assembly plants were still misplacing parts, but now even if the lost ones appeared to be shortages, the new parts arrived early enough to cover for the missing parts. The machining division, in the matter of two months, went from being the worst internal supplier to the best. Their success was all about creating valid plans and then using the supporting processes to execute them.

We have heard a thousand times the response when telling an MRP Planner to work all the messages daily: "Are you crazy? We could never get through all of them." Our response is always simply, "Have you ever tried it with a valid plan (aka, a valid Master Schedule and accurate data) with educated and trained MRP Planners?" Their answer is always, "No." Can an MRP Planner resolve thousands or even hundreds of messages in a day? Of course not! Can they work 20? Of course they can. The key is improving data accuracy and the way the planning system is managed so that you can work with valid plans and minimum nervousness. As we have said, what gets measured gets done, so you should measure the performance of action message clearance, by planner. The system will provide the data management needs to make it visible and the planners need to act. See later in this chapter the performance measurement for MRP Planners.

What you just read is not fiction. We experience the same in many companies and for those client companies we have coached the result is the same, providing they have followed our coaching advice. Working all the messages daily was not a dream for them but a reality. Plan nervousness and churn disappeared, employees no longer needed to spend their entire day reacting, and they were for the first time able to contribute to business success, with significant financial benefits. What they had not realized was the impact these improvements would have on the quality of their work life balance and job satisfaction, a real motivator.

Material Planning Objectives

Before we get into scenarios, let us define the MRP material planner's objectives:

- **Execute the Master Supply Schedule:** The Master Schedule represents the agreement between all the major resource managers (Finance, Production, Sales, IS, HR, Purchasing, etc.) about:
  - What will be produced.
  - When the items will be produced.
  - How many of the items will be produced daily, or even hourly.

■ **Optimize Resource Utilization:** The plan must meet the customers' requirements and optimize production efficiency. Almost any company can deliver to their customer on time or operate with maximum productivity; an excellent company does both and with the expected/planned cost base.

■ **Provide detail schedules for the parts or components by item number that:**
  ■ Are configured properly.
  ■ Reflect accurate quantities.
  ■ Provide realistic and valid dates.
  ■ Provide forward visibility.

An MRP Planner will encounter many issues in achieving these objectives, so we will explore a few examples to demonstrate how they are effectively managed. These approaches can be applied to many other issues as they arise. A key aspect to note is that MRP Planners need to be disciplined, organized, and, most of all, dedicated to using the processes. If the process is found to be deficient then they must own the need to develop and implement the required solution; if they do not, that dreaded churn will return.

MRP Worksheet

Figure 6.2 is an example MRP worksheet to provide a basic understanding and then to describe how MRP should be managed; see Figure 6.3 for the related Bills of Material (BOMs).

Item: Description:
OH: LT:
OQ: SS:

	Period							
	1	2	3	4	5	6	7	8
Projected Gross Requirements								
Open Orders								
Projected Available Balance								
Planned Order Receipts								
Planned Order Release								

FIGURE 6.2 MRP Worksheet

Please note the following definitions for this example:

- **Periods:**
  - Weekly time buckets, weeks 1–8 (software can provide daily or hourly buckets).
  - Planning horizon, in this example, is eight weeks (software enables a longer-term horizon of at least two years or more to cover the cumulative lead time of manufactured or purchased items). Planning horizons need to be carefully established as they can vary product by product and company by company.
- **Projected Gross Requirements:** The number of units required in each week based on the:
  - Master Schedule – End item or option (dark gray and white computers*).
  - Dependent Demand – Parent items requiring this component (dark gray and white cases*).
  - Independent Demand – Spare parts/direct sales (computer screen*).
  - * See Bill of Material.
- **Open Orders:** Actual released parts orders in hand which increase the Projected Available Balance of the item.
- **Projected Available Balance:** The quantity of that item that will be in inventory during each period based upon the starting inventory decremented by Projected Gross Requirements and incremented by Open Orders.
- **Planned Order Receipt:** The period in which a computer planned order is scheduled to be received.
- **Planned Order Release:** The period in which a computer planned order is scheduled to be released.
- **Item:** The item/part number that is being planned.
- **Description:** States in the company's commonly used term a description of the part being planned; most companies utilize a disciplined naming nomenclature.
- **OH:** On hand, the quantity of that part currently available in inventory and not already committed to (decremented from available inventory).
- **LT:** Lead time for either a manufactured part or a purchased part. Manufacturing lead time should match that time documented in the Routing; purchasing lead time should match the time documented in the item's

master data record and should be agreed with the part supplier. Both are discussed in later chapters.

- **OQ:** Order quantity, the quantity documented in the item's master data record and used by the planning system whenever an order is planned or released. The following order quantity types and rules can have a significant impact on inventory levels and availability:

  - *Fixed Order Quantity:* This is the same quantity for all orders regardless of what is needed and is usually set based upon an economic order quantity.

  - *Lot-for-Lot:* The quantity matches only what is required to cover requirements for that specific period. This order quantity type is selected normally when there is very little setup time. It also results in no residual inventory of that part.

  - *Economic Order Quantity:* This is determined by a formula that considers the annual demand, setup time, and inventory carrying cost to determine the optimal size of each order. This lot size option may enable the MRP Planner to calculate optimal lot size but should never be used in the automatic mode because formula elements are variable and any change in them and MRP recalculates, driving nervousness throughout MRP.

  - *Period Order Quantity:* This calculates the quantity during several time periods prescribed by the MRP Planner. Every time requirements change in that prescribed number of time periods, the planning system recalculates the order quantity. While this order quantity option allows the MRP Planner to stay within inventory goals, it creates significant nervousness and disruption in the material plans. Do not use this option!

- **SS:** Safety stock, which is documented in the item master for each item, allowing the MRP Planner to maintain an inventory amount that buffers demonstrated variations in demand, scrap, operational losses, and so forth. A new planned release will be created for that item when the projected available balance for that item reaches the safety stock level, not when the inventory falls to zero. A planning system can be configured to not show the safety stock quantity in the projected available balance, but we do not recommend that configuration.

- **Modifiers:** Most planning systems offer the use of many more modifiers to the MRP Planner. Before any of these modifiers are utilized, the MRP Planner must understand completely each modifier and its impact on material and supplier plans. Sound procedures regarding authorization of each modifier's use must be documented and followed.

▪ Types of Orders

- ▪ *Open Orders:* Orders that have been authorized for execution by the MRP Planner (e.g., a released shop order or released purchase order). Inside the planning system these are usually described as open orders, but on external MRP displays, these are normally displayed as scheduled receipts.

- ▪ *Planned Orders:* Orders not yet released by the MRP Planner. These orders are controlled and modified as necessary by the planning system, which will automatically move and/or recalculate the order quantity as inputs change from day to day.

- ▪ *Firm Planned Orders:* Orders that have not yet been released by the MRP Planner but have moved inside the emergency time fence, to enter the firm zone, or manually firmed by the MRP Planner to take control of the order away from the planning system. If and when the planning system recognizes an imbalance between supply and requirements of a component, it cannot change that order's quantity or time but sends an action/exception message to alert the MRP Planner of that imbalance. Chapter 7, Mastering the Master Schedule, describes the use of firm planned orders by the Master Schedulers through cumulative lead time.

The simplest things can often create big problems in developing valid material plans. For instance, the MRP Planner must be knowledgeable of his or her item numbers and related descriptions to fully understand what has been ordered and what is being planned inside the planning system.

Why is this so important? Consider this example. While touring a manufacturing site where a company's largest lift trucks were produced (15,000- to 62,000-lift capacity), the GM asked the Materials Manager, "Why have we had two 62,000 truck frames in the yard for a couple of weeks?" Component and sub-assembly inventory was the Materials Manager's responsibility. Returning to the office, the Materials Manager asked that question of the MRP Planner responsible for truck frames. The Materials Manager was stunned to learn that someone had added to the truck frame's material master a safety stock level of two. The MRP Planner, who was new to the business, explained that the recommendation to add a safety stock level of two to the item master for all parts "just in case" came from one of the senior MRP Planners. This is also a great example of why management by walking around is so important; this is discussed in Chapter 18.

We describe the appropriate use of safety stock later in this chapter but recognize that adding safety stock "just in case" is not one of its appropriate uses! This specific example identifies that this MRP Planner had a serious lack of knowledge regarding the parts being planned. The solution to improve that knowledge was to immediately provide all less-experienced MRP Planners time in the plant departments where their parts were produced so that they fully understood the plants' needs and could make good planning decisions. Corrective action was taken, as described later under the safety stock section of this chapter.

What about the Senior Planner who recommended the safety stock? Education and training are not always followed, because old habits are hard to break. Just a glance from the Materials Manager and he knew he had been caught and decided to change his behavior.

The Calculation

This is a simple example of the calculations performed by the planning system countless times each day in determining net requirements for components in two very simplified computer products, one white and one dark gray. Figure 6.3 is a depiction of the two products' Bills of Material.

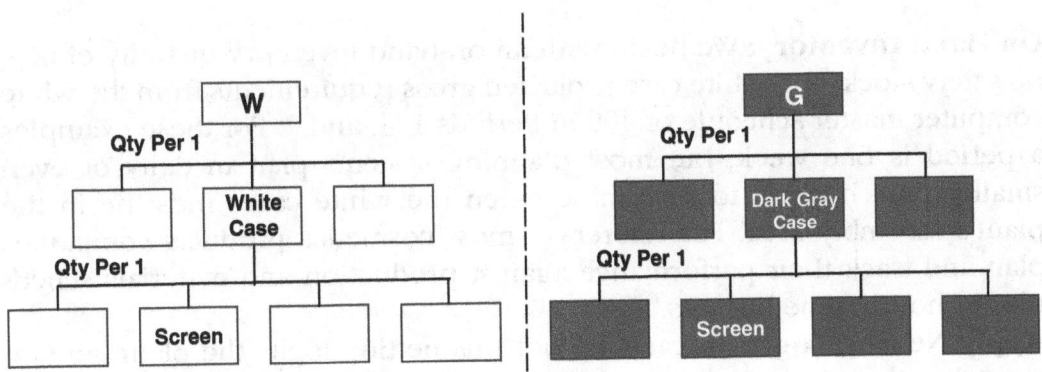

FIGURE 6.3 Computer Bills of Material Example

Netting Process

To be sure we are on the same page, we start by explaining the netting process using the white case component (see the BOMs above and follow the white case time-phased planning grid calculation table, Figure 6.4). Referencing the definitions previously described.

	Master Schedule (Release Date)							
	Period							
	1	2	3	4	5	6	7	8
White Computer	400			400			400	

Item: C345   Description: Case, White
OH: 600   LT: 2 Wks
OQ: 350   SS: 0

		Material Requirements Planning (MRP)							
		Period							
		1	2	3	4	5	6	7	8
Projected Gross Requirements		400			400			400	
Open Orders									
Projected Available Balance	600	200	200	200	−200 150	150	150	−250 100	100
Planned Order Receipts					350			350	
Planned Order Release			350			350			

FIGURE 6.4 Using Your Data to Populate Your Planning System

- **On-Hand Inventory:** We begin with an on-hand inventory quantity of 600, no safety stock, and white case projected gross requirements from the white computer master schedule of 400 in Periods 1, 4, and 7. For these examples a period is one week, but most planning systems plan in daily or even smaller time buckets to determine when the white cases must be in the plant's assembly area. For reference, most cosmetics products companies plan and track their performance against production and materials schedules in hourly time buckets.
- **Apply Netting Logic:** In carrying out this netting logic, the planning system takes the white computer planned order release date (the start date for assembling a lot of white computers) from the white computer master schedule and drives it down into the projected gross requirements (due date) in the white case time-phased plan.

- **Netting Calculation:** Since there are already 600 white cases in stock and only 400 required in the assembly area, the netted projected available balance becomes 200 white cases. Since there are no projected gross requirements in Periods 2 and 3, the projected available balance is unchanged in those periods and remains the same at 200 units.
- **Negative Balances:** In Period 4, there is another projected gross requirement of 400, but there are only 200 white cases in stock. Whenever the planning system projects a negative balance of white cases, it reacts by placing a planned order receipt of 350 (the order quantity in the white case material master and in the planning system determined in this case by the EOQ formula) in Period 4.
- **Applying Lead Times:** The MRP planning system then applies the material master lead time of two weeks and places a planned order release of 350 in Period 2.
- **Projected Gross Requirements:** Ongoing calculation logic:
  - With the 200 white cases remaining in stock and the 350 to be received in Period 4, inventory in that period will grow to 550 units. When the 400 required by white computer assembly are sent to the assembly area, the projected available balance at the end of Period 4 will be 150 white cases. There are no projected gross requirements in Periods 5 or 6, so the white case projected available balance remains 150 through those periods.
  - In Period 7 there is another projected gross requirement of 400 white cases, which again drives the projected available balance negative and causes MRP to place a planned order receipt of 350 in Period 7 and a planned order release of 350 in Period 5, resulting in a projected available balance of 100 at the end of Period 7.
  - There are no projected gross requirements in Period 8, so the projected available balance remains 100 white cases through that period. This netting process continues at the speed of light throughout the planning horizon (one to two years).

MRP can be refreshed countless times, and so long as the basic data regarding requirements, inventory, lead times, and so forth do not change, the system recommendations will remain the same. It is not MRP that injects plan nervousness, but the planning data accuracy and changes entered.

Rescheduling Process

If there is a change to any MRP input, it modifies the plan beyond the planning time fence, the cumulative lead time. If the modified plan affects orders inside the cumulative lead time and before the emergency time fence, the trading zone (i.e. a released order or a firm planned order) should be modified; MRP will send an action/exception message to the MRP Planner with a recommended course of action. In Figure 6.5, MRP is suggesting that an open order receipt be moved out one period, indicating that an input must have changed since the previous plan update. The change could have been a demand change (change in customer order or demand plan) or a supply change (additional inventory found). Whatever the reason, the MRP Planner must respond (decide) to the action message. In this case MRP is telling the MRP Planner that the inventory at the end of Period 2 is unnecessarily large and that the open order in Period 2 is not needed until the beginning of Period 3.

Master Schedule (Release Date)								
Period								
	1	2	3	4	5	6	7	8
Dark Gray Computer	200	200	200	200	200	200	200	200

Item: C567   Description: Case, Dark Gray
OH: 600   LT: 1 Wk
OQ: 650   SS: 0

Material Requirements Planning (MRP)									
		Period							
		1	2	3	4	5	6	7	8
Projected Gross Requirements		200	200	200	200	200	200	200	200
Open Orders			600						
Projected Available Balance	500	300	700	500	300	100	−100 500	300	100
Planned Order Receipts							600		
Planned Order Release						600			

Scheduled Receipts:
Work Order: 123
600 Due Period 2
Action Message: Reschedule Out 1 Period

FIGURE 6.5 The Effect of Rescheduling

The MRP Planner must decide whether to move the open order receipt into Period 3. That decision will be based on the MRP Planner's knowledge of the dark gray computer business. With no other information, the MRP Planner should move the order to Period 3. Yes, that will cause some plan nervousness within assembly and, perhaps, with the supplier if the supplier's plan can even be changed, but passing along the adjustment for agreement by the factory or the supplier is worth the effort. If there are capacity issues in assembly or at the supplier, we do not want them working on this order if the component is no longer needed at the beginning of Period 2. There are also situations in which the order should not be moved. For example, if the capacity plan has identified a constraint in week 3 and moving this order would further overload capacity in that week, the order would not be moved. The MRP Planner should annotate the firm planned order, indicating the reason for rejecting any action/exception message to move the open order receipt from Period 2 to Period 3. This note is critical because the next time MRP runs it will send the same message. With the note in place, the MRP Planner, or a vacation replacement MRP Planner, avoids the work of researching the message again. The bottom line: the MRP planning system message is a suggestion, but the MRP Planner understands the business and is accountable for making the best decision.

Requirement Explosion

Joe Orilicky's biggest breakthrough innovation in converting a simple parts list into MRP at J. I. Case in 1961 was exploding component requirements from one BOM level to the next lower BOM level. Based upon the earlier BOM, the screen is one of four white case components and is common to both the white and dark gray cases. Therefore, when either white or dark gray case assembly is due to begin, the screens must be available. MRP takes the order start date for each parent (white case or dark gray case) and drives those quantities into the projected gross requirements of all case components. The term "dependent demand," in this case vertical dependency, comes from this logic. That logic takes assembly requirements (case assembly) and explodes those requirements through the BOM down to case component (child) quantity requirements. In the instance of the white case, Figure 6.6, the 350-piece quantity from the

Item: C345   **Description: Case, White**
OH: 600   **LT: 2Wks**
OQ: 350   **SS: 0**

		Period							
		1	2	3	4	5	6	7	8
Projected Gross Requirements		400	0	0	400	0	0	400	0
Open Orders									
Projected Available Balance	600	200	200	200	150	150	150	100	100
Planned Order Receipts					350			350	
Planned Order Release			350			350			

Item: C567   **Description: Dark Gray**
OH: 500   **LT: 1 Wk**
OQ: 600   **SS: 0**

		Period							
		1	2	3	4	5	6	7	8
Projected Gross Requirements		200	200	200	200	200	200	200	200
Open Orders			600						
Projected Available Balance	500	300	700	500	300	100	500	300	100
Planned Order Receipts							600		
Planned Order Release						600			

Item: S678   **Description: Screen**
OH: 900   **LT: 3 Wks**
OQ: 1000   **SS: 200**
Independent Dmd: 100/Wk   Allocated: 0

		Period							
		1	2	3	4	5	6	7	8
Projected Gross Requirements		100	450	100	100	1050	100	100	100

FIGURE 6.6 How the Planning System Deals with Gross Requirements

planned order release line in Periods 2 and 5 become the screen projected gross requirements of 350 since each case requires one screen. Similarly, the dark gray case planned order release of 600 in Period 5 explodes to a projected gross requirement of 600 screens in Period 5 of the screen time-phased planning grid. Now, since both white and dark gray cases use the same screen, the assembly requirements for all screens in this simple example have been passed on to that component's time-phased planning grid. In this same manner, no matter how many other parent items require the same screen, the screen's time-phased material plan will include all required screens across the full planning horizon.

To complicate matters in this example, the screen has proven to need spare parts (repair parts) over time totaling, on average, 100 screens per week. Since that supply is not driven directly by parent requirements, that demand is called "independent demand," must be forecasted, and is simply shown as an additional screen-planning parameter along with the other planning parameters, such as the description, safety stock, on-hand inventory, and order quantity, on the screen time-phased planning grid. That independent demand must be added to the dependent demand to reflect total screen projected gross requirements. Since this repair item is independent demand, there will be some demand variation and, therefore, a need for some screen safety stock, as shown in the screen planning parameters.

The result in our example for screen projected gross requirements is shown in the final time-phased planning grid, Figure 6.6. There is a projected gross requirement of only 100 spares in Period 1; 100 screen spares and 350 white case assembly units in Period 2; 100 spares in Periods 3 and 4; a total of 1,050 spares and white and dark case assembly units in Period 5; and 100 spares in Periods 6, 7, and 8. The large demand spike in Period 5 is termed by some as lumpy demand, which is caused by assembly requirements but more so by large order quantity lot sizing. Large lot sizes can cause many problems in detail capacity planning and should be subjected to continuous improvement techniques (see Chapter 16) to reduce their size, inventory holding costs, and planning complexity.

Should the forecast of the independent screen demand prove to be variable from period to period, it could be shown as a separate row in the screen time-phased planning grid, but we chose to keep it simple for this example, Figure 6.6.

Order Release

If MRP runs now, the time-phased planning grid, Figure 6.7, would appear.

Note that in Period 4 there are 150 screens remaining as the projected available balance, but since there is a safety stock requirement of 200 units, the balance has fallen below the safety stock, and the MRP planning system will place a planned order for 1,000 units, the order quantity, in Period 1. In Period 5 the same logic is used.

Notice that in this display, demand detail (the origin of the demand) and action messages (the planning system's recommendations) are shown to facilitate the MRP Planner's decisions.

In this case the MRP, rather than automatically changing the plan, would send an action message recommending releasing a screen order for 1,000 units

Item: S678   Description: Screen
OH: 900   LT: 3 Wks
OQ: 1,000   SS: 200

Material Requirements Planning (MRP)

Independent Demand: 100 / Wk		Period							
Allocated: 0		1	2	3	4	5	6	7	8
Projected Gross Requirements		100	450	100	100	1,050	100	100	100
Open Orders									
Projected Available Balance	900	800	350	250	150 1,150	100 1,100	1,000	900	800
Planned Order Receipts					1,000	1,000			
Planned Order Releases		1,000	1,000						

Demand Detail (Pegging)

Period	1	100 Spares
Period	2	100 Spares
Period	2	350 White Computer
Period	3	100 Spares
Period	4	100 Spares
Period	5	100 Spares
Period	5	350 White Computer
Period	5	600 Dark Gray
Period	6	100 Spares
Period	7	100 Spares
Period	8	100 Spares

Action Messages

Release Order	Period 1	1000
Release Order	Period 2	1000

FIGURE 6.7 Based on the Planning Inputs, Running MRP confirms Order Release

in Period 1, indicating the recommended change is inside the cumulative lead time. An experienced MRP Planner would review that message and, before taking any action, would review the plan to determine any alternatives that would avoid such a near-term change. For example, the MRP Planner could consider releasing an order for 2,000 in Period 1 if this is a purchased part and transportation and handling costs could be saved with one shipment rather than two, or if there are quantity discounts from the supplier on orders above a given size to be balanced against inventory holding costs for the increased quantity. But before releasing an order for 2,000 units, the MRP Planner must also check warehouse and supplier production capacity availability. A little creativity and effort can save significant inefficient churn later. The good news is that MRP Planners become familiar with their items and their supply chain so that the amount of time they need to investigate these situations goes down significantly and quickly.

Safety Stock

Safety stock is an option in MRP software that gives the MRP Planner the ability to add additional supply to the plan but is often misused. In this example, Figure 6.8, different from the example above, the time-phased planning grid, shows dependent demand for a computer mouse. The MRP Planner has decided to carry a mouse safety stock of 10 even though there is no independent demand (i.e., spares) for the item. In Period 2, the planning system nets the 200 projected gross requirements out of the 200 on hand, recognizes that the projected available balance has dropped below the safety stock requirement, and creates a planned order for 1,000 units, the authorized order quantity, even though all requirements have been met. When the 1,000 units arrive at the beginning of Period 2, they will sit in inventory for five periods before there is another planned requirement of 200 units. A safety stock setting of 10 units is unnecessary waste given the forecasted projected gross requirements and the lead time of only one period. Huge, unnecessary inventories can result from the improper use of safety stock, but even more inefficient is that the MRP Planner is placing unnecessary capacity requirements on potentially constrained resources to produce materials that are not needed. The MRP Planner's priorities, in this case, are wrong and the plan is invalid.

Item: M178 OH: 200 OQ: 1,000	Description: Mouse LT: 1 Wk SS: 10	Material Requirements Planning (MRP)							
		Period							
		1	2	3	4	5	6	7	8
Projected Gross Requirements			200							200
Open Orders									
Projected Available Balance		200	200	1,000	1,000	1,000	1,000	1,000	1,000	800
Planned Order Receipts			1,000						
Planned Order Release		1,000							

FIGURE 6.8 Dealing with Safety Stock

The earlier example regarding lift truck frames that sat in inventory for 12 weeks, very expensive inventory held for no reason, precipitated development of a policy requiring the Material Manager's approval for adding safety stock to any component that did not have independent demand. Occasionally, the MRP Planner and the buyer would recommend safety stock for a purchased item because the supplier was consistently missing its delivery dates. Adding safety stock for this reason should be a temporary solution while the real issue with the supplier is being resolved. There must be a set of actions taken to get the supplier on schedule so that eventually the safety stock can be removed permanently, or, if that does not work, a new supplier should be qualified. Adding safety stock for the item's requirements also covers up the fundamental issues so that the supplier need not correct them. In that actual case, safety stock should be approved only if there is a realistic action plan with a reasonable chance for success. It should also be recognized that adding safety stock raises the demand on the supplier making the situation even worse. When the supplier demonstrates a sustained ability to meet delivery dates, the safety stock should be eliminated. Safety stock addition could also be approved during the transition period if the action plan is to change suppliers.

Bottom-Up Replanning

"Stuff" happens in the best-laid plans. Take for example the plan for the white and dark gray case computer screens. Suppose the buyer receives a call from the supplier with the information that the 1,000 screens expected in Periods 1 and 2 are not going to be available. In fact, no screens will be available for delivery until Period 6, and then only 300 per week thereafter. Of course, the buyer immediately begins to pressure the supplier, including stating that the issue will be escalated to the Purchasing VP and the supplier's Sales VP if there is not an immediate resolution. The supplier explains that escalation will do no good because the critical machine that makes the screens experienced a major breakdown and is not repairable. A replacement machine is on emergency order and is due to arrive next week, but it will not be operational for an additional three weeks. The two companies have a good relationship, as do the supplier's representative and the buyer; the buyer believes the representative. What are the options? Push the bad news that this shortage will cause the computer company to miss customer deliveries? This buyer is well educated, experienced, and smarter than that, and believes there might be a better course of action. The buyer meets with the Master Scheduler to explain the situation. The Master Scheduler reviews the master schedule in detail, but unfortunately, finds no immediate relief for the shortage. The Master Scheduler next reviewed the white and dark gray case inventory in the planning system. If the white case assembly order quantity could be reduced to "lot-for-lot" (a lot size of 1), only 200 screens would be required in Period 2 and 400 in Period 5, see Figure 6.9.

Item: C345 **Description: Case, White** **Material Requirements Planning (MRP)**

OH: 600   LT: 2 Wks
OQ: 350   SS: 0

		Period 1	2	3	4	5	6	7	8
Projected Gross Requirements		400	0	0	400	0	0	400	0
Open Orders									
Projected Avaiable Balance	600	200	200	200	~~150~~ 0	~~150~~ 0	~~150~~ 0	~~100~~ 0	~~100~~ 0
Planned Order Receipts					~~350~~ 200			~~350~~ 400	
Planned Order Releases			~~350~~ 200			~~350~~ 400			

Item: C567 **Description: Case, Dark Gray** **Material Requirements Planning (MRP)**

OH: 500   LT: 1 Wk
OQ: 600   SS: 0

		Period 1	2	3	4	5	6	7	8
Projected Gross Requirements		200	200	200	200	200	200	200	200
Open Orders			600						
Projected Avaiable Balance	500	300	700	500	300	100	~~500~~ 0	~~300~~ 0	~~100~~ 0
Planned Order Receipts							~~600~~ 100	200	200
Planned Order Releases						~~600~~ 100	200	200	

Item: S678 **Description: Screen** **Material Requirements Planning (MRP)**

OH: 900   LT: 3 Wks
OQ: 1,000   SS: 0
Independent Demand: 100/Wk   Allocated: 0

		Period 1	2	3	4	5	6	7	8
Projected Gross Requirements		100	~~450~~ 300	100	100	~~1050~~ 600	~~100~~ 300	~~100~~ 300	100
Open Orders									
Projected Available Balance	900	800	500	400	300	0	0	0	0
Planned Order Receipts						300	300	300	100
Planned Order Releases			300	300	300	100			

FIGURE 6.9 Bottom Up Replanning

A similar conclusion is reached when examining the dark gray case screen requirements. With lot-for-lot, the dark gray case needs 100 screens in Period 5 and 200 in all the following periods. Wow, just by changing the lot size on the cases, no customer deliveries will be missed, even with the delay from the supplier. Still, the buyer must monitor the supplier closely to make sure its delivery commitments are being met. The MRP Planners could declare a plan vulnerability to raise awareness and ensure that the supplier is monitored to ensure the issue is resolved as they have planned.

The only drawback is the efficiency, which could be negatively affected in the case assembly area because of the reduced lot size. So, for the future, a recommendation should be made to implement some continuous improvement activities to reduce the set-up time to avoid efficiency loss even with smaller lot sizes. A later chapter on Lean/Agile (Chapter 16) will elaborate more on this improvement opportunity.

MRP Planner Action/Exception Messages

Many MRP software systems offer a wide variety of action/exception messages that are unnecessary and should not be used. We recommend using only the basic messages listed below. Planned orders are automatically rescheduled by the planning system so that no action messages are required. Action messages are provided only for released and firm planned orders, most of which are in the firm and trading zones. The basic action messages we recommend utilizing include:

- **Reschedule Out** – Due to a change since the last run, the plan provides unneeded inventory; a firm planned or released order should be pushed out to a later date.
- **Reschedule In** – Due to a change since the last run, there will be a parts shortage. A firm planned or released order for that part should be pulled into an earlier date.
- **Cancel** – Due to a change since the last run, there is no unmet requirement for that part across the entire planning horizon, and any firm planned or released order for that part should be canceled.
- **Release Planned Order** – This is a system recommendation to release a planned or firm planned order.
- **Other Messages** – Use of any other system available action/exception messages should be carefully evaluated to see if they are really needed and that they provide value. They consume valuable MRP Planners' time and typically add little to no value. All messages must be acted on daily and be recognized by the MRP Planners as critically important in ensuring the MRP Planners' and the company's success.

Silence Is Approval

To fully benefit from a MRP system, the company culture must include some fundamental behaviors. One of the most important is "Silence is approval." Whenever a plan is put in place, everyone responsible for executing that plan must review it to confirm that their part of the plan is achievable. If it is not achievable, they must speak up immediately so that the plan can be made valid. For instance, if Production finds a capacity constraint during the detail capacity planning process (explained in Chapter 12), the MRP Planner must be informed immediately so that the problem can be resolved before the schedule is disrupted. The same applies to Procurement so they can work with their suppliers. "Silence is approval" also means that if something disruptive happens during plan execution, the appropriate MRP Planners must be informed immediately so that corrective actions can be taken to avoid disruption.

MRP Planner Responsibilities

MRP Planner responsibilities include:

- **Valid Plans:** Creating and maintaining valid material and capacity plans (accurate and achievable).
- **Act:** Reviewing and acting upon the planning system's action/exception messages daily and responding to change requests from other areas.
- **Bottom Up Replanning:** Use bottom up replanning when necessary to maintain maximum plan stability.
- **Make Decisions:** Determining what actions are "practical" versus "impractical" when reviewing action messages, a determination that often requires communicating with other departments.
- **Communicate:** Providing immediate feedback whenever an approved plan cannot be executed.
- **Maintaining Planning Data:**
  - Item master file.
  - Order file.
  - Maintain data accuracy, ownership, and its change management.

Implementation

One of the biggest mistakes companies make is to put MRP implementation into the hands of IT (information technology). Yes, it is software, but what it must do in support of the business has to be understood by the users to properly configure the planning system. A colleague of ours accepted a new job as MRP system Implementation Manager for one of four divisions of a large electronics firm. The four divisions included 18 sites. This division consisted of four component plant manufacturing sites. During day 1, it was a great surprise to learn that the Implementation Manager would report to the IT Manager. Arguing against this with the boss secured a discussion with the new IT Manager. When they meet, the Implementation Manager made the case that if the planning system implementation were driven by IT, it would be perceived as an IT project and users would not take it seriously. Ownership would be in the wrong department. The new IT Manager listened intently and said, "So, you are suggesting we be partners. You will take the responsibility for the operational requirements and users; I have responsibility for implementing the hardware and software." Our colleague responded enthusiastically with, "Yes!" The IT Manager smiled and said, "I love it. I'm tired of implementing systems that users don't use and that don't deliver the expected return on investment." That started a great working relationship that ended with a huge success story and four Class A certifications.

The other 14 sites sent their MRP Planners to Corporate for systems training. The company President had an Oliver Wight Class A Certification as a company objective. Selected to coach this company's transformation, we built our implementation based on the Oliver Wight Proven Path (explained later in Chapter 19). Instead of just training employees on software use, we created an education and training program using Unparalleled Business Planning and Execution Practices as a starting point, followed by business process redesign and configuration of the software to enable successful deployment of the new ways of working. The user design team decided which system capabilities to use and how they would use them. When his four sites' education and training program was completed, our colleague relocated to one of those component sites as their planning system implementation Project Manager. That site's GM was committed to achieving Class A, his rationale being that if they did not achieve those improvements the site would be out of business. His was the 12th of 18 sites to implement the software but the first to achieve Class

A Certification, less than one year from the first project team meeting. The other three component sites were not far behind, but the 14 remaining sites were hopelessly lost. Just prior to the Class A Certification celebration, the other divisions complained that their failure was the fault of the planning software. When our colleague's site, having been considered initially by Leadership to be the worst performing, reached Class A, that poor software excuse had little credibility, given the results the other four component sites were achieving. Other divisions began recruiting and hiring the MRP Planners from the Class A sites. Their problem, however, was that they wanted Class A Certification but did not want to change their basic behaviors. Many of MRP Planners who went to other divisions wanted to come back.

Our colleague's division began with 30 MRP Planners. One said he would not follow the new procedures; he was terminated. Another said there was too much responsibility, was moved to a job putting folders and prints together for released orders (something the MRP Planners were doing in the past), and was very happy. Just a year after Class A Certification and new planning system software implementation, the number of MRP Planners, all producing valid schedules that resulted in incredible improvements for that site, was down from 30 to 12. Inventory was reduced by 50% and on-time delivery increased from 16% to 98%. What happened to the 16 MRP Planners who were no longer needed? All MRP Planners received promotions inside the company or chose to move to other companies. The organization lost some of their best people, but they still delivered outstanding outcomes resulting from the disciplined processes put in place, and the performance discipline that became part of the culture.

The conclusion to draw from this example is that providing education to a broad array of people can ensure shared understanding. With this new knowledge, those people can then participate in Facilitated Application Workshops (described in Chapter 19) to apply their new knowledge, ensuring that planning processes are redesigned to capture Unparalleled Business Planning and Execution Practices. Finally, and only after the education and process redesign, they can work with the implementation manager and planning system experts to configure the software to support the redesigned planning processes. It is rare for off-the-shelf software to completely support newly redesigned business processes. However, the new knowledge allows the implementation team to have much better trade-off discussions. With properly configured software installed, users must be trained in its use, their specific roles and responsibilities, and how their work integrates with their colleagues' activities. During this training, the discipline required to ensure the software is always used and used properly must be emphasized, even if there are still some configuration issues. Any issues raised must be resolved immediately to ensure that the planning system is not blamed, which could cause people to then return to their spreadsheets and firefighting culture. Effective leadership and management will ensure success, which always results in significant, sustainable improvements and results, often exceeding the objectives used to justify the transformation initiative.

Measuring MRP Planner Performance

All previous chapters have included documented performance measures. Many companies create MRP Planner performance measures that simply are not effective performance measures of the MRP Planner. A measure that, for example, tracks the number of messages each MRP Planner receives is not a valid measure of their performance, unless research shows that they are not working their messages. As discussed earlier, the largest number of action messages are caused by other areas. The only proper MRP Planner performance measure is plan validity. To determine whether that plan is valid, the plan must be reviewed by a knowledgeable person. The review, or audit, begins by seeing if there are any messages that have not been worked. Is there is safety stock on an item and if there is, what is causing that need? What order quantity is being used and why? The list goes on. What is item validity accuracy for the items under that planner's control? If any item master data element is incorrect or cannot be explained, that item is counted as a miss (see the measure below). Obviously, it takes a skilled, unbiased person to perform the audit. When this path is followed with clients, it is amazing just how fast improvements are made. It never fails. The measurement is:

$$\text{Valid plan accuracy} = \frac{\text{Number of valid plans}}{\text{Number of plans reviewed}}$$

The minimum acceptable is 95%.

Summary

What seems to be most difficult about the education and training, process redesign, and planning system configuration and implementation discussed in this chapter? Spending the time and money to ensure a proper education and training program is developed and implemented. There is always pressure to chase the shiny, expensive thing, the software. But the biggest obstacle to success is changing the culture and discipline required in following approved procedures. The education and training program must address this issue at all levels but starting with Leadership. MRP will not work well if Leadership does not demonstrate their commitment and willingness to hold people, including themselves, accountable, or if Integrated Business Planning processes are not operating and following Unparalleled Business Planning and Execution Practices.

Without great Leadership it is a long, uphill, and disappointing battle. With great Leadership, the benefits exceed all expectations.

To learn more about Class A, the Proven Path for implementation, and its benefits, review the following books:

> *Achieving Class A Business Excellence, An Executive's Perspective* by Dennis Groves, Kevin Herbert, and Jim Correll (John Wiley & Sons)
> *An Executive's Guide to Achieving Class A Business Excellence* by Dennis Groves, Kevin Herbert, and Jim Correll (Oliver Wight International)

For additional but more specific reading please visit the Oliver Wight Website and gain access to the extensive library of White Papers.

CHAPTER 7

Mastering the Master Schedule: Meeting Customer Requests at Optimal Cost

This chapter reinforces the use of Master Scheduling to ensure that planning the end item is fully appreciated. Previous chapters have discussed nervousness in Material Requirements Planning (MRP) plans and schedules,

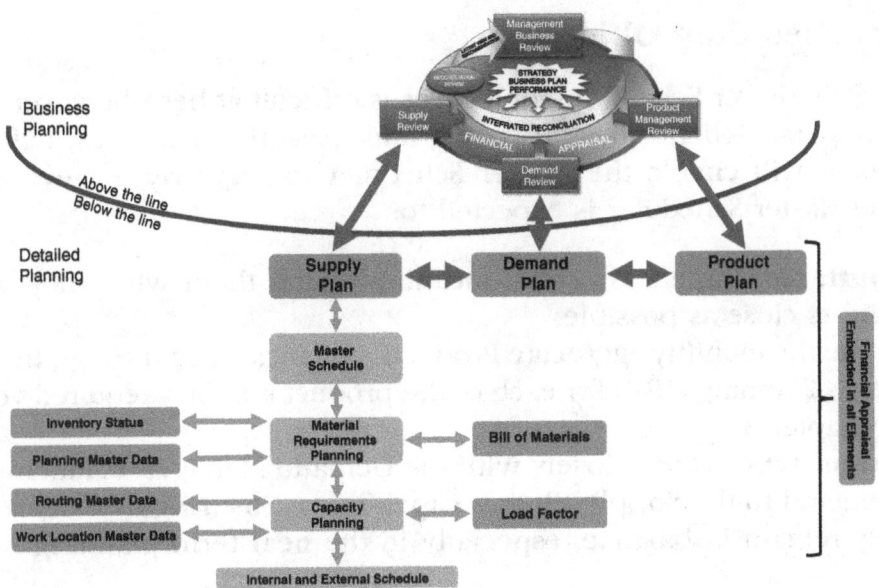

FIGURE 7.1 Business Excellence Planning

and how underlying data inaccuracy contributes to that nervousness. But nothing drives more nervousness than improper use of the Master Schedule (MS). The Master Scheduler (Supply Planner) operates between Sales and Marketing (the internal customers) and Supply (the internal supplier). It is a key and a challenging role that is, all too often, very understated. Coaching a client who was implementing a new MRP system with Class A behaviors (Chapter 18), one of the Master Schedulers made the observation that the Master Scheduler is between "a rock and a hard place." Our answer was a quick "absolutely." In fact, one of our recently retired colleagues used to refer to that existence as "living between the dog and the fire hydrant"! This chapter describes the critical processes and behaviors needed to enable the Master Scheduler to operate effectively in this environment.

Figure 7.1, Business Excellence Planning, shows where Master Scheduling sits in an integrated planning process. It drives MRP, relying on accurate Bills of Material (BOMs), inventory, and item masters, the same as MRP. MRP receives independent demand for items like spares, but the Master Schedule receives its independent demand as actual orders and the demand plan; see Chapter 10. One exception to this occurs when two-level master scheduling is utilized for product options planning, explained later.

Master Scheduling Objectives

Achieving all Master Scheduling objectives is difficult at best; however, following the Unparalleled Business Planning and Execution Practices, outlined in this chapter, will enable the Master Scheduler to regularly achieve most of them. The Master Scheduler is expected to:

- **Support:** Sales and customers, meaning giving them what they want or coming as close as possible.
- **Execute:** the monthly aggregate Production Plan, agreed through Integrated Business Planning (IBP) for each of the product families' required volumes. (See Chapter 8.)
- **Collaborate:** working closely with the Demand Manager, balancing product demand to the Supply Chain's capabilities. Ensuring that demand and supply remain in balance, especially in the near-term planning horizon,

is critical. More supply than demand results in excess inventory and degradation of bottom-line results; more demand than supply results in missed customer deliveries and degradation of both top- and bottom-line results.

- **Communicate:** Regulate responses to Sales/Customers who seem to be changing their minds. Understanding this fact of life, the Master Scheduler must serve as a shock absorber to dampen manufacturing schedule disruptions as much as possible while supporting customer service.
- **Manage:** resources, meaning minimizing the tremendous amount of churn that can occur in the company and across the entire Supply Chain when reacting to customer changes inside agreed lead times. The Master Scheduler (Supply Planner) must support the customer but also keep Supply organizations operating efficiently (there is that rock and hard place again).
- **Be Cost Effective:** Minimize inventory investment, a significant challenge since excess inventory might, but does not always, satisfy changing customer requirements, but that will also increase product cost and reduce ROI, making Finance less than happy!
- **Optimize:** business results through regulating response to changing market conditions, managing supply resources, optimizing inventory and supporting the customer. This means the Master Scheduler (Supply Planner) must develop an optimized plan based on Leadership's strategy.

Master Scheduling Challenge – Valid Schedule

The first challenge the Master Scheduler(s) faces is how to maximize customer service while also minimizing inventory and operating costs. A valid Master Schedule (accurate and achievable) is the key to the process. A valid Master Schedule means that the:

- **Sales organization** (internal customer) agrees with the schedule.
- **Supply Chain organization**, while making known any resulting inefficiency, commits to delivering the schedule.
- **Agreement:** when reached, the Master Schedule is valid.

The Master Schedule drives MRP through all levels of the bill of material (BOM) and into supplier schedules for all master scheduled items, which could be hundreds or even thousands of items. Any question now about why the schedule must be valid?

Master Schedule Logic

The logic is the same as that used for MRP but with some additions to help manage change. Figure 7.2 is a simplified spreadsheet to explain the logic. Master Schedule and MRP Planning logic assumes the world is predictable and that what is displayed in the schedules is reasonably accurate and will actually happen. The logic is not designed to deal with a world of ever-changing numbers, inaccurate data, and so forth, but this chapter addresses how to manage the process to reduce the impact of this imperfect world.

		Period							
		1	2	3	4	5	6	7	8
Forecast	"A"								
Production Forecast	"A"								
Actual Demand	"A"								
Total Demand	"A"								
Projected Available Balance	"B"								
Available-to-Promise	"B"								
Master Schedule Receipt	"C"								
Master Schedule Release	"C"								

FIGURE 7.2 Basic Master Schedule Worksheet

A definition for each of the worksheet labels is provided below.

Periods
- **Weekly Buckets:** These are weekly buckets 1–8 (planning software can provide at least daily buckets over a planning horizon of 12 to 24 months and beyond).

Demand "A"

- **Forecast:** This is the Sales department's best estimate of what will be sold in the future by item/option and by period. However, the sales forecast by itself is not always adequate for production because end items requiring the availability of spares must also be forecasted, by period, to provide the full needs.
- **Production Forecast:** This is the production planner's projection of how many end items and derived subassemblies must be produced, in specific periods, to satisfy planned end item demand. Independent demand for spares and any demands from other Demand Managers, if production is supplying other business units beyond its own Sales organization, must also be included.
- **Actual Demand:** Customer orders already received that have consumed the forecast for that period.
- **Total Demand:** Sales forecast unconsumed + Actual demand + Production forecast (see definitions above).

Supply "C"

- **Master Schedule Receipt:** The period in which a master scheduled item production order is scheduled to be received.
- **Master Schedule Release:** The period in which a master scheduled item production order is scheduled to be released.
- **Types of Orders:**
  - Released Orders (purchased or manufactured item): Orders that have been authorized to have work done on them by the Master Scheduler.
  - Planned Orders: Orders that have not yet been released and are controlled by the planning system, which automatically generates suggested orders and regenerates them upon system refresh.
  - Firm Planned Orders: Orders that have not yet been released but the Master Scheduler has taken away the planning system's ability to change quantity, lead time, or both, and to move the order. If the computer recognizes an imbalance, it sends an action message regarding that firm planned order to the Master Scheduler.

Critique "B"

- **Projected Available Balance (PAB):**
  - The on-hand and calculated projected inventory for each item in each period.

- Creates action messages for the Master Scheduler when the master schedule demand and supply are out of balance.
- **Available-to-Promise (ATP):** The calculated quantity of end items not yet committed to a customer. These items are, therefore, available for customer promising. The ATP calculation is one of the most powerful tools in the planning system.

Calculating the Master Schedule

Header Information:

Referencing the time-phased planning grid, Figure 7.3:

Item: A123   Desc: Pencil
OH: 30   LT: 3
OQ: 50   Cum. LT: 7
Safety Stock: 0

		Period							
		1	2	3	4	5	6	7	8
Forecast		10	10	10	10	15	15	15	15
Production Forecast									
Actual Demand									
Total Demand		10	10	10	10	15	15	15	15
Projected Available Balance	30	20	10	0	40	25	10	−5 45	30
Available-to-Promise									
Master Schedule Receipt					50			50	
Master Schedule Release		50			50				

FIGURE 7.3 An Example of a Basic Master Schedule, Time-Phased Planning Grid

- **Item:** The item number being master scheduled.
- **Description:** The name of the item; most companies have a disciplined naming nomenclature.
- **OH** (on-hand inventory): The quantity of that item currently in inventory.
- **LT** (lead time): The demonstrated lead time required to manufacture an item (i.e., to convert the components of a single-level BOM from level 1 to level 0). Lead time is derived from the Routing.
- **OQ** (order quantity): The quantity that the Master Schedule will plan; a fixed order quantity should ideally be used as the quantity is constant providing a measure of planning stability.

- **CLT** (cumulative lead time): The time required, beginning with no components in inventory and ending when the product has been completed. To determine the required time, first examine the lead time for each BOM leg by adding up the individual component lead times level-by-level for each leg. Select the leg with the longest lead time. The lead time associated with that leg, including the final assembly time and quality control release time, if necessary, is the cumulative lead time (CLT).
- **SS:** (safety stock): The amount of additional inventory the Master Scheduler plans to keep on hand. When planning a new order the planned safety stock level of that item has been, or is projected to be, depleted by actual orders or forecast of that item. For options, safety stock can be added for flexibility of forecast error.
- **Over Planning:** A method to put extra product in the master schedule for two-level master scheduling that minimizes inventory that safety stock would put into inventory.

Following the time-phased planning grid, Figure 7.3:

- There is a Forecast of 10 units per period, jumping to 15 per period in Period 5. There is no additional requirement for this item caused by another Master Schedule item, there is no production forecast, and there is no actual demand (orders).
- Total Demand is then 10 per period through Period 4 and 15 units beginning in Period 5.
- Since there are 30 units in the stock room (on hand) and 10 are expected to be consumed in each of Periods 1–3, the projected available balance (PAB) drops to 0 in Period 3. With no safety stock requirement, the planning system's master schedule is still happy with the current plan.
- In Period 4, inventory is projected to fall below zero, so there is a projected need for a scheduled receipt in Period 4 for 50 units (the order quantity) and a scheduled release of 50 in Period 1 since the lead time is three periods. When the 50 units arrive in Period 4, 10 satisfy demand, leaving 40 as the PAB. The forecast jumps to 15 each of the Periods 5–7, resulting in the need for another scheduled receipt of 50 in Period 7 and an associated scheduled release in Period 4. With the receipt in Period 7, the PAB in Period 7 will be 45, and in Period 8 it will be 30.

Point of Reflection Back to Data Accuracy

This is a good time to reflect on the earlier data accuracy discussion. Consider the impact to the Master Scheduler if the data shown by the system above is 50% accurate. In that case, the CLT might be anywhere from 3.5 to 10.5; LT might be anywhere from 1.5 to 4.5 periods; the OQ could range from 25 to 75; the OH could be anywhere from 15 to 45; the Master Schedule Receipt could be 25 up to 75. Overall, the planning system output would be a complete mess and the Master Scheduler would rush back to using trusted spreadsheets. Accurate data is essential.

Planning Time Fences

The planning time fences (emergency and cumulative) when understood and honored, are the most powerful schedule stabilizers between the Master Schedule and MRP. To have MRP stability plans must be stabilized from the top down, this begins with Integrated Business Planning, the feed to Master Scheduling. Every time the Master Schedule is changed, schedules for hundreds, or even thousands, of items in lower BOM levels could be affected. There must be a decoupling of demand for resources from supply because of the chaotic nature of unmanaged demand. To achieve this stability, the Master Schedule must prevent the MRP planning system from moving or creating planned orders inside the planning time fences.

In Figure 7.4, the horizontal line represents the timeline starting with point of delivery (when the product ships) and extends out as far as the planning system extends, typically two years. The firm time fence (often referred to as the emergency time fence) is three periods, as represented by the light gray vertical line on the time-phased planning grid. This vertical line, which can be, and should be, different for every item, represents the emergency time fence, or firm time fence. The CLT for this item is seven weeks, represented by the dark gray vertical line. Different software packages vary in how they deal with creating near-term stability. Some are overly complicated and cause more work than necessary. A simple solution is for the Master Scheduler to release orders at the firm time fence, and to firm planned orders at the CLT, thus taking control of quantity and timing away from the planning system. If the MRP system recognizes a Demand/Supply imbalance that indicates a need to move a firm planned order, it notifies the Master Scheduler through action/exception messages. The Master Scheduler analyzes the message and the situation to see what products and components are impacted and then reviews each to determine how reasonable the system-generated recommendation is. Usually only a few products and components would be short if the plans have been valid, and the Master Scheduler could easily address the situation unless the course of action would affect demand. If the Master Scheduler performs properly, responses to most plan imbalance decisions are not just made in a vacuum, by the Supply Chain organization, but must be made in partnership with the Commercial/Sales organization. Otherwise, decisions will always be made based on optimizing cost.

However, the imbalance situation could be extremely complex, requiring considerable analysis with many alternative courses of action to resolve the issue. Most companies, due to the frequency, aggravation, and frustration caused by these imbalances, tend to simply and quickly change the master schedule and force the myriad of resulting schedule changes with little understanding of consequences and costs. The churn then begins and ultimately either the customer promise, which was made inside the agreed lead time, is missed or other customer promises are missed or both. Yes, it takes more work for Master Schedulers to maintain schedule stability, but in doing so, they make the work of MRP Planners and Buyers significantly simpler, eliminate factory and supplier schedule churn, save money, and learn how to meet nearly all customer requirements.

With a well-managed, stable Master Schedule, data accuracy, and a planning system providing logical action/exception messages, an MRP Planner can plan and manage effectively, several thousand items. The applied Unparalleled Business Planning and Execution Practices must be documented in the Master Scheduling Policy and related procedures, which clearly state what is to be done, by whom, and by when to resolve demand and supply imbalances. Of course, the policy and procedures must be available and followed.

Time Fences must be:

- **Available:** for every master scheduled item.
- **Established:** for firm and trading zones (additional time fences may be added as appropriate for some companies). Should Leadership's desire be to reduce the total lead time required for a product, inventory of the longest-lead-time items may be maintained.
- **Used:** to decouple demand from supply.
- **Realistic:** developed and managed by the Supply Chain and supported by Leadership.

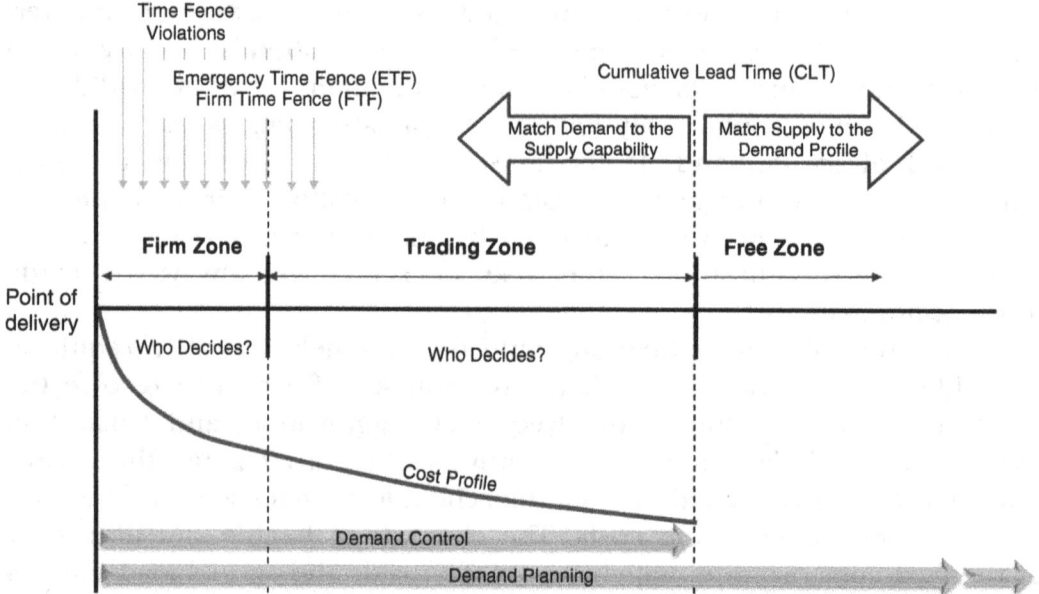

FIGURE 7.4 Time Fences

A typical cost profile is included in Figure 7.4. This cost profile would vary from product to product, but as the change decision moves closer to the point of delivery the cost of change will increase exponentially.

Also included in the diagram are two arrows. The demand planning arrow goes out through the whole horizon, which means that the demand planning process (see Chapter 10) covers the entire planning horizon. The demand control arrow extends only to cumulative lead time fence. Above those arrows are two more arrows. The one pointing to the left, "Match Demand to the Supply Capability," recognizes that changes in demand within the CLT are very costly, as the Supply Chain is already charged to deliver the approved Master Schedule; if increased demand is needed longer term, then Supply needs to make a rec-ommendation as to how this will be achieved. Until this has been done, the concept is to get Sales and Marketing to match the demand; they see to the current Supply Chain Capability. The arrow pointing to the right, "Match Supply to the Demand Profile," means that any demand increases are acceptable, as there is time for Supply to cost-effectively increase its capability to match the demand. However, this does not include a new product being introduced with a lead time longer than the existing CLT.

Just how important are time fences? The Materials Manager at an equipment supplier was "blessed" with a new GM who was not provided Unparalleled Business Planning and Execution Practice education on the planning processes or planning system. One day that new GM wandered into the planning office to inform the Materials Manager that he had committed delivery of a vehicle to a sales representative on a specific date. He mentioned that meeting the delivery date was also important to him personally since the sales representative presented him with an expensive bottle of wine as a thank-you gift for his flexibility. The Materials Manager asked for a few minutes to check whether it was even possible to do what was being asked but was quickly told, "Just make it happen." The Materials Manager forced the change request into the plan, but that was the only vehicle not to meet its scheduled delivery date that year.

Master Schedule Change Process

Now that the requirements of a valid master schedule are clear, how does the Master Scheduler deal with the real world in which orders (shown as the vertical time fence violation arrows in Figure 7.4) inside the cumulative lead time are requested regularly or changed? The following is a starting point – a list of questions to be asked and answered:

- **Has demand really changed?** Demand change requests should be processed through the Demand Manager, who may be able to resolve the change without affecting the Supply organization. But when the Master Scheduler receives a demand change request, the first question of the Demand Manager, Order Entry, or Sales is whether this changed demand represents a real emergency. The number of true emergencies is remarkably low. The requirement to escalate the change request to a senior manager for review and approval quickly reduces the frequency of requests and ensures that only real emergencies receive resolution attention and resources.
- **Can we get the required materials?** Depending on the timing of the change request, the question can be answered easily by checking ATP, or if not in ATP by having the Buyer or MRP Planner contact the supplier (see Chapter 13).

- **Can we get the required capacity?** This question can be answered easily and quickly if there is a detail capacity planning process in place (see Chapter 12).
- **How much will the change cost?** This can be difficult to determine but is extremely important and hence warrants good analyses. The costs are often underestimated because the resulting churn is not fully understood and is therefore difficult to assess accurately.
- **Is the change worth the cost and churn?** This question most often must be answered by Sales and Supply Chain Leadership.

The bottom line is that there are just two questions: First, *"Can we do it?"* and second, *"How much will it cost?"* Armed with these answers, the Master Scheduler (if the decision is within the Master Scheduler's decision boundaries) or Leadership (depending on authority levels documented in policy) can make a good decision.

Some time ago, we were helping a large heavy equipment manufacturing company reach Class A. The Chairman of that company asked each of his division managers if they could do more in the final quarter of the year to improve the company's results. One division manager, with whom we were working, asked if pulling in equipment orders was a Class A behavior. We asked the question "Can you do it, and how much will it cost? Based on that information, make your decision." His Master Schedulers reviewed the situation, found vehicles they could pull in, and estimated the cost to be $1 million. At that cost, the division manager needed to escalate the decision to the Chairman. The Chairman was pleased and approved the recommendation. When it was all said and done, all vehicles were delivered on time at a premium cost of $2 million. Afterwards, in response to the question of whether they would have made the same decision knowing the elevated cost of the move, the GM's answer was a resounding "yes." Always remember that the planning system does not manage your company; you do. Because the right approach was taken, all Business Objectives were met. Had this company just thrown more vehicles into the plan without examining which specific vehicles it made sense to pull in, they probably would not have met the original schedule, let alone the additions to the plan.

Master Schedule Change Zones

There are typically three planning zones (depicted in Figure 7.4) within which changes are often requested, and these must be managed carefully. The zones characteristics are as follows:

1. Firm Zone (inside the firm time fence and often referred to as the emergency zone)
   - The required date for any order added in this zone is close, inside the agreed lead time.
   - Materials for orders in this zone either have been received or will be received prior to the item's production start date.
   - Available capacity in this zone has been committed and the production cycle has begun.
   - The schedule in this zone is not flexible without significant capacity, cost and inventory impact, and usually a significant lowering of productivity.
   - *Typically, it is very expensive to make the change in this zone.*
   - Change request approval must be escalated to Supply and Demand Leadership.

2. Trading Zone (between firm time fence and cumulative time fence)
   - Any order added inside this zone violates the planning guideline that requires materials to have been ordered and capacity to have been reserved in-house and in third-party suppliers.
   - The schedule is somewhat flexible in this zone if change requests involve similar products, setups, and materials; changes are normally approved by the Master Scheduler after consultation with the Production Managers.
   - *Changes in this zone will have relatively modest cost, capacity, and inventory impact.*

3. Free Zone (beyond the cumulative time fence)
   - The required date provides the time necessary to order all materials and to plan capacity.
   - Material orders are planned but not firmed or released.
   - Capacity is planned in aggregate but not for specific items.
   - The schedule is very flexible, and orders are normally automatically processed.
   - *There is little to no expense* incurred in changing the schedule in this time zone.

In summary, the nearer the required date, the higher the cost of making a change; the increase in cost is exponential, particularly when the delivery date is near. The further out in the planning horizon the required delivery date is, the easier and less costly it is to approve the change request. When considering the impact of the change, remember that small changes are relatively easy but large changes can be overwhelming. Frequent change requests provide an incentive to initiate a "lean/agile" manufacturing project. Reducing lead time allows the firm time zone to be reduced and provides more flexibility for schedule changes, provided that third-party suppliers also have similar flexibility in their processes or in-house sites are permitted to carry additional inventory of constrained components.

The cost profile from the cumulative lead time (CLT) to the point of delivery must be clearly understood and used to support decision making. In the trading zone, the cost of change for orders added close to the CLT will be relatively small. However, as the change request date approaches the firm time zone, the cost of change rapidly escalates. Similarly, for violations allowed between the emergency time fence and the point of delivery the cost will further increase exponentially. Approval authority for these near-term changes must be controlled, and clear decision-making authority must be documented in policy. Just as an example, approval of the Supply Chain or Commercial Director may be required for changes in the firm zone, and the Procurement Director for the trading zone. All change request decisions must have Commercial/Sales Leadership involvement; otherwise decisions will always be based upon cost implications ("Is it worth it to the business?").

It is worth noting at this point that any changes approved in the firm or trading zones will rarely have a positive impact on overall business results. Nearly all changes approved will help one customer but often at the expense of others and will significantly increase supply costs.

Planning, Supply, Sales, Marketing, Product, and Commercial teams must all understand and honor time zones, understand change request implications, and honor approval procedures to optimize business results and customer service.

Available-to-Promise

Available-to-Promise (ATP) is one of the most powerful Master Scheduling features, but it is generally not understood, not used, or not used effectively by too many companies.

To understand how ATP works, reference the same worksheet as before, but customer orders received are now shown in the actual demand row, and the ATP quantity is calculated for each period (see Figure 7.5). In this example, there is actual demand (customer orders) in Periods 1 and 2 for 10 units each. In Period 3, there are orders for an additional 5 units. In Period 4, actual demand is 2, and in Period 5, actual demand is 1. Note that actual demand consumes the forecast (actual demand is deducted from the forecast). Again, in this example, adding the unconsumed forecast and the actual demand together equals total demand, which remains the same at 10 for each period. A stable Supply plan is maintained even though orders are still being received.

Item: B789 Desc: Blue Pens OH: 30 LT: 3 OQ: 50 Cum. LT:7 Safety Stock: 0		Period							
		1	2	3	4	5	6	7	8
Forecast				5	8	9	10	10	10
Production Forecast									
Actual Demand		10	10	5	2	1			
Total Demand		10	10	10	10	10	10	10	10
Projected Available Balance	30	20	10	0	40	30	20	20	0
Available-to-Promise		5			47				
Master Schedule Receipt					50				
Master Schedule Release		50					50		

FIGURE 7.5 Available-to-Promise and Its Link to Master Schedule Receipt

Forecast consumption is essential to maintain the anticipated total demand requirements as provided by Demand Management (see IBP and Demand, Chapters 8 and 10). If this does not happen each time an actual order is entered in the system, the demand for that item would be increased by that new order amount. In turn, plan instability would be introduced as the increased demand would cascade to the Master Schedule, MRP, and so forth. Master Scheduling consumption logic must be thoroughly understood by all planners to ensure that the planning system is configured correctly.

The next step in calculating ATP is to determine the number of planning periods remaining until the next Master Schedule Receipt. In this case the first Master Schedule Receipt is due in Period 4; so, the inventory on hand now must last until the end of Period 3. Actual demand for Periods 1, 2, and 3 totals

25. Total demand is 30 (same as inventory, meaning the master schedule matches demand) during those same three periods. Therefore, Customer Service can promise delivery of 5 additional units prior to the next Master Scheduled Receipt in Period 7. When can we sell and promise those units? Right now, since they are in inventory. ATP becomes 5 in Period 1 and 0 in Periods 2 and 3.

Next, total actual demand from the time the first Master Schedule Receipt in Period 4 until the Master Schedule Receipt in Period 8, or two in Period 4, one in Period 5, and 0 in Periods 6 and 7 for a total actual demand for Periods 4 through 7 of three. The Master Schedule Receipt of 50 in Period 4 less the three units ordered in Periods 4 and 5 leaves an ATP of 47 in Period 4. Since there is no actual demand in Period 8, all 50 units in that Master Schedule receipt remain ATP.

How powerful is this capability? Assuming the company is executing its plans, the ATP row can be used by Order Entry to receive orders and instantly reply with better than 99% confidence that the products ordered will be available on time, assuming a valid plan at all planning levels. Why not 100% confidence? Simply because "stuff happens" outside the company's control, but companies operating with Unparalleled Business Planning and Execution Practices commonly operate with customer service above 99%.

What happens if there is no ATP when the customer wants product? If the Demand Manager concludes that product is a priority for that customer, Order Entry works directly with the Master Scheduler to resolve the problem. Our experience is that in more than 80% of the cases, the Master Scheduler and the planning team meet the customer requests because the vast majority of customer orders are now being committed to and delivered by our clients on time with very little churn.

Here is the big caution. Plans must be valid, and they must be executed well throughout the company. How is that accomplished? Do what is recommend in the other chapters, and it becomes a way of life. Let one area of the organization fail to follow the new procedures, and the expected results will not be achieved.

Supply Chain Strategy

A key Supply Chain strategic decision that affects all aspects of planning is determining where to meet the customer (Figure 7.6).

➤ Level that enables us to meet the customer and best balance our business objectives

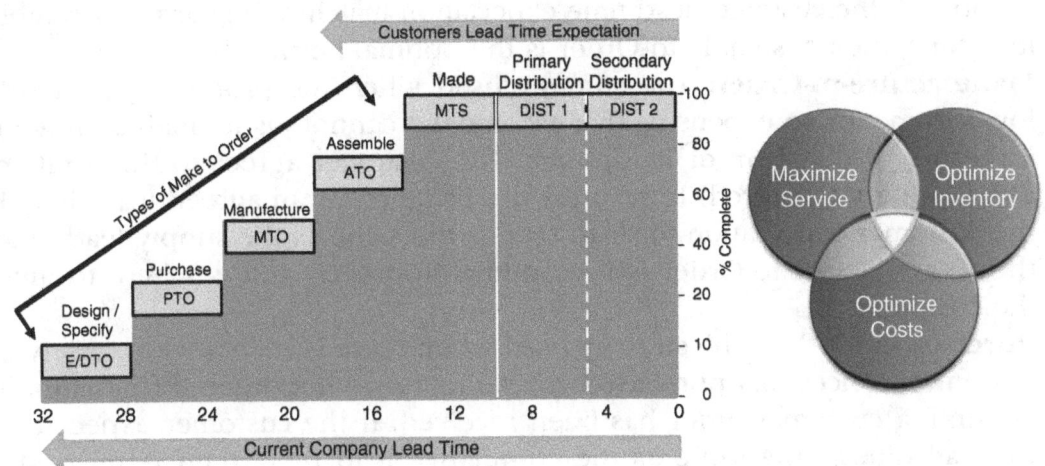

➤ Level that gives you maximum control based on the shape of the product profile

FIGURE 7.6 Where You Meet the Customer

The approach to meeting customer lead time expectations is to meet the customer from:

- **Distribution 2:** A strategy of meeting the customer from a secondary distribution center located very close to the customer, usually a major strategic customer, allowing maximized flexibility in meeting the customer needs, often responding with same-day delivery.
- **Distribution 1:** A strategy of meeting the customer from a regionally centralized distribution center intended to reduce lead time in that region and to reduce distribution costs, often with delivery within two to three days.
- **Make-to-Stock:** The strategy of meeting the customer from a centralized warehouse or from regional warehouses (Distribution 2 or Distribution 1) and used when the customer will not wait for the product; if it is not in stock, they buy a competitor's product.
- **Assemble-to-Order:** The strategy used when there are many product options. The options are planned and ordered by the Supply function in advance of the Customer order. When the customer order arrives, the

options are selected, and the product is assembled to the customer's specifications. If the customer lead time expectation matches the current assembly lead time, then Assemble-to-Order is the optimal approach.

- **Manufacture-to-Order:** The strategy used when the product is complex, low volume, or so expensive that a company cannot justify maintaining an inventory of that item or its options. The customer agrees to this strategy and is willing (required) to wait for the product for an agreed lead time. If the customer expectation for lead time is the same as the supply lead time, then Manufacture-to-Order is the optimal approach and is where to meet the customer.

- **Purchase-to-Order:** The strategy used when there is such a wide variety of customer choices that purchased components are not ordered from suppliers until a customer order has been received. If the customer expectation for lead time is the same as the cumulative lead time, then Purchase-to-Order is the optimal strategy and where to meet the customer.

- **Engineer-to-Order:** The strategy used when products are extremely complex, with design specifications that require unique design solutions. In this case, inventory is held in the form of engineering and design resources applied only when a contract has been signed. If the customer expectation for lead time is the same as cumulative lead time including Design Engineering, Engineer-to-Order is the optimal strategy and where to meet the customer.

For Purchase-, Manufacture-, and Assemble-to-Order and Make-to-Stock, all of the preceding work must be completed in order to meet the customers' expectations; this work is usually managed through a process called Proceed at Risk.

When asked which strategy they use, people in the room often disagree; it is not uncommon for a company to employee all seven. Take a Manufacture-to-Order company that swears it does not do any Make-to-Stock supply. When asked if they must produce spare parts for their products, and they do, we then ask if they have any spares in stock. We hear only silence. Then there is the Make-to-Stock company that makes some of their new products only after they receive a Customer's order. The bottom line is that most companies have different strategies for different products. The primary strategy does not make any difference – the appropriate master scheduling technique(s) must be used to support customer requirements for each product. The explanation of the various techniques and how to select the proper "where to meet the customer" technique for each product is best described in our good friend John Proud's book, *Master Scheduling: A Practical Guide to Competitive Manufacturing*, third edition (see the recommended reading at the end of this chapter).

It is, however, worthy to note that the best strategies to minimize inventory are Make-to-Order and Purchase-to-Order, but they come with the downside of extending customer lead time. Their use depends upon the customer's response expectations. The best approach, however, is to maximize flexibility and agility, as the company could well miss out on orders from customers who are not prepared to wait for long lead times.

Component Manufacturing Master Scheduling

Component suppliers often believe that they may not require master scheduling techniques since their demand comes directly from their customers. Of course, they would like to believe that their customer requirements are always accurate, and that their customers honor the agreed time fences, but, of course, they know better! Our experience is quite the opposite. Customer planning processes typically range from poor to terrible. Receiving volume and timing changes every day is disruptive, but that can't always be controlled. What is unacceptable is allowing those changes to flow through directly to the sites; that can be and must be controlled. The planning organization determines the best response option to satisfy the customer rather than forcing the churn. The solution for minimizing that churn is for component suppliers to master schedule their end items.

In the example shown in Figure 7.7, there are three finished product facilities, two component facilities, and two sub-component facilities, all interdependent. Poor scheduling in the finished product facilities causes uncontrolled churn in all the other facilities. Imagine being the planner in one of the sub-component facilities if the component facilities also have poor planning processes. Never-ending churn! Looking at the right side of the figure, component requirements flow down from the finished product facilities' Master Schedules to MRP then to MRP at the next level, then at the level below that, and so on. This approach guarantees churn at every level, high costs, and unacceptable resource utilization. The recommended approach is to plan requirements as shown on the left side of the figure, from MS through MRP at the finished product facilities, then to MS and MRP at the component facilities, then to MS and MRP at the sub-component facilities. This approach always works and allows each facility to stabilize their schedules, optimizing customer service, costs, and resource utilization.

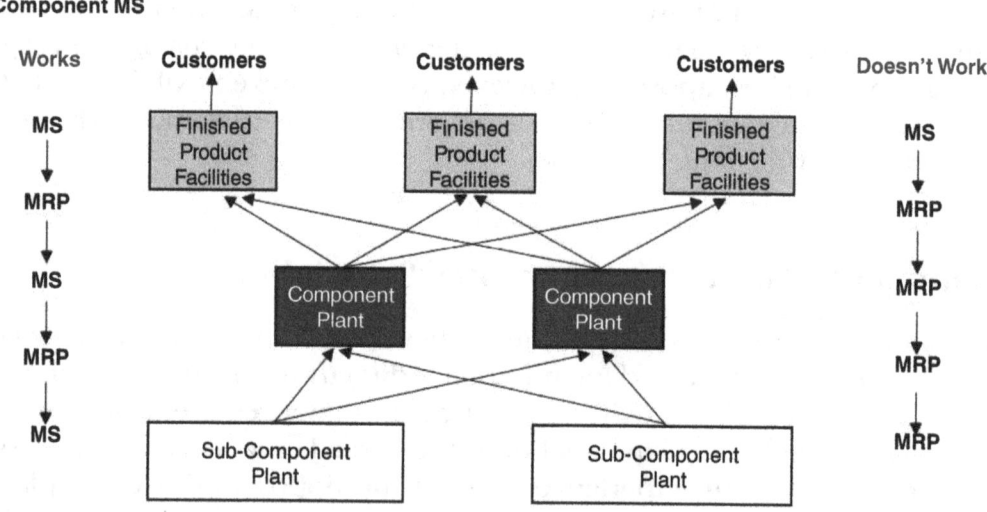

FIGURE 7.7 Utilizing the Master Schedule for Control – What Works?

How does this work in practice? The component and sub-component facilities create firm planned orders for all their end items, out through the cumulative lead time. Each time the customer violates the agreed CLT, the planning system sends an action message to the facilities' Master Schedulers noting those violations and recommending action. This does not mean that the change requests should be refused (you will be out of business quickly) but that the affected facility's Master Scheduler should investigate the need and response options in collaboration with the internal customer, or Sales if an external customer, to determine a course of action that optimizes results for both parties.

The following are some proven options that work effectively in many companies:

- **Challenge the Change:** Very often the challenge will result in a more reasonable request, or even eliminate the change request. Making change easy tends to drive very bad behavior; people just request changes because they can. Also, consider the message the customer receives if the answer is always "yes" when they call. The unintended message is that their forecast is not needed and that you have infinite, cost-effective agility. A customer would be happy to believe this, so, at an appropriate point in time, this customer misconception must be corrected. Time after time it has been proven that getting a customer to forecast, accurately, its business also gives them significant competitive advantages.

- **Charge Extra:** If change requests fall into the trading zone, levy a minimal charge for the change. If the change request falls into the emergency zone, levy a significant charge for the change, which typically results in more operating income to the supplier's bottom line. This is often a negotiated fee with the ability to offer a discount from the initial pricing position reflecting improved customer scheduling stability over time.
- **Develop an Unconstrained Demand Plan:** One of our clients continuously complained about poor customer forecasts and change requests making planning nearly impossible. We suggested taking the offense by developing their own forecast using input from their Sales organization. Their forecast accuracy became so reliable that their Finance VP offered all their customers a 5% discount if they could provide a forecast better than their own. No customer was able to capitalize on the offer.
- **Reduce the Cumulative Lead Time:** Do this through Lean/Agile techniques (Chapter 16, Business Improvement). This approach provides significant customer value by reducing the lead time, thus eliminating many of the requests.

Key responsibilities in a Supply Chain customer-supplier relationship include:

- **Customer (Orders the Components):**
  - Establishing and communicating requirements.
  - Honoring time fences.
- **Supplier (Makes the Components):**
  - Satisfying customer requirements.
  - Controlling its own destiny.
  - Owning rescheduling.
  - Optimizing its product costs.

Master Scheduler Performance Measures

Just as with the MRP Planner, the real measure of Master Scheduler performance is whether their plans are valid. The only way to determine whether a Master Schedule is valid is to audit the Master Schedule with a competent and knowledgeable person.

The Master Scheduler's job is far more complex than that of the MRP Planner. For example, they have personal authority to establish finished product inventory quantities required to better serve the customer. Therefore, it is necessary to measure and track the inventory investment planned by a Master Scheduler. The master schedule planning system must be able to total inventory and projected inventory by Master Scheduler and by product line. Most planning systems have that capability, but if not, it is an easy program to add.

When there is excessive churn due to time fence violations, it is important to measure how many violations occur by period and the cause of that churn. This measure provides visibility and the awareness needed to systematically understand each violation and to eliminate its root cause.

Other useful performance measures include Master Schedule Adherence and Supplier Schedule Adherence, both requiring consistent minimum adherence of 95% to enable valid plans.

Master Scheduler Responsibilities and Planning System Capabilities

The best way to define the Master Scheduler responsibilities and required planning system capabilities are to separate the two:

1. Master Scheduler:
- Creates and maintains a valid master schedule for all items assigned.
- Evaluates proposed changes for Supply Chain impact.
- Provides input to negotiate customer dates.
- Maintains master schedule credibility by keeping it up to date (daily) and valid.
- Accountable for master schedule validity (i.e. positive rewards and negative penalties).
- Requires data accuracy in the planning system.

2. System Capability:

- Stores all information needed to perform required calculations.
- Displays the information in a manner that supports the master scheduling process described here and in John Proud's book. Not always available in master scheduling systems because code writers often do not know or understand Unparalleled Business Planning and Execution Practices.
- Calculates the projected available balance and available-to-promise quantities.
- Critiques the plan status and sends action messages alerting the Master Scheduler of all supply/demand imbalances.
- Uses the data provided whether accurate or not. Unfortunately, management often blames the system for invalid plans when the real problem is inaccurate data and poor Master Scheduler decisions. Even worse, in a firefighting environment Master Schedulers are willing to blame the system rather than to understand and eliminate the real causes. Committed and knowledgeable Leadership is essential in driving continuous performance improvement and in not accepting a culture of firefighting.

Remember the earlier comment that the Master Scheduler is between a rock and a hard place? The rock is the constant pressure to respond to customer change requests, and the hard place is Supply resisting those changes because it makes them inefficient. The Master Scheduler must effectively decouple demand from supply in the planning system to maximize plan control. Without a valid and stable Master Schedule, MRP must be controlled manually to ensure component inventory does not grow based on an inaccurate forecast. In addition, Demand Control (see Chapter 10) requires a valid Master Schedule for critical customer service information as available-to-promise (ATP), projected available balance (PAB), and forecast consumption.

Summary

The Master Scheduler is a critical player in a comprehensive planning process, but at the same time decoupling demand and supply. This is a management role, not a clerical role. In this chapter we presented only some basic Master Scheduling behaviors, but they are the behaviors we see violated most often and the ones that cause the most havoc in MRP plans. John Proud's expansive

Master Scheduling book (see the recommended reading) presents far more detail on this subject. It is not a casual read, but it is a must-read for all Master Schedulers and their Managers.

The skill required to Master Schedule properly is extremely high and is dependent upon knowing and using Unparalleled Business Planning and Execution Practices. Many Master Schedulers we have encountered do not understand those required practices and do not have sufficient knowledge of their businesses to effectively carry out their responsibilities. Leadership must understand Master Scheduling fundamentals and benefits, insist that educated and trained individuals are placed in those roles, and must hold them accountable in order to utilize the planning system effectively, support the effective planning culture, and realize the bottom line benefits of effective Master Scheduling.

Recommended Reading

Groves, Dennis, Kevin Herbert, and Jim Correll. *Achieving Class A Business Excellence: An Executive's Perspective.* John Wiley & Sons.

Groves, Dennis, Kevin Herbert, and Jim Correll. *An Executive's Guide to Achieving Class A Business Excellence.* Oliver Wight International.

Proud, John F. *Master Scheduling: A Practical Guide to Competitive Manufacturing,* third edition. John Wiley & Sons.

For additional but more specific reading please visit the Oliver Wight Website and gain access to the extensive library of White Papers.

CHAPTER 8

Integrated Business Planning: Leadership from the Top

As described in Chapter 2, MRP has multiple inputs. Chapter 7 described master scheduling and its direct and powerful impact on MRP. This chapter describes the impact of Integrated Business Planning (IBP) on the planning

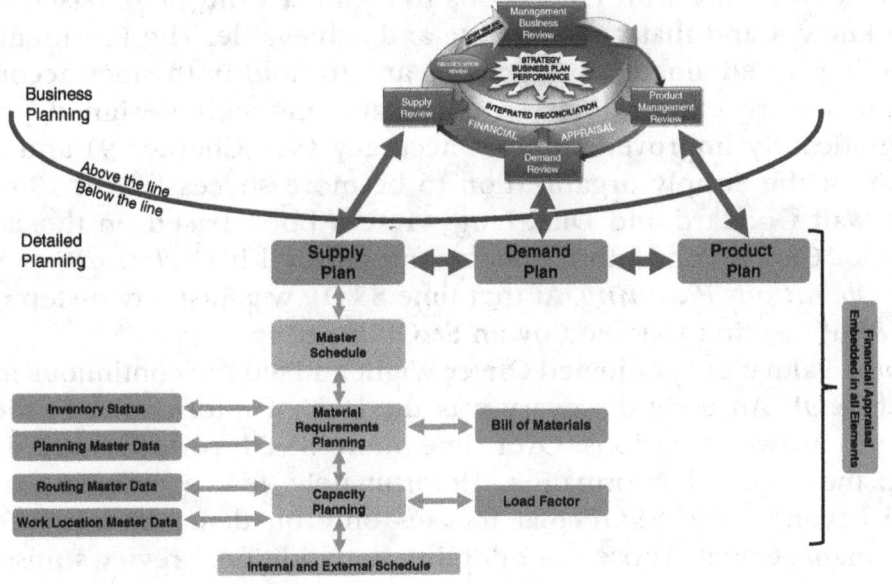

FIGURE 8.1 Business Excellence Planning

process. As shown in Figure 8.1, IBP links business strategy to execution and is the primary driver of the Master Schedule.

Integrated Business Planning had its earliest beginnings on the supply side of the business. Companies realized that with increasing market complexity and change, they needed to plan their resources more frequently than once a year. Several companies began to do Resource Requirements Planning (RRP) monthly using the fundamentals of Rough-Cut Capacity Planning (RCCP) but carried out at the aggregate (category, family) planning level. The label for these monthly resource planning meetings became "Production Planning." It became apparent that these monthly Production Planning meetings required a credible demand forecast to determine resource requirements. The need for improving forecasting was becoming increasingly apparent and led directly to the Oliver Wight Company's coaching a number of companies in this effort. A particularly important event occurred when an Oliver Wight Principal had what he thought was a Master Scheduling problem with a Nevada client. He investigated and discovered that the forecast was changing so fast in the client's combined Make-to-Stock (MTS) and Make-to-Order (MTO) environment that there was no way Master Schedulers could keep up with the changes. He enlisted the help of George Palmatier, the Nevada company's Sales and Marketing VP. They agreed that Sales would meet monthly with Operations to create a valid plan, based on truth as they knew it and that was accurate and achievable. The President was in the meetings to eliminate any impasses and to hold both sides accountable. The results were extraordinary. George and his staff designed processes that significantly improved forecast accuracy (see Chapter 9) and made it possible for the Supply organization to be more successful. In 1988 Oliver Wight's Walt Goddard and Dick Ling wrote a book based on those experiences with George, and other clients, and entitled it *Orchestrating Success: Sales & Operations Planning*. At that time S&OP was just a two-step process, a pre-S&OP meeting followed by an S&OP meeting.

George Palmatier later joined Oliver Wight and led the continuous improvement of S&OP. An early discovery was the lack of information in the S&OP meeting to answer questions. Over time, more S&OP reviews were added to develop the required information. Unfortunately, few companies have progressed beyond basic S&OP that focuses only on demand, supply, and inventory management. Those not adopting the additional reviews miss out on greater benefits. On the other hand, those who have adopted S&OP principles and have implemented the newer version of S&OP, branded by Oliver Wight as Integrated Business Planning (IBP), use this as the primary process to run the business.

Integrated Business Planning (IBP)—Linking Strategy to Execution

Figure 8.2 shows the IBP process developed by Oliver Wight.

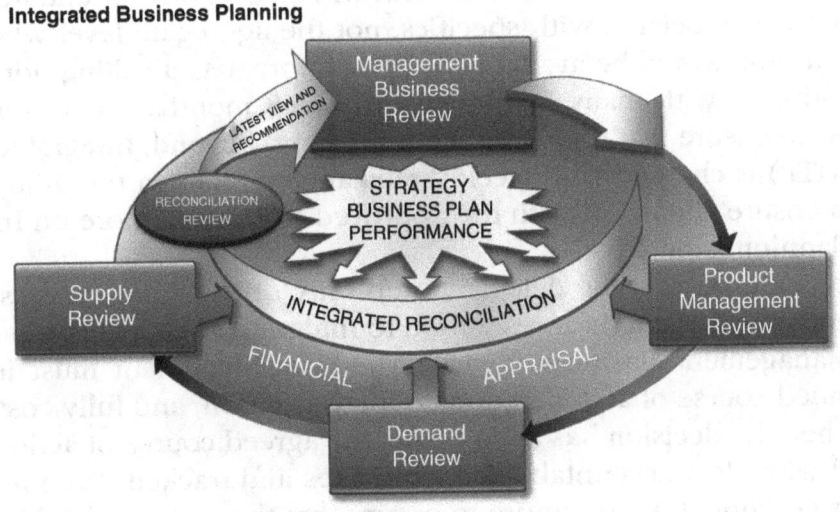

FIGURE 8.2 Integrated Business Planning

Source: © Oliver Wight International.

It is a closed-loop monthly process described, along with its key interfaces and characteristics, in the remainder of this chapter. This abbreviated description of IBP is described in more detail in the recommended reading, which provides implementation and operating details that enable IBP to become the process used by Leadership to run the business effectively and efficiently.

Fundamentally, IBP is a decision-making process. Decisions are necessary to approve updated aggregate sales, production, and inventory plans and to approve actions required to close gaps to strategic, business, and annual plans.

It is an exception-based process, meaning that it is assumed that a "good" plan was approved by the Leadership last month, so only the changes from last month to this month need to be highlighted, understood, and managed in the lead up to each Review. IBP is not about approving plans for individual products, end items, or SKUs (stock keeping units). It is conducted at an aggregate level (categories, product families, or segments) to highlight business trends and quickly uncover gaps. The further into the future gaps are identified, the more cost effectively they can be eliminated without churn/firefighting. Gaps detected in the near term are more costly to resolve because the number of options are fewer, which drives firefighting, higher costs, and wasted resources. Moreover, gaps discovered in the near term will involve SKU or end item detail, so the gaps are associated with specifics, not the aggregate level where more options and time would be available. IBP, therefore, has a rolling horizon of 4 to 24 months or, with many companies 36 or 48 months, to cost-effectively close gaps. To ensure that the focus is month 4 and beyond, Integrated Tactical Planning (ITP) is charged with weekly rebalancing plans in the 0- to 3-month horizon to ensure alignment with the approved IBP plans (more on Integrated Tactical Planning later).

If actions are beyond the delegated authority of IBP Core Process leaders, the issue must be escalated for resolution to Integrated Reconciliation and possibly to Management Business Review. The issue document must include a recommended course of action, rationale for that action, and fully costed alternatives. When the decision has been made, the agreed course of action is communicated with clear accountabilities, due dates and tracked. IBP must detect these gaps far enough in the future to ensure that they are resolved before the issue becomes a crisis in the near term, causing churn, inefficiency, and increased cost. Every IBP Review must maintain visibility of agreed action plans to ensure that they are progressing as expected.

The Leaders and Owners of the IBP Core Process and its Review are those on the Leadership Team for that part of the business. For example, and depending on the type of business:

- The Product Review Owner could be the Marketing VP, Engineering Director, or R&D VP, the individual with accountability for shaping the product/service portfolio. The Product Review Leader reports to the Owner, facilitates the Review, and ensures that activities feeding the Review are managed effectively.

- The Demand Review Owner could be the Sales and/or Marketing VP. If the Marketing VP owns the Product Review, the Sales VP would own the Demand Review. The Demand Review Leader is the Demand Manager, with responsibilities like those of the Product Review Leader.
- The Supply Review Owner could be the Supply Chain VP, Operations VP, and so on. The Supply Review Leader is the Supply Manager for the business.
- The IBP Process Leader is the Owner and Facilitator of the Integrated Reconciliation Process and Review (IRR). The IBP Process Leader has the full delegated authority of the President to deploy and manage IBP. To ensure the validity of projected financial results, the CFO, Financial Director, or Company Accountant ensures engagement of finance representatives in each of the IBP reviews.
- The Management Business Review, owned by the President, is the culmination of the monthly cycle in which escalated decisions are made and aggregate plans are approved.

Product Management Review (PMR)

The scope of the PMR is confirmed through design workshops; in short, it is a business process focused on ideation, innovation, and R&D through project selection and execution to launch. It then manages the resulting portfolio and additions/deletions to ensure that it delivers the anticipated revenue and margin while ensuring that it is more attractive than the competition's offering. The PMR must receive information that enables decisions or escalation if the required decisions exceed the team's delegated authority. Decisions are about any aspect of the process or product offering, such as resource requirements, current or future resource capabilities, project performance, product performance, margin projections, portfolio rationalization, or gap analysis. The PMR is designed to compare expected progress and results to actual, what has changed since the last PMR, why the difference, if any, and what is required to close any gaps.

By its very nature, the PMR is very strategic, as it deals with decisions about the future health of the portfolio (collection of offerings). A clear strategic roadmap, developed from the company vision, mission, strategic plan, and Sales & Marketing Roadmap, provides clear direction and enables effective decision-making.

Although Project Management is deployed companywide, often through a Project Management Office (PMO), the PMR is vital to decide on projects and programs associated with the offering. For this we advocate the use of a Stage and Gate process to track projects and programs, to enable decisions, and to kill projects that fall short of expectations before resources are wasted.

At one client's facility, the Product Development VP stated that he knew the design of a new product, intended to replace a current product, was three months late, but was keeping the date unchanged to put pressure on the engineers. His decision resulted in new materials being received before they were needed (excess inventory) with some needing to be remanufactured or scrapped because the design was still changing. An even more disastrous effect was that the planning system was not recommending release of materials for the product to be replaced during those three months, resulting in significant shortages and customer dissatisfaction. This underscores an important Class A Principle to tell the truth as we know it, no matter how uncomfortable, because the truth eventually becomes self-evident!

Multi-functional teams are generally required for developing and launching new products. Consequently, Resource Requirements Planning (RRP) is needed for development resources to ascertain if adequate resources are available to complete all projects in the pipeline.

Some of the required resources may not be part of the team and must be requested from other departments. Their need must be accurately planned or they will not be available when needed, causing the product launch to fail.

In the IBP example, it was evident that dates were constantly being pushed out. The Engineering VP claimed the reason was a shortage of engineers. We suggested that engineering skills be included in a Resource Requirements Plan (see Supply Review). With our coaching the capacity plan was completed with a recommendation to add nine engineers; this was escalated to the IR Review and then to the MBR. The President's response was less than calm because the corporate ratio of engineers to sales dollars was higher than in any other division. He was under increasing pressure to reduce, not increase, it. The President asked for our thoughts. Our explanation was simple enough. Wherever there is a capacity constraint, more capacity must be added or the capacity load must be reduced. Before anything else could be said, the President asked to review all the current Engineering projects through IBP to verify that any decisions made were within the IBP Process. As this was very important, the President asked for an extraordinary IBP session, as the decision could not wait for the next monthly cycle. The team accomplished this over the next few days. From the recommendations and revised data, the President decided to cancel more than half the projects that had little or no return on investment.

This signaled that gate reviews were not working; projects falling short of their objectives were not being killed and some not meeting the initially approved Business Case were even getting through the front-end filter. Clearly, there was bias in the analyses and, in some cases, less scrutiny of pet projects. These behaviors are symptomatic of an undisciplined process.

To note from the example is that IBP, if carried out properly, identifies many issues that, when resolved, significantly improve the company's performance.

For the PMR, or any other IBP Review, to be successful and become a decision-making forum, pre-work must be completed and distributed 24 hours in advance. All the required analyses, gap-closing alternatives and recommendations, previously approved action plan updates, and "what-if" analyses, including cost impact, must be completed. These activities follow a mapped process from the completion of the last MBR through to the current cycle's PMR. The process must be mapped and supported with documented roles and responsibilities to ensure that all IBP requirements and timings are formalized every month. These processes are often called the Feeder Process or the Preparation Cycle to each review.

Demand Review

The Demand Review focuses on Sales, Marketing, and Demand Management using a multi-input Demand Planning Process. It results in an agreed Unconstrained Demand Plan that is based on truth as they know it, summarizing what customers are expected to buy from the portfolio of offerings reflecting both volume and value across the IBP rolling horizon and importantly, ignoring views on supply constraints. The Demand Review provides the business with its first view of the revenue and profit potential, should all other areas perform.

The primary intent is to optimize profitability of the go-to-market strategy using the existing product and service offering. Uncertainty regarding projections is managed through documenting vulnerabilities and opportunities and by continuously scanning the IBP horizon with what-if analysis and contingency plans to mitigate, faster than competitors, vulnerabilities and to leverage opportunities as they materialize. Linked to the Supply Chain, the unconstrained demand plan is the sole signal for Supply to charge the Supply Chain, prepare for uncertainties, and gain a potent competitive advantage.

As mentioned earlier, the Demand Plan is at the aggregate level, not the detailed SKUs or end items. This is to ensure that trends, normally masked by demand volatility at the item level, especially beyond the Trading Zone, can be used to identify gaps and enable effective decisions.

Unconstrained means that the demand plan is not constrained by the availability of products or resources to ensure that the true market potential is known. Of course, it is constrained by pricing, competitors, customer choices, and so forth, but not by the Demand Team's view of Supply's capability. These constraints are examined by Supply in the Supply Review.

The output of the PMR is integrated into the Demand Plan through the Demand Planning process, ensuring that product launch dates and end-of-life plans are incorporated and visible to Supply. For new product launches, volumes, timing, revenue, and margin are taken from the latest business case if Sales and Marketing have not yet determined the actual market potential.

As mentioned, the unconstrained demand plan is the sole signal to Supply to prepare, unless there are products they provide to other parts of the business, which must be added to the plan.

On receipt of the unconstrained demand plan, Supply determines what they can and cannot provide based on demonstrated and planned resource capacities. If Supply, after examining all available options, confirms that the unconstrained demand plan exceeds its capabilities, then Supply and Demand Management meet to resolve the imbalance. The Demand Review Team is responsible for analyzing the impact and determining which customers will receive their orders in full and which customers will have their orders constrained. In addition, the Demand Team must inform those customers whose orders are affected and when they can expect delivery.

Should there be a long-term Supply constraint that has been agreed through IBP, the unconstrained demand plan must then reflect that constraint, but maintain the full unconstrained potential. The MBR team must be aware of the lost revenue and margin caused by the Supply constraint to understand why Supply may recommend capital expenditures as part of gap-closing plans.

Although assumptions, vulnerabilities, and opportunities are used in all IBP Reviews, they are especially important in the Demand Review to control volatility and ensure that any volume changes can be related to changes to the underlying assumptions. Demand Plans are not wrong, although they can be inaccurate; incorrect underlying assumptions cause Demand Plan inaccuracy and provide insight in how to improve the accuracy.

Measurement for accuracy, volatility reduction, and the elimination of bias is essential. Bias is a behavior that ensures that the unconstrained demand plan is deliberately and continuously understated or overstated; that behavior must be eliminated. Either way, it introduces numbers into the planning system that will cause Supply to begin second-guessing those numbers. In essence, the Supply Manager will then take over the Demand Manager's forecasting role to avoid building excess or inadequate inventory – not a recommended solution. Reasonable volume variation around the Demand Plan is manageable. Overages offset under forecasts from month to month if there is no bias. When is there bias? For three consecutive months when actual demand is either continuously above or below the plan; either must not be tolerated.

Supply Review

Upon receipt of the unconstrained demand plan, the aggregate must be analyzed quickly to determine if there is adequate key resource capacity, over the full planning horizon, using Resource Requirements Planning (RRP) techniques, which are detailed in Chapter 12. If there is an imbalance between demand and supply for one or more product in any month, they must be disaggregated to the detail level through a disaggregation algorithm. Armed with these weekly volumes, the Supply Manager and Master Scheduler can then use Rough-cut Capacity Planning to determine which specific deliverables are overloading the same key capacity resources, discussed in greater detail in Chapter 12.

Comparing key resource capacity required with capacity available quickly identifies gaps and enables the Supply Review Team to either find alternatives and confirm the plan or have the Supply Manager meet with the Demand Manager to explain the magnitude and duration of the constraint and begin developing alternative approaches to manage customer needs. Note that capacity planning can identify a lack of required capacity, but it can also identify a situation in which there is excess, expensive idle capacity. Both are issues that must be resolved. Should there be a constraint, however, it is the Supply Team's responsibility to confirm the magnitude of the constraint and when and how it will be eliminated. It is essential that the Supply Team work honestly using demonstrated capacity and performance (truth as we know it) to ensure that plans for the future are built upon current reality, not on wishful thinking. Often, Supply plans with their demonstrated numbers, but Finance uses standards that are typically set by Industrial Engineering. This introduces two sets of numbers, leads to no ownership in Supply, and financial gaps that are often hidden through the use of financial plugs, because it is too late to economically close those gaps.

A recent example involved a company's Supply Manager, who explained that they worked an eight-hour shift but were only able to produce product during five of the eight hours – in this case, five units at a standard time of one hour per piece, as per the accounting system, over the eight-hour shift. Since only five hours of work were being completed in an eight-hour shift, actual performance was 62.5%. The result of this calculation is known as the load factor (see Chapter 12). Using the standard of one hour per piece is completely wrong; the true demonstrated performance in an eight-hour shift was five standard hours of work. Planning was using eight standard hours per shift, resulting in unplanned overtime and a financial variance. When demonstrated performance replaced the previously used standard in the planning system, the company eliminated the need for overtime and reduced its product costs by $1 million. Resolution of supply constraints can happen quickly, for example, using subcontractors or through changes to the unconstrained demand plan, because Sales is actioned to manage the customers. On the other hand, a capacity constraint may need a capacity investment, which could take an extended period of time. If this investment is approved through IBP, the unconstrained demand plan would then be constrained until the additional capacity is online.

When the proposed unconstrained demand plans are sent on to Supply, Supply can test its capability to deliver those plans using Resource Requirements Planning (RRP) techniques, mentioned earlier. If a capacity gap is identified, Supply must develop a plan to close that gap. The critical question is how soon additional capacity is needed. The phrase "do the best you can" is inadequate and does not result in the accountability necessary to deliver the required capacity. It is an indication of poor leadership.

In another client company, the President wanted to implement IBP because major customers were lost due to poor on-time delivery performance. The company had four plants producing the full range of portfolio products, with some of the products being made in multiple plants. When capacity plans were produced as part of the Supply Review, it became apparent that a work location (work center) in one plant was overloaded while the identical work location in another plant was underutilized. The overloaded plant had a record of late deliveries while the other plant was underproductive. During the Supply Review, the recommendation to balance the work locations, based on future volumes from the unconstrained demand plan, was authorized, enabling on-time delivery performance to exceed 99%, eliminating the customer losses.

The Supply Review is concerned not just with internal capabilities, but also with the overall End-to-End Supply Chain capabilities and Performance. Constrained supplier resources must be added to Resource Requirements Planning considerations to keep plans valid. The same can be said for engineering, facilities and maintenance, quality, logistics, and warehousing capacities.

Financially, the Supply Review's objective is to meet customer requirements and achieve, or reduce, planned product costs. Any cost implications in the plan or in planned changes must be reviewed across the IBP planning horizon to determine their overall impact on projected results. If costs are escalating the company must either enact a price increase or, preferably, implement cost reduction projects to ensure adequate future margins.

Having completed the Product, Demand, and Supply Reviews the information and presentation decks, already shared and discussed between Product, Demand, and Supply Teams, are sent to the Integrated Reconciliation Team to update business results, agree on recommendations for escalation, and incorporate data regarding companywide projects and support functions into the presentation deck that will be sent to the MBR, once agreed by the Reconciliation Team.

Continuous Integrated Reconciliation and the Review

Product, Demand, and Supply Teams focus on their part of IBP to maximize their contribution to the business. Integrated Reconciliation with additional inputs from the support functions and companywide projects focuses on the whole, developing a month-by-month projection of the overall business results in terms of volume and value. This requires quickly produced rough-cut P&L, Balance Sheet, and Cash Flow statements.

Reconciliation, process and review, is driven by the IBP Process Leader on behalf of the Leadership Team. The IBP Process Leader must ensure that

Reconciliation is not just a financial exercise, but one that identifies all business gaps to plan over the entire rolling planning horizon and then develops recommendations and alternatives for their resolution. In addition, the IBP Process Leader ensures that the MBR Deck includes action plan updates, performance metrics, recommended aggregate plans, and recommendations, and requested decisions are communicated 48 hours in advance of the MBR. Following completion of the MBR the results are communicated to key IBP players for execution in the next cycle and key highlights to the broader organization.

Throughout the month, the IBP Process Leader ensures that Product, Demand, and Supply Teams are working together, as required, to ensure that cross-process issues are resolved efficiently and effectively, sometimes involving teamwork among all three teams and financial analysts.

Continuous Reconciliation occurs at any point during the month when an issue is identified while preparing the various formal IBP Reviews. When a Facilitator identifies an issue, it is discussed with the other Facilitators and the appropriate Finance Leader; for example, the Controller. If the resolution is within the decision authority of the Review Owner or Facilitators, action is taken and reported in the involved Review presentation deck. If not, the team begins to draft an issue document that includes a recommendation and alternative solutions for escalation and decision.

The Integrated Reconciliation Review deck (ultimately the MBR deck) is prepared through a four-step preparatory process like the steps followed in developing the PMR, Demand, and Supply decks. The four steps include:

1. The IRR Team receives the presentation decks from the Product, Demand, and Supply Reviews. These decks are received in that sequence over a two-week period, or as dictated by the monthly review dates. To facilitate easy understanding, analysis, and development of a comprehensive business results and future plans, they must have standard formats and templates.

2. The IRR Team also receives required information from support functions and from companywide project teams to complete the financials and complete resource view.

3. Having received these presentation decks from support functions, the Team creates bottom-up, rough-cut P&L, Balance Sheet, and Cash Flow statements.

4. The IRR Team then compares the current bottom-up results with the committed top-down requirements and objectives that are based on the

strategic, business and annual plans. The objective is to identify any gaps between the bottom-up projections and the top-down objectives and prepare recommended gap-closing action plans and alternatives to be forwarded to the MBR.

An experienced CFO of a recent client, when asked how IBP and the IRR have helped him, responded by saying, "For the first time in my career, I can sleep at night." Another CFO of a generic pharmaceutical company, who initially doubted the validity of aggregate financial projections, agreed after two IBP cycles that the aggregate financials were "close enough" to the financials developed from time-consuming detailed analysis, enabling him to rapidly analyze IBP what-if scenarios with confidence.

A continuous improvement culture allows the IRR Team to ensure that they are receiving the information needed, with improved accuracy of underlying assumptions and projections. Ensuring that delegated authorities are used, the Team improves their process to provide their deck to the MBR Team 48 hours prior, allowing Leadership time for pre-read.

Please note, the IRR is also designed to:

- Stop Leadership from wanting to dive into unnecessary detail.
- Ensure that decisions escalated are beyond their delegated authority.
- Provide the MBR deck, which includes pre-read and the material for the review.
- Ensure that the MBR presentation deck is succinct, provides information to enable decisions, and is not a data dump that hinders the pre-read desire.
- Use "truth as we know it" to highlight gaps, not hide them.
- Create the MBR agenda.

We were coaching a heavy equipment manufacturer on IBP and ran into a problem in the MBR with the GM. He was constantly questioning Supply's issue response alternatives to deal with several significant capacity constraints and proposing what he thought were better solutions. Our first reaction was to attend the next IRR and challenge the Supply team. We believed that they should have better anticipated the GM's challenges and prepared for them. They agreed and improved by the time of the next MBR. The MBR was better, but the GM still had lots of challenges. We went back to them again, trying to get them to consider all the possible alternatives and to choose the best to present. Again, there was improvement, but the result was the same. A coach must sometimes step up and address the real issue. We took our own advice and met directly and alone with the GM. We told him he should demonstrate more confidence in his team and that his constant challenges were demoralizing the team and delaying action. The GM smiled and agreed but said that challenging was just his nature to try and improve things. He said, "Please sit next to me next time and kick me when I start challenging unnecessarily." We did; end of the problem and he sustained this new approach himself. Culture changes flow down from the top of the organization, not up from the bottom!

Management Business Review

Finally is the Management Business Review, chaired by the President, facilitated by the IBP Process Leader, and attended by the full Leadership Team. It is designed to be an efficient and effective decision-making forum lasting between 1.5 and 2 hours, when the process has matured. To be efficient and effective, the MBR must be exception based, meaning that only changes from last month's plan, the implications of those changes, and required decisions are addressed; attendees must be prepared to make decisions when they come to the MBR by completing all pre-reads. Only agenda items may be discussed, and there are to be no surprises that would lead to unstructured discussion rather than decisions.

The Process Leader, following the timed agenda, introduces the topics to be discussed, invites the owner of the agenda item to explain that item, and identify, if any, decisions required.

An inability of the Leadership Team to decide indicates a process failure. Either insufficient information was provided or the Business Leader is just not capable of making tough decisions. The answer in each instance, experience has shown, is obvious. This situation represents a valuable coaching opportunity. If there is not enough information to make the decision, the Process Leader must take careful note of what information is missing and ensure that information is made available in the next cycle or schedule a follow-up MBR to enable the decision to be made in this cycle.

At the end of the MBR, decisions made and expected communications to the IBP Teams and broader organization must be reviewed and agreed. Closing the loop is essential in ensuring that the process is top-down and bottom-up and is valued across the company.

A President's style will influence how the MBR is run. One GM of the largest division of a heavy equipment company scheduled a time slot of 90 minutes for the MBR, and it would end precisely at that time. No one was ever late to one of his MBRs (or any of his meetings), and no one was ever unprepared.

The President of a medical company initially was not restrictive about the duration of the MBR. When the Review began, he would drill down until he got the information he needed to make a decision, which in the beginning could take as much as four hours. Over time, and with continuous process improvement, the time required was reduced by better preparation and standardization of the MBR presentation deck. Everybody began to realize that IBP was not just another meeting but was the process with which the President was running the business. Improved preparation was essential to their success.

There is no standard for the length of an MBR or of any of the other Reviews. The length of the meeting depends upon, for example, the size of the company, the complexity of its products and services, and the issues that must be considered. The time required can vary from cycle to cycle. What is important is that the MBR stays focused on the agenda and decisions required and is not allowed to get entangled in unnecessary detail. This is an aggregate planning process; all presentations must be crisp and complete.

To maximize commitment to using the process to run the business, the President cannot dominate the MBR. The GM of a client company wanted to increase production. The Sales VP pointed out that the demand increase was solely the result of dealers increasing their stock and that there was no increase in end customer demand. The GM was pushing hard to increase production volume when he suddenly paused in mid-sentence, looked over at us and said, "I'm not supposed to do that, am I?" A simple nod answered his question. They did not increase production, which turned out to be the right decision. Once again, culture change begins at the top!

Load Leveling

A major expectation of IBP is load leveling done at the aggregate level. Chapter 12 describes Resource Requirements Planning, Rough Cut Capacity Planning, and Detail Capacity Planning. Detail Capacity Planning will be a nightmare if loads are not leveled at the aggregate level using Resource Requirements Planning (RRP) as part of the Supply Review.

IBP Calculation

The following is a basic explanation of a make-to-stock worksheet used in IBP. The attributes of the worksheet are:

- **Product Type:** Make-to-stock/make-to-order (this is a make-to-stock example).
- **Time Resolution:** Months.
- **Horizon:** This display shows three months of history and just five future periods. History may be increased if that provides value, but the future horizon must be at least 18 to 24 months. Some companies display a longer planning horizon if their cumulative lead time or equipment/facility increases require a longer lead-time. Beyond 24–36 months that moves into the strategic planning horizon.
- **Product Group:** Family.
- **Family:** A group of SKUs, typically organized by market/customer. The overall IBP process for a business should limit the number of families to 20. More than 20 encourages people to get into too much detail and quickly becomes unmanageable.

This worksheet has three sections – Sales, Production, and Inventory – and is, therefore, sometimes referred to as the SPI worksheet.

Sales
- **Plan:** The last approved demand plan (actual history and anticipated future volumes).
- **New Plan:** The proposed new Sales plan (future only).
- **Actual:** The actual amount sold (history).
- **Difference:** Subtracting the Actual from the Plan, which can be a positive or a negative number (history).
- **Cumulative Difference:** The cumulative difference between Plan and Actual over the period of history displayed (three months in this example).

Production
- **Plan:** The last approved production plan (history and future).
- **New Plan:** The proposed new production plan (future only).
- **Actual:** The actual quantity produced (history).
- **Difference:** Subtracting Actual from Plan, which can be a positive or a negative (history).

■ **Cumulative Difference:** The cumulative difference between Plan and Actual over the period of history displayed (three months in this example).

Inventory
■ **Plan:** The resulting inventory from the last approved Sales and Production plans (history and future).
■ **New Plan:** Inventory quantity resulting from the proposed new plan (future only).
■ **Actual:** The actual quantity in inventory (history).
■ **Difference:** Subtracting Actual from Plan (history).

MBR Conversation Using the Example

Looking at the numbers in Figure 8.3 as a company President, sales have exceeded the planned in each of the past three months. Cumulative sales for the past three months have accumulated to 25 units above plan. The President

Period		-3	-2	-1		Curr	+1	+2	+3	+4
Sales										
Plan		120	120	120		120	125	125	125	125
New Plan						125	130	130	130	130
Actual		125	130	130						
Difference		+5	+10	+10						
Cumulative Difference	0	+5	+15	+25						
Production										
Plan		125	125	125		125	125	125	125	125
New Plan						130	135	135	135	130
Actual		110	110	115						
Difference		-15	-15	-10						
Cumulative Difference	0	-15	-30	-40						
Inventory										
Plan		108	113	118		123	123	125	123	123
New Plan						108	113	118	123	123
Actual	103	83	58	38						
Difference		-25	-55	-80						

FIGURE 8.3 Make-to-Stock Worksheet

asks the Sales and Marketing VP why the plan has been oversold. The VP replies that there is a lot of difficulty getting the Sales Team to stop including bias in their numbers, and consequently they are consistently understating what they expect. "Okay," the President says with a lot of frustration, "But what is causing this bias? They know we want a plan built on 'truth as we know it'!" The Sales and Marketing VP shifts uncomfortably and says, "The way we are measuring their performance is driving this." "What?" the President snaps. The Sales and Marketing VP responds, "We measure them only on sales, and this determines their bonus. Consequently, they consistently understate their numbers to ensure they get the maximum bonus when they exceed plan." The President, with even more frustration, snaps, "So, you know what they are doing, and you have been allowing this for months? Just look at the history!" The Sales and Marketing VP says, "That is true when you look at the history, but behaviors are difficult to change when they are paid the way they are. I have been asking them for an accurate plan, but their income is more important to them. We need to change how we measure their performance." "Okay," says the President, "but I want your proposal this afternoon. But first, let's look at what effect this bias has been having on Production to make sure we do not implement a solution that generates even more problems."

The President then turns to ask the Production VP about her consistent shortfall in each of the past three months. Her response is very common: "Based on the Sales Plan, I develop a Production Plan to build the inventory to satisfy the Demand Plan without too much overtime. I get challenged every month on our overtime percentage. Unfortunately, true demonstrated performance was not used in developing this plan. The result is that our actual production is under plan by 40 units over the past three months." "So," says the President with complete exasperation, "even with Sales giving you a plan that is lower than they require you still cannot deliver to it! All of us sat right here at this table and agreed to an operating strategy to build inventory to a level of 123 units to cost effectively deliver our customers' needs. But today I am hearing that we have massively reduced our inventory from 103 to 38. All I can say is well done, team." "Again," says the President to the Production VP, "the plan clearly shows you have been underperforming – just what is going on?" The Production VP goes on to explain that she had not believed the true demonstrated performance being presented by her team and had instructed them to work with a load factor of 90%, not the 70% they had presented. After further, more detailed, investigation she realized that the load factor should be by work location and that these numbers would be different based on the past performance. Consequently, she now realizes that using an average was wrong, because some key work locations had significantly different load factors.

The President responds abruptly, "And with what logic did you come to that decision?" She starts to reply, but Finance interrupts the conversation.

The Finance VP confirms that the net effect of Sales understating their plan and Production underperforming has meant that inventory has not been built to plan and is now at 38 units, not the planned 118. The Finance VP continues, "Just how do you think we are going to deliver the future customer needs based on what I'm seeing here? I suggest we get to a plan right now that reflects truth as we know it. If we do that quickly enough, we might then deliver to customer needs, at the right cost with the right number of units. The President jumps in, "I really do not need you to repeat what I have been saying. Why from a financial point of view have you not raised this as a problem before now, anyway? How can we be recovering our overhead expenses with this type of production performance, and why do we pay Sales bonuses when the business is in such a mess?

"Come on people, this is not rocket science! We must stop playing games and make sure we all contribute plans and decisions that support our strategies. As I look at where we are now, it's as though we have all been burying our heads in the sand!"

This is when the President's leadership style becomes apparent. At this point, the President turns to the Sales and Marketing VP and asks when a new Sales Plan will be ready, and then adds, "Your job depends on getting it reasonably right!" The Sales and Marketing VP responds that he can have one ready in three days. The President then turns to the Production VP and says, "Missing the Production Plan will no longer be tolerated. Is that understood?" The Product Development VP responds by saying that they are using the new detail planning process to develop and plan new product development with this latest launch and all new ones. "The new scheduling process has all of the new projects on schedule." The President smiles and says, "Well, at least we are making progress in some areas." The President then turns to the HR VP and instructs him to look into the measures and bonus scenarios with the Sales Team and come back with recommendations to eliminate the volume bias immediately and develop a measurement to drive plan accuracy not just bonus payments. Finally, he turns to the Finance VP and says that the VP should have highlighted this issue in the IBP Financial Appraisal and in the IRR months ago and should never allow such a poorly developed plan get to the MBR. The President then admits he is ultimately at fault for not paying closer attention in earlier Reviews and not being firm enough about holding his VPs accountable.

He then reschedules an emergency MBR in three days. He asks his VPs if they will be ready and receives an affirmative answer.

Is the President's approach too brutal? His reaction was probably fueled by frustration and past reviews where "truth as we know it" was not being presented. With this level of error and lack of integration you can see why a President may become more aggressive than constructive when he realizes his team was not making decisions based on reason and an integrated approach.

Hundreds of companies have implemented S&OP and IBP to ensure an integrated approach with one set of accurate numbers. In every case, with those who chose to drive for Class A, a member of the Leadership Team took control with the right level of empowerment and the company was successful; those that did not have a member of Leadership driving the implementation and did not use an appropriate level of "tough love" in its leadership style tended to fail.

This simple example represents a company with extremely low process maturity (see Chapters 2 and 19). In a mature company, a volume-based IBP worksheet would not always be necessary in the MBR unless a specific issue is being addressed. These worksheets are more likely to be used in the Supply and Demand Reviews, to better understand how well supply is balancing against demand and to control the resulting inventory. Discussions about meeting or not meeting the Demand Plan or the Supply Plan at the family and sub-family levels must occur in those Reviews. For this example's results to have continued to fall short three months in a row suggests that the company's weekly Integrated Tactical Planning (ITP) process is not working well or is completely absent.

There are some significant differences between creating Sales Plans and Production Plans.

Forecasting is by far the most challenging task in planning the future since it involves determining what customers are going to do in the future, sometimes far into the future. Therefore, larger tolerances are put in place for Sales Plan accuracy depending upon the families, and at different points over the planning horizon. For example, a client had a product that sold only two units per month, but each of those units delivered $1 million in profit. They also had a product family that on average sold 100 units per week. Sales Plan accuracy was consistently above 90% for the high-volume family but was consistently below 50% for the low-volume family. Realistic measurement tolerances reflecting those and other differing characteristics must be assigned to each product family. Production Plan performance tolerance assignment is markedly different from the Sales Plan performance tolerance. If the Supply Chain VP has a Class A process in place, data accuracy and results will be consistently at least 95% or higher in delivering the approved Plan. Finance should now be able to deliver their financial projections, providing there is a good costing system in place, since plans by family are now valid. In fact, one of our Class A certified clients consistently hits the company financial numbers within 0.5%, month in and month out. This caused a bit of interesting friction with the other divisions that did not commit to achieving Class A certification and could never get close to the same performance or accuracy.

Charts versus Spreadsheets

Sending a stack of spreadsheets full of numbers for leadership to review before the MBR is not helpful, bordering on a complete waste of time. Each person who looks at the numbers will likely come up with different conclusions and different questions. Leadership need information, not just piles of data. Converting spreadsheet data to graphical presentations is helpful; it very quickly identifies issues and promotes a deeper dive, when that is necessary, to better understand the issues. Graphs make it easy to see what is happening with trend development and gaps to those trends, without sorting through the numbers. Seeing an obvious issue on a graph, leadership often turn to the numbers to facilitate decisions.

Figure 8.4 is a Demand Review graph for one product family. This chart graphs three months of history and 24 months of future projected demand displayed in both volume and value. Each IBP family and subfamily must have similar graphs.

It is easy to see that the new plan numbers are significantly higher in the future than the prior plan's. The first question to be anticipated would be the cause of the increase. There had better be a good explanation of what is driving the volume up and not just the volume required to make budget. The next question would be whether the new plan meets the budget over the next two years. In this case it appears graphically that the budgeted revenue will be exceeded. The next question would be about Supply's capacity to meet these increased volumes.

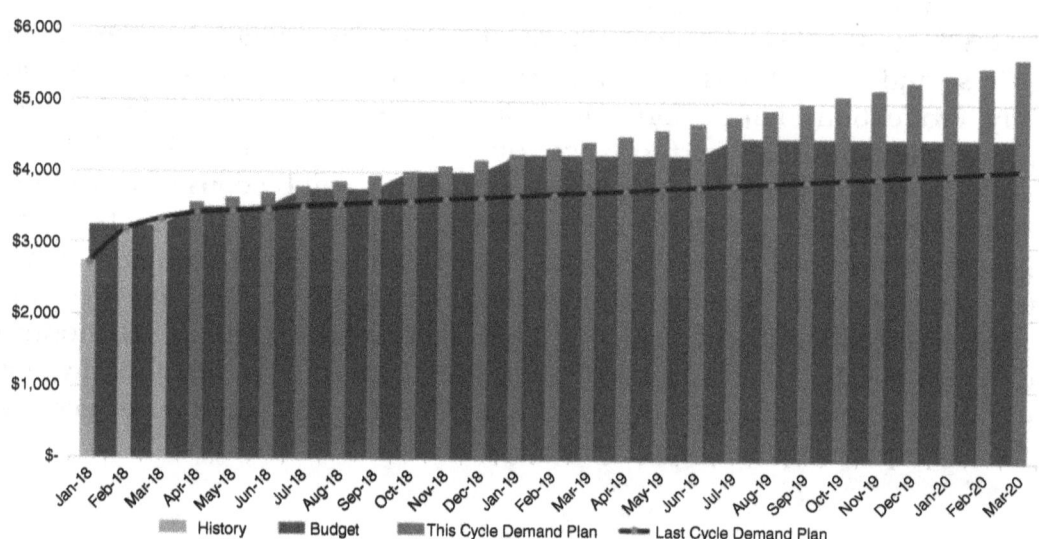

FIGURE 8.4 Demand Review Chart – One Family

When, in this example, Demand (Sales) distributed their new unconstrained demand plan, Supply (Resource managers) immediately developed supply plans, by family, to meet the unconstrained demand plan. Figure 8.5 shows what this Supply team came up with for this family. The one question that finance might be concerned with is the inventory increase, for this product family, caused by the plan. Supply would develop similar plans for each family.

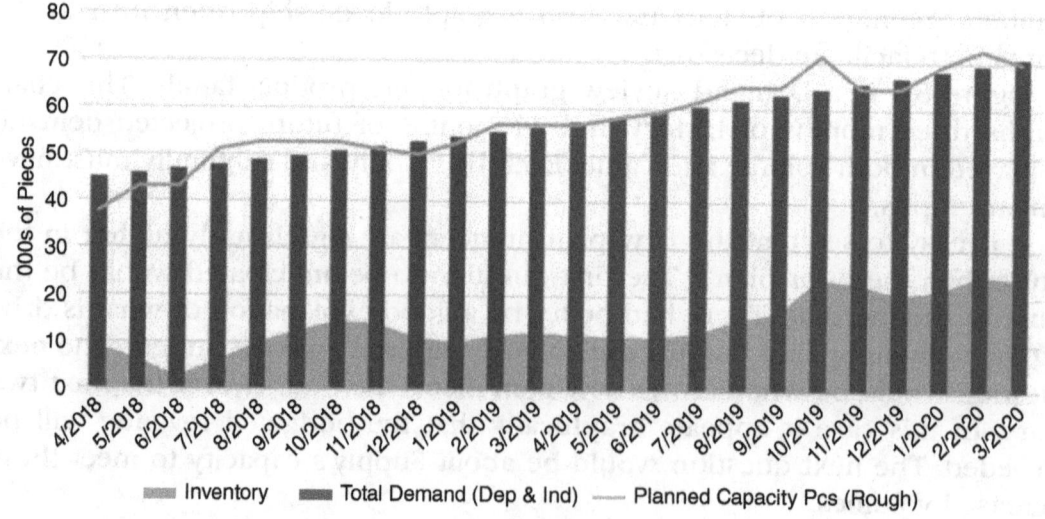

FIGURE 8.5 Supply Plan versus Demand and Inventory Consequence

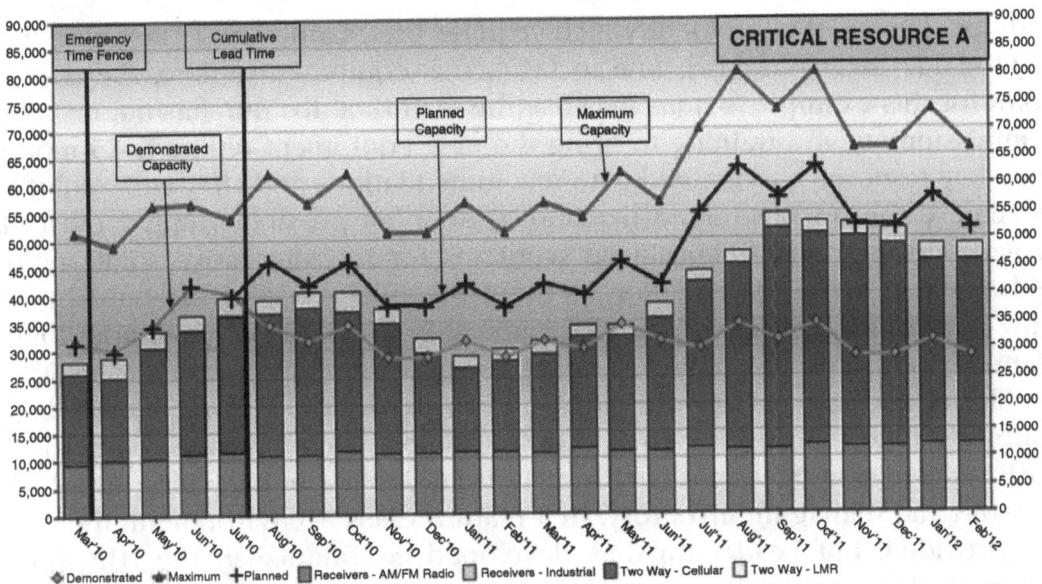

FIGURE 8.6 Resource Requirements Plan, All Families Planned and Maximum Capacity

Next the new Supply Plan is tested for validity using Resource Requirement Planning (RRP) techniques. An RRP (see Figure 8.6) is developed for each key resource with all the demand. Based on this information, when demand exceeds capacity, alternatives, and a recommended action plan to close the capacity gap are developed, along with the financial impact associated with the new plan. Supply can quickly develop RRP plans, like the plan in Figure 8.6, for all key resources (see Chapter 12, Capacity Planning).

The graph displays Demand Plan requirements on one key resource for three families, the stacked bars showing how resource requirements change through the planning horizon. Based on Demonstrated Capacity, it is apparent that additional capacity is going to be required for month 6. The black line (+) represents additional capacity, Planned Capacity (based on demonstrated performance plus or minus changes – see Chapter 12, Capacity Planning), which includes overtime production hours and a third shift. This is the first decision point. Often Supply VPs want this as a decision point because they do not want to justify the overtime and/or third shift cost increases that would occur in the following months. Another decision will be required in June 11 to cover future planned demand increases as they exceed current Maximum Capacity. The Maximum Capacity line reflects the total capacity available, without adding capital resources. In this case Supply is recommending buying and installing an additional piece of equipment which changes the Planned and Maximum lines, in June 11. Given the lead time to bring this equipment online, the decision point for this example is *now*, because the lead time for purchasing, installing, commissioning, and training to bring the new equipment online is 15 months. Each key resource is examined with recommendations and alternative solutions to achieve the unconstrained demand as soon as possible. Supply must also provide detailed and financialized scenarios for the alternative solutions that will result in a recommendation to the MBR, once verified through the IRR. Now it becomes a decision point for leadership in the MBR. Remember that all planned and maximum capacities *must* be based on demonstrated capacity.

Charts and graphs are very helpful in explaining and recommending a course of action during the MBR, but their display is not always required. The MBR is a decision-making review, not a discussion about balancing supply and demand and managing inventory. In a mature Class A environment, the charts are provided, but Leadership has developed confidence in the IBP Review Teams to deliver valid plans and bring trusted recommendations to the MBR for decision. One client had a history of debating nearly every capacity increase decision endlessly over a six-month period. When Class A had been implemented and the culture had changed, those decisions were made in the MBR in as little as five minutes, a much better use of Leadership's time and a much quicker return on investment!

An example of a one-page Sales, Production, and Inventory Plan for a product family is shown by Figure 8.7. The intent of this display is to consolidate the basis of the recommended plan on a single page for the leadership.

Components of the one-page summary include:

- **Assumptions:** Each person who contributes to the summary documents captures their thinking through an assumptions database. Assumptions are used to develop volumes and to explain any changes from one month to the next. Additionally, new information coming into the summary should be tested against the current assumptions. If the new information does not change the current assumption, then the plan should not be changed. If the new information does cause an assumption to be modified, then the plan is changed. Formal, documented assumptions provide planning value by capturing knowledge, enabling better decisions, and ensuring that original thinking is not lost should something change in the future. Revisiting documented assumptions after the fact improves assumption accuracy over time

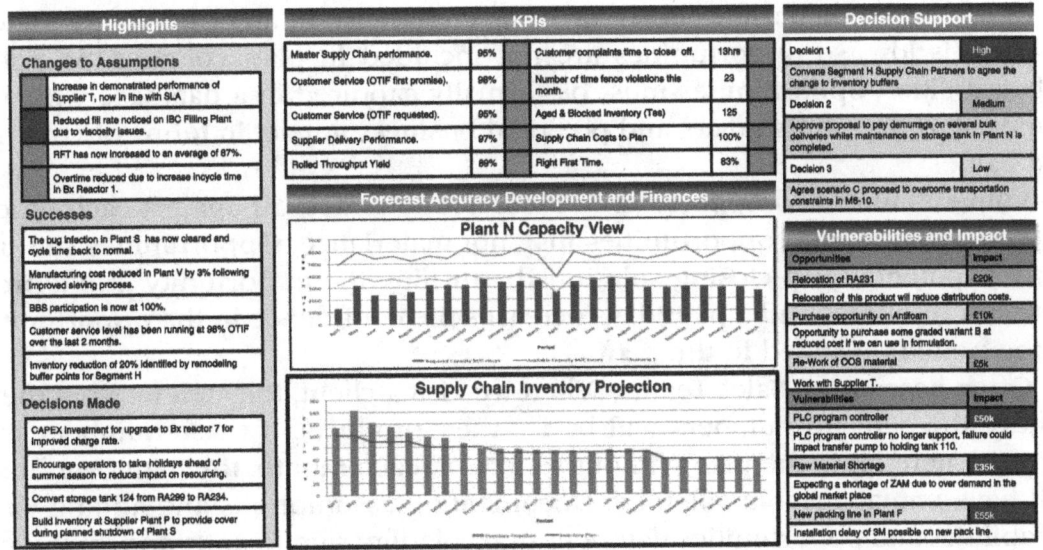

FIGURE 8.7 Supply Review One-Page Summary

and enables continuously improved planning accuracy. The number is not as important as the thinking behind that number.

- **Vulnerabilities and Opportunities:** Vulnerabilities are used to identify potential downsides in volumes included in Product, Demand, and Supply plans. Vulnerabilities and Opportunities are applied in the plan differently and are used for different purposes and must be clearly defined and understood.

When a plan has been developed and agreed on, the plan's accuracy will be measured. However, since the plan covers a lengthy planning horizon, some issues in the future could materialize and affect the plan.

Vulnerabilities, potential downsides, as they are sometimes called, while they are not expected to happen, should be listed as vulnerabilities to ensure that they are continuously watched and managed. Vulnerabilities are included in the plan and are part of the measurement. Vulnerabilities should be formally captured in a database that includes the owner, the date the vulnerability could be anticipated, and its potential impact on the plan in terms of volume and value.

Opportunities, on the other hand, are potential future issues that could have a positive impact on the plan, upsides, as they are sometimes called.

However, based on current understanding, confidence in an opportunity materializing is low, so opportunities are not included in plan volumes. As with vulnerabilities, opportunities must be formally captured in a database with an owner, start date, finish date, and potential business impact in terms of volume and value.

Vulnerabilities and opportunities must not be netted off against each other as vulnerabilities and opportunities may not materialize. Opportunities can be used as potential gap-closing solutions by turning the opportunity into a project with resources and a plan that increases the confidence in the opportunity to the point it is added to the plan.

Often heard from Sales Teams: When we visit a client, they tell us what they believe the demand numbers will be for their products. If these numbers are simply entered into the plan without validation each month, the plan over time will have unmanageable volatility. Documenting assumptions and adding vulnerabilities and opportunities dampens that volatility significantly and improves plan accuracy.

Consider this example. A customer historically has ordered 250 units per year. This year, their order is for 500 units. Sales must investigate the difference in order quantity, decide what to include in the plan, and capture the assumptions underlying that number. Their investigation revealed growth each year of roughly 50 units, but nothing to suggest growth of 250. Their conclusion and assumption, therefore, could be to enter 300 units into the plan to accommodate the growth trend but then document an opportunity of 200 to capture the customer's more optimistic number. With 300 units as an assumption, a vulnerability of 50 units could be documented to ensure that this part of the 300 happens. If, on the other hand, the customer has provided a clear, logical reason for their increased order quantity of 500 units, the increased volume should be added to the plan. One logical explanation that could be documented as the assumption underlying the increased plan could be the onboarding of a new Sales Director who has refocused the entire Sales Team, which has successfully entered a whole new market. The 500-unit quantity is now completely reasonable and would represent the most likely outcome, not just an upside opportunity. The point is that there must be a good understanding of the plan's assumptions to determine what vulnerabilities and opportunities to document.

- **Decisions:** The power of IBP is its ability to enable effective and efficient decisions, based on facts. Decisions already made within the scope of the Reviews leading up to the MBR are documented; the decisions required are listed under Decision Support, provided in advance of the MBR. These are costed recommendations requiring a yes or no before the conclusion of the MBR. To support good decision making there is a need to ensure the entire process is supported with good up-to-date information. This information is based on accurate and concise explanations of changes, the improvements being made in performance through clearly presented KPIs and how gaps to plans have been identified. From these trusted recommendations are developed plans to close gaps.

The chart in Figure 8.7 includes examples of what could be included in the one-page family summary. We kept the descriptions short, but anything included in the summary must have a solid basis. MBR participants will have 48 hours to ask probing questions and expect answers before approving the plans presented. An explanation of the reason for improved productivity such as employees will be working harder and smarter is not acceptable. That could imply that the manager of that area currently allows people to waste time and should be fired! There are many logical approaches to improving productivity. The action plan behind this increase must be documented in detail with dates and accountabilities for the plan to be approved in the MBR.

Management Business Review Agenda (MBR)

The MBR agenda is designed to meet a company's specific needs but should ensure that decisions are made and the Sales, Production, and Inventory (SPI) Plans for each product family are approved. Regardless of industry or company, Unparalleled Business Planning and Execution Practices have been proven to be effective.

Figure 8.8 shows the MBR attendees and a routine agenda.

At the end of every IBP Review, including the MBR, a formal critique should be conducted to identify continuous improvement opportunities. This critique also signals the official end to the Review.

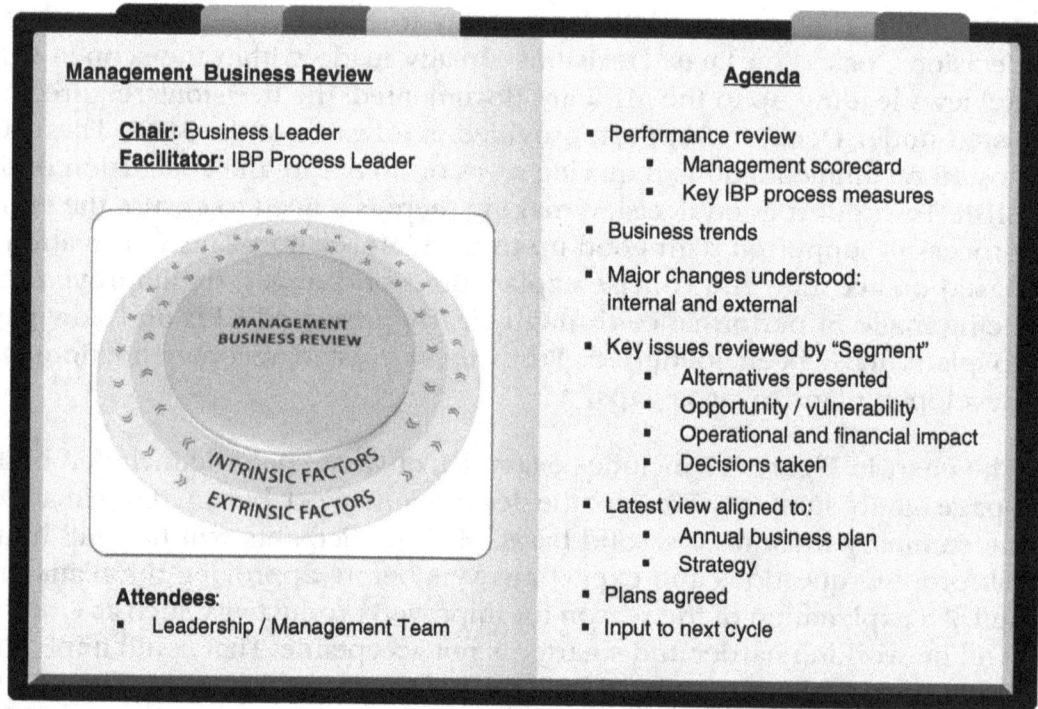

Management Business Review

Chair: Business Leader
Facilitator: IBP Process Leader

MANAGEMENT BUSINESS REVIEW

INTRINSIC FACTORS
EXTRINSIC FACTORS

Attendees:
- Leadership / Management Team

Agenda

- Performance review
  - Management scorecard
  - Key IBP process measures
- Business trends
- Major changes understood: internal and external
- Key issues reviewed by "Segment"
  - Alternatives presented
  - Opportunity / vulnerability
  - Operational and financial impact
  - Decisions taken
- Latest view aligned to:
  - Annual business plan
  - Strategy
- Plans agreed
- Input to next cycle

FIGURE 8.8 Example of a Typical Management Business Review Agenda

Principles for Success

Unparalleled Business Planning and Execution Practices provide the roadmap for achieving business success. The following structures, practices, behaviors, and principles, when embedded in the company's culture, will transform the company and ensure business success:

- IBP is owned by the President and driven by the IBP Process Leader with the Leadership Team's full delegated authority.
- The Leadership Team is fully engaged and actively demonstrates its commitment to IBP as "the way we run the business."
- IBP is the engine that delivers the deployed strategy and links that strategy to execution.
- IBP plans are built upon truth as we know it, with all gaps and assumptions openly displayed and used to develop fully costed gap-closing recommendations and alternatives.

- IBP ensures that there is one set of valid plans and numbers used by all functions to run the business.
- IBP is a decision-making process, with all analysis performed in feeder processes and Reviews.
- IBP empowers people at all levels, through clearly documented decision authority boundaries, to make decisions and escalate to the MBR only those decisions that can only be made by the Leadership Team.
- IBP gradually moves the organization from a functional focus to a business process focus, ensuring that all support functions are aligned and execute the approved Sales, Production, and Inventory Plans.
- IBP is an aggregate, monthly, rolling process with at least a 24-month planning horizon and focus on months 4–24. Management of months 0 to 3, to ensure delivery of the previously approved plans, relies on Integrated Tactical Planning (ITP), described later, not IBP, unless a significant change to those previously approved plans is warranted and must be escalated to the MBR for decision. See Figures 8.9, 8.10, and 8.11 for more on this horizon discussion.
- IBP is simplified through focusing only on changes from the previous month's approved plans, accompanied by documentation of the cause of those changes.
- Scenario planning, modeling, and issue documents are used to determine future options and provide recommended courses of action to enable efficient and effective decisions for closing gaps to plan and to strategic business objectives.
- No IBP decisions are made outside the IBP process. If supporting function decisions are required and are within the decision boundaries of those support functions, those decisions are reported to the IRR team for inclusion in the MBR presentation deck.
- IBP information and decisions must be disseminated in a way that eliminates the need for additional, unproductive meetings.

Figures 8.9, 8.10, and 8.11 have been included to diagrammatically represent why it is important to move from a budget (annual plan) year focus to a rolling 4- to 24-, 36-, or 48-month horizon.

In month 1 of the budget year you have a 12-month outlook; in month 2 it becomes 11 months and so is referred to as a myopic budget year. Traditionally, the real focus with this approach is the short term, often the next three months

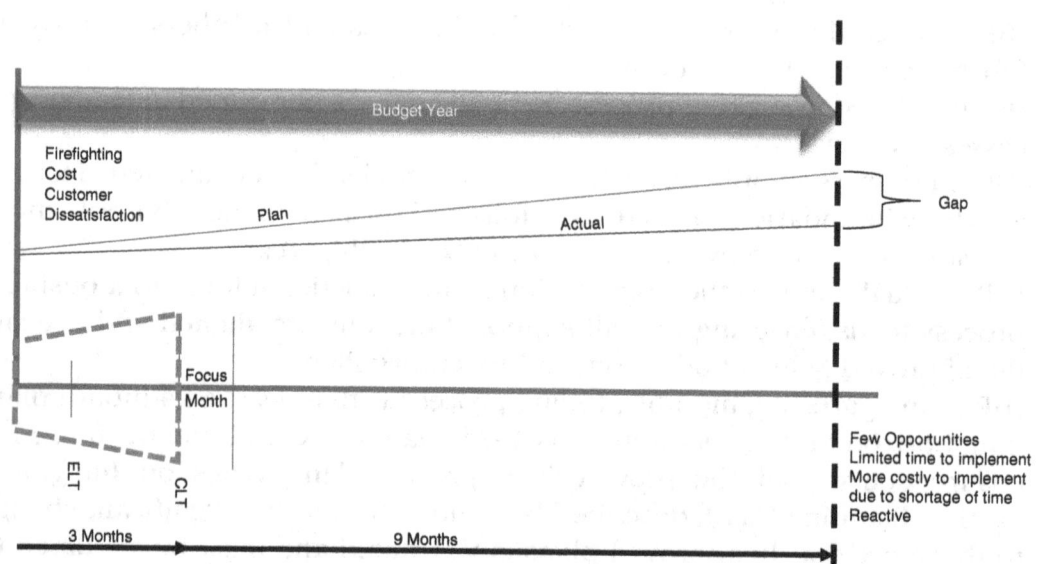

FIGURE 8.9 Typical Budget (Annual Plan) Year Focus

with possible focus into month 4, the area within the dotted trapezoid. As the focus tends to become so short term there is little opportunity to improve as the focus is about the here and now and satisfying customer demands and changes to those demands. However, the real firefighting (churn) is driven by internally generated problems that do not get the time for sustainable resolution. The result is higher cost and customer dissatisfaction and low employee morale. Even if there was a mechanism to investigate the 12-month horizon there is still too limited time and few opportunities to improve. This whole focus tends to be very reactive and drives an "eyes down and look in" management style – clearly, not an IBP approach.

Figure 8.10 shows three budget years laid out sequentially, as this identifies an additional issue with this approach.

In laying three budget years out in sequence, we can see in Figure 8.10 a potential 36-month horizon; however, as the focus is still budget year there is always a restart at the end of every 12 months, with each 12 months continuing with the problems described for Figure 8.9. So, what are the issues at the end of each budget year that explain the need for the restart? Typically, with a budget-year focus you see traditional financing maintained, so there is a quarter-, half-, three-quarter-, and full-year focus. Equally, the only time the second budget year receives any focus is during the budget process, which tends to

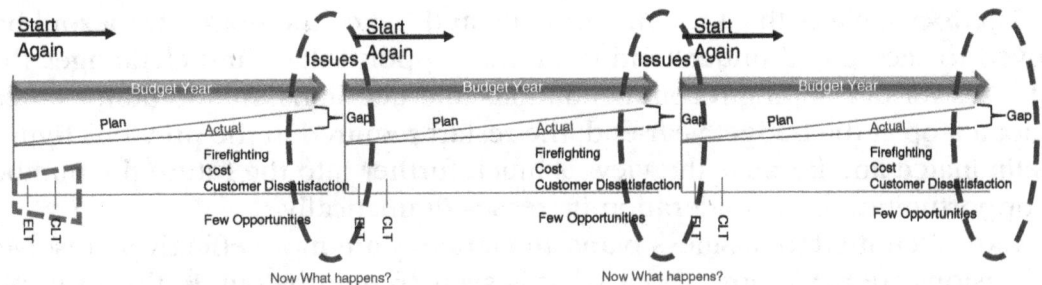

FIGURE 8.10 Sequential Budget Years; is this 36 months?

use assumptions that become outdated when the year starts. The year-end issues that then impact the start of the subsequent year are driven by the need to maximize results for the current budget year, which often means demands for the first quarter in the subsequent year are pulled forward to augment the current year result. The overall impact is a compromised start to the new budget year – again, not an IBP approach.

To overcome these frequently encountered symptoms associated with a sole budget-year focus, introduce a rolling horizon that, depending on your business needs, could be 4 to 24, 36, or 48 months. Figure 8.11 shows this recommended approach, which IBP needs for success.

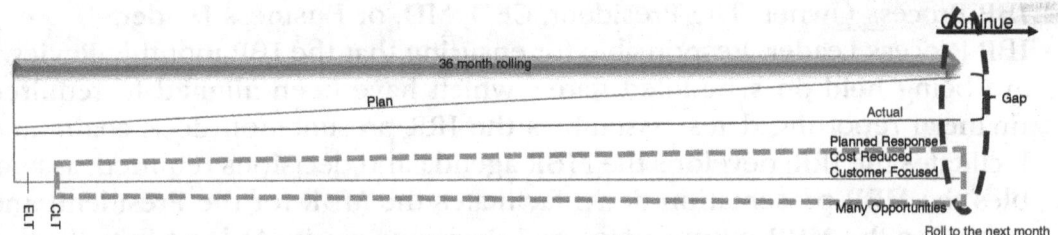

FIGURE 8.11 A Diagrammatic View of a 36-Month Rolling Horizon and Focus

In this approach there are many advantages to the previous two figures that are used by IBP to enable decisions to be made out into the future so there is time to cost-effectively ensure that they happen. Make what happen? For example, decisions associated with capital expenditure to enable Supply Chain capacity improvements to meet future customer demands. Often Supply Chain investments take much longer than 12 months to execute; consequently, with a budget-year focus, this cost-effective approach is lost and becomes reactive or rushed.

The focus is months 4 to 24, 36, or 48, and hence the dotted trapezoid has moved to secure and understand the future opportunities and challenges that IBP uses for developing recommendations and decisions. In addition, as there is not a stop at the budget year-end, the restart required in the previous figures is eliminated and because the view is much further into the future the number of opportunities for consideration increases dramatically.

Gaps identified to business plans and strategy are more effectively resolved if decisions are made now about what is seen 36 months out, in this example. This is a significant advantage to the maximum 12-month view provided by a budget year.

Figure 8.11 shows the need for the short-term horizon to be managed separately from the rolling horizon and hence the link between the two needs to be established through Integrated Tactical Planning, explained in the following sections.

The rolling horizon needs to be reviewed case by case because all businesses have different needs; however, today many companies are moving to the 36- and 48-month rolling horizon.

IBP Organization Structure

- IBP Process Owner: The President, CEO, MD, or Business Leader.
- IBP Process Leader: Responsible for ensuring that the IBP monthly Reviews are being held on scheduled dates, which have been aligned to required financial reporting dates; assembles the IRR presentation deck chairs and facilitates the IRR; develops the MBR agenda and decisions required; assembles the MBR presentation deck; facilitates the MBR for the President; and publishes the MBR output notes and decisions made. At least initially, this is a full-time role that is strongly supported by the President through continuous reinforcement of the President-delegated authority. Responsible for execution excellence.
- Product, Demand, and Supply Review Facilitators: Directly report to their Core Process Owners; gather and organize their Review agendas; ensure that their Reviews are held on the scheduled dates; facilitate their Review chaired by the Core Process Owner. Activities required to carry out these responsibilities occur throughout the month and normally result in these roles being full-time.

- The Product Review Facilitator is often referred to as the Product Manager, who is responsible for developing the aggregate Product Plans for developing and modifying the Portfolio.
- The Demand Review Facilitator is often referred to as the Demand Manager, who is also responsible for developing the aggregate Demand Plan covering the full IBP planning horizon and the detailed SKU forecast covering the first few months (SKU by week by shipping point).
- The Supply Review Facilitator is often referred to as the Supply Manager, who is also responsible for developing the Supply Plan covering the full IBP planning horizon and, with the Master Schedulers, the detailed plans covering the first few months (SKU by week by production site).
- Review Participants: Typically total not more than 10 participants for each Review (but note that people should only attend if they have an agenda item), which averages 1.5 to 2 hours in duration. Additional attendees may be invited as required to provide clarifying information for specific issues being discussed. Those core team members and additional attendees are each responsible for a Review agenda topic to be presented. Each Review Team includes a Finance representative to provide finance implications of topics and changes discussed. Note, these reviews are not about sharing information.

Matrix IBP

In more complex businesses with regional or global reach, it is often necessary to view the application of the IBP principles discussed in this chapter differently.

Oliver Wight has pioneered the Matrix approach because the application of an IBP process with global and regional organizations to keep the cadence monthly needs to be done looking at the global structure and where decisions are made.

Often, when looking into the Matrix IBP design the decision-making process, as is, will be challenged, as the IBP design will often introduce new opportunities for decision making that challenge the current approach. This is another "turkeys voting for Christmas" issue.

Figure 8.12 shows a generic example of this approach and highlights the use of a "swim lane" approach to facilitate the flow of the monthly process from the Product Review through to the MBR or Corporate Review, depending on the organization's structure.

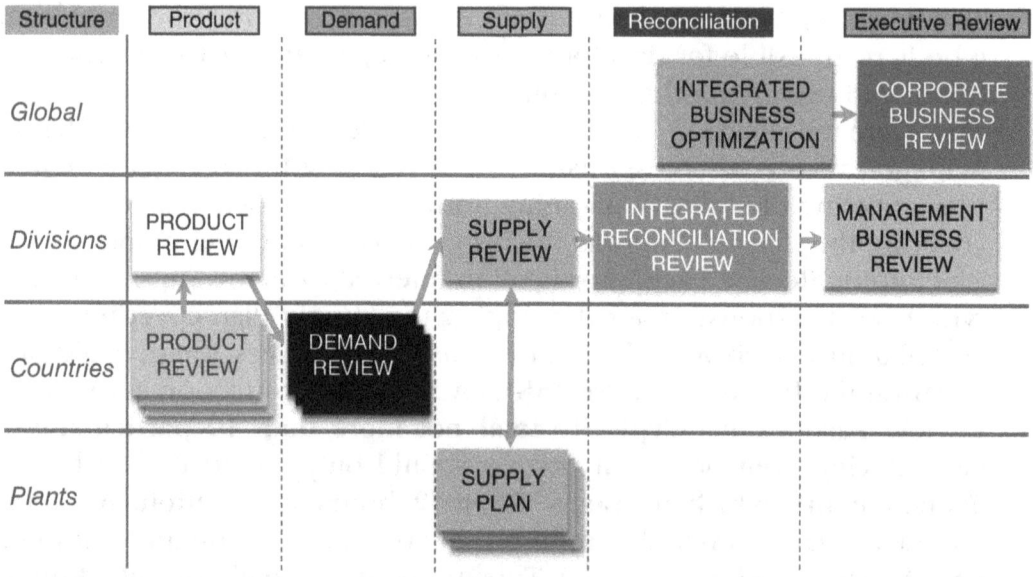

FIGURE 8.12 Generic Example of a Matrix IBP Design

The first step is to confirm the organization dimensions to enable the structure to be confirmed in the first column. This can be very different for different organizations; the above is a simple example. With this structure in mind it is then possible to build each step of the IBP process column by column, starting with the Product Review. The arrows indicate how information will flow and the position of each review against the structure indicates a level of decision making.

Some of the issues that must be considered in a Matrix design are:

1. Supply Chain is separated from demand for efficiency and focus.
2. Sales territories potentially have multiple supply sources, all of which must achieve consistently high service levels.
3. All markets and business units rely on a common product management process that must be effective on multiple levels.
4. Demand Management processes must be consistently deployed to support the pan-regional organization.
5. Sales territory plans must be aligned with longer-term, broader-based marketing plans.
6. Process is designed to recognize organizational accountabilities.
7. Behavior of power players is crucial as their boundaries are challenged.

This is just meant as an introduction to a very important design consideration for the IBP process that must be discussed business by business, as so many have such different global/regional structures and challenges presented by their different markets.

Integrated Tactical Planning (ITP)

The ITP process, to work effectively, requires reliable execution, such that senior management can focus on strategy and the longer term, assuming everything is on track, unless formally notified otherwise. This is known as "silence is approval." The process that interfaces between IBP (the domain of leadership) and weekly/daily execution of those plans already approved (the domain of middle management) is known as Integrated Tactical Planning.

In every business, planning takes place at different levels, or planning layers, spanning different time horizons and involving different levels of detail. As discussed in this book so far, Strategic Planning, IBP, Annual Planning, Master Scheduling, and Material Requirements Planning all have different objectives but must be orchestrated to achieve clear and documented business objectives. In too many companies, these planning layers are performed in isolation, with a focus on functional success. In companies that employ the Unparalleled Planning and Execution Practices, these planning activities across all layers are completely integrated, their objectives are met, and significant bottom-line benefits are achieved.

The North American region of a global consumer goods company that achieved Class A reported a recurring annual savings of $1 billion on annual revenue of $13 billion, an inventory reduction of $1 billion, increased customer service performance, and improved quality of work life. Operating with a single set of plans and numbers drives enormous benefits to the bottom line. Regarding time horizons and level of detail, the rule of thumb is the further into the future of the planning horizon, the more aggregate level of detail is adequate for planning; the nearer portions of the planning horizon require more granular information planning. The challenge is ensuring that these levels of planning and execution always remain aligned and congruent. Even within IBP there are several of these levels, as shown in Figure 8.13.

Figure 8.13 shows the IBP planning levels and their related planning horizons. While IBP is designed to "operationalize" strategy and provide monthly, aggregate execution direction to the rest of the organization, ITP is

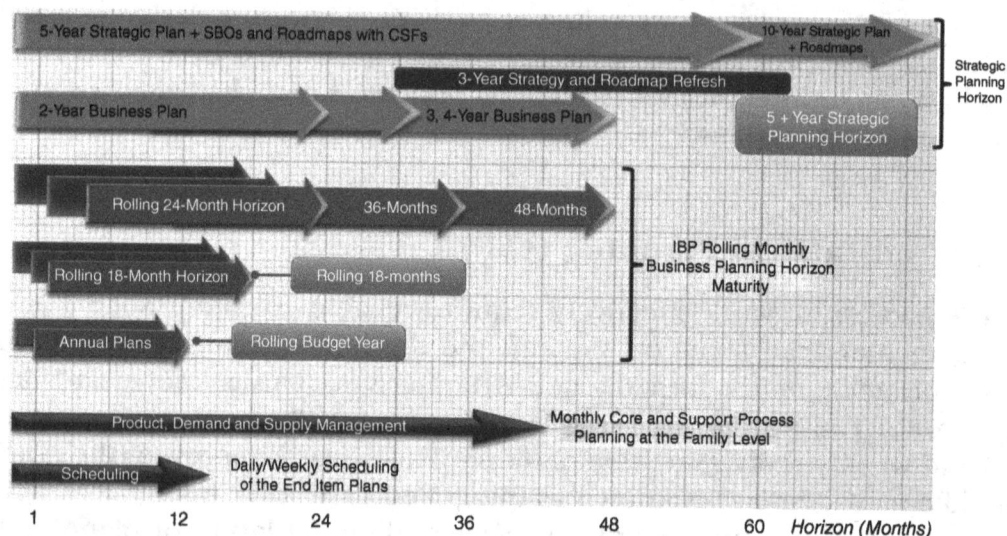

FIGURE 8.13 Business Planning Horizons – Strategy to Execution

designed to operationalize IBP and provide weekly and daily detail execution direction to the below-the-line organization over the tactical horizon (e.g., a rolling 13 weeks) and provide information back to the above-the-line (see Figure 8.1) organization if there are issues with being able to deliver the approved aggregate plans in that time horizon. This then closes the loop from the strategic planning horizon to the daily execution planning horizon and back again.

So, ITP is a near-term process for optimizing and synchronizing changes as they occur in the IBP Product, Demand, and Supply Plans, along with their associated financial and inventory change implications. ITP operates across the Firm and Trading Zones, as distinct from the IBP horizon, which focuses on month 4 and beyond. Even if the Firm and Trading Zones cover less than 13 weeks, the ITP planning horizon should remain a rolling 13 weeks since its primary intent is to stay on track to deliver reliably the previously approved first three months of the IBP plans and thereby ensure Leadership's confidence in the middle management team, allowing them stay focused on the longer term.

This planning structure creates a seamless interaction of the core processes – Product, Demand, Supply, and their resulting financial and inventory plans – from the longer-term, monthly, aggregate management plans, to the nearer-term weekly/daily, detailed execution of those plans. While the monthly IBP process validates the available resources and supply capabilities to meet the Product and longer-term Demand Plans, the key concept of ITP is managing the Product and Demand Plans to meet the typically less flexible Supply resources and capabilities inside the firm and trading time zones.

As Figure 8.14 shows, inside the planning time fence, the boundary between the trading zone and the free zone, is where the aggregate IBP plans are disaggregated to a lower-level of detail, usually by SKU (stock keeping unit) or end item by week or even by day, by shipping point, with the intent to rebalance Demand Plans to match Supply Plans. It should be noted again that these aggregate plans have previous MBR approval, which includes approval of the associated costs and resources required to deliver those aggregate plans. Therefore, ITP is required to proactively identify change, rebalance the detailed plans if possible, and escalate issues when required.

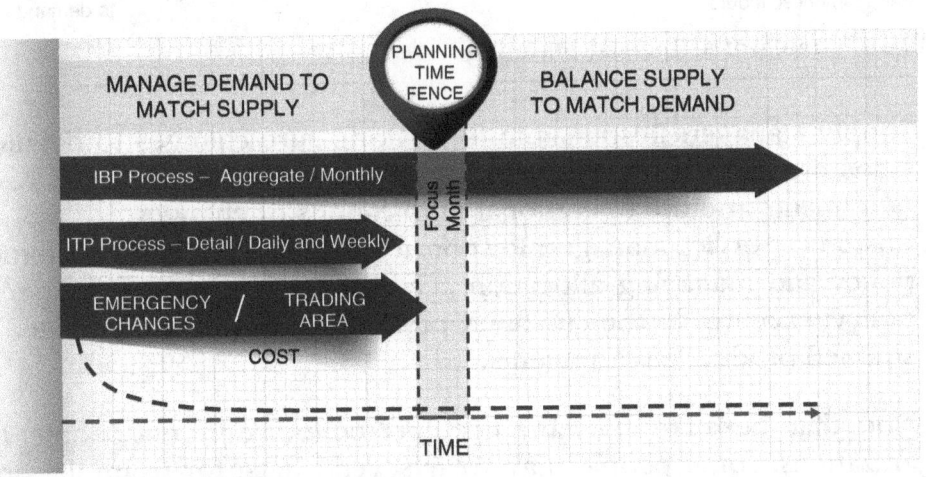

FIGURE 8.14 Planning Time Fences

To effectively manage and execute ITP, the ITP team must include four critical roles that constitute the required quorum.

As shown in Figure 8.15, these roles include:

1. **Product/Project Manager:** Responsible for executing the product launch schedules and volumes against launch expectations.
2. **Demand/Execution Manager:** Responsible for managing requests for changes in demand and "sensing" sales-order patterns that depart from the approved demand plan.

FIGURE 8.15 Integrated Tactical Planning

3. Supply Manager: Responsible for making sure changes to detailed supply plans are made cost effectively, taking into consideration all resource requirements and the operational implications of changes.

4. Customer Service Manager: Responsible for executing the customer service policy and managing allocation according to the segmentation/allocation policy; executes to the customer promise, in both unconstrained and constrained product environments.

Note that these are roles and need not be four different people. In smaller organizations, some people may wear several hats; for example, one person may fill both the customer service and demand execution manager roles. In larger organizations there may be several people with the same title, such as Supply Scheduler by plant or Product/Project Manager by product category. The two roles that should never be combined, however, are the demand and supply manager roles. It is critical for those roles to fairly represent their aspects of the plans. Combining them most often results in making the easiest decision in a supply-demand imbalance situation rather than the right business decision.

The two primary objectives of ITP are to:

1. Optimally manage changes in near-term Product, Demand, and Supply execution plans (i.e., inside the planning time fence), to deliver the previously approved IBP Plans;

2. Save time, reduce costs, and increase flexibility by truly empowering individuals throughout the organization, through documented decision boundaries, to make the right decisions at the right time without the need for escalating every decision.

So, as each day, week, and month passes, this IBP/ITP model allows people closest to the near-term operational capabilities to make the changes required to most effectively meet shifting circumstances, deliver the aggregate plans, and avoid costly uncontrolled churn and firefighting. Empowering people closest to near-term changes is how senior management increases its confidence in the capabilities of middle management and frees Leadership to focus on longer-term strategic objectives and actions.

Summary

The length of this chapter indicates the importance of IBP and its evolution from S&OP. It also indicates the importance of enabling senior management to focus its attention on aggregate plans in the 4- to 24-month planning horizon. Figure 8.16 summarizes the key differences between the more executional S&OP process and Oliver Wight's more strategic IBP process.

Sales and Operations Planning compared to Integrated Business Planning—what are the key differences?

S&OP	OW IBP (and historic S&OP)
Supply and Demand Balancing	Business Planning
Execution based	4- to 24-month decision-making
Focused on Demand and Supply	Focus on integrating the whole business
SKU and Detail	Family or Aggregate level (trends)
Production output	Gap closing
A plan	Modeling and scenario planning
Meetings dominate to review numbers	Integrated business plan and deployed strategy
Firefighting	Planned Agile response
Managed environment	Empowered environment
People-dependent processes	Nonpeople-dependent processes
Functional approach	End-to-end process based
Possible multiple agendas	Integrated with one direction
Traditional Budget focus	Rolling business plan of a minimum 24 months

FIGURE 8.16 Key Differences between S&OP and IBP

A robust Integrated Business Planning process requires an equally robust weekly Integrated Tactical Planning replanning process. ITP aligns and optimizes detailed plans inside the planning time fence, keeping the detailed plans aligned with the previously approved aggregate plans and, in turn, provides direction to those executing the detailed plans.

Recommended Reading

Correll, James, and Kevin Herbert. *Gaining Control: Managing Capacities and Priorities*. John Wiley & Sons.

Crum, Colleen, with George Palmatier. *Demand Management Oliver Wight Best Practices: Process, Principles and Collaboration*. J. Ross Publishing.

Groves, Dennis, Kevin Herbert, and Jim Correll. *Achieving Class A Business Excellence, An Executive's Perspective*. John Wiley & Sons.

Groves, Dennis, Kevin Herbert, and Jim Correll. *An Executive's Guide to Achieving Class A Business Excellence*. Oliver Wight International.

Palmatier, George, with Coco Crum. *Enterprise Sales and Operations Planning: Synchronizing Demand, Supply and Resources for Peak Performance*. J. Ross Publishing.

Palmatier, George, and Coco Crum. *Transitioning from Sales & Operations Planning to Integrated Business Planning*. White paper. Oliver Wight website.

For additional but more specific reading please visit the Oliver Wight Website and gain access to the extensive library of White Papers.

CHAPTER 9

Product and Portfolio Management: Offer What Customers Need, Not What You Think They Need

An often-forgotten element of Business and Detailed Planning is the need to integrate Product and Portfolio Management. It is essential that your current and future offering, your Portfolio, is developed to attract customers and successfully eliminate challenges brought by your competition. As can be seen in Business Excellence Planning, Figure 9.1, Product Management, which includes the management of the Portfolio, plays a key role in both Integrated Business Planning and Detailed Planning to support your Supply Chain's ability to deliver to customer needs. This chapter explores the suite of activities required to make this aspect of your Business and Supply Chain successful.

Strategically Driven

To develop and maintain a competitive Product Portfolio (the offering you take to market), it is essential to understand the direction of the business over at least a 5-year horizon. Strategic Planning should be supported with a process that progressively involves various levels of the organization to ensure multiple views have been obtained.

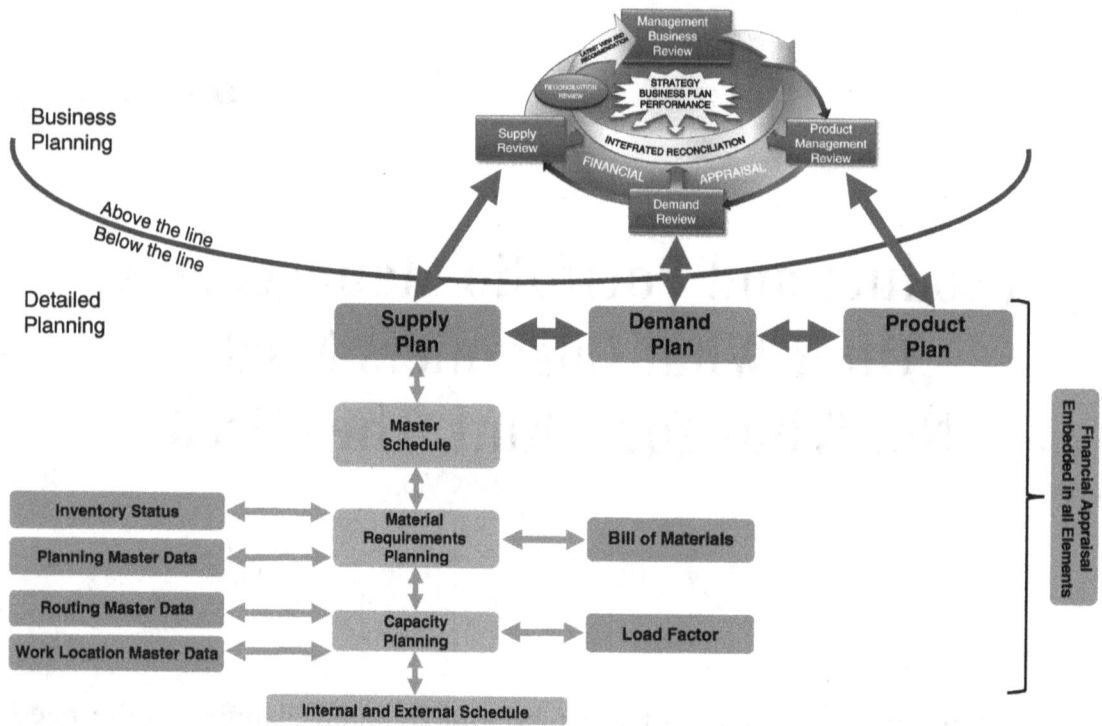

FIGURE 9.1 Business Excellence Planning

Please note: *Product* refers to the products and services being offered to customers and consumers.

All too often company strategies are just communicated through Vision and Mission Statements with very little granularity to support understanding and real decision making. We recommend developing integrated Roadmaps, stated in yearly buckets over the strategic planning horizon, that clearly identify the direction and objectives of the business.

There are Driving Roadmaps (Sales and Marketing; Product and Portfolio; Supply Chain and Finance) and Supporting Roadmaps (Human Resources; Information Technology; Quality and Legal) that should be developed through a process of one building off the other to ensure an integrated and shared direction.

Each Roadmap should clearly identify how the political, economic, social, and technological landscapes are changing and what impact/opportunity will result. The Strategic Planning process, therefore, enables you to bring the future into today, Figure 9.2.

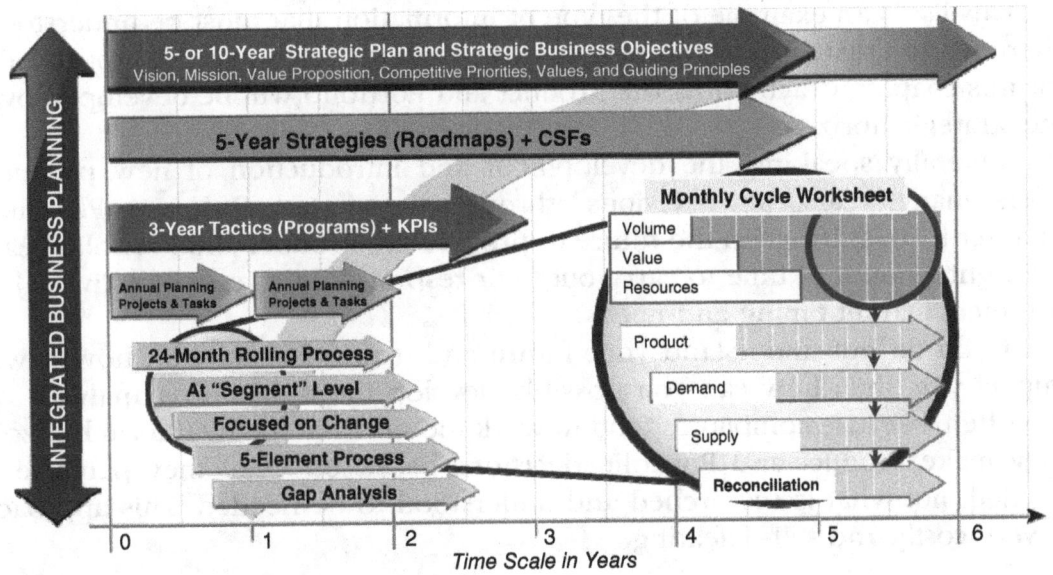

FIGURE 9.2 Bringing the Future into Today

To develop a competitive Product Portfolio that supports all the Strategic Business Objectives, it is essential to provide the team with clear direction that enables decisions associated with:

- The Families, Categories, or Segments needed to ensure that a competitive, attractive, and profitable offering is developed and maintained.
- Understanding market dynamics and whether any growth aspirations will be enabled through all Families or just certain Families. How the Business plans to invest in the envisioned future and what this investment means to the Product/Portfolio mix.
- Essential understanding of the investment in detail – whether this investment is to support growth, productivity, profitability, rationalization, and so forth, and then establishing how Product and Portfolio activities will support the objectives.
- The investment focus: Does this investment objective require increased supply capacity, implementation of new technologies, expanded team knowledge, acquisition, or a combination of all these and even more?
- The introduction of new legislation and regulations and the impact on the offering due to changes in materials, chemicals, safety, and so on.
- Parent Company demands and investment strategies.

This list is an example of the type of information that must be understood, shared, and utilized in developing a clear business response and, specifically for this chapter, exactly how the Product and Portfolio will be developed over the strategic horizon.

Generally speaking, the development and introduction of new products takes many years, so decisions, through Integrated Business Planning, Chapter 8, must focus on the future to provide the Product and Portfolio Team the right amount of time to carry out their responsibilities cost effectively, but still meet market timing and needs.

If you do not understand your future and make decisions on how it will impact you, then how can you possibly develop the right needs analysis? All too often, because companies tend to work too much in the near-term horizon, they make Product and Portfolio decisions based on what they perceive is needed, not what is researched and understood to be needed. This approach is very costly and self-defeating.

New Product Development and New Product Introduction

Clear, documented processes must be established for New Product Development (NPD) and New Product Introduction (NPI) to ensure all required activities can be executed on time and cost effectively.

For NPD to be successful, it must be fed from a very good Ideation Process that takes inputs from multiple sources on expected market demands well into the future. The Ideation Process creates a pool of ideas that have been approved to become Programs or Projects when appropriate resources become available.

The NPD timescale dictates an idea's viability for selection as a Program or Project. If a decision is made to move forward, but the execution time available is insufficient, then the decision must be changed to select an alternative. Hope does not result in success.

NPD initiatives must be authorized based upon an agreed and recognized market need, and the decisions to secure the market potential must provide the Program or Project Team sufficient execution time.

In many companies, NPD Projects/Programs take several years to reach the market. Therefore, the IBP horizon must be based upon the NPD time requirements, see Chapter 8.

NPI comes into play at the end of an NPD Project/Program and clearly identifies the steps required to take the new offering to market. Often, these "Go to Market" steps utilize a Stage and Gate approach (see Stage and Gate later in this chapter) and are sometimes included as part of the overall Stage and Gate Project/Program Plan. The main message is that there is a process in place to effectively manage introduction of New, Modified, or Discontinued Offerings.

For NPD and NPI, it is essential that the required resources are available at the time they are needed, both in the near term but also to align with future anticipated requirements. This is not just about headcount; it is also about having the right mix of skills available to cover all development and introduction needs, especially if these needs are changing over time. See the section on Resources later in this chapter.

Project/Program Management (Stage and Gate)

Countless Stage and Gate books and papers are already broadly available. This section will not repeat what is already available. Rather, this section emphasizes the keys for Stage and Gate effectiveness, namely being *formal* and *disciplined*.

Figure 9.3 illustrates a basic Stage and Gate model that emphasizes discrete and separate Gates and Stages. The first thing to be pedantic about is to emphasize that it is referred to as Stage *and* Gate, not "StageGate," as is often used, suggesting that the Stages and Gates are blended. They are not.

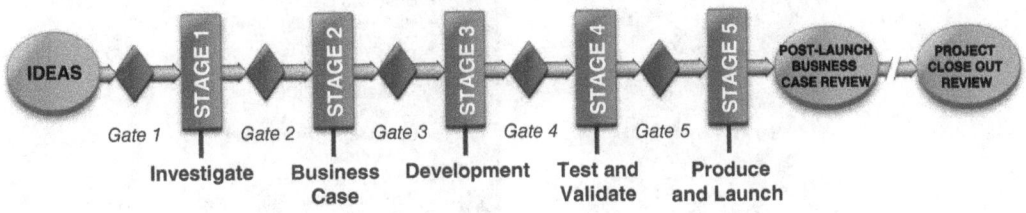

FIGURE 9.3 Basic Stage and Gate Model

This discipline mentioned is vital for a Stage and Gate process to work effectively and for the benefits it delivers to be realized. If these are not adhered to, then it is not worth investing in the Stage and Gate education and training for your people.

Businesses use Stage and Gate 10 times more than any other equivalent methodology because when used as intended it will:

- Involve Leadership early.
- Shorten time to market.
- Kill projects early that are not going to deliver their Business Case, allowing resources to be redeployed and better utilized.
- Stop the perpetuation of pet projects.
- Force visibility and decision-making.
- Enable longer-term resource management based upon headcount and skill requirements.
- Provide a standardized Project/Program Management approach, one that is not people dependent.
- Enforce priorities.
- Reduce the amount of rework.
- Protect you against you.
- Increase launch success.

Stages and Gates are very different aspects of the methodology and must be clearly designed and specified with clear roles and responsibilities to ensure that the key elements identified in Figure 9.4 are understood and deployed.

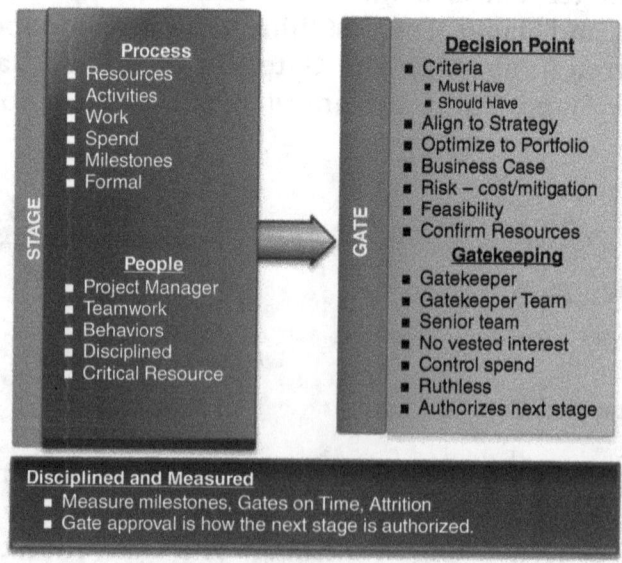

FIGURE 9.4 Key Elements of Stage and Gate

At a high level, the definitions of Stage and Gate are:

Stages
- Gather information.
- Multifunctional with parallel activities.
- Drive uncertainty down.
- Where work is done.

Gates
- Decision points for the next Stage – GO/STOP/RECYCLE.
- Serve as quality and prioritization control steps.
- Are predefined and specify a set of deliverables.
- "GO" authorizes resources for the next Stage.
- "Staffed" by senior managers.

It is very important to be clear about the governance ownership at the Gates; Gate Criteria must be defined along with the role of the Gatekeeper and the purpose of the Gatekeeper Team Review.

With respect to Gate Criteria, there are basically two elements: the Must Have and the Should Have:

- Must Have
  - An updated and valid Business Case and Plan.
  - Completed the planned work in the preceding stage.
  - Funding to continue to the next stage.
  - A stage plan for the next stage of work.
  - All required multifunctional resources available to plan.
  - An agreed date for the next Gate review.

- Should Have

  - Work not on the critical path completed to plan.
  - Identified unique visible benefits, cost advantages, higher quality for the same cost, higher value for the investment.
  - Market attractiveness, higher volumes, more share, and so on.

- Easier to sell, uses customer base knowledge, enables distribution simplification.
- Easier to manufacture, lower investment, and so on.
- Resource Requirements to be established for the Must and Should Have criteria.

The Gatekeeper:
- Should have, whenever possible, no vested interest in the Project or Program.
- Is accountable for the business success of the project.
- Says "Yes" when it makes business sense and authorizes the next Stage.
- Says "No" when Gate Criteria are not met and takes one of the following four decisions:
  1. Authorizes the project for the next stage of work.
  2. Kills the project.
  3. Reworks the stage to ensure the "Must Have" criteria are achieved.
  4. Puts the Project on hold.
- Should be selected based upon the focus of the Gate:
  - Gates 1 and 2, often Marketing.
  - Gate 3, often Finance, as this is when major spend/investment is authorized.
  - Gate 4, often Supply Chain, to confirm they can supply the product or service.
  - Gate 5, often Sales.

The Gatekeeper Team Review: The review agenda is constructed with two distinct halves:

- **Team Review Meeting Agenda: First Half focuses on Criteria achievement:**
  - The work anticipated during the preceding stage has been completed.
  - The quality of the work completed.
  - The full scope of work anticipated has been completed.
  - The "Must Have" criteria have been achieved.
  - The "Should Have" criteria are reviewed.
  - Takes one of four decisions:
    1. Approve the Project to continue to the next stage.
    2. Kill the project.
    3. Place the project on hold.
    4. Re-work the stage.

- **Team Review Meeting Agenda: Second Half focuses on the next Stage and Gate:**
  - Confirm the Stage activity and timeline.
  - Agree on the date of the next Gate Review.
  - Agree on the dates for in-stage milestone reviews.
  - Confirm availability of the required resources:
    - Critical Resources.
    - Gatekeeper for the next Gate Review.
  - Ensure funding is available for subsequent stages.

Governance and the Project Management Office (PMO)

The PMO must be very clearly integrated with the Integrated Business Planning process to ensure clear ownership and accountability, alignment to Strategic Business Objectives, and to enable escalation when the PMO identifies a conflict.

Governance
- Policy development.
- Make decisions (Gate Reviews).
- Reviews "Must Have" and "Should Have" data and recommendations.
- Interprets strategic roadmaps and associated initiatives.
- Approves budget and resources for the next stages.
- Responsible and accountable for the final Gate decisions.
- Protects the company from waste.

Project Management Office (PMO)
- Becomes the Information Center.
- Develops and makes recommendations.
- Prioritizes projects.
- Maintains resource data.
- Evaluates project performance.
- Supports idea/project Business Case development.
- Establishes a Master Product Development Schedule (MPDS) and provides a picture of funnel health.
- Recommends projects for selection, deselection, delay, or termination.
- Continuous improvement.

Leadership Visibility

For Stage and Gate to be successful, it is essential that Leadership are involved to set clear policies, decision-making rights, and that they themselves have clear responsibilities and the required information to make decisions:

- **Leadership Responsibilities**
  - Time and budget tracking.
  - Project issues mitigation forums.
  - Resource planning and allocation.
  - Project governance – Stage and Gates funding and approval.
  - Standardized and simplified project delivery methodology.
  - Ongoing portfolio assessment and reoptimization activities.
- **Leadership's Visibility of Performance**
  - Distribution of effort.
  - On-time launch rate.
    - Time to Volume.
    - Time to Profit.
  - Milestone adherence.
    - Planned use of resources.
    - Project benefits realization.
    - Project estimated versus actual hours.
  - PPD – Perfect Project Delivery.
  - Ideation: "No's" generated, attrition rate.

When implementing a formal and disciplined process people often resist because:

- Isolated groups resist and avoid processes and process discipline.
- There is a belief that formality stifles creativity and entrepreneurialism.
- Processes slow down time to market.
- There is a lack of accountability and follow-through.
- There is resistance to transparency and tracking.
- There is an absence of rigor around structured documentation.
- The business's reluctance to commit to a specific ROI.
- Project Management capability is poor.
- People do not accept empowerment.
- Fear of being second-guessed – decisions are not made, but often escalated.

Stage and Gate is an excellent way of managing Projects and Programs and must be implemented with Leadership's full support and understanding. The highlighted issues in this section just scratch the surface and have been made visible to ensure that the key aspects of discipline and formality are well understood and appreciated.

Generic Stage and Gate Project/Program Profiles

Figure 9.5 illustrates how your Stage and Gate design can be simplified when dealing with less complex Projects/Programs.

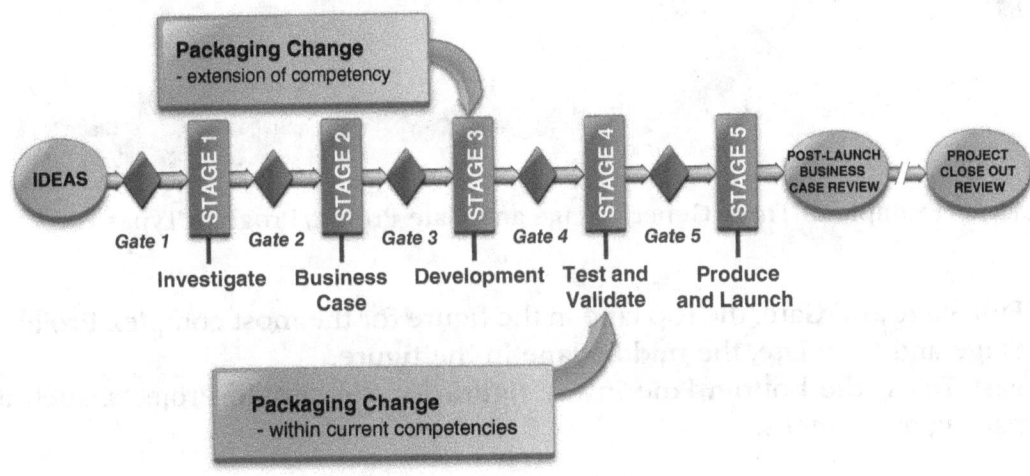

FIGURE 9.5 Stage and Gate Simplification Thoughts

It is important to develop these designs and then have the profiles matched with resource requirements based on historic Projects/Programs, experience of Project/Program Managers who have managed the same, or similar, Projects/Programs in the past.

Over time, you will develop generic Project/Program profiles that can then be used to develop a resourcing profile across the planning horizon; see additional comments later in this chapter.

When this exercise has been completed you will then have several generic designs; the number will depend on your specific industry and business needs. This results in your being able to specify the types of Project/Programs, made clear through a naming convention, common to your business. Figure 9.6 is just an example.

The three examples in Figure 9.6 are:

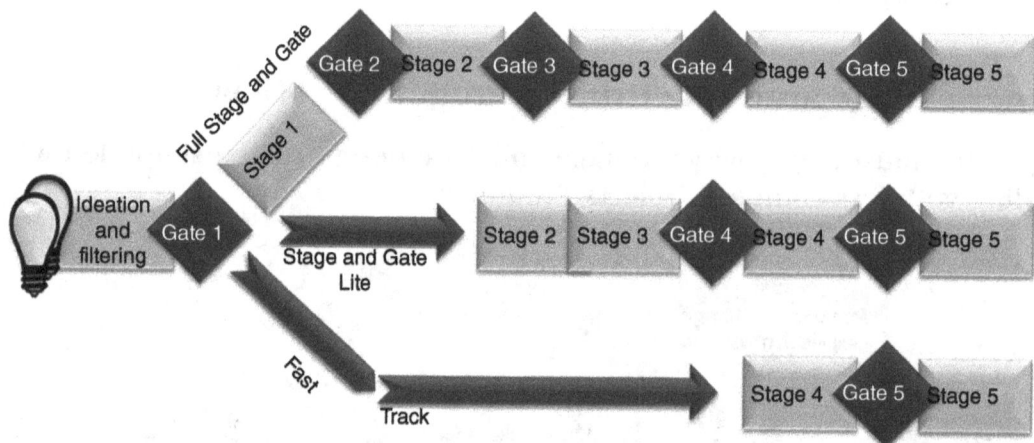

FIGURE 9.6 Example of Three Generic Stage and Gate Project/Program Types

- Full Stage and Gate, the top lane in the figure for the most complex Projects.
- Stage and Gate Lite, the middle lane in the figure.
- Fast Track, the bottom lane in the figure for the simple Projects, such as packaging changes.

Some companies may need more Stage and Gate lanes, but for most companies the three shown here are sufficient. An example of a different approach is one of our clients, who had about 70 launches per month and was successful in far less than 50% of the launches over the past many years. We had them not use Full, Lite, and Fast Track, but had them be more specific in the profiles. They developed a profile for packaging changes, one for component changes, one for flanker products, and one for completely new products. Within a year, they improved to above 99% launch success and launched an entire new brand with over 700 new items on the same day without missing a single shipment!

Eliminating the middle Stage and Gate may be appropriate in some instances, but the starting and final Gates and Stages must remain the same.

Resource Requirements Planning

The most common cause of failure with Product and Portfolio Management (P&PM) is the lack of resources in the right quantities, with the required skills and competencies at the right time. In business, the P&PM Team is one of the earliest examples of a multifunctional team since employees are required from across multiple areas of the company. All too often, many of these team members come from areas of the company not under the direct control of P&PM. Consequently, if the need is not established and requests are not made in advance for their involvement, the likelihood of them being available is zero, leading to frustration, delay, and lost opportunity.

Assuming Stage and Gate has been implemented and each project type has been designed it is then possible to establish a view of the resource need and mix over the full planning horizon.

With the "Must Have" and "Should Have" criteria established, for each design, you can then determine the work required during each stage, the mix of skills required, and where they will come from. Obviously, when accomplished for all Project/Program types, you will have a P&PM resourcing profile.

The resources to be considered would normally come from the areas shown in Figure 9.7, but are not limited to these sources.

RESOURCE FROM:

Program Managers	Testing	Supply Planning
Project Managers	Laboratory Technicians	Engineering
Product Managers	R&D	Suppliers
Design Engineers	Technical	IT
Manufacturing Engineers	Quality Assurance	Quality Control
Process Engineers	Supply	Production
Packaging Design	Sales	Manufacturing
Purchasing Officers	Commercial	Assembly Areas
Product Costing	Marketing	Demand Planning
Finance	Shop Floor	Shop Floor

FIGURE 9.7 Types of Resources to Consider for Stage and Gate

Utilize the steps in Figure 9.8 to build the resource profile out over your planning horizon of 36 to 48 months, or more, depending on demonstrated Product Development lead times.

- Use the New Product Master Plan (NPMP) to profile the actual use of resources on authorized and proposed projects/programs.
- If using Stage and Gate, what are the Gate resources needed?
- If using Stage and Gate what are the Generic Project types you are using?
  - Full.
  - Express.
  - Fast Track.
- From experience build up the typical resource profile for each project type:
  - Multifunctional, from R&D; marketing; engineering; QA; supply; labs; etc.
  - PMO – Program Managers, Project Managers etc.
  - If time writing has been used then use these as they should be more accurate.
- Using your Strategic Roadmap for Marketing, develop your Product and Portfolio Roadmap.
- Use the Roadmap to lay out the anticipated projects required beyond those authorized in the NPMP.
- From the NPMP + future projects use the generic resource profile to build a rough monthly view of the resources needed and show this graphically.
- If there is a gap, over or under, what are the decisions?

FIGURE 9.8 Process Steps to Build a Resource Profile for Projects and Programs

Figure 9.9 will be the result of this effort and will enable a clear view of the resources, skills, and capabilities required. Armed with this information, decisions can then be taken for:

- The availability of the resources required and the potential impact their use may have on the business.

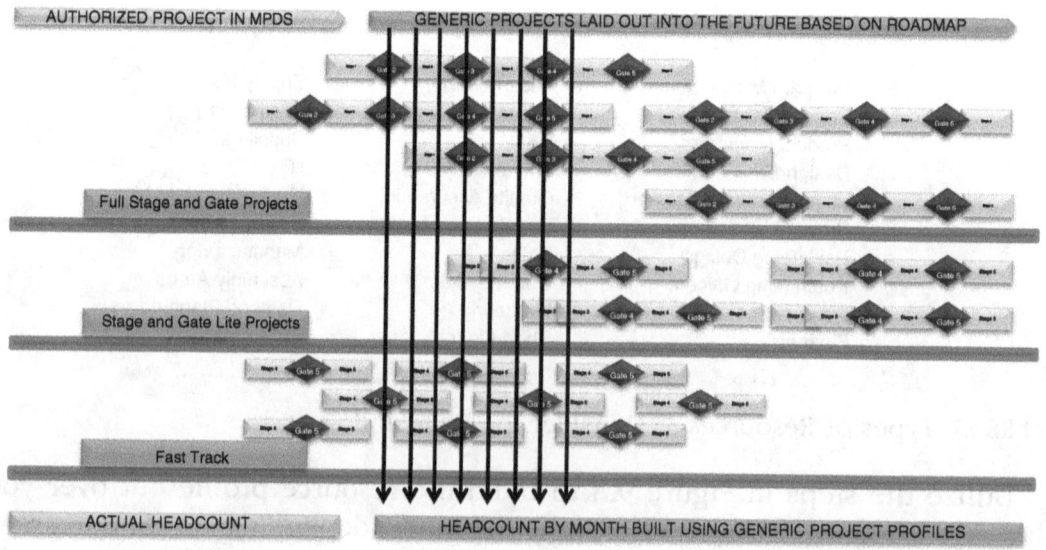

FIGURE 9.9 Build your P&PM Resource Plan for All Projects and Programs

- The skills required and the skills available. What education and training do these indicate may be required?
- Skills that may be missing and, hence, recruitment that may be needed.
- Decisions that must be made about how many Projects/Programs will be possible and whether the desired number generates a gap to the business need. Gaps would require issue escalation to IBP with recommended courses of action.
- Imbalances requiring a decision to either expand the resources or reduce the number of projects.

In Figure 9.9, the two bars at the bottom indicate actual headcount and generic headcount. The actual represents projects that are currently authorized, have been allocated the required resources, and are monitored as part of the New Product Master Plan (NPMP).

Detail Capacity Planning

Often more detail is required for not only capacity planning but for priority planning. Using the planning system, a bill of material with item numbers for development resources can be created for each step in the stage and gate process. A Routing (see Chapter 5) can then be created for the steps inside that stage with run times for each. The system will then calculate Detail Capacity Plans (Chapter 12) for each resource type and Routing operation start and due dates (see Chapter 11). When using this process, one of our clients that did "black" (military secret) projects delivered the company's first project on time and on budget.

Very importantly, ensure that there are no other projects being worked on outside this schedule. Why? Because they will invisibly consume resources that will affect near-term planning and IBP, utilizing resources that, through the formal processes, have been allocated elsewhere. This common problem in many companies must be stopped as it undermines decision-making, will cause Projects and Programs to fail, and significantly undermines the ability for launch dates to be achieved when the market needs them.

The P&PM Resource Plan enables a view over the next 12 to 24 months; again the horizon will need to be developed for each specific business and used to feed IBP. This view is roughly right rather than being precisely wrong as it is built up from the generic profiles, the actuals only being fully understood when the project/program specification is fully understood after authorization.

As the horizon extends further into the future, the generic mix of Projects and Programs has greater potential to be changed. Consequently, Resource Requirements Planning is used to support decision-making, again through IBP.

The use of Demonstrated Capability should also be reinforced, just like Demonstrated Capacity discussed in Chapter 12. Basically, this is understanding your demonstrated ability to deliver Projects and Programs compared to plan. For example, let us assume you have a plan to deliver 10 Projects/Programs each month; however, the demonstrated completion is only 8. Why plan to complete more than 8 until the issue causing the shortfall has been resolved? This analysis would identify a gap to plan and an issue escalation to IBP with recommended courses of action.

Measurement

As with all other chapters in this book, it is important to establish, based on the current level of Business Maturity, what measures will be used to summarize performance. The following are some of the measures that might be used for this analysis:

- New Product – On Time in Full – All Requirements Achieved on Time:
  - To Volume.
  - To Market.
  - To Profit.
- Master (Product) Schedule – On-Time Launch.
- Project Milestone Adherence.
- Gate Performance – Gates Achieved versus Gates Scheduled.
- New Product Vitality – Revenue and Margin versus expectation.
- Break Even Time (BET) – Investment Recovery.
- PM Contribution – Gap Value, Vitality, Other.
- Time to Market – Development Time in Days.
- Budget Control – NPD&I Spend to Plan by Project.
- Project Attrition Rate – Starts versus Launches.

In addition, there are some additional important Class A measures:

- Perfect Project Delivery (see more detail further on).
- Right-First-Time Quality.

- Resource Productivity.
- Profitability Tracking.
- Gates achieved.
- Gates failed (which should be a success, as it means the process is working).
- Cost/Schedule tracking.
- Education/Training to plan.
- Resource to Plan.
- BOM accuracy.

Perfect Project Delivery (PPD) is much more than Milestone Adherence, which, in a Stage and Gate process, for example, would simply be your success in achieving predetermined Milestone checkpoints such as Gate Reviews and specific Milestones on the way to a Gate Review.

PPD considers a much broader view. Consider the following as a definition:

A Perfect Project does not only finish on time and on budget, but delivers the right end product or service, at the pre-determined market price, using the most appropriate Project Management Options.

Delivering Perfect Projects requires adherence to the following steps:

- **Starting with the "best" solution:** From your ideation process, data, information, and options are provided to knowledgeable people who, after reviewing different Business Case scenarios, select the best idea to become a project.
- **Beyond Project Completion:** Project decisions are made based upon the anticipated life cycle of the product or service to be launched into the market. Will this launch achieve the customer and consumer expectations and the Business Case?
- **Beyond the basic Business Case:** The Perfect Project is often part of a bigger Brand, Family, or Aggregate Grouping. The deployment of new ideas must enhance their benefits to the business and the marketplace.
- **Perfect Projects achieve schedules:** The concept with Stage and Gate is to "kill early" to ensure that resources are used to the best benefit of the business. Good, speedy decisions keep projects moving ahead and to schedule.
- **Good communication and visibility:** Simple and effective information is developed to communicate progress, decisions needed and made, and next

steps. Progress is supported by effective communication of risk, governance, performance, and clear shared roles and responsibilities.

- **It delivers expectations:** The Perfect Project delivers the scope initiated through the Business case. Additional elements are added should an imperfection occur; this approach aids learning and process improvement.
- **Team-Based:** All involved become part of a multifunctional team – suppliers, stakeholders, individuals, and possibly the customer – to create a collaborative environment to deliver mutual benefits through trust and openness.
- **Decisive:** Through good collaboration and availability of trusted data and information, decisions are made early.

Project Management Options, mentioned earlier, refer to the type of Stage and Gate project and the steps to be followed. It builds on Figure 9.10.

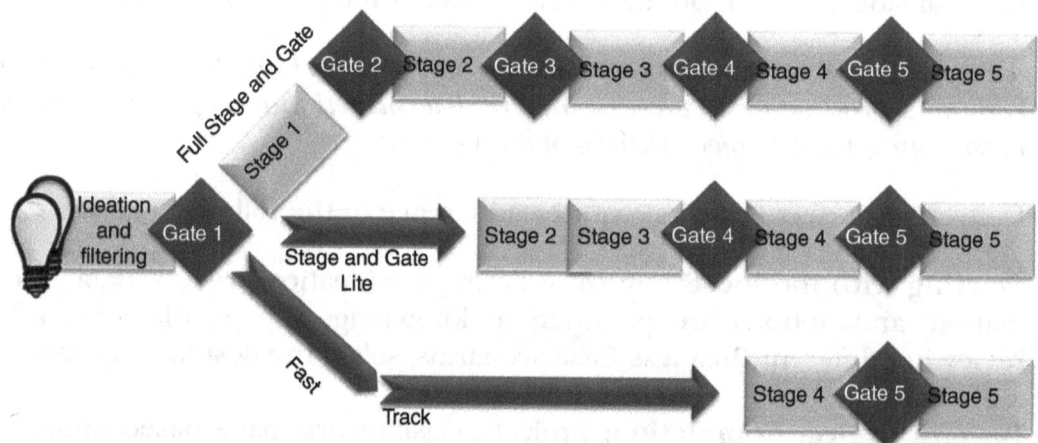

FIGURE 9.10 Stage and Gate Types, Some Examples

To gauge your Perfect Project delivery performance, consider the following additional measures:

- **Gate Reviews:** The number of Gate Reviews achieved on time; the measure would be the number of gates on time/number of gates planned during the month.
- **Gate Failures:** The number of Gates that have failed to be achieved on schedule; the measure would be the number of gates causing the project to be placed on hold, projects killed, or projects requiring rework of the

previous stage divided by number of Gates planned in the month (each failure type could also be measured). Indeed, there should be an expected level of attrition, especially at early Gates. Kills should be celebrated, not denigrated. Having Gate kills means that the process is doing its job!

- **Funnel Health:** The health of the development funnel is fed from a healthy ideation process, so measures associated with this should exist. The measure would be the number of ideas accepted as project ready divided by number of ideas generated monthly.
- **Ideation Timescale:** The timescale for the ideation process should be measured as time elapsed from when the idea was listed to the time the idea was accepted as ready to become a project. A graphical plot will show the trend.
  - As with the previous bullet, but by Project type, how long is it from the idea being accepted as a new project to the idea being ready to launch?
  - If the elapsed time is too long, how can process velocity be accelerated?
- **Project Completion:** Another interesting measure, depending upon what is considered as project completion. Is completion represented by time launched, time to expected volume, or time to expected profit? The maximum learning opportunity would be time to profit based on the lifecycle view. However, this can be quite a long time, and maintaining a project team for that long would be counterproductive. Transfer of product ownership (e.g., to Sales) would still be required before then, so when the measure of volume or profit has leveled out, the time can be documented.
- **Product Performance Management (see more information later in this chapter):** Product Performance Management (PPM) is a measure used to gauge the product or service once in the market. Measures would include whether the customer/consumer got what they needed; number of sales in the month divided by sales predicted in the business case; number of sales in the month divided by sales anticipated in the Unconstrained Demand Plan.
- **OTIF:** Supply Chain performance should also be added into this list, for example orders delivered OTIF.

Perfect Project Delivery Calculation

For Perfect Project Delivery, as mapped in Figure 9.11, the end-to-end set of processes must be orchestrated well. Obviously, this end-to-end picture must be mapped for each project type and individual measures established for each.

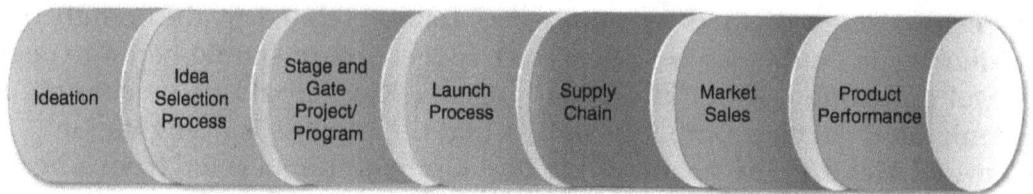

FIGURE 9.11 Mapped Project/Program Execution Steps

With this picture in place, it is possible to show how the measures relate to each other, like a Supply Chain where each node delivers to the next. In a Supply Chain this is referred to as the overall yield and is based on the multiplication of performance of each node. For example, if there are six nodes in the chain, each performing at 95%, yield is calculated as:

$$0.95 \times 0.95 \times 0.95 \times 0.95 \times 0.95 \times 0.95 = 0.735 \text{ or } 73.5\%$$

This should be graphed to show how this yield is trending based upon improvement projects executed in some or all the Supply Chain Nodes.

A similar approach can be taken with mapped Ideation through to Offering Portfolio processes feeding into market processes and would provide a Perfect Project Delivery view.

Perfect Project delivery, the mapped process, may be as shown in Figure 9.11.

Product Performance Management

When a Product or Service has been successfully launched into the marketplace, it is then available to customers and consumers. The Product or Service was selected as a Project or Program because it had a Business Case identifying desired potential.

Now in the marketplace, it should be a priority to determine its actual performance to confirm that it is contributing to the business as anticipated by the Business Case. To do this, there should be a focus on two main aspects, Technical Performance and Financial Performances.

- Technically, does the Product or Service do what it is specified to do? If not, what are the issues and how can they be fixed?

- Financially, does the Product or Service provide the consumers, customers, and business with the financial rewards anticipated? If not, why, and what can be done?

Figure 9.12 summarizes some of the performance considerations that should be of interest.

FIGURE 9.12 Product or Service Performance Considerations

Link to Demand Management and, More Specifically, Demand Planning

Product and Portfolio Management issues and conclusions must be fully integrated with Demand and Supply. This is accomplished very effectively through the Integrated Business Planning process and, more specifically, through IBP Demand Planning. See Chapters 8 and 10.

A decision for each business is when to add NPD launch dates into the Unconstrained Demand Plan. Chapter 10 identifies this as one of the key feeds into the Demand Planning process since the Demand Plan is the sole signal to Supply to determine the Supply Chain's ability to deliver. There must be a clear policy identifying which Gate is used to authorize entering the launch date into the Demand Plan, including volume and value, using Business Case numbers until actual Sales figures are available.

Portfolio Management

To ensure that what you offer to the marketplace continues to be attractive, competitive, and profitable, it is essential to continuously analyze performance of the Product and Services Portfolio and how it is contributing to business success.

Many tools are available to make this analysis. In this section, a few have been selected to explain the type of work required. This work, however, is useful only if it is then used to make decisions about the shape of future marketplace offerings based on the business strategy, customer/consumer needs, competitor activity, and Leadership's ability to take difficult decisions.

The insights gained provide an input to the Ideation Process for New Product Development, Product Improvement, Product Rationalization, and Product Discontinuation. Portfolio Management includes a suite of tools and processes that must be integrated to ensure effective execution; the results become a key feed into Integrated Business Planning with recommendations for decisions. Figure 9.13 shows a high-level view of required Portfolio processes.

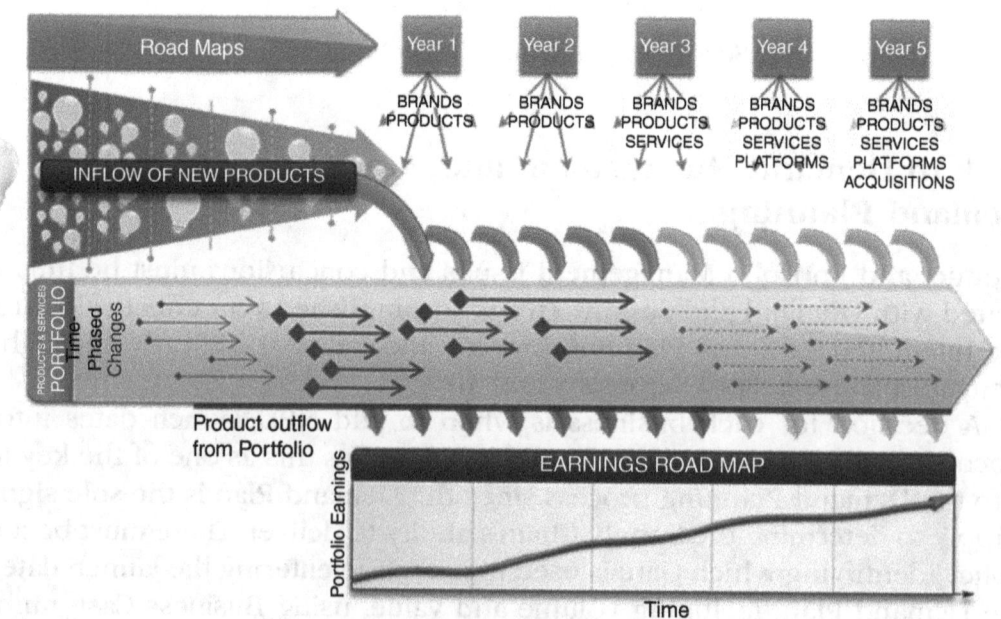

FIGURE 9.13 High-level View of Portfolio Management

Figure 9.13 illustrates the importance of a clearly communicated strategy through a Roadmap that identifies how the Portfolio is expected to change year by year. In this figure, year 1 focuses on Brands and Products while in year 5, it now includes Services, Platforms, and Acquisitions.

From the Stage and Gate "funnel" there is an inflow into the plan of New Products, Rationalized Products, and so forth, selected to grow the business and support the business strategy.

There is an outflow from the Portfolio reflecting agreed discontinuation of Products and Services. This part of Figure 9.13 is often missing, which means the Portfolio simply fills up and up with items that never really sell, undermine sales of new item, reduce overall profitability, and increase costs. And of course, while these items are still in the portfolio they consume time and resources to maintain them.

The final aspect in the illustration is the Earnings Roadmap to determine if the current and future Portfolio will generate the expected margin and, hence, profitability.

Portfolio Management requires Leadership to be ruthless; there is no room for maintaining any Product or Service that is not profitable, unless there is a conscious strategic decision to do so by the Leadership Team (for example, trying to get a foothold in a specific market by positioning a loss leader or to maintain pharmaceutical ethical drivers for life-saving drugs that may not be available from other sources).

To support Leadership's decision-making, executives must be confident that tools are being used to analyze their Products and Service. A few examples of available tools follow.

The Boston Matrix

Figure 9.14 shows the Boston Matrix and how the portfolio can be analyzed to provide information to support decision-making.

The Boston Matrix is a tool that allows an organization to sort its portfolio into a matrix, based on two driving criteria:

1. How effective is that part of the portfolio in sustaining market share?
2. Is that part of the portfolio operating in a high- or low-growth market?

This portfolio perspective provides insight into the organization that says to concentrate scarce resources on the "Stars" and "Cash Cows," take some time to

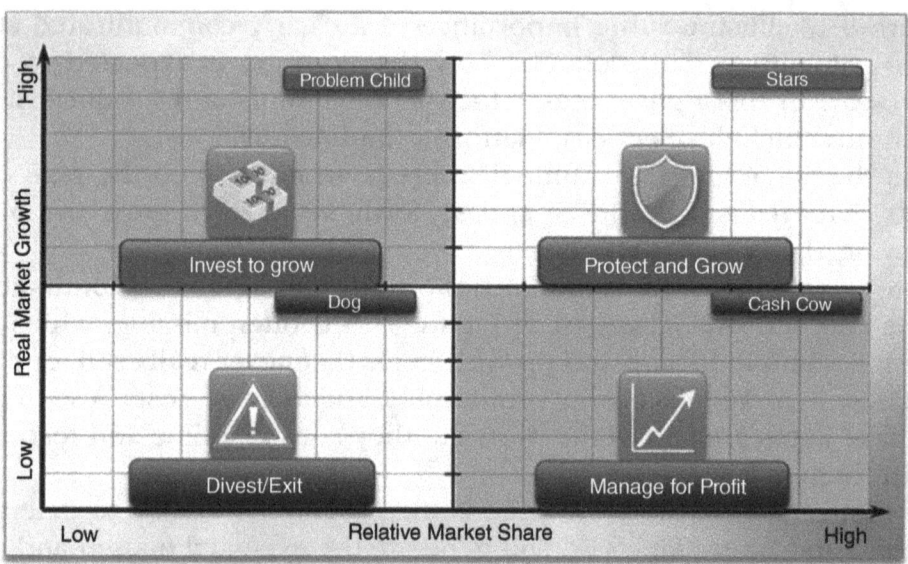

FIGURE 9.14 The Boston Matrix

consider the investment strategy in the "Problem Child" category, and plan to divest or discontinue the "Dog" category. What is insightful with this approach is that it highlights products and services perceived to be producing value (low market share and slow market growth) while the important message is one of focus – not deflecting resources from where their value can be maximized.

Financial Perspective

When it comes to achieving buy-in across the organization, presenting the business case as clearly as possible will always be important. As mentioned, understanding the true cost of maintaining a portfolio product or service is quite often grossly underestimated. What is required is a TCO (Total Cost of Ownership) approach whereby true costs can be applied and presented transparently, see Figure 9.15.

To achieve this, a structured TCO model appropriate for a given business must be developed and approved by the executive team. The model can draw on a broad range of potential considerations, with the approach being to achieve a level of robustness, to avoid too many challenges to the model design, to focus on the 80:20 rule of the big cost factors, and to keep the model as simple and transparent as possible.

TCO: What to Consider in Your Model?

Marketing	Product	Supply Chain	Finance	Business
• Unclear, poorly deployed, and unused Business Strategy. • Attractiveness to new markets. • Cost to keep Product active. • Influence of competition, reducing share. • Difficult to sell, aging, old technology, etc. • Requires too much people time to manage. • Customer complaints. • No repositioning strategy for Products	• Drain on critical resources. • Low Product performance when being used. • Old technology. • No longer viable against competition. • Cost and time to manage. • Portfolio Management too concentrated on the 'Dogs and Problem Childs'. • Sales continuing to sell delisted product, which takes volume predicted for the new listing. • DFM, DFT, and DFS implications.	• Falling sales volumes means higher costs. • Hundreds of small-quantity orders, too much planning time. • Too many change-overs, reduced output. • Poor Supply Chain Strategy to deal with increased small batches. • Frustrated Suppliers pushing for price increases. • Increasing inventory. • Capacity designed for volume being used for multiple short runs. • Poor customer service.	• Price should be increased as volumes fall; often sales maintain original prices, so margin erosion. • Emerging cost not matching planned costs. • Overtime due to firefighting and change in the short-term horizon. • Under recovery of overheads. • Cash flow cycle extending with a need to buy larger quantities of raw material than needed for small batches.	• Short term dominates the Long term, the organization compresses, and the business becomes very top-down. • Revenue and profitability gap to Business Predictions. • Traditional cost control implemented, which reduces the ability for all to manage. • Lack of Capex investment to support repositioning

FIGURE 9.15 Considerations for the Design of a Total Cost of Ownership Model

Life Cycle Management

Figure 9.16 illustrates a typical life cycle curve, a very useful picture for understanding the Products and Services you are offering.

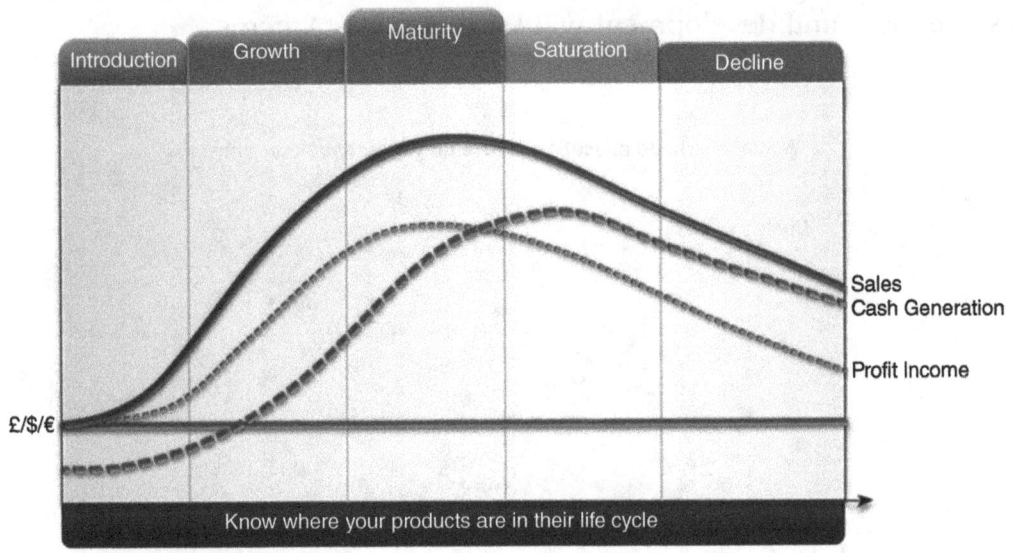

FIGURE 9.16 Typical Life Cycle Curve

There is nothing very new about tracking life cycle curves, assuming they are relevant to your business. However, they must be used in conjunction with other tools to understand why the Product or Service has reached Maturity or Saturation and what actions must be taken.

It is also important to understand that Profit and Cash tend to lag Sales, so this must be considered when developing Business Cases. If not understood, expectations may not align with reality and good products could be wrongly discontinued.

ABC Analysis

Figure 9.17 illustrates the different classes of Products to be considered when applying this methodology to understand how these different classes contribute to the business and what decisions should therefore be made.

- **Class A:** the most valuable products or customers in your portfolio. The products that contribute most of your profit without overutilizing resources. This is the smallest category, reserved exclusively for the biggest contributors.
- **Class B:** middle-of-the-road products or customers. Often believed to be those who contribute to the bottom line but are not significant enough to receive the required attention. However, Class B is about potential and with some focus and development will become Class A items.

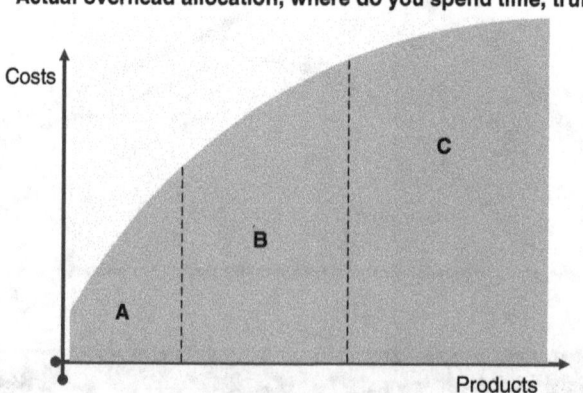

FIGURE 9.17 ABC Analysis

- **Class C:** all about the hundreds of tiny transactions that are essential for profit but do not individually contribute much value to the company. This is where most of your products or customers will live. It is also where you should try to automate sales to drive down overhead costs and minimize management attention. Often the C Class will divert management attention from the A and B, which is where their focus should be.

Why Use an ABC Analysis?

To improve your ability to deal with large and complex data sets by breaking them down. These classes, categories, or segments define the priority for the data being used.

When the data is broken down, it is easier to focus and use it in a meaningful way. Using three classes helps you prioritize more clearly.

First, divide the products into each of the three classes based on volume and value contribution.

The products with the most value will go into the high-priority Class A, while less important products would be placed in the bottom class, C. Products that remain are Class B.

This classification allows you to understand your most valuable products. Often the classification will spring some significant surprises, products you believed to be highly profitable are in fact not, and vice versa. Understanding this allows you to develop action plans and apply resources accordingly.

Please note that this approach could be used with customers as the focus.

As mentioned earlier, many tools are available to analyze a portfolio; those described here are just a few of the tools available. Others are highlighted in Figure 9.18.

Summary

All too often, Product Management is left isolated when in fact, as has been described, it must be clearly presented to be fully integrated with Demand and Supply to enable all business organizations to perform well. Product Management is very strategic since it develops the marketplace business offerings and, based on NPD lead times, identifies when decisions must be made regarding changing that offering.

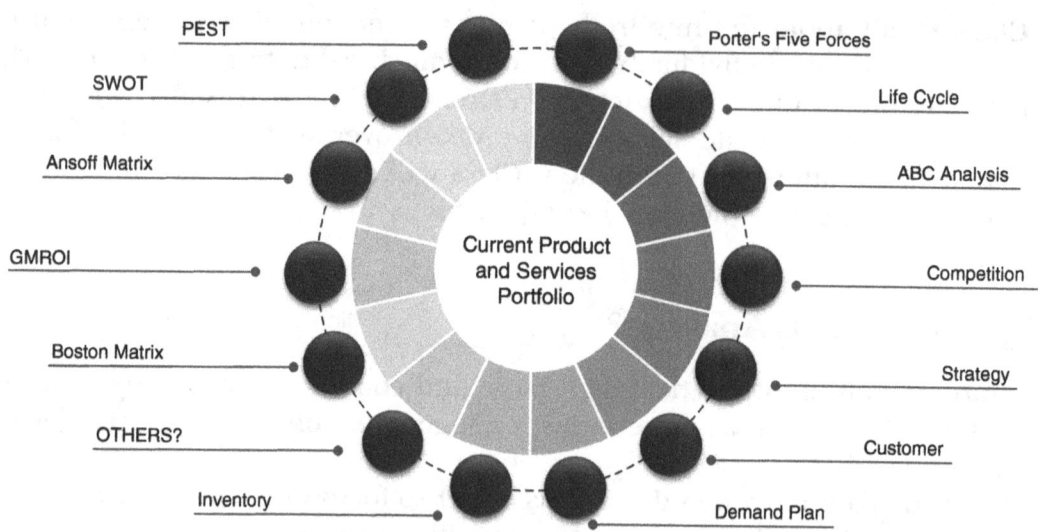

FIGURE 9.18 Examples of Portfolio Analysis Tools

This chapter introduces the key concepts regarding Product/Portfolio Management (P&PM) and highlights the scope of considerations required to ensure effective portfolio management and integration. Managing this aspect of the business effectively is critical to the success of near-term planning and execution and medium-to-long-term planning through Integrated Business Planning. Most importantly, it is fundamental to enabling closed-loop decision-making at all organization levels.

Recommended Reading

Correll, James, and Kevin Herbert. *Gaining Control: Managing Capacities and Priorities*. John Wiley & Sons.

Crum, Colleen, with George Palmatier. *Demand Management Oliver Wight Best Practices: Process, Principles and Collaboration*. J. Ross Publishing.

Groves, Dennis, Kevin Herbert, and Jim Correll. *Achieving Class A Business Excellence, An Executive's Perspective*. John Wiley & Sons.

Groves, Dennis, Kevin Herbert, and Jim Correll. *An Executive's Guide to Achieving Class A Business Excellence*. Oliver Wight International.

For additional but more specific reading please visit the Oliver Wight Website and gain access to the extensive library of White Papers.

CHAPTER 10

Demand Planning: The Art of Demand Planning and Execution

One of the most challenging elements of our Business Excellence Planning model, Figure 10.1, is creating the Demand Plan because those who create it must investigate the future and predict what people will buy at that time.

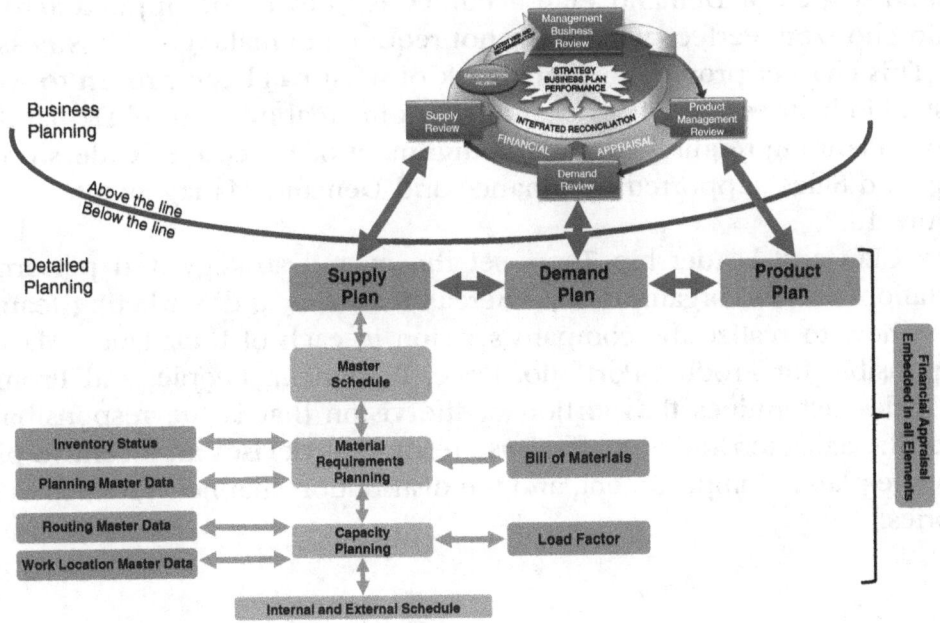

FIGURE 10.1 Business Excellence Planning

Imagine that we could accurately predict the future to make exact projections of the largest variable facing an organization – the products or services your customers will order 3, 6, 12, 18, and even 24 months from now. If we could make accurate predictions like that, we would head directly to Las Vegas on the next plane and not ever have to worry about working again. But, it seems, that does not work so well. All those casinos are making a ton of money because people who believe they can accurately predict the future outcomes fall well short of doing so.

The aggregate Demand Plan is a direct input to Integrated Business Planning (IBP); the detailed Demand Plan is a direct input to the Master Schedule, which, in turn, feeds the Material Requirements Plan (MRP) for dependent demand and, separately, provides input for planning independent (spare parts) demand. It is challenging because we know that the plan will never be 100% accurate across the future planning horizon of 24 months for aggregate planning and 3 months for detailed planning. IBP, with its minimum 24-month rolling horizon, presents the greatest challenge because of the ambiguity associated with such a long planning horizon, but future planning in the aggregate presents less volatility and uncertainty than future planning at the detailed SKU level. The good news is that even an imperfect Demand Plan is nevertheless useful in enabling the Supply Chain to satisfy customer needs, especially if the demonstrated degree of Demand Plan accuracy is known and applied across the planning horizon. Perfect accuracy is not required to make good business decisions. This chapter provides a framework of what has been proven to work in almost all industries and what does not work in creating a useful Demand Plan. Demand Planning requires input and alignment of Executive Leadership, Marketing, and Sales supported by Finance and Demand Management, as shown in Figure 10.2.

The CEO and Leadership Team set the overall strategy and performance expectations for the organization, whereas the Sales and Marketing teams determine how to realize the company's vision in each of their lanes. Marketing is responsible for Product/Portfolio, Price, Placement, People, and Promotion plans. Sales determines the portion of the vision that is the responsibility of each of the Sales territories, staffs those territories, devises an incentive plan to encourage plan accomplishment, and the distribution channels for each of those territories.

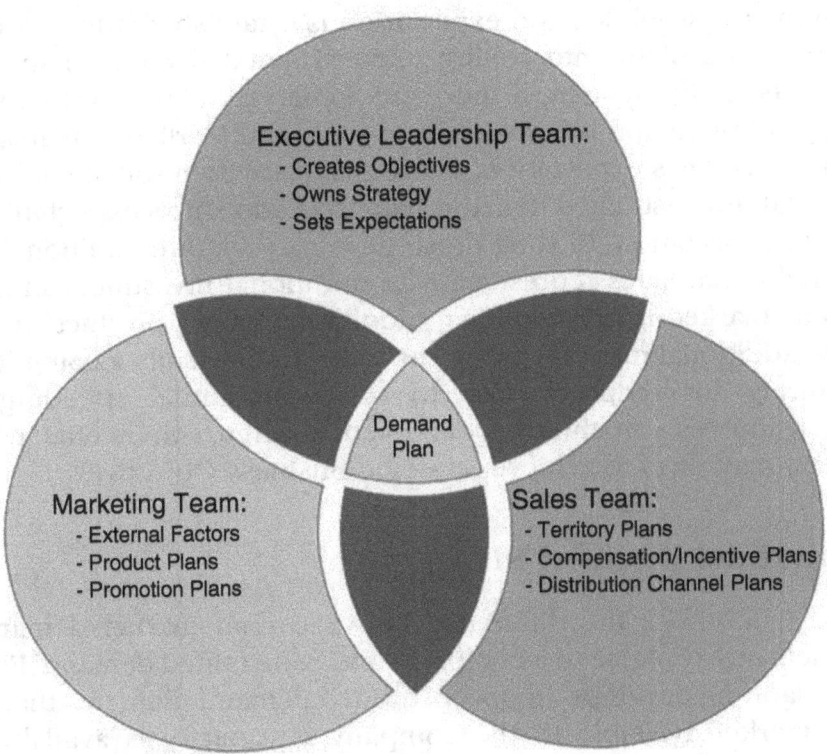

FIGURE 10.2 Demand Planning Convergence

Basic Approach: Start with Last Year's Sales with Puts and Takes

Basic Demand Planning in most companies begins with a top-down directive from leadership to establish expected demand volume and revenue over the following years. This is typically carried out by first looking at last year's sales volumes by territory and then assembling a high-level list of assumptions to either increase or decrease those volumes across the planning horizon. Rarely have we seen a senior management team develop an initial plan with lower than the prior year's actual sales, but it can be appropriate in certain circumstances. For example, a client company that we assisted moved away from the unprofitable portion of their business to increase sales in more profitable lines to increase bottom-line profits while decreasing total unit volume sold.

When the top-level demand expectation is established, the task of developing the minimum 24-month rolling unconstrained demand plan by product family (occasionally by item, if there are some very significant end items), by customer, and by region is handed off to Sales and Marketing teams to achieve senior management's expectation. Those plans are then rolled back up to compare the total unconstrained demand plan to Leadership's expectations to identify gaps to expectation. Closing those gaps may require additional resources, such as additional Sales representatives; additional investment in advertising, sales, and marketing promotions; additional new product development resources; additional manufacturing capacity; and possibly a commitment from Manufacturing for reduced costs to offset additional spending. Demand Planning resources can then be deployed to align commercial resources to appropriate market(s) to achieve Strategic Business Objectives.

Unconstrained Demand Plan

Figure 10.3 describes the difference between total market demand, unconstrained demand available to a company, and constrained demand. Each month, Demand Planning develops an unconstrained demand plan, i.e., that portion of the total market available to the company if capacity is available. That is, Demand assumes Supply has the necessary capacity to meet those unconstrained volumes. Obviously, the Demand Plan will have commercial con-

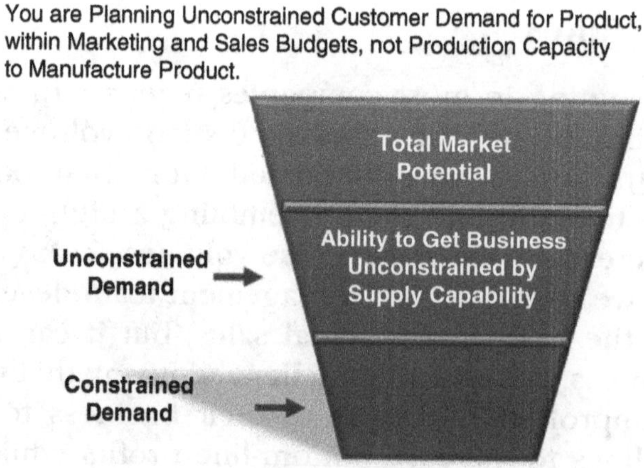

FIGURE 10.3 Principle of Unconstrained Demand

straints related to price, competition, the current portfolio offerings, customer choices, reputation, product performance, and so forth, but we do not want Sales or Marketing to assume any Supply constraints and reduce the plan based on those suspected constraints. Recommending constraint of an unconstrained demand plan is the responsibility of the Supply Manager after consultation with Manufacturing, Operations, or Supply Chain and presentation of constraint recommendations to the Demand Manager for alignment on the optimum use of the constrained resource(s).

Demand Planning's "truth as we know it" view of what is planned to be sold over the rolling 24-month horizon, without regard to any Supply constraints, provides Leadership a view of what could be achieved if Supply constraints were eliminated. So, when Supply develops and submits a capital expenditure to eliminate some or all the constraints, Leadership has the full picture of why the capital expenditure is needed and the resulting revenue and margin benefits to enable an informed decision.

If Supply has a long-term constraint for a particular family or families, and a capital expenditure is approved through Integrated Business Planning, the Demand Plan may be reduced accordingly to eliminate the need for Supply to present the same constraint every month until the approved resources are added. Note, however, that the Demand Plan should continue to show the full unconstrained potential unless the business decision is not to pursue that business opportunity. Then that potential demand is eliminated from the unconstrained demand plan from that point forward.

It is fair to say that Sales and Marketing sometimes struggle with this unconstrained demand approach since it requires more accurate interpretation of marketplace potential. It requires more ownership and accountability for predicting future potential. Equally troublesome is a belief that the unconstrained demand potential is 100% of the market, potential that is rarely, if ever, realized, since doing so would require a market monopoly. Required Demand Planning behaviors are crucial to Demand Plan accuracy and highlighted throughout this chapter.

Another key concept in developing the unconstrained demand plan is looking not only backward (i.e., the actual demand experienced in the past) in developing the new plan but also looking forward to anticipated future volume changes, such as new product launches, movement into a new category, Sales and Marketing pricing initiatives, customer promotions, and expansion into new territories. Looking only at history to develop an unconstrained demand plan would be like the driver in Figure 10.4, using only the rear-view mirror to navigate the road ahead. A crash would be inevitable and would usually occur within minutes. Yet this is how many companies develop their Demand Plans. If they operate their company by only looking backward, they will live in a culture of continuous churn and firefighting and fall far short of the business results available to them. Companies must look forward to anticipating the changing road ahead and be ready to turn when the road curves! Anticipating the future requires multiple inputs to the unconstrained demand plan.

FIGURE 10.4 Would you drive forward only using the rear-view mirror?

The Importance of Multiple Inputs to the Demand Plan

One of the most fundamental principles of Demand Planning is that there must be a single owner of the process, typically the Sales and Marketing VP. When, as some companies believe, everyone owns the Demand Plan, the reality is that no one owns the Demand Plan. A second principle is that all Demand-related organizations must contribute to the process. Thousands of Class A companies over the past 50 years have reinforced the Unparalleled Business Planning and Execution Practice that a company benefits whenever there are multiple views feeding into the Demand Plan. Input must be solicited from multiple internal functional areas within the company as well as from outside the company, such as directly from the customer base. The Demand Planning Wheel, Figure 10.5, summarizes available inputs that should be included.

This principle also builds accountability and commitment to the Demand Plan across all company Demand functions and, if done well, even among those in the Customer base who input into the plan. Far too many companies place inordinate reliance on statistical tools to generate the Demand Plan with little or none of the other inputs displayed in Figure 10.5. This statistics-limited approach ensures that the Demand Plan is far less than accurate and develops absolutely no result ownership. It also results in the Supply Manager beginning to second-guess the Demand Plan and in developing a second set of numbers. The best companies have a true unconstrained demand plan that is owned by the Sales and Marketing VP, the individual who is held accountable by the senior executive for its accuracy and delivery. It is refreshing to see that Class A companies also measure the accuracy of customers' input and then review the results with them so that they begin sensing the importance of their input in the improvement efforts.

FIGURE 10.5 Multiple Inputs Are Required to Build an Unconstrained Demand Plan

Source: © Oliver Wight International.

Demand Planning Elements: Predicting, Influencing, Communicating, Managing

One of the largest complaints we hear is that the forecast is never accurate. That is precisely when we remind companies that Demand Planning is more than just forecasting what orders will come in. It is planning future demand, incorporating those actions that the Sales and Marketing teams will take as part of their go-to-market plans and initiatives. This includes demand influencing, communicating, and managing demand, through a demand control process, as new orders flow into the company's order backlog.

Demand influencing includes activities like trade show attendance, promotions, advertising, discounting, placing inventory closer to or at customers (consignment programs), service level or flexibility guarantees, and use of other market variables. We have seen some of the simplest approaches to demand influencing yield the largest results. At a large business-to-business (B2B) custom electronics solution manufacturer, the Inside Sales team used customer-supplied SKU level forecasts to solicit orders whenever there was unconsumed forecast inside the individual product's published order-to-ship lead time. This led to significant forecast accuracy increases, stability in manufacturing schedules, and efficiencies across the End-to-End Supply Chain, along with an increase in customer satisfaction. Customers appreciated that their supplier was double-checking with them at product lead time to ensure they had not missed a trigger on their side to place an order. The Inside Sales team was also able to gain "intel" when the customer opted not to place an order. If the customer chose not to place the order, a follow-up question was asked to find out why, and then the Demand Plan would be adjusted according to the customer's feedback.

The importance of the communicating portion of Demand Planning cannot be stressed enough. Simply put, this is all about keeping the Demand Plan as accurate as possible in real time. Whenever there is new information regarding how actual Demand is materializing, there *must be* a methodology for reflecting this new reality in the Demand Plan. This underscores the importance and use of assumptions (see the assumptions section later in this chapter). Too often, we see a lack of robustness in companies' communications that results in failure to use available information. What good is it that a Sales representative learns that a customer is going to double its demand next quarter if the company does not build that information into the Demand Plan? When the actual orders hit the system the demand exceeds capacity, and churn and fire-fighting begin. Again, keep it simple; ask just two questions of the Demand Plan stakeholders:

1. How will the information just learned impact the Demand Plan (volume or due date)?
2. Who else needs this information (resource requirements to source, make, or deliver the changed volume or due date)?

If the answers to these two questions are driven into the Demand Plan and are part of a company's core behaviors, that company has a great chance of responding successfully to changes in actual demand. Techniques for responding to demand will be explained in more depth in Chapter 11 under the heading Compressing Lead Time.

Demand Planning Key Principles

First, some basic principles of Demand Planning:

- **Constructed:** by using as few product families as possible (see IBP, Chapter 8).
- **Use Statistical Forecasting:** to develop a baseline plan to modify with other inputs regarding future initiatives, internal and external.
- **Continuously reduce:** bias, volatility, and variability.
- **Formally:** document assumptions, vulnerabilities (risks), and opportunities to improve accuracy and manage demand.
- **Review and update:** frequently (remember that a demand change does not always require a Production Plan or manufacturing schedule change).
- **Measure:** to continuously improve.

Demand Planning, covering the rolling, 24-month planning horizon, can sometimes go awry when it is the responsibility of Sales and Marketing. Their sense of information sharing urgency in keeping Supply in the loop is not always what it should be regarding day-to-day demand changes. Demand Planning must be a real-time, continuous process to be successful. A close working relationship between and co-location of the business unit's Demand and Supply Managers ensures that the required information is easily and continuously shared.

Formal Demand Planning requires regular attention, much like physical exercise. Like a muscle, it must be exercised regularly to make gains in process efficiency and strength. Initially, gaining Sales and Marketing commitment to participate in a formalized monthly process can be challenging, given frequent travel requirements and customer communications requirements. One of our recently retired Principals described himself, when he was the Sales and Marketing VP for a client company just beginning to implement S&OP, as the company's anchor. Not that he was the stabilizing force in the company, but that he had to be dragged along behind the ship as it moved! That changed dramatically when the light went on and he began to see improvements in his customer service, revenue, and margin. It is rare to find someone in the commercial side of the business who is excited about signing up for another program and having their performance measured yet another way, especially regarding Demand Plan accuracy. Add to these challenges that Demand Planning software requires a level of technical capability that is not high on the priority list of those in customer-facing roles such as Sales, and that these technical skills, when acquired, are perishable. So, if a company is expecting a Sales representative to input significant amounts of data into a computer system monthly, the task had better be:

1. Intuitive, so that it requires little to no training, and
2. Streamlined, so that it takes little time.

So, how should a company engage its Sales and Marketing people in the Demand Planning process?

Sales and Marketing, supported by Demand Management, own the unconstrained demand plan and must maintain accuracy of the aggregate product plans. They have access to the prior cycle's aggregate, product-level Demand Plan and the customer hierarchy, along with the statistical forecast and all customer collaborative input. This gives them the keys to understanding the data and enables them to own the total unconstrained demand plan and the underlying assumptions.

In the near term, a detailed Demand Plan at the SKU level is required; it is therefore essential to keep the conversion from the aggregate to the detail as simple as possible for Sales and Marketing. Most companies expect Sales representatives to forecast individual detailed SKU quantities by customer for the near-term months or weeks. Except for consistently large SKUs, these quantities are extremely variable and, to a great extent, impossible to forecast in detail. Asking for this level of detail from Sales representatives is a waste of their time and inaccurate. Nevertheless, individual SKU quantities are required by week within the firm and trading zones. These quantities are more reliably and efficiently developed through disaggregation of accurate product family quantities by the planning system through algorithms, updated at least quarterly, for product mix, and percentages distributed from each shipping point. These quantities can also be adjusted with information regarding promotions, customer initiatives, and so forth. Common weaknesses in Demand Plan input from Sales and Marketing include:

- **Product Cannibalization:** Cannibalization is often unaccounted or under-accounted for, leading to surprises when the new offering reduces demand for the older product at a rate much higher than planned, leaving unsellable product in inventory.
- **Product Rationalization:** The true cost and benefit of individual products is rarely understood or examined with any precision. As a result, products that should be discontinued often remain in the portfolio well beyond their viable lifespan. Sales normally contributes to this weakness due to a reluctance to take any item out of the portfolio that could possibly produce revenue, and Sales representative bonus, at some point in the future.
- **Visibility of Customer Promotions:** Especially for manufacturers with custom part numbers (meaning its product SKUs are exclusive to each customer), it is vital that the company understand their customers' detailed promotional calendars.
- **Supply Lead Times:** It is important that Sales and Marketing understand how their products are replenished based on their business strategies (ETO, MTO, ATO, MTS, etc.; see Chapter 7, Mastering the Master Schedule) and typical lead times, including Purchasing, Manufacturing, and Distribution lead times. Clearly, understanding these lead times will help Sales and Marketing provide timely, detailed demand input for proactively planning their response.

Another key Demand Planning process is documenting assumptions, the list of internal and external factors expected to impact demand and, therefore, influence the unconstrained demand plan, either positively or negatively. Fundamentally, assumptions capture the thinking underlying an input into the Demand Plan. Each assumption must be documented, quantified, and measured, after the fact, for accuracy. The more complete the underlying thinking, the more accurate the unconstrained demand plan. Most companies do an adequate job of capturing Demand Plan assumptions during their annual planning processes, but as soon as these annual plans are approved, assumptions are rarely reviewed until the following year's annual planning cycle begins again. This major mistake can cost companies significantly by delaying decisions necessary to address large Demand Plan changes caused by changes in those underlying assumptions.

For instance, several oil fracking companies documented annual planning process assumptions showing the price of a barrel of oil remaining above $50 across their entire planning horizon. Then OPEC increased production, and the price plummeted. Some fracking companies failed to recognize the full impact of that assumption until their next annual planning cycle began. Some of those went out of business because they continued to operate unprofitably. Had they reviewed and updated their assumptions each month and reacted appropriately, they might have survived.

Using assumptions to manage the unconstrained demand plan is essential. Consequently, all Demand Plan inputs must be supported by key assumption documentation, including assumption owners' names. If new information is received and considered different from the current assumption, then the assumption must be modified, and the plan adjusted accordingly. If the new information is not different enough to modify the current assumption, the plan remains unchanged, but the new information is retained for continued understanding until it can either be used or discarded. Documenting and using assumptions reduce Demand Planning volatility (see description at the end of the chapter) and results in greater plan stability.

Another Demand Planning concern is bias, for example, Marketing's wearing "rose-colored glasses" to justify new product introductions by planning unrealistically high market share for those products. Sales inputs, on the other hand, must be reviewed to ensure that they are not understated, making it easier to earn bonuses for exceeding the quantity, but risking customer service by understating the quantity to be produced.

Consistent high-side bias results in the company's bearing unnecessary Supply Chain costs, excess capacity, inventory, and overhead, all of which reduce profits. A recent client benefited from this type of bias when they expanded by taking over a former large online marketplace's warehouse at a significantly discounted rate per square foot. The online marketplace had expanded their distribution network too quickly based on an overoptimistic Demand Plan and then consolidated its distribution network and corrected their biased Demand Plan soon after. Although they have experienced impressive growth since then, their early mistakes resulted in years of losses before they became profitable.

Negative Demand Plan bias is equally bad because it leads to delayed or lost revenue. When companies experience actual demand consistently greater than their Demand Plan, service levels suffer because tight capacity reduces flexibility if the mix is not perfectly predicted, expediting efforts increase, overtime increases, and operational efficiency decreases. If these conditions continue for a prolonged time, the continuous churn and firefighting results in decreasing efficiency, maximum overtime, increased first-aid and recordable injuries, decreased quality, and staff burnout.

Bottom line: Demand Planning bias is a behavioral issue that must be addressed and eliminated through the implementation of a good program of metrics, such as Demand Plan Accuracy (aggregate and detail) and Forecast Consumption. These measures are designed to provide feedback to the Demand Planning organization on trends and the degree of bias present so it can be entirely eliminated. Along with Bias, Demand Plan accuracy is measured monthly, however, the plan is only as accurate as its inputs so the accuracy of assumptions used to create the plan must also be measured monthly. Improving the accuracy of the assumptions will improve the accuracy of the plan so the view of the assumptions better directs continuous improvement efforts.

Finally, bias must be eliminated by the person introducing it into the plan. Left to someone else, that bias may be removed but the behavior of the person introducing it will not change.

Assumptions, Vulnerability, and Opportunities

It should now be clear that assumptions must be documented so that their accuracy can be measured, updated, and improved, as necessary. The next point to be addressed is clarifying the types of assumptions to be documented, along with the types of vulnerabilities and opportunities that should be documented.

Assumptions, both internal and external, are factored into the Demand Plan. Internal assumptions are inward facing with associated action plans such as hiring a Sales Manager and Sales representatives for a new territory. These assumptions must have documented owners and due dates to track progress and on-time completion. External assumptions deal with demand influences outside the company, such as governmental actions (e.g., tariffs) or anticipated competitor actions. These assumptions require monitoring so that the organization can quickly recognize when they are proven to be accurate and gap-closing actions can be initiated. Assumptions can be quantitative, meaning they can be converted to numbers, or qualitative, meaning they are based upon agreed subjective judgments but are not easily stated in quantitative terms.

Plan vulnerabilities are Demand Plan risks. These risks may materialize, and if they do, they will have a detrimental impact on the Demand Plan. Vulnerabilities are probable, not certain, to occur. Therefore, their associated volumes are included in the Demand Plan and are included in the Demand Plan accuracy measure. Vulnerabilities are documented to ensure they are monitored and not overlooked. They are not a list of every possible negative demand impact that could happen to justify reducing the number that actually occur. They are specific, quantifiable, and probable risks (not, for example, the sun may not come up next week) that must be managed and then prioritized for mitigation. Vulnerabilities at the top of the priority list require action plans, with owners and due dates, so that if the vulnerabilities materialize, they are immediately ready to be executed to mitigate any negative impact.

Opportunities are not included in the Demand Plan but provide upside potential requiring actions if they materialize and/or are needed to mitigate the impact of a vulnerability that has materialized. Many companies overthink this list by including every single Sales bid. In terms of adding an opportunity to the Demand Plan, only those significant opportunities requiring cross-functional effort to enact are added to the Demand Plan. Opportunity documentation requires quantification (i.e., the size of the prize), probability of occurrence and a suggested plan on how to increase that likelihood, and an executions plan. Each opportunity requires an owner and a due date to drive decision-making and track progress when executed. Keep in mind that executing opportunities may cause competing demands on limited resources; prioritization and decisions to execute must balance likelihood, resources required, cost, and benefit (a trade-off analysis).

As the planning horizon extends further into the future, so does the number of vulnerabilities and opportunities. It is important to recognize that it is much more cost effective to execute future opportunity action plans than those in the near term.

Using the Appropriate Technique

When building the unconstrained demand plan, it is essential to align techniques with the type of demand variability and volume expected or experienced historically for product families. There are four approaches as described below and summarized in Figure 10.6:

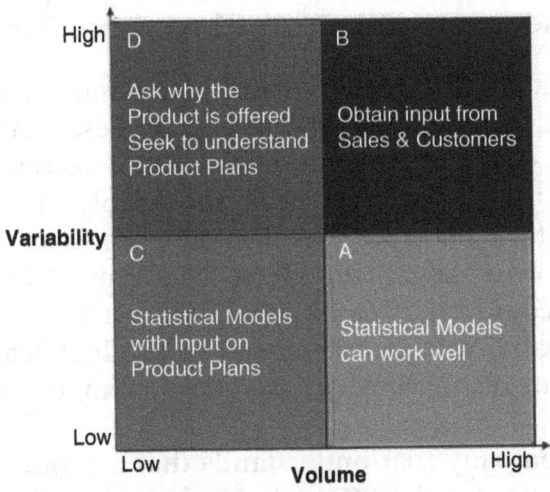

FIGURE 10.6 The Four Demand Planning Categories

1. **Category A:** Products have high volume and low demand variability. Planning system algorithms typically do a good job of predicting future patterns. System-generated demand models still require Sales and Marketing review, inclusion of future initiatives, and approval.
2. **Category B:** Products have both high volume and high demand variability, requiring more Sales and customer input to better predict future demand. Promotions, campaigns, and customers initiatives should be factored into the plan for these families and items.
3. **Category C:** Products have both low volume and low demand variability. These products can make use of statistical models, but a company should carefully review and include product plans to ensure that any volume growth efforts are included.
4. **Category D:** Products have low volume and high variability. Typically, these are Engineer-to-Order or Make-to-Order products. The continued existence

of these products should be continually examined by weighing their costs against their benefits. Just as important is considering any product plans that will impact volume growth and demand variability to stabilize current demand patterns. A product may start out as an Engineer-to-Order or Make-to-Order item and eventually become a higher volume item.

Coping with Inaccurate Demand Plans and Forecasts

It is vital to note that virtually all Demand Plans and forecasts are imperfect, but if there is a disciplined Demand Planning process, accuracy will improve. The amount of error over the planning horizon also becomes more predictable and can be successfully planned for within the Supply Chain to maximize both profitability and customer service. For instance, products that have inherently high variability and error negatively affect the Demand Plan. However, when that variability is recognized, it can become a positive if Lean techniques are used to increase flexibility. Lean techniques will reduce lead times and enable greater flexibility in responding to demand changes; this is agility, not firefighting.

Additionally, a company that understands that a product family has a consistent 20% forecast error at the SKU mix level can intelligently plan its inventories and safety stocks to achieve its desired service level with high confidence despite that variability. These Supply Chain linkages are invaluable in enabling the entire organization to understand the Demand Plan and to plan effective responses when there are unplanned demand changes. This includes being aware of Supply's constraints in meeting unconstrained demand to achieve the end goal of maximizing profitability over the long term. Companies that use only historical sales or shipments in Demand Planning are not following Unparalleled Business Planning and Execution Practice. They do not understand the amount of business they are leaving on the table and are not taking steps to maximize revenue and profitability.

Demand Manager Responsibilities

The role of the Demand Manager is paramount for the success of Demand Planners, Demand Analysts, and Demand Controllers in developing the unconstrained demand plan and in managing the Demand Plan and its accuracy. Key responsibilities include:

- **Establishing:** For Sales and Marketing, the Demand Management organization and its successful development into a key business team integrated, through Integrated Business Planning, with Product, Supply, and Finance.
- **Creating:** A Demand Planning process supported with the right data, from multiple sources, and using this effectively to develop a presentation deck for the Demand Review that is also shared and used throughout IBP for decision-making and other plan development.
- **Coaching/Mentoring:** Assisting Sales and Marketing in Demand Planning and Demand Control/Execution processes to drive accuracy and stability.
- **Generating:** The unconstrained demand plan, having this agreed through IBP as the first indication of what the business could achieve if Supply has no constraints.
- **Monitoring:** The timeliness of data and information submission in meeting process deadlines.
- **Ensuring:** All data sources are supported by detailed assumptions that are used to explain any changes. These inputs should have owners and clearly provide a view into the future as to why a plan needs to look like it does.
- **Communicating:** The unconstrained demand plan to Supply Planning for its review, approval, or identification of key resource constraints that may constrain the unconstrained demand plan.
- **Resolving:** Any Supply constraints to the unconstrained demand plan collaboratively with the Product, Supply, and Finance Managers (continuous IRR) for inclusion in the IBP presentation deck submitted for the IRR and MBR.
- **Implementing a Measurements Hierarchy:** That drives Demand Plan accuracy, eliminates bias, improves customer satisfaction, reduces volatility, and enables stable Supply Planning.

We are often asked where the Demand Planning group should reside organizationally. Without question, the Demand Manager and the Demand Planning organization should report to the Sales and Marketing VP to place accountability in the organization that most directly influences demand. Companies that place Demand Planning in the Supply Chain organization, especially if they place it under Manufacturing Operations, experience nearly identical outcomes shown below:

- Specifically, Sales and Marketing demonstrate no ownership of or commitment to achieving the approved Demand Plan.
- They operate independently, creating churn, and a culture of firefighting.
- Blame Supply for poor customer service results.

Demand Planning Performance Measures

Peter Drucker was correct when he said, "What gets measured gets managed," and doing so with the Demand Plan is no different. If Demand Plan performance is not measured and tracked, Demand Planning might as well be replaced by throwing darts against a wall to predict demand and make business decisions. Customers and shareholders would not be happy. As stated earlier, the Demand Plan is not expected to be perfectly accurate, but measuring performance is not about perfection. Measuring Demand Plan performance is about accountability and continuous improvement. Measuring Demand Plan performance comes down to two essential questions:

1. Did we generate the Demand that we planned (volume)?
2. Did the product family mix of items match what we planned (mix)?

Since the Demand Plan is used for decision-making, we recommend that the two essential attributes of volume and mix accuracy be measured at various points in time across the planning horizon, and that the team be held accountable for continuous improvement across the suite of Demand Plan metrics. When we say volume and mix accuracy at various points in time, we mean thinking about major decisions and decision points needed across the entire planning horizon and then plotting those decision points as points at which Demand Plan accuracy is to be measured and understood. It is important to note that when we talk about mix accuracy in relation to the planning horizon, we are not always talking about SKU level accuracy measures. Most major IBP decisions are based on the Demand Plan at different lead times (offsets or lags) such as annual budgeting, quarterly financial forecast locks, strategic material planning supplier volumes, monthly actuals versus plan, direct labor headcount changes, capital equipment investments, tactical purchase order releases, and detailed labor scheduling and work order releases. Common specific measures include:

- **Budget/Annual Business Plan Formation:**
  - Metrics: Forecast consumption percentage and straight comparisons.
  - Scope: Overall plan and multiple levels of product hierarchy for year-to-date (YTD) actuals, total year (TY) plan (YTD actuals + YTG plan) and 24-month future horizon compared to the Demand Plan and original budget. Recommend graphs, not just metrics.
- **Demand Plan Actuals versus Forecast:**
  - Metrics: Demand Plan and forecast accuracy; bias; and volatility; see notes below.
  - Scope: Monthly results versus the forecast at multiple levels of the product hierarchy.
- **Firm Zone/Mix Detail Scheduling:**
  - Metrics: Weighted mean absolute percent error and bias at finished goods SKU level.
  - Scope: At finished goods SKU level at lag (offset) equal to the firm zone.

Another Word on Bias

Demand Plan bias, both aggregate and detailed, is overlooked by far too many companies because they believe they can achieve their objectives using accuracy metrics alone. This ignores the huge leverage that bias offers in improving the Demand Plan. See the "The Overlooked Forecasting Flaw: Forecasting Bias and How to Tackle It" article referenced in the recommended reading list at the end of the chapter.

More on Volatility

Use of volatility as a measure in the early days of establishing a Demand Plan Accuracy is acceptable. People with low Phase 1 Business Maturity should work on reducing the volatility in their Demand Plan to then help focus more effectively on bias elimination and then onto more pure Demand Plan Accuracy based on weighted absolute percent error or mean absolute percent error. See Figure 10.7.

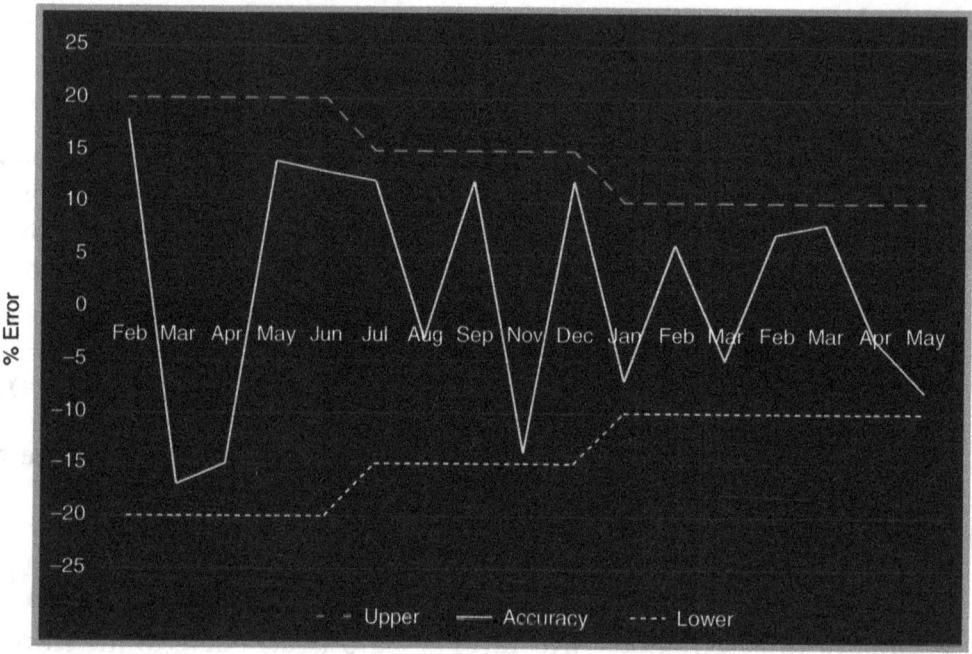

FIGURE 10.7 Demand Plan Volatility: Upper and Lower Lines

The upper and lower lines identify the "outliers," which should be progressively eliminated to systematically bring the volatility down. A Demand Plan with huge swings like this is useless for short-term planning as it contributes to huge instability. Working with the clients and Sales Team to aggressively eliminate these huge swings then enables bias, and then Demand Plan accuracy, to be focused on more effectively.

Summary

Making improvements to the demand planning process can be a challenging endeavor, often because it involves instilling more discipline and accountability in areas of the organization that are not used to being measured on much beyond the basic achievement of the aggregate sales target. This chapter laid out the case for going much deeper so that the demand plan represents a true consensus resulting from the collaborative efforts of multiple functions within the organization for the benefit of the entire organization. The accuracy of the demand plan does not have to be perfect in order for it to be useful; however, like all areas outlined in this book, it must be measured and evaluated for possible improvements so that its contributions allow for better decision making.

To learn more about Demand Planning in IBP and S&OP, review the following books and articles:

> *Demand Management Best Practices: Process, Principles and Collaboration* by Colleen Crum with George Palmatier (J. Ross Publishing)
>
> *Enterprise Sales and Operations Planning: Synchronizing Demand, Supply and Resources for Peak Performance* by George Palmatier with Coco Crum (J. Ross Publishing)
>
> *The Overlooked Forecasting Flaw: Forecasting Bias and How to Tackle It* by Jim Bentzley, LinkedIn Pulse

For additional but more specific reading please visit the Oliver Wight Website and gain access to the extensive library of White Papers.

CHAPTER 11

Managing Internal Priorities: Delivering Products on Time

This chapter describes how to take the "valid" (realistic and achievable) plan from Master Scheduling (MS) and Material Requirements Planning (MRP) and convert it into valid internal schedules. Valid internal schedules enable

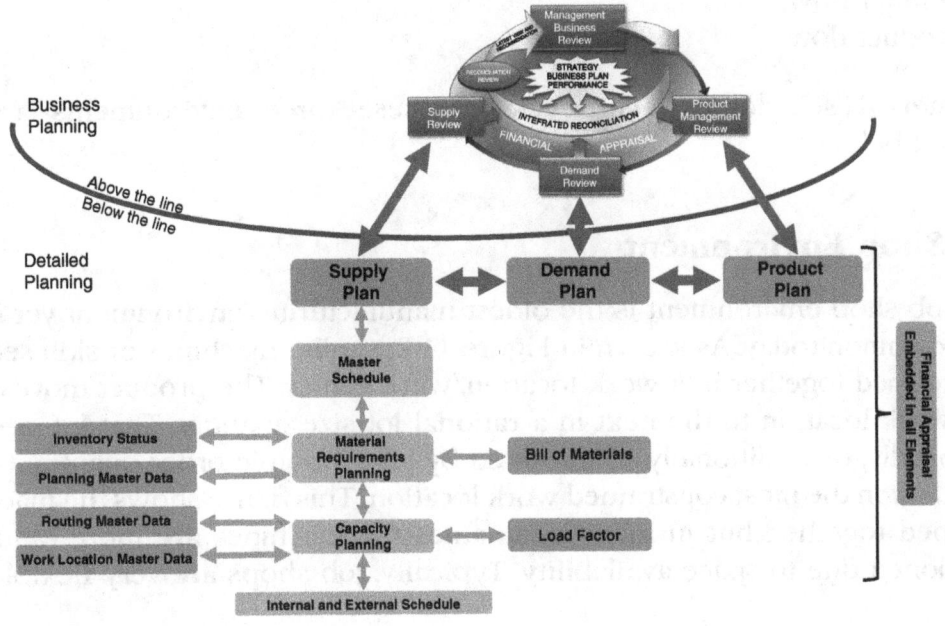

FIGURE 11.1 Business Excellence Planning

supply to meet at least 95% of MRP due dates while significantly increasing productivity and quality. Perhaps the most rewarding result is improved quality of work life; Supply employees ending every day being able to say, "I have done an excellent job and feel valued today."

Internal schedules are found at the very bottom of Figure 11.1, Business Excellence Planning (BEP). Planning and resource validation activities performed in the steps shown above internal schedules provide valid plans for the supply. This last step, often referred to as the Dispatch List, Priority Schedule, or Work to List, tells the workforce when specific operations must be completed to meet due dates. These dates should be believable (intellectually and emotionally) since capacity planning (see Chapter 12) has been completed in advance of scheduling.

As can be seen in Figure 11.1, capacity planning takes place before internal schedules are developed. However, it is important for the reader to learn about operations scheduling to understand how detailed capacity planning is performed. For this reason, this chapter is sequenced prior to the capacity planning chapter.

There are three basic workflow environments:

1. Job shop
2. Cellular flow
3. Product flow

Internal scheduling techniques for these three environments are described below.

Job Shop Environment

The job shop environment is the oldest manufacturing environment yet is still very common today. As shown in Figure 11.2, similar machines or skill sets can be grouped together in a work location/work center. The product moves from one work location to the next in a rational lot size quantity. That lot size that is typically, or traditionally, determined by an economic order quantity (EOQ) based upon the most constrained work location. This figure shows the machines grouped together, but in many companies the machines are more randomly positioned due to space availability. Typically, job shops are very flexible and

Product

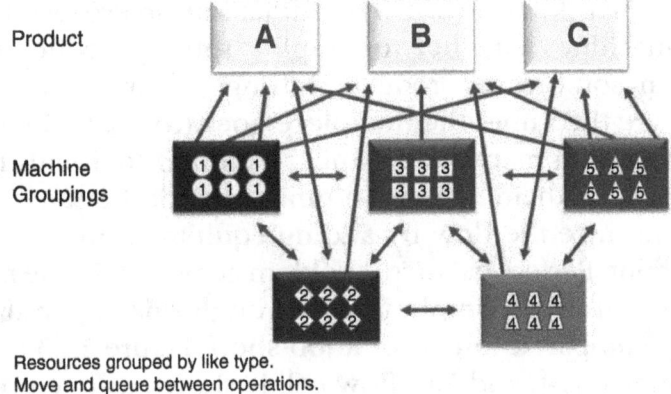

Machine
Groupings

Resources grouped by like type.
Move and queue between operations.

FIGURE 11.2 Workflow: Job Shop Environment

can make a wide variety of products. The job shop, however, does have challenges. Total production lead times are much longer because each operation for the entire lot is completed before the lot moves to the next work location and sits in a queue. This approach is often referred to as "batch processing" and adds move and queue time (waiting to be worked on) between each operation. In the example shown in Figure 11.2, one item going into product A has the route Machine Group (MG) 2 to MG 3 then finally to MG 1. Product B has one item that takes the route MG 4 to MG 3 to MG 5 and then MG 1. Product C has an item with the route MG 4 to MG 3 to MG 5. As each internally manufactured item is routed by Engineering (Industrial, Manufacturing, etc.) there could be any combination of machine groups, as shown by all of the arrows. Each step is identified in the Routing as an operation (see Routings, Chapter 5). The combinations and sequences can be infinite if the company is an Engineer-to-Order company. It is also not uncommon for a product to have as many as 20 or more operations.

Item Flow Cell Environment

When volume is high enough, an alternative approach to the job shop is to take machines out of like groupings and put them together to create a flow cell. In the following example, a machine from job shop MG 2 has been paired to machines from MG 3 and MG 4. The Industrial or Process Engineers have arranged these machines together to simplify routing, reduce manufacturing lead time, and, in some cases, reduce staffing requirements. In this design (when run times are the same) the first piece goes from 2 to 3 immediately and a new piece is started in machine 2, similarly from 3 to 4 with no wait, move, or queue time between them. If the run times are not the same, then the engineers try to synchronize the flow by adding equipment or decreasing the run time of the constraint. Perfect balance is seldom achieved, so the faster machines sit idle for a time. An order simply flows through this cell, reducing the lead time significantly compared to that of a job shop. Figure 11.3 shows a second flow cell of machines, 1, 4, and 5. A flow cell is shown as one operation on the routing, significantly simplifying routings and routing maintenance (see more about Lean and Agile in Business Improvement, Chapter 16).

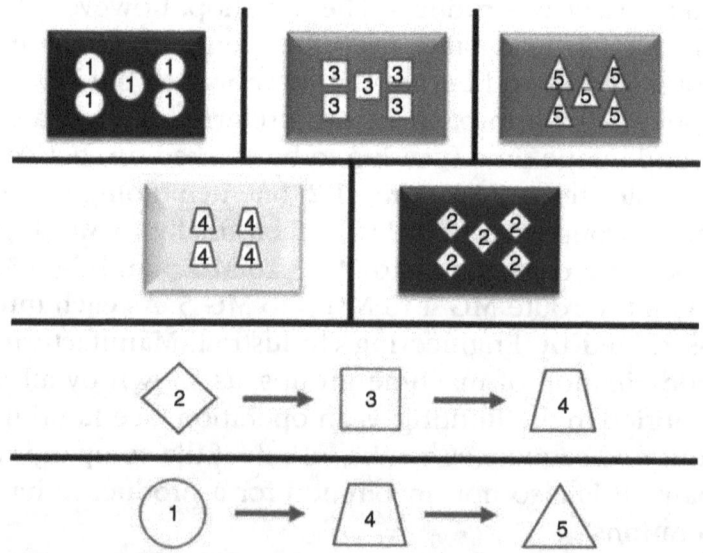

FIGURE 11.3 Workflow: Item Flow Cell Diagram

The primary advantage of this environment is a significant reduction in product lead time, since the items move in a one-piece flow through a series of machines, at the low cost of relocating machines. Another advantage is that often only one person is required to operate the cell while the job Shop example required at least three operators. Quality is also improved because a problem in machine 2 that impacts machine 4 is caught after only a couple of pieces, whereas in the job shop the entire order would have been run through machines 2 and 3. The disadvantage of this environment is that a limited number of items can be produced in this cell.

Many companies create cells to put like products together, but stay with the batch environment as the product moves through the cell. Therefore, they must use a multiple-step routing with queue and move time between operations. A flow cell eliminates the move and queue between steps. Keeping the batch environment, even though a cell has been created, does not take advantage of the lead time reduction offered by the flow cell.

Product Flow Environment

The third basic environment is product flow; see Figure 11.4. Products with very large volumes, large lot sizes, and rapid processing times requiring multiple assets are best suited for this workflow environment. In this environment a new batch is started on a line and is finished completely. No surprise, the inventor of this environment was Henry Ford, but this environment is not limited to assembly lines. For example, it is the predominate workflow environment in consumer goods manufacturing. Raw materials are processed continuously and completely through multiple pieces of processing equipment in a single location and are often transferred continuously to the packaging work location that is also comprised of multiple pieces of packaging equipment,

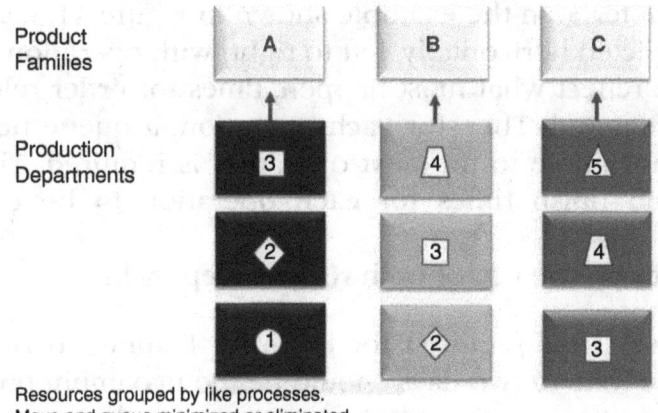

FIGURE 11.4 Workflow: Product Flow

such as fillers, cappers, labelers, weight checkers, automated case packers, and automated palletizers in another single work location. The advantage of the product flow environment is again a huge reduction in lead time, minimal setup time, large volume processing, and minimized product cost. As with flow cells, product flow environments minimize the required number of operators. The disadvantage of the product flow environment is the cost to construct them and a limitation of what types of products can be processed through them.

Internal Manufacturing Priorities

MRP identifies the order's start and finish times, which is fine for a flow cell environment since the time from start to finish is short. But in the job shop environment, where numerous operations are required, and in the flow cell environment, where additional operations are often required before and/or after product goes through the flow cell, more information is required to ensure that orders progress in a timely manner. Each operation must know what order is coming next and when the current operation must be completed. Most MRP planning software has an Operation Scheduling Module that uses the routing to develop required detailed schedules.

Operation Scheduling

How does operation scheduling work? It starts with the accurate routing, as described in Chapter 5. In the example shown in Figure 11.5, a two-step routing has been depicted horizontally, left to right, with operation 05 followed by operation 10. To reflect what must happen, times for order release and store-room pick are required. Then for each operation, a queue time, setup time, run time, and move time to the next operation is required. This information enables start and finish times for each operation to be determined and documented.

Considerations on the use of each routing step include:

- **Order release:** Time required for the MRP Planner to review the order before release (one to two days should be the maximum time allowed).
- **Pick:** A realistic time for the store's operators to pick the required materials (one to two days).

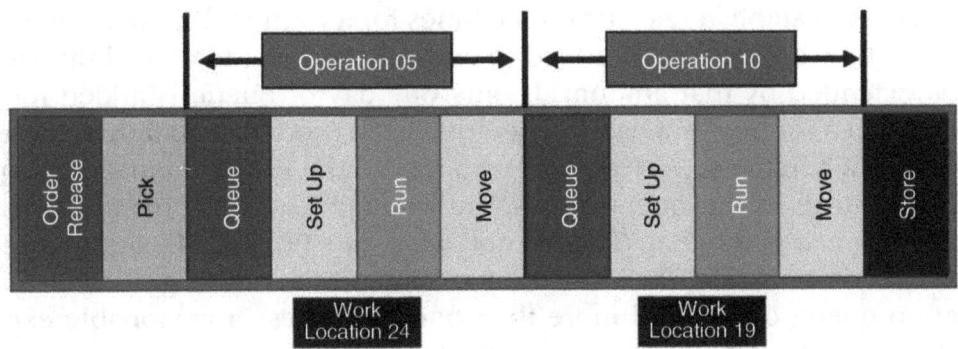

FIGURE 11.5 Operation Scheduling Elements

- **Queue:** Queue time is listed by machine (or required skill) and should be minimal except for machines at or near maximum capacity. In that case, the time should be just enough to keep the location busy if there is a break-down in the prior location(s) or a lumpy workload.
- **Setup:** As listed on the routing (see the referenced article on routing accuracy).
- **Run:** The required time listed on the routing to run one piece multiplied by the number of pieces on the production order, the calculation performed by MRP planning software. Planners need not manually calculate the run time for every order.
- **Move:** The time required to move the order from one routing work location to another. If the next operation is in the same work location, move time should be zero; if the next operation is in the same department, another department, or another site, the move time will vary. Realistic, demonstrated times must be established.
- **Store:** The time required to receive and put away the order in the stock/storeroom, not the time that the order might remain in storage.

Establishing these times can be somewhat challenging. Remember one of the key principles, "truth as we know it." Truth eventually becomes self-evident, so knowing it earlier than later is essential. This is not easy because it is not the culture in many companies. In those companies there is a tendency to "kill the messenger" so the behavior leans toward "telling them what they need to know, want to hear, or will accept for self-preservation" or to "make yourself look good." For instance, an MRP Project Manager at one client site asked supervisors to establish realistic queue times for a routing. Please keep in mind that every time an increase is added to an operation, the total lead time for the item is extended by that amount. If only one day of queue is added for each operation on a routing that has 10 operations, the product lead time is increased by 10 days. When the supervisors, in response to the Project Manager's request, finished putting in the queue times, the average lead time for all items had doubled from the original. This is not what the Project Manager expected! Based on this outcome, the MRP Project Manager added a guideline that no operation queue could total more than one day unless a reasonable explanation was provided. After review, only a few queue times were more than one day.

Operation Scheduling Example

For this operation scheduling example, times have been added in the version shown in Figure 11.6. To keep the example simple, times added are in days, but planning software offers more realistic and useful times – hours or even minutes. In this example, MRP planners determined that one day is required for order release; stores confirmed that two days were required to pick materials and one day to put away the product in stores; Material handlers established the move times: one day for the move from Work Location (WL) 24 to WL 19 since they are in the same department, and two days from WL 19 to stores since the storage facility requires transport from WL 19. The queue time for WL 24 is set at one day, with two days allowed for WL 19 since that work location includes a very expensive piece of equipment that cannot be "starved."

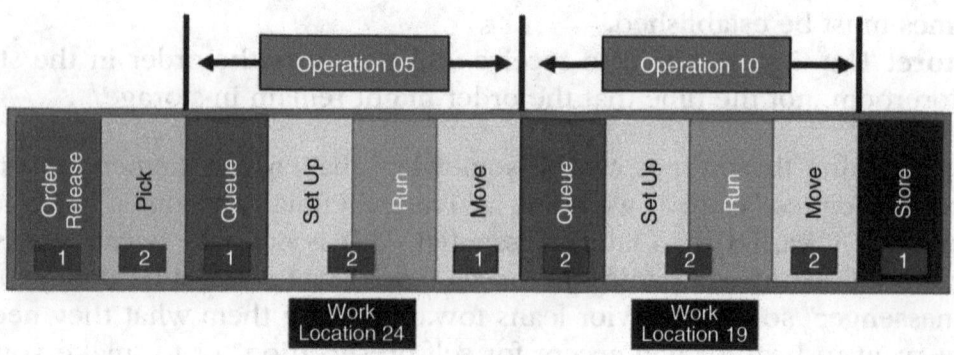

FIGURE 11.6 Operation Scheduling with Times

A decision was made to run it near maximum capacity rather than buy an additional or new machine. Setup and run times have been combined for simplicity in Work Locations 24 and 19.

Operation Scheduling with Dates

Loading this information into the planning system enables the calculation of start and completion dates. In the example shown in Figure 11.7, back scheduling (from the due date backward) logic has also been used (see later explanation). Additionally, a manufacturing day calendar has been used (using only scheduled workdays) for ease of calculation. The order due date is obtained from MRP as manufacturing day 412. Since it takes one day to store and two days to move, the operation due date for WL 19 is manufacturing day 409, calculated as 412 – 3. Therefore, operation 10 must be completed three days prior to the MRP due date. Since operation 10 requires two days for setup and run, the setup start date is day 407. Allowing two days for queue and one day for the move from WL 24 to WL 19, the completion date for operation in WL 24 is manufacturing day 404. Allowing two days for setup and run for operation 05, WL 24's start date for operation 05 is day 402. Backing out one day of queue,

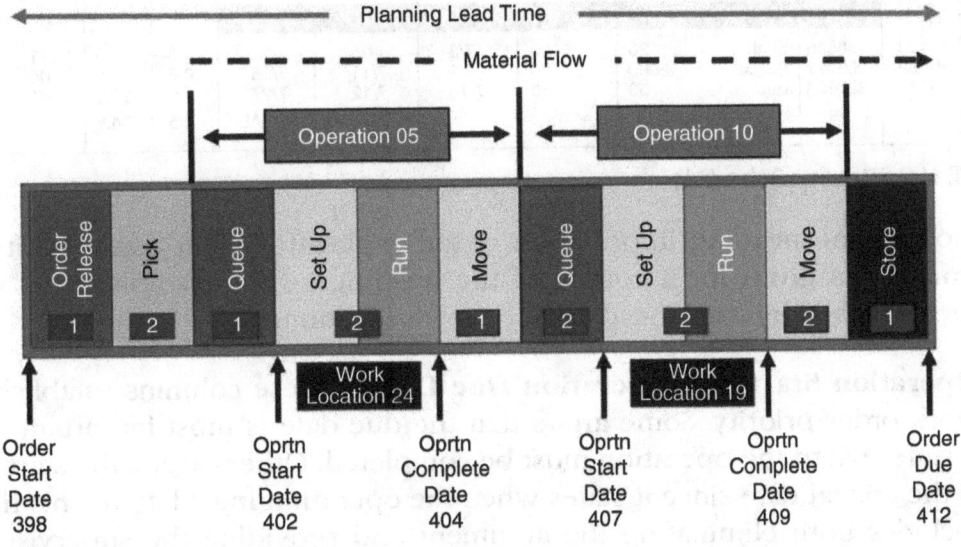

FIGURE 11.7 Operating Schedule with Dates

two days to pick and one day for order release, the order start date is calculated as manufacturing day 398.

This is the same simple back-scheduling logic that is used by the planning system thousands of times each day to calculate when to start an order and to ensure that it moves on time, operation by operation, to meet the due date.

Manufacturing Priority Schedule

When operation scheduling has been completed, the planning software can lift that information and sort it by work location. An example of a Priority Schedule for WL 24 is shown in Figure 11.8.

Order No.	Part No.	Part Description	Qty	Operation No.	Operation Start Date	Operation Due Date	Order Due Date	Setup Hrs	Run Hrs	Next Current
WORK LOCATION NO.: 24				DESCRIPTION: Lathes			DATE: 7/2			
		JOBS CURRENTLY AT THIS WORK LOCATION								
W123	144398	Shaft	200	20	6/26	7/19	7/19	0.0	7.0	04
W123	144398	Shaft	200	30	6/29	7/2	7/19	1.0	10.0	07
W124	428876	Bolt	3000	30	6/29	7/3	7/24	2.0	30.0	07
W110	330246	Gear	500	20	6/28	7/3	7/18	1.0	15.0	07
W120	407211	Bolt	4000	30	7/2	7/5	7/20	2.0	50.0	07
W112	163726	Hub	40	20	7/3	7/5	7/23	3.0	8.0	07
W128	118132	Gear	400	20	7/5	7/10	7/24	2.0	40.0	07
							TOTAL	11.0	160.0	
		JOBS COMING TO THIS WORK LOCATION								
W129	186846	Shaft	20	20	7/3	7/5	7/12	1.0	4.5	01
W138	258721	Spacer	2000	20	7/9	7/11	7/25	0.5	20.0	05
W140	321406	Hub	50	30	7/10	7/12	7/27	1.0	30.0	01
							TOTAL	2.5	54.5	

FIGURE 11.8 Priority Schedule

Most of the heading information is self-explanatory, but some additional information is given for a couple of the headings. This example uses "work center," which is interchangeable with "work location."

- **Operation Start and Operation Due Dates:** These columns establish the work order priority. Some argue that the due date is most important since it states when the operation must be completed. Others argue the start date is the critical date since it states when the operation must begin. This figure includes both eliminating the argument and providing the supervisor all information required to track work through the work location. Some planning systems have codes that can indicate priority, but the codes do not relate well to work location operators. They need to see the actual dates. Start and due dates are clear and explain what should be happening hour by hour in the work location. We strongly recommend using dates.

- **Order Due Date:** This date, unrelated to a specific work location, allows Production to review options to get back on schedule. The order due date provides guidance of what operations must be completed and by when to meet the product work order due date. Production personnel, creatively working together, can often meet product due dates even if some operations fall behind schedule.
- **Jobs Currently at and Jobs Coming to This Work Center:** The planning system can list separately the jobs currently in the work location from the jobs coming to the work location as in this example or it can have some indicator so it is easy to see what jobs are available to work on.
- **Next/Current Work Center:** For jobs currently at the work center this column shows where the work order is headed next. For jobs that have not yet arrived it shows what work center the job is currently at. This information allows a production supervisor to check the status of the job so they can make preparations if it will be late. The importance of having this information readily available is demonstrated by the following example.

A company was having severe shortage issues with its internally manufactured gears. The Machine Shop Manager, who was responsible for machining the gears, was constantly criticized during the daily shortage meeting for gears being late. These gears passed through multiple departments and operations, so it was virtually impossible to tell where they were and what state they were in. Using a Priority Schedule report for the first time from their newly implemented planning system, the Machine Shop Manager looked in the "Jobs Coming to This Work Center" column titled "Next/Current" and was amazed to see that the large number of past due jobs were in the saw work center. As he checked each of the Priority Schedules for all work locations that manufactured gears, he found the same thing. The saw was the very first operation and was in the Plate Shop department. It took him very little time to learn that the saw area was not following the Priority Schedule. He met with the Plate Shop Manager and explained why his gears were always late. The Plate Shop Manager sheepishly agreed to use the Priority Schedule for the saws. From that point forward, with the Priority Schedule being followed by the sawing operation and across the entire Machine Shop, capacity planning became effective (see Capacity Planning, Chapter 12) and gears began flowing through the operations as scheduled. Shortages disappeared.

Priority Scheduling Rules

Effective Priority Scheduling requires strict adherence to documented rules. Critical rules include:

1. Honor no "hot list," "shortage report," "personal expedites," or "do me a favor" requests.
2. If a work location falls behind schedule, prioritize the open orders by operation due dates.
3. If the work location is on or ahead of schedule, sequence the orders to optimize resource utilization without missing any operation due dates.
4. If a work location is going to miss an operation due date, communicate that delay to downstream work locations so they have time to plan how to make up the lost time and still meet the product due date.
5. If a product work order is going to miss its work order due date, easily determined since the due date is on the Priority List, communicate this delay to the MRP Planner with the anticipated order competition date.
6. Practice "management by walking around." See the recommended additional reading list at the end of the chapter.

A planning system implementation example in a large electronics firm's machining and fabrication site where we were coaching might help reinforce the importance of these rules. Tom Peters' book *Management by Walking Around* was a favorite of the GM. We encouraged the GM to do "Management by Walking Around *with a Purpose*" by suggesting that he should, when visiting a work location, see if the work location is on schedule according to the Priority Schedule (that was the purpose). If it was not on schedule, he was to ask what was being done about it (see rules 4 and 5). The GM agreed and started following our recommendation immediately. One afternoon, at the beginning of the second shift, he "walked around" into Maria's subassembly area and asked to see her Priority List. When he asked Maria if she would make all her operation due dates, she responded, "Yes, except for one order which is missing a component because of an inventory accuracy problem." When the

GM followed up by asking what she was doing about the shortage, she responded that she had talked with the Shear Area Supervisor and the Press Area Supervisor to see if they could rush through the missing component. They refused, citing priority scheduling rule #1 (no personal expedites). The GM, being a man of action, told Maria that he would solve the problem and headed immediately for the Shear department. He asked the supervisor, Anna, if Maria had been to see her about the shortage. She confirmed Maria's visit, but declared that she was not going tear down the machine and lose capacity just to make the missing item. She continued, citing the rules and then showed him a copy of the Priority Scheduling policy that he had signed. The GM's face turned red as he grabbed the policy, ripped it in half, and said, "Sometimes you just have to make things happen around here." Anna, being a quick learner, raced over to the operator and ordered him to change over one of the shears.

The Press Area Supervisor was walking by the Shear area and overheard the conversation between Anna and the GM. By the time the GM arrived at the Press area, the Supervisor was already tearing down one of the presses. He was also a quick learner.

The GM went back to Maria and proudly informed her that he had solved her problem. She was singing his praises when the MRP Planner walked into her area with the missing brackets in hand. He explained to a surprised Maria that the day shift supervisor had called about the missing bracket that was threatening the schedule and learned that the Spares department had an excess number of brackets in inventory. Spares had double-ordered all spares items because their suppliers rarely delivered on time. Maria looked down at her desk and found a note from the day shift supervisor informing her of the problem and the solution. In the meantime, both a shear and a press were changing over to make the no longer needed parts. The press area lost valuable manufacturing time because presses were constraint machines. The GM quietly returned to his office.

The next morning that story was the talk of the entire facility. When questioned by his leadership team about the incident, the GM said, "I'll never do it again." Despite this one setback, the GM was the key to successful implementation of the Priority Setting implementation. Yes, he occasionally stumbled, as in this example, but he was quick to admit his errors and proceeded full steam ahead in supporting the process. All 18 company divisions were chartered by the President to implement Unparalleled Business Planning and Execution Practices. This GM's division was the twelfth to implement the new planning software but the first to be awarded Class A Certification. The GM's clear commitment and leadership made all the difference.

Accurate Reporting

If you have read all the previous chapters, you know without question the importance of accurate and timely data in creating valid plans. Accurate data includes accurate operational data, otherwise the Priority Report and Detail Capacity Plans (see Chapter 12) are not worth the paper they are printed on. Data accuracy is undermined immediately by reporting behaviors that lack integrity. For example, when teams are measured for their on-time job completion performance, and team members enter invalid complete dates and times, the next team in line pays the price. They will lose production time searching for the missing items and miss their operation due dates. Documenting the process is essential to success, but not by itself. People must be held accountable for following the approved process. They must understand that inaccurate reporting is not tolerated, understand the problems it causes, and understand that they are expected to report accurately in order to optimize resource utilization, reduce product cost, and enable continuous improvement by identifying and eliminating performance failure root causes. This is a perfect example of where management by walking around can expose people not following the Priority Scheduling rules.

Forward Scheduling or Backward Scheduling?

The debate between forward scheduling and backward scheduling can be controversial.

Backward scheduling was demonstrated in the example earlier in this chapter. The total elapsed production lead time remains the same whichever method is used. Unfortunately, controversy arises when an order is requested inside the stated lead time and it is added to the schedule because production confirmed that it will not interfere with the completion dates of other work orders. Backward scheduling with a short lead time will immediately show the initial work location(s) behind schedule for that order but the downstream orders on time. Forward scheduling will show the initial work locations on schedule, but the downstream operations will be after the MRP order due date. This is the worst possible situation because the order due date will not be met and will create a customer service issue.

We visited a company whose leadership supported forward scheduling. Supervisors and managers were happy with the new system because whenever they missed an operation due date, the planning system simply moved out downstream operation due dates as well as the due date for that product work order and other product work orders. While this may have been convenient for supervisors and managers, it was unsatisfactory for Sales and their customers. The Sales Director began spending most of his time apologizing to important customers for missed deliveries that had been rescheduled numerous times because the new system had been set to "forward schedule." The customers were clear; if the problem was not fixed quickly, they would take their business elsewhere. If short lead time orders are requested frequently, one method of coping is to compress lead times.

Compressing Lead Time

Neither backward nor forward scheduling, by themselves, will solve the problem of orders being received inside agreed lead times. If a plant is operating with Unparalleled Business Planning and Execution Practices (≥95% of all orders are released with full lead times which have been continuously reduced through valid scheduling and lean efforts), then compressing operations move and queue times equally across all operations is an option, so long as order due dates are not violated.

Compressing lead times requires absolute agreement of all production areas. At one client company, production departments agreed to automatic work order release so long as move and queue time compression did not exceed 60%, and the number of inside lead time orders added to the schedule didn't exceed 5% of total orders scheduled. That company continued to deliver 98.9% of product orders on time.

But what can be done next if setup and run times already have been reduced through application of lean and agile techniques (see Chapter 16) and move and queue times also have been compressed when orders are received inside the reduced lead time? One option is to split the normal lot size and produce only the quantity needed to fill that order. The reduced lot size reduces run time considerably so the order due date can be met on time. The remainder of that lot must be rescheduled in the planning system to accurately reflect its new need date. That option is not "free," of course, since two setups instead of one are required; production capacity is lost and productivity is reduced. Another option is to run a few pieces at one operation while setting up a machine in the next routing work location. This option is essentially a one-time use flow cell. A recent client using this option was able to run in a single day a product with a normal lead time of two weeks. The Manufacturing team celebrated its accomplishment, until they understood the disaster left behind in terms of reduced productivity, lost capacity, and the number of other items delayed.

The moral of the story: Manufacturing can work miracles occasionally, but when the need for miracles becomes commonplace, productivity goes out the window and meeting due date commitments is a thing of the past. Churn and firefighting begin to undermine the organization's culture.

The Lead-Time Loop

As discussed previously, valid planning requires realistic lead times. We also encourage using lean activities such as creating flow cells to continuously reduce lead and setup times. Unfortunately, many companies do not understand lead time and misuse it in trying to solve other problems.

Foremost is the misuse of lead time in trying to solve capacity problems (see Chapter 12). Inflating or overstating lead time does absolutely nothing to help with capacity constraints. In fact, it makes the situation worse. A simple example is trying to increase the flow of water through a hose by increasing its length. The flow of water does not change but the time it takes to get the water through the hose increases in direct proportion the increase in hose length. Similarly, increasing a product's lead time only increases the number of orders in backlog, extends the time customers must wait for their product, and increases the number of orders that will be received inside lead time. Increasing lead time solves no problems; it creates churn.

During a client company shortage meeting, the Production Manager and Materials Manager argued about lead times. The Production Manager kept saying he was late on deliveries because the lead times for his products were too short. Finally, the Materials Manager said he would increase all the Production Manager's items' lead times. After a week the Production Manager said the increase helped and asked for lead times to be increased a second time. With no argument the Materials Manager agreed. The Production Manager again asked for an increase in lead time for the third time, but this time the Materials Manager pushed back. He informed the Production Manager that he actually had been decreasing lead times, and at this point they were finally realistic and should not be changed again. You could have heard a pin drop in the room.

Other Priority Scheduling Applications

Discussions, so far, have focused on priority setting in manufacturing operations; however, other areas can also benefit from the use of Priority Scheduling in the planning system. A client that makes satellites was experiencing significant problems delivering on time and meeting budgeted costs; in fact, they never did. The main problem was that Design Engineering was always late or too early and production had to scramble to build most of the items while others were completed early, driving up inventory. Following coaching advice they structured a new and unique item number, described as "Design Engineering," and added it as the last item in the BOM. They then attached a routing to the item number reflecting the steps/operations that Design Engineering had to perform to meet the required need date of the purchased or manufactured item. Now, due dates were established by the Master Schedule driven down through MRP, giving Design Engineering a due date that was completely aligned with production requirements. The routing enabled Design Engineering to detail a capacity plan for each skill set (next chapter) and gave each skill set the operation due dates required to complete the design on time. Bottom line, the very first contract scheduled including Design Engineering in the BOM was the very first contract delivered on time and on cost.

This exact same approach, with the exact same results, was used recently with a global cosmetics company that planned to launch 70 new products each month but could not deliver any new products on time. In this case, instead of Design Engineering operations, the addition to the BOM and routings involved the Product Development organization that was late with every new product design. Subsequently, the company planned to begin shipping on one given date an entirely new brand with over 200 new SKUs. Not a single shipment was shorted. This approach can be and should be used broadly in every company and industry.

Summary

This chapter describes the interface between planning and execution, exactly where the rubber meets the road. But is this worth all the effort? We could report countless examples of improved results reported by client companies. From their perspective, the answer to the question about whether the effort is worth the work it is a no-brainer. The personal benefit for those involved comes from the sense of a job well done and the elimination of full days of never-ending churn and firefighting. As stated by a client's Supply Chain Director, "After many years of working 10 hours a day, usually six days a week and missing all my son's baseball games over the past two years, this year I am coaching my son's Little League baseball team!" His answer was indeed a no-brainer!

It does take a lot of work initially to change the way companies operate and their culture, but far less work after implementation of Unparalleled Business Planning and Execution Practices to run the business and realize significantly improved results.

To learn more about Operation Scheduling, review the following books:

Achieving Class A Business Excellence: An Executive's Perspective by Dennis Groves, Kevin Herbert, and Jim Correll (John Wiley & Sons)

An Executive's Guide to Achieving Class A Business Excellence by Dennis Groves, Kevin Herbert, and Jim Correll (Oliver Wight International)

Gaining Control: Managing Capacity & Priorities by James G. Correll and Kevin Herbert (John Wiley & Sons)

Management by Walking Around by Tom Peters

For additional but more specific reading please visit the Oliver Wight Website and gain access to the extensive library of White Papers.

CHAPTER 12

Capacity Planning: Short, Medium, and Long Term

Much has been written about capacity planning. A popular message is to find and eliminate the constraint and then move on to the next one. While this is good in theory, capacity planning must first answer the

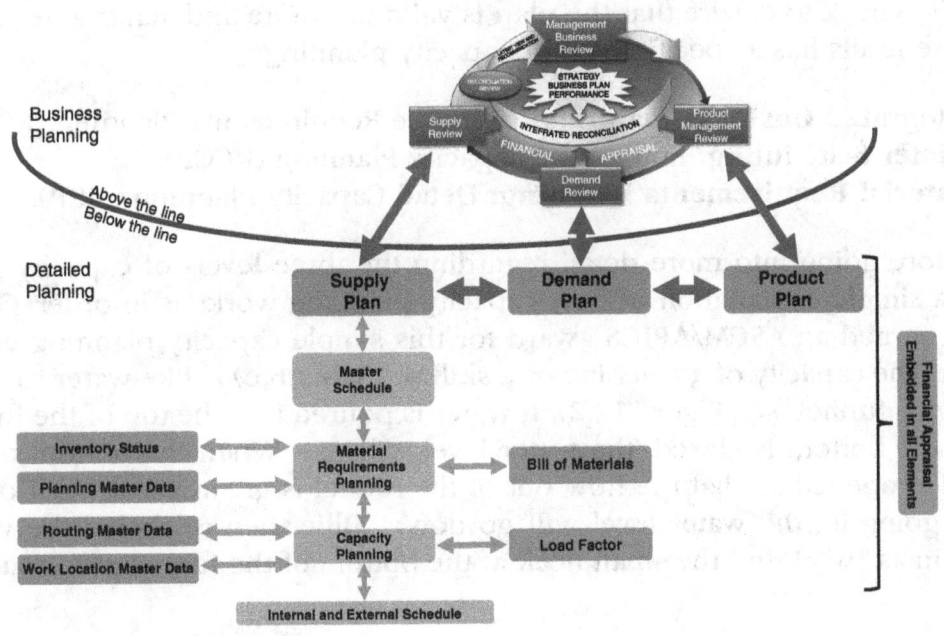

FIGURE 12.1 Business Excellence Planning

question of whether the production area can reliably execute the proposed schedule. The capacity constraint may change when the schedule changes or when the product mix changes. In fact, a schedule change could result in multiple constraints. This chapter is about using the Business Excellence Planning process, Figure 12.1, to identify and resolve capacity constraints related to the schedule presented. Management must be able to identify the constraints, eliminate those constraints, or change the schedule. If those options are not addressed, the schedule is invalid, the churn begins, and life gets worse!

Material Requirements Planning (MRP) is priority planning driven by dates. The planning system believes, without question, that the data that it has been given is accurate. Effective MRP requires, as discussed in previous chapters, data accuracy, a valid Master Schedule and Demand Plan, both aggregate and detailed, and detailed schedules that are reasonably accurate to the best of the company's knowledge. In order to have an overall "valid" plan (accurate and achievable), each of three planning levels must be tested to determine if the products are needed and if required resources are, or will be, available when needed to support the plans and schedules.

Each of the three planning levels shown in Figure 12.1 (Integrated Business Planning, Master Scheduling, and Material Requirements Planning) requires a capacity check to ensure that the plan is valid (accurate and achievable). Each of these levels has a specific type of capacity planning:

- **Integrated Business Planning:** Resource Requirements Planning (RRP).
- **Master Scheduling:** Rough-Cut Capacity Planning (RCCP).
- **Material Requirements Planning:** Detail Capacity Planning (DCP).

Before going into more detail regarding the three levels of capacity planning, a simple explanation of how capacity planning works is in order. Oliver Wight earned an ASCM/APICS award for this simple capacity planning explanation. The capacity of a machine or a skill set (resource) is like water running through a funnel (see Figure 12.2). If water is poured into the top of the funnel when the bottom is closed, the water level will rise. When the bottom of the funnel is opened so that the flow out of the funnel is greater than the flow of water going in, the water level will go down. Ollie then relabeled the water going in as "Work In," the small neck at the bottom of the funnel as "Capacity,"

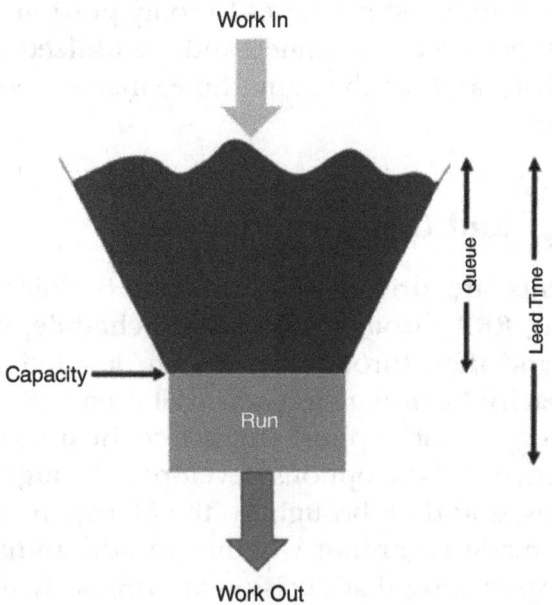

FIGURE 12.2 Capacity Funnel

and the water flowing out as "Work Out." Water sitting in the funnel is called "Queue," like work orders sitting in front of a work location/work center. The time it takes the water to flow through the neck and out of the funnel is the amount of time work is being performed, or "Run Time." Adding queue time to run time results in the lead time for that operation. Typically, in a job shop environment (see Chapter 11), 80% of Manufacturing lead time is queue and move time.

Preventing the funnel from running over or running out of water requires balancing the water flowing into and out of the funnel. In Ollie's example, the job is to balance work location capacity with the work entering the work location. To balance the capacity in work locations with multiple machines and operators, determine first the capacity of each machine and the number of operators required. For instance, a machine requiring only one operator may be needed for only one shift, so only one operator is hired. If Work In increases, a second shift or third shift (a second or third operator) can be added. When the Work In exceeds the capacity of the machine already running three shifts, adding another operator will not add capacity. Another machine is required.

A well-run shop schedules most machines for only portions of the shifts so that all operators/assemblers are cross-trained and are utilized continuously, which maximizes productivity and, at the same time, meets operation and product work order due dates.

Capacity Strategy and Capacity Planning

Capacity requirements are driven from Integrated Business Planning, with plans validated using RRP, through the Master Schedule, with schedules validated using RCCP, and then through MRP with detailed schedules validated using DCP. The Capacity Planning strategy, a vital part of a company's overall Manufacturing Strategy, must support Integrated Business Planning. When a constraint is determined and the options developed through the Supply Review, Reconciliation Review, and then brought to the Management Business Review, a decision must be made regarding whether to add additional capacity. The determining factors in making that decision are primarily demand volume that exceeds current capacity and the cost of adding that additional production capacity.

If capacity is not available to service the increased demand, business will be lost to competitors. If demand is not available when additional capacity is brought online, expensive equipment will sit idle – the machine cannot run if not authorized from IBP. Approving Production capital investments can be a very expensive decision. The biggest questions are: What does the future hold? Is the projected demand realistic? Can the Demand Plan be trusted? Excellence in Demand Planning (Chapter 10) and Integrated Business Planning (Chapter 8) and trust in the recommended courses of action are critical in enabling efficient and effective capacity decisions. Another important consideration is Leadership's perspective. Being either overly conservative or overly aggressive presents risks that must be understood. Some companies adopt an overall strategy of leading (aggressive) or lagging (conservative) with capacity, which helps when making individual capacity decisions.

A manufacturing strategy with its included capacity strategy must be clearly documented. The capacity strategy must include these principles:

- **Balance:** Required Capacity and Planned Capacity that does not meet Planned Demand must be brought into balance by either increasing capacity or reducing demand.

- **Committed:** Resource owners are accountable for producing the volumes to which they commit.
- **Confirmed:** Planning must confirm the capacity used to create their plans and schedules is or will be available when needed.

Capacity Terminology

Important capacity planning definitions include:

- **Gross Capacity:** Amount of time available (machine or operator) to work. For example, if there is one machine requiring one operator but running two shifts then the gross capacity is 16 hours.
- **Standard Times:** Setup and run times maintained in the Routing file, typically established by an industrial engineer.
- **Theoretical Capacity (Gross/Rated):** Production output per hour that should be available if all planning data is 100% accurate and the manufacturing operation works perfectly without interruption. This is most often a meaningless statement of capacity since nothing ever works perfectly. For example, if a production line is designed to run at 100 units per hour, its theoretical capacity is 100 units per hour.
- **Demonstrated Capacity:** The actual production output per hour of production demonstrated over a recent period, often a rolling three months. Demonstrated capacity represents the demonstrated output per hour that is used in determining how many production hours are needed to complete a work order, and considers production efficiency, breakdowns, unscheduled maintenance, and other unplanned disruptions. To determine the number of hours that must be scheduled to realize the required production hours, see "Load Factor" below. This demonstrated capacity number is not an industrial engineer's number nor is it management's hoped-for output. It is a realistic, proven, hourly output based on history (trailing 4–12 weeks) and knowledge of the environment during that period. Caution must be exercised in using that historical number; what was happening during that past period of time could indicate the appropriateness of scrubbing a non-occurring event, such as a fire drill, tornado evacuation, exceptional level of absenteeism due to illness, and so forth, from the database and to adjust the number to reflect a more realistic number going forward. If this demonstrated capacity does not meet management's expectations, Engineering

and Manufacturing must develop an action plan to increase the average hourly output that is achieved over a span of 4 to 12 weeks of actual production before the increased demonstrated capacity number can be used by capacity planners and production supervision. The load factor uses these actual production hours in its calculation and is what typically exposes opportunities for improvement.

- **Load Factor:** A percentage factor that is determined by dividing the actual number of standard hours that a resource has been demonstrated to run by the number of gross hours that were scheduled. For example, a production line, cell, or skill set may have been scheduled one shift, or 40 hours per week. However, the resource may not achieve that many standard hours because of inefficiencies (operators not meeting the standard), breaks, scheduled maintenance, sanitization, meetings, material, or operator problems, and so forth. The resource may run only 30 standard hours during the week. This results in a load factor of 75% (see the following formula). Dividing required production hours by the load factor percentage determines the number of production hours that must be scheduled to complete a production order. In this example, if 40 standard hours are required to complete a work order, the resource must be scheduled for 40 ÷ .75 = 53.3 hours.

$$\text{Load factor} = \frac{\text{Actual standard hours output}}{\text{Gross hours available}}$$

- **Required Capacity:** Production capacity at all planning levels required to support the IBP aggregate Production Plan, the Master Schedule, and MRP schedules.
- **Planned Capacity:** A statement of demonstrated capacity +/− capacity changes that are planned and funded in the future. For instance, a second production shift could be added to a single-shift operation and double the demonstrated capacity. However, if new employees must be trained, second-shift output will be less than current demonstrated capacity and slowly increase over time throughout the learning curve. If this learning curve is not considered by the planners and schedulers, the schedule developed and distributed will deliver fewer products than required.
- **Maximum Capacity:** The maximum output that can be expected from a work location without the addition of capital equipment. A work location

normally scheduled to run two shifts per day for five days each week could be scheduled for three shifts per day, eight hours per shift, and seven days a week at its demonstrated capacity production rate to reach maximum capacity for a period of time. Scheduling at maximum capacity presents high risks of equipment breakdown and negative employee impacts such as increased absenteeism and safety incidents, especially, for example, when a resource is scheduled to run two 8-hour shifts and operators are asked to work 12-hour shifts to achieve maximum capacity. Further, demonstrated capacity used to schedule the resource will quickly become overstated due to postponement of maintenance, operator fatigue, and so on. Most companies choose a more moderate approach such as running three shifts per day, eight hours per shift, but only six days a week to allow for maintenance on the seventh day and for the health and safety of the operating crews. Any maximum capacity plan must be based upon a demonstrated, unquestioned, production rate, not a desire or wish, and must be approved by Leadership, and it must be based upon planned capacity, not theoretical capacity.

- **Move and Queue:** The demonstrated amount of time allowed between operations to move the material from one operation or work location to another, plus the amount of time a work order will sit in front of the next operation or work location before it is put into production (see Chapter 11).

- **Product Costing:** The operating cost per hour used to determine a product's cost is dependent upon the work location's capital value, operating crew hourly wages, and overhead cost distribution. Taking a "peanut butter" approach and applying the same cost for all work locations is not acceptable. Invest the time required to develop accurate data to improve financial system accuracy. As an example of the importance of finance system accuracy, a client company producing and selling three different types of paper products in the same operating division held up for years one of the product lines as the "shining star" and most profitable of the three. When the business continued to grow and a decision was made to separate the three product types into three separate operating divisions, requiring detailed analysis of actual operating costs for each product line, corporate leadership discovered that its shining star product line had actually been subsidized by the other two and was the only one of the three operating at a loss.

While these are all important definitions that Capacity Planners and Production Supervisors (see a description of accountabilities later in this chapter) must understand, their primary focus is balancing planned capacity with required capacity. If Capacity Planners and Production Supervisors fail to balance these two, either customer needs will not be met or inventory will build unnecessarily. Productivity and product cost will be negatively affected.

Resource Requirements Planning

As mentioned in Chapter 8, Integrated Business Planning's Resource Requirements Planning (RRP) is used as part of the Supply Review to test key resource capacity available to support the aggregate Production Plan. RRP starts with the Demand Plan's unconstrained demand plan quantities for each family. The next step in calculating RRP is identifying potential internal and external capacity constraints. There are normally a relatively small number of potential constraints depending on the mix and volume of products in the unconstrained demand plan. This effort need not become a science project. The easiest way to identify potential production constraints is by asking production supervisors in each major manufacturing area to identify the two resources that could cause work to back up. They know what these are and it takes only a few minutes to develop the list. The same can be said of other areas such as engineering, quality, marketing, and raw/packaging materials supplier capacity. One client's operating area was forced to curtail operations when a controlled substance by-product storage vault filled to capacity. The next RRP analysis included that storage vault capacity as a key resource. Identifying key constraints for RRP is simple enough that it takes little time to identify key constraints that were missed in the past and those that can be removed from the list.

This chapter focuses on Supply constraints but recall that the Integrated Business Planning chapter referenced Product Engineering's skilled key resource requirements using RRP in the Product Review, exactly the same process used for analyzing Supply Review capacity except for different key resource equipment and skill sets.

The third step is developing a Capacity Resource Profile to identify how much of a key resource's capacity is consumed by each unit of a family going through that resource. The capacity consumed is determined as the time-weighted average, based upon the current product mix within that family, and of all the items in that family routed through that. Again, extensive Industrial Engineering studies are unnecessary and simply take too long to complete. Rather, the Bill of Material (BOM) and Routing can be used to identify what items in a family are routed through a constraint and the time required to process each item. Often something as simple as a quick discussion with an experienced operator in the constraint work location can quickly confirm the validity of the result from the BOM and Routing. The resulting Capacity Resource Profile provides a weighted average of the time it takes for each unit of a family to go through a key resource, or, said another way, the capacity of a key resource consumed by each item scheduled and produced in that family, as shown in Figure 12.3.

Product Family	A	B	C	D	E	F
Lathe (hrs)	2	3	4	–	1	6
Mill (hrs)	1	3	2	–	4	5
5 Axis (hrs)	1	2	1	1	–	4
Inspect (hrs)	2	3	–	2	–	–
Warehouse (cube)	2	3	–	2	5	10
Supplier A (Gal)	2	3	1	–	3	–

FIGURE 12.3 Capacity Resource Profile: Product Families A–F

In this table, A through F represent six product families. Key resources include the lathe, mill, 5 axis, inspect, warehouse, and supplier A (raw material) capacity. Note that the list includes some potential external constraints, such as inspection hours, warehouse capacity and a supplier's capacity to provide a component, all external to the production area. The Capacity Resource Profile then has the average number of demonstrated hours per unit (or 100 units or 1,000 units, depending on typical volumes), required of each key resource to support the aggregate Production Plan. The number of hours in the figure are rounded to whole hours for simplification of the example.

The proposed Production Plan meeting the unconstrained demand plan is tested against the key resource requirements for that proposed Production Plan by multiplying the monthly family Production Plan quantities by the consumed hours from the Capacity Resource Profile. In the example shown in Figure 12.4, representing the Production Plan for a single month, producing

Product Family	A	B	C	D	E	F			
Quantity by Family	40	10	50	10	60	6			
Key Resources	Production Plan Quantities (Family Quantity x Key Resource)						Required Capacity	Planned Capacity	Maximum Capacity
Lathe (hrs)	80	30	200	–	60	36	406	484	621
Mill (hrs)	40	30	100	–	240	30	440	380	400
5 Axis (hrs)	40	20	50	10	–	24	144	140	180
Inspect (hrs)	80	30	–	20	–	–	130	100	240
Warehouse (cube)	80	30	–	40	300	60	510	550	610
Supplier A (gals)	80	30	50	–	180	–	340	500	640

FIGURE 12.4   By Family Monthly Production Plan

40 units of family A requires 40 × 2 or 80 hours of lathe capacity. Producing 10 units of family B at 3 hours of capacity consumes an additional 30 hours of lathe capacity. That calculation continues through the remaining product families to determine the total hours of lathe capacity consumed by the proposed Production Plan. Notice that product D does not go through the lathe, so family D consumes none of its capacity. The total lathe hours needed to support the proposed Production Plan is called required capacity, in this case 406 hours. The same calculation procedure is followed for each family and each key resource for each month in the minimum 24-month planning horizon.

Having calculated the required capacity hours for each key resource to support the proposed Production Plan means little until it can be compared to planned and maximum capacity available. Reviewing the lathe key resource, the required capacity is less than the planned capacity and far less than the maximum capacity. To get a full view, the process is repeated for each month across the IBP horizon. By looking across the horizon the pattern for the lathe indicates excess equipment or people. Those decisions are not acted on until the Detail Capacity Plan is examined because it is more accurate. The mill, however, presents a serious problem. Required capacity exceeds not only planned capacity but also maximum capacity. If it is the beginning of a continuing issue across the planning horizon, then action needs to be taken. Supply must develop an action plan to resolve the supply/demand imbalance. Options could include buying another machine, subcontracting part of the workload, or putting some of the work on another machine. These all come with price tags that are important in making the decision. The Supply Manager should begin developing an issue document stating the issue, background on how the issue developed, a recommended solution from the Supply perspective, rationale for that recommendation, and a listing of other alternative courses of action considered, all fully costed. The Supply Manager would then work with his IBP Product and Demand Leaders with their Finance business partners (see IBP, Chapter 8) to determine if Product or Demand alternatives might also resolve the issue, or to agree to a recommended course of action in escalating the issue to the IBP Integrated Reconciliation Team and possibly to the Management Business Review.

Note that in a Class A IBP process, this RRP capacity constraint would have been recognized many months into the future, allowing time for a more cost-effective response unless there was a major, unplanned change to the unconstrained demand plan. But if, in this case, the additional mill capacity cannot be obtained soon enough to satisfy the demand, a chart like the one in Figure 12.4 extended across the full horizon will support the IRR and MBR Teams in determining, for example, product families they should constrain or which customers' demand to constrain in order to keep from overloading the factory. If the adjustment is not made formally, the result will be, you guessed it, churn that will cause even more products to miss schedule. In this case C (100) and E (240) are the most likely candidates because they have the most volume, but Sales, Marketing, and Finance must make those decisions.

RRP's purpose is to identify when large capacity issues are developing. This needs to be out beyond the decision points, so they can be addressed before the Sales, Production, and Inventory Plans are forwarded to the IRR for approval. This simple process is used to identify those issues, make decisions during the IBP MBR, and ensure that aggregate plans are valid.

Rough-Cut Capacity Planning

Should a product family show significant capacity consumption of an over-loaded key resource in the RRP calculations, then this raises an additional question, beyond the question discussed in the previous paragraphs. Are any specific items within that family inordinately consuming the overloaded resource capacity? To examine whether this is the case the Supply Manager uses Rough-Cut Capacity Planning (RCCP), a procedure identical to RRP. RCCP examines capacity requirements of each Master Scheduled item, within the family, to determine which consumes the greatest amount of overloaded key resource. RCCP still uses monthly time buckets and the same key resources identified in RRP. Since there are many Master Scheduled items in each product family, developing the RCCP Resource Profile is more complicated than that of RRP and often requires Industrial Engineering support to complete.

RCCP is conducted at the discretion of the Supply Manager, using the business unit's Capacity Planner and Master Scheduler with support from Finance. It is essential to understand the financial impact of having to constrain the demand. The Master Scheduler, having completed the RCCP analysis, provides the resulting information to the Supply Manager. With the Product, Demand, and Finance Manager, the Supply Manager then determines the course of action to constrain the demand, agree on ways to eliminate the constraint, and/or escalate recommendations to the IRR and MBR.

Detail Capacity Planning

When, through the MBR, aggregate plans have been approved, they are disaggregated across the planning horizon by the planning system into detail plans by item, day, and distribution point. This enables a focus, by Demand and Supply, on schedules in the firm and trading zones. Recall that the planning system, if configured properly, is not permitted to automatically reschedule orders within those time zones.

Supply conducts the third level of capacity planning to ensure detailed schedules are valid, that is, that the required capacity will be available when needed. Detail Capacity Planning (DCP) requires an entirely different approach from Resource Requirements Planning and Rough-Cut Capacity Planning in that it does not use a profile but examines capacity of every work location (see later) and resource. Using information from item masters, routings, and work location masters (see Routings Accuracy, Chapter 5), the planning system runs an Operation Scheduling program. There is a detailed description of how the Operation Scheduling program works in the previous chapter (Managing Internal Priorities: Delivering Products on Time, Chapter 11). Building on the same example (see Figure 12.5) used in the Chapter 11 that rounded up setup

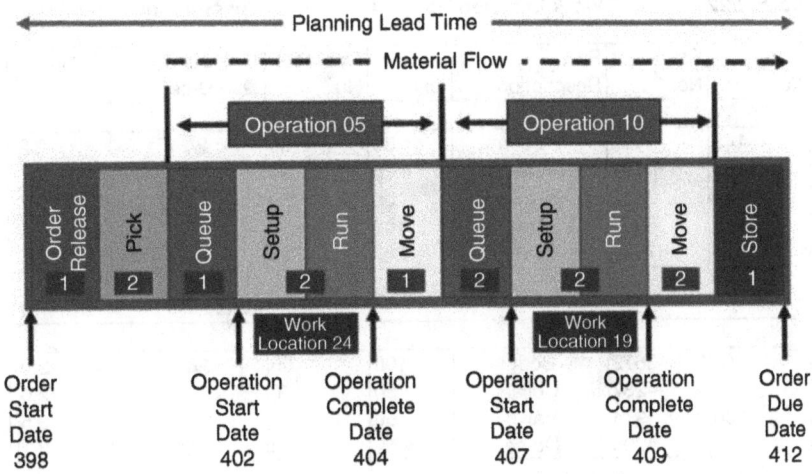

FIGURE 12.5 Establishing the Planning Lead Time

and run times for simplicity, in calculating Detail Capacity Plans the times will not be rounded up to days since the calculations must be more accurate. While setup and run times for both operations were rounded up to 2 days, their capacity hours differ. Work Location (WL) 24 has a setup time of 2 hours and a run time of 2.6 hours. The order for 100 units, therefore, requires a setup time of 2 hours and a run time of 26 hours for a total of 28 hours. Since the work location is running 2 shifts, or 16 hours, the order for 100 units is scheduled for 2 days. WL 19 requires 1 hour for setup and has a run time of 0.13 hours. Therefore, the work order for 100 units requires a run time of 0.13 hours times 100, or 13 hours for a total of 14 hours. Since WL 19 is running only one shift per day, the work order is also scheduled for 2 days in that work location.

Any operation or work location capacity overloads must be resolved by a site's Capacity Planner, Master Scheduler, and Production Supervisor or escalated for resolution. With valid, required hours determined, the Detail Capacity Planning program organizes the work orders first by work location and then by job, listing the setup and run hours in weekly buckets as shown in Figure 12.6. This summary is for WL 24 showing the work order in the example, work order 148, on the first line of the second weekly time bucket. The manufacturing day calendar used in the Chapter 11 description is now displayed as scheduled weeks' calendar dates.

Date: 2/22			Work Location No: 24				Description: Lathe		
Week Starting	Order No.	Part No.	Part Description	Qty	Operation No.	Operation Due Date	Setup Hrs		Run Hrs
2/20	145	4422	Sleeve	30	50	2/21	2.2		19.6
2/20	138	4897	Connector	15	90	2/22	1.0		27.6
2/20	142	3517	Nipple	30	50	2/22	3.7		10.0
2/20	140	8052	Arm	100	10	2/23	0.5		25.0
2/20		7196	Cover	200	20	2/23	0.5		22.5
						Totals	7.9		104.7
2/27	148	3672	Body	100	05	2/27	2.0		26.0
2/27	136	4287	Collar	50	70	2/29	2.6		35.0
2/27	130	914	Valve	50	20	3/02	3.5		10.5
2/27		4290	Dome	52	60	3/03	3.2		60.6
						Totals	11.3		132.1

FIGURE 12.6 Capacity Requirements Detail

Required production hours in each work location are now clearly documented in detail for the current and coming weeks. How good is the information? How good is that schedule, and how accurate is the data used by the planning system? With good (not perfect) planning and data accuracy, on-time completion *by operation* in most companies implementing these procedures exceeds 95% and realizes a 20% to 50% productivity improvement. How far into the future can this information be viewed? It is available across the entire MRP horizon.

As presented in previous chapters, a graphical presentation such as Figure 12.7 is much more useful than a chart full of numbers in quickly pointing out future potential capacity constraints and inefficiencies. Once a potential issue is identified graphically and the detailed data shown, Capacity Planners and Production Supervisors can focus their attention on the specific weeks, and the data for those weeks required to resolve capacity problems and to determine staffing levels to meet on-time delivery and planned productivity objectives.

Detailed Capacity Plan

What is measured improves. All previous chapters have provided planning and execution measures related to the subject processes. The measure of Detail

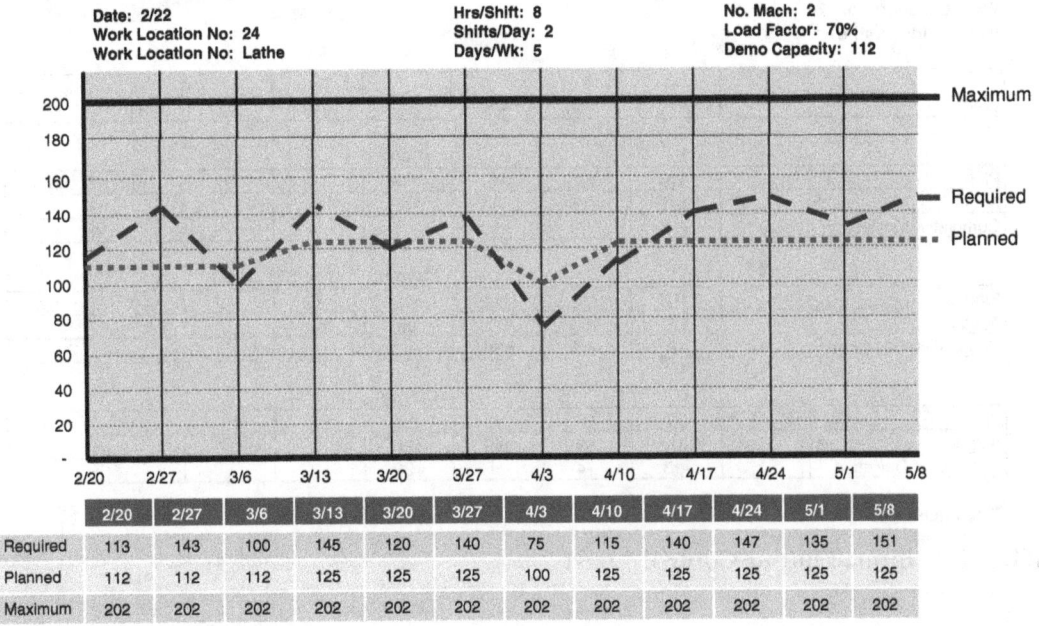

FIGURE 12.7 Detailed Capacity Plan

Capacity Planning effectiveness is called Capacity Input/Output Control. This is a measurement report not typically available in commercial software but is easy to develop.

The report shown in Figure 12.8 is divided into three sections: Input, Output, and Queue, showing four weeks of history and then the next four weeks, although the number of weeks displayed can be modified as desired. Each section of the chart is broken down further:

- **Input** (combined output coming from upstream work centers/work locations)
  - Plan: The standard setup and run hours directly from the capacity requirements detail.
  - Actual: The number of standard hours of work that came into that work center that week based on shop floor reporting.
  - Cumulative Deviation: The cumulative difference between plan and actual hours.
- **Output** (this work location)
  - Plan: The number of standard hours of work committed by production in this work location.

Work Location No: 24   Date: 2/22
Description: Lathe

Week		1/23	1/30	2/6	2/13	This Week	2/27	3/6	3/13
Input									
Plan		115	120	110	118	113	123	100	145
Actual		100	125	80	132				
Cumulative Deviation	0	−15	−10	−40	−26				
Output									
Plan		112	112	112	112	112	112	112	125
Actual		110	100	90	90				
Cumulative Deviation	0	−2	−14	−36	−58				
Queue									
Plan		50	58	56	62	63	73	61	81
Actual	47	37	62	52	94				
Cumulative Deviation		−13	+4	−4	+32				

Tolerance: +/− 30 Hours   Desired Q: 50 Hours

FIGURE 12.8 Input/Output Control Chart

- Actual: The number of standard hours of work produced.
- Cumulative Deviation: Cumulative difference between plan and actual work hours.
- **Queue**
  - Plan: The desired hours of work in queue for this work location.
  - Actual: The actual hours of queue in front of this work location.
  - Cumulative Deviation: The cumulative difference between plan and actual hours in queue.

To make the process work effectively, the Capacity Planner (described later) and Supervisor review this data in a weekly meeting to monitor the performance of each work location under that supervisor's accountability. The meeting begins with a review and update of the work location file for the first work location. Next, they review the Input/Output Report for that work center to determine actual performance against plan. The Capacity Planner is responsible for the Input, and the Supervisor is responsible for the Output.

Input/Output Control objectives include:

- **Monitoring:** The workflow through the factory.
- **Measuring:** Input and output plan performance to ensure promised work location input (Capacity Planner), and output (Production Supervisor) hours

are delivered as planned. If there are discrepancies, the Capacity Planner and Supervisor do the research necessary to identify what caused the difference and improve the future plan accuracy.

- **Performance:** Measuring the performance of the Capacity Planner and Supervisor.
- **Maintain:** Establishing and maintaining demonstrated capacity.
- **Managing:** Establishing and managing queues.

Work Location (Work Center) Accuracy

Measuring work location accuracy is not complex. During the weekly Detail Capacity Planning meeting (including Input/Output Control) the Capacity Planner and Supervisor review the work location planning parameters. It is the Supervisor's responsibility to ensure they are accurate (an effective Supervisor should know this information) and the Capacity Planner updates the file. The work location data is shown in the header of the Detailed Capacity Plan, Figure 12.7. This is the same information used in Resource Requirements Planning and Rough-Cut Capacity Planning for key resource work locations.

Accuracy is calculated as follows:

$$\text{Work location accuracy} = \frac{\text{Number of accurate work locations}}{\text{Number of work locations checked}}$$

If any data element is incorrect the work location is recorded as incorrect, or a "miss." As stated earlier it is done at the beginning of the Detail Capacity Planning meeting. If changes are necessary they are executed. If the Detail Capacity Planning meeting is under the "truth as we know it" principal, then this audit should always be 100% accurate.

Work location header information must be in the MRP system. Use of ad-hoc systems is unacceptable.

Detail Capacity Planning Meeting

Let us "listen in" on the conversation between Samantha (Sam) (Capacity Planner) and Joe (Supervisor) in the Detail Capacity Planning meeting. They

Work Center No: 24   Date: 2/22
Description: Lathe

Week		1/23	1/30	2/6	2/13	This Week	2/27	3/6	3/13
Input									
Plan		115	120	110	118	113	123	100	145
Actual		100	125	80	132				
Cumulative Deviation	0	−15	−10	−40	−26				
Output									
Plan		112	112	112	112	112	112	112	125
Actual		110	100	90	90				
Cumulative Deviation	0	−2	−14	−36	−58				
Queue									
Plan		50	58	56	62	63	73	61	81
Actual	47	37	62	52	94				
Cumulative Deviation		−13	+4	−4	+32				

Tolerance: +/− 30 Hours   Desired Q: 50 Hours

FIGURE 12.9 Detailed Capacity Planning

have reviewed the Detail Capacity Plan in Figure 12.7 above. They are now reviewing the Input/Output report in Figure 12.9. The Input/Output is the performance measure of the Capacity Planner and the Supervisor and is critical in capacity planning.

Sam: "Joe, you have not made your output numbers again this week. You are now well outside the 30-hour tolerance we agreed on. What is going on?"

Joe: "Well, those 30 hours you didn't give me on 2/6 caused me to fall behind, and I am trying to catch up!"

Sam: "Come on Joe. You know that is a phony excuse. Look at the work center queue; you never ran out of work. I go by that work center often, and it has been down on many occasions, even with plenty of queued material. I know last week's input was down, but as soon as I saw that I followed up with the MRP Planner and Purchasing. The material that caused the shortage was rejected in inspection, but the supplier jumped through hoops to get the material here as fast as possible. Those input hours only showed up this week. Come on, Joe, let us be honest with one another."

Joe: "Okay, Okay. You're right. The real cause is that the first-shift operator came down with the flu and gave it to the second-shift operator. I lost both operators for a full week. I learned a valuable lesson and now have operators cross-trained on that machine. Everyone is in good health now, and we will catch up by working this Saturday."

Sam: "What do you want to do with the Planned Output of 112 hours in the future? Do you want to change the load factor and modify your demonstrated capacity for that work center?"

Joe: "No, the planned capacity is still accurate. I just need to manage better using this process, and somehow I think you will help me do that, whether I like it or not."

Detail Capacity Planning Accountabilities

Accountabilities by role include:

- **Production Supervisors ensure that (listed by priority):**
  - People work safely.
  - Work locations produce quality products.
  - Operation due dates are met by ensuring equipment availability and assigning operators correctly.
  - Delays are immediately reported to other Supervisors and/or Capacity Planners.
  - Participate in the Detail Capacity Planning process and maintain agreed-upon capacity levels. When there are multiple shifts, the Production Manager typically attends these meetings.
  - Ensure data integrity/accuracy of reporting and feedback on routing, work location, and BOM accuracy.
  - Continuous productivity improvement.

- **Expeditor:** The need for an occasional expedited order will never be eliminated, but with the processes described in this book there is no need for someone to fill an Expeditor role. Reductions of expediting churn significantly increases time available to improve safety, costs, productivity, and so on.
- **Capacity Planner:**
  - Maintains and monitors shop priority list.
  - Reviews past due operation dates.
  - Analyzes capacity plans.
  - Maintains Work Location file.

- Leads Detail Capacity Planning Meeting.
- Communicates with MRP Planners.
- Assists Supervisors in resolving problems.
- Provides capacity management and scheduling system technical expertise.

Carrying out significant Capacity Planner accountabilities implies an addition of headcount in many companies, usually a point of resistance. However, in most cases, it does not require additional personnel. When this position is filled, the need for expeditors (a formal position in many companies, to chase shortages) is eliminated and Supervisors become far more effective. Overall, the Capacity Planner role, if new in a company, results in a significant total headcount reduction. Moving a Supervisor to a capacity planning position allowed a Machine Shop Manager to reduce shortages from over 100 per day to 1 per day and improve productivity by 10 percentage points in 5 months.

The Internal Scheduling section of this chapter references Engineering's use of the Priority List (Dispatch List). Industrial Engineering also uses the Capacity Requirements Planning process just explained. If new equipment has been approved and installed it needs to be used to eliminate capacity constraints and in so doing improve overall efficiency.

Demonstrated Capacity

Perhaps one of the most important capacity planning concepts to be addressed by Leadership and Management is Demonstrated Capacity. Maintaining accurate demonstrated capacities enables planners to create plans and schedules with a realistic expectation of what will be produced. Using the Input/Output Control process, accuracy of load factors and capacities can be monitored, and this will signal when modification is needed. This ensures that the best capacity information is being used for all three capacity planning levels. Capacity planning charts should include work location load factors to ensure that the difference between scheduled hours and required hours is clear.

It is interesting to watch a company President during the IBP MBR when informed, following a Sales and Marketing VP celebrating a great unexpected sale, that there is not enough capacity to meet this additional demand. It gets even more interesting when the President is told that the load factor for the constraining resource is at 50% (half the gross capacity is unavailable to produce product). Sparks fly and blame is passed between the Production and

Manufacturing Engineering VPs as to why the load factor issues have not be resolved. Nobody wins; both VPs have their excuses, but the President and customer lose since it is too late to accommodate this order due date, even though it is unexpected. The solution is to immediately identify and resolve the root causes of the capacity loss, for any constrained resource, with a load factor less than 85%.

Priority versus Capacity

What is more important, priority planning or capacity planning? The answer is that both are equally important. If the priority is correct but you do not have the hours, you will be late even though the orders are in the right sequence. If the hours are right but the priority wrong, you will also be late because you are producing items that are not yet needed. It is only through using both, with a valid plan, that you will be "on time every time" in delivering customer service requirements.

The "Muscle More in to Get More Out" Myth

Unfortunately, it is common to hear leadership say, "Put a little more in the plan, apply muscle to it, and you will get a little bit more out." That is simply not true and the opposite will happen; you get less out of a resource or work location because it demotivates – a workforce knows what the problems are and see leadership applying ignorance. Let us consider a simple example:

A is the finished assembly made from two components, X and Y. They both go through Work Location (WL) 11 and are the only items using that work location, taking 1 hour each. WL 11 has a maximum capacity of 200 hours. From the capacity planning process 100 A's are recommended – 100 hours to machine X and 100 hours to machine Y. But Leadership wants to "muscle more in to get more out." So, in response, the Master Scheduler schedules 110 A's. That means 220 must be machined. WL 11 produces 110 X's and then starts on the Y's but runs out of time when only 90 Y's have been produced (total 200 hours). So, 90 A's were assembled, falling 10 short of schedule, which is 10 less than WL 11's capacity if it were not overscheduled. A simple example, but imagine this approach with hundreds of machines and thousands of items. Inefficiencies, missed customer commitments, and a culture of continuous firefighting becoming the norm. Remember people, processes, and then tools; shared knowledge through education dispels many myths.

Capacity Planning Comparisons

Effective capacity planning is a critical enabler in successfully managing a manufacturing company. Figure 12.10 compares the three levels of capacity planning: Resource Requirement Planning (RRP), Rough-Cut Capacity Planning (RCP), and Detail Capacity Planning (DCP).

	RRP / RCCP	DCP
Inventory	No	Yes
Lead Time Offset	No	Yes
Resources Reviewed	Constraints	All
Relative to MRP	Before	After
Focus	Production Plan / Master Schedule	MRP and Internal Priority List

FIGURE 12.10 Capacity Planning Comparison Template

Expanding on the template, RRP/RCCP and DCP differ in the following ways:

- **Inventory:** Only ending aggregate finished goods inventory by family is considered in developing the Production Plan and analyzing RRP-indicated needs; only Master Scheduled item inventories are considered when developing the Master Schedule and analyzing RCCP needs. However, all inventory items are considered in MRP and DCP.
- **Resources Reviewed:** For RRP and RCCP the focus is on key resources, those that could constrain the unconstrained demand plan, based on volume and mix or both, are reviewed in order to simplify the process and speed up "what-if" analysis. The objective of RRP and RCCP is to identify and resolve major constraints that require a long lead time to resolve. DCP is used to identify and resolve constraints in the near-term horizon, to make decisions on the best use of capacity to enable delivery. This visibility will also identify opportunities for continuous improvement. Since any resource can be a constraint or require balancing to optimize efficiency, all work locations and resources must be included. DCP enables cost-efficient

capacity adjustments using overtime, temporary hires, or moving employees to constraint work locations, usually with minimum lead time.

- **Relative to MRP:** DCP accuracy is high (if you follow this book's recommendations) because it is determined after MRP and uses MRP data. RRP and RCP are calculated prior to MRP to ensure the aggregate and master schedule level plans are valid before MRP runs in the planning system, so no detail planning data is available.
- **Focus:** RRP is performed for Leadership with a focus on months 4 to 24–36 or more to ensure validity of IBP plans. This enables future constraints, which often require expensive long lead-time resolution, to be determined and authorized. RCCP is performed by the IBP Supply Manager with the support of the planning team to identify specific items that may be causing aggregate constraints to ensure adequate availability before the Production Plan is sent for approval. When released the aggregate Production Plan is disaggregated for detailed scheduling. DCP is performed by detail Capacity Planners and Production Supervision with a focus on the near-term horizon, to identify and resolve any minor constraints as explained above. The aim is to execute the near-term action plans required to meet the operation due dates to ensure delivery to plan.
- **Accuracy:** The DCP is far more accurate than RCP and RCCP if there is a valid plan. Therefore, the DCP output should be compared to the RCP and RCCP information to assure regularly to confirm their accuracy.

Common to each capacity planning level is that the required capacity and planned capacity must be in balance. When an imbalance is recognized, it is up to the Planning Team and Support Functions to get creative. Some alternative courses of action to resolve a constraint have been mentioned in this chapter, but we have seen creative Supply Managers, Planners, and Operators overcome seemingly unsolvable imbalances while at the same time they optimize resource utilization, increasing productivity, reducing costs, and improving customer service.

Summary

Capacity Planning is a critical and often misunderstood component of Business Excellence Planning. Performed well at each of the capacity planning levels described in this chapter, valid plans and schedules will be executed reliably and on time, assuring on-time delivery of customer orders, significant productivity improvements, and cost reduction. Effective capacity planning eliminates the churn created unnecessarily by imbalances between demand and supply not recognized until it is too late to regain balance effectively and efficiently.

To learn more about Capacity Planning, review the following books:

Achieving Class A Business Excellence, An Executive's Perspective by Dennis Groves, Kevin Herbert, and Jim Correll (John Wiley & Sons)

An Executive's Guide To Achieving Class A Business Excellence by Dennis Groves, Kevin Herbert, and Jim Correll (Oliver Wight International)

Distribution Resource Planning: The Gateway to True Quick Response and Continual Replenishment by Andre Martin (John Wiley & Sons)

Gaining Control: Managing Capacity & Priorities by James G. Correll and Kevin Herbert (John Wiley & Sons)

For additional but more specific reading please visit the Oliver Wight Website and gain access to the extensive library of White Papers.

CHAPTER 13

External Sourcing and Supplier Planning: Reaping the Benefits of Valid Scheduling

In the Demand Planning chapter, Chapter 10, demand planning was identified as the most challenging of all the Business Excellence Planning activities because it requires looking into the future and predicting what customers will

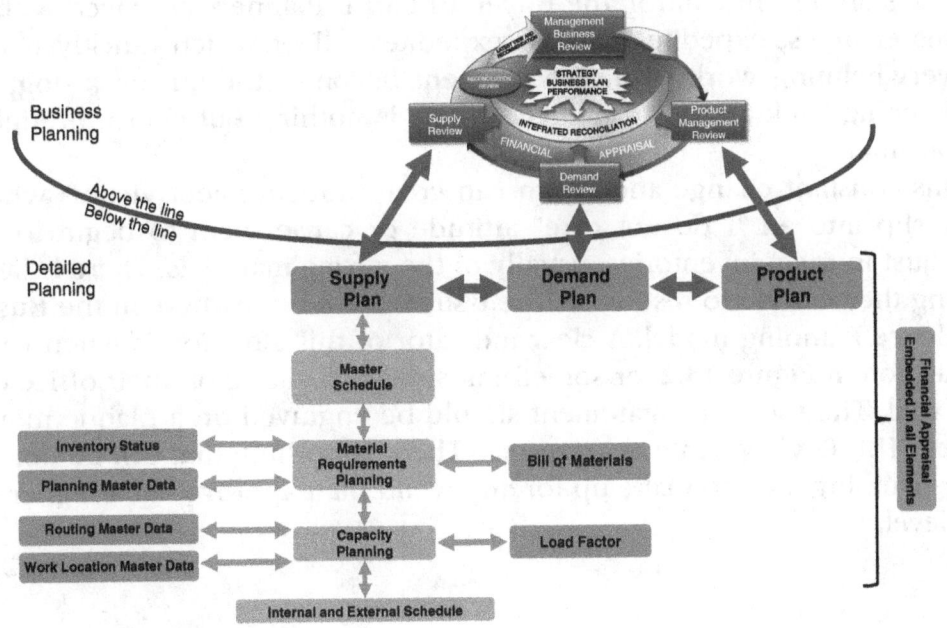

FIGURE 13.1 Business Excellence Planning

be buying. Nevertheless, it is an essential task in running a business. With Unparalleled Business Planning and Execution Practices, demand planning processes are superior to simply looking at history or just guessing. The most troublesome of all planning activities can be procurement, represented in Figure 13.1 as External Scheduling. Tracing Figure 13.1 down from Integrated Business Planning to Master Scheduling to Material Requirements Planning to Capacity Planning, you finally arrive at Internal and External Schedule. That means that absolutely any errors or changes at any level in these prior planning activities caused by inaccurate data or human error fall on Procurement to react to and deal with.

To make it worse, all manufactured parts and products begin with a purchased part or materials (the lowest level of every bill of material is a purchased item). So, not only must Procurement be aware of everything that is happening in all planning levels, but also be aware of what is happening or failing to happen in manufacturing operations. If the business is operating with Unparalleled Business Planning and Execution Practices, life in Procurement is far more rewarding since few items each day require supplier communication and schedule adjustment. Most of the days and weeks can be spent continuously improving customer-supplier relationships, reducing inventories and costs, and consolidating the supplier base. But if the planning and execution processes are not in control, the Buyer and MRP Planners are faced with continuous changes, expedites, and de-expedites, all of which quickly result in an overwhelming work load. Procurement becomes the tail on a dog, a tail that is going back and forth like crazy. Life is nothing but churn, firefighting, and burnout.

This constant change and churn can create Procurement victims who can easily slip into an "I do not care" attitude or cause them to begin to order large "just-in-case" inventories, usually of the wrong materials. There is literally nothing they can do to resolve all the issues caused elsewhere in the Business Excellence Planning model. A clear indicator of this situation is when you see the cartoon in Figure 13.2, or something similar, hanging on their office or cubicle wall. The following statement should be engraved on a plaque mounted in every IBP Review conference room: "There is nothing that can be done at a lower planning level to make up for an invalid plan approved at a higher planning level."

FIGURE 13.2 The Impact on People

Another attitude that often emerges can be called "cantankerous." For example: Fred had just moved to a new corporate headquarters role in a plant location and needed a set of tires for his personal car. He was advised by Pat that he could go to the Procurement department and they would get them for him at a great price. "It's just down the hall," Pat advised. Fred did not know the size of the tires, but Pat advised him that John would know what size he needed. Fred found John, who asked him in a very sour tone what he wanted. Fred thought it might be a good idea to just introduce himself and leave, but he proceeded against his better judgment. When John asked the size of the tires needed, and Fred said he did not know, John exploded, asking why Fred was wasting his time by asking him to buy something without the necessary information. When Fred returned to his work area, Pat and a half dozen others were waiting, eager to celebrate Fred's initiation into the group, laughing about his first introduction to John and his bad temper and stubbornness. Pat told Fred that John's nickname was Cruncher; Fred now knew what it meant to be crunched. John, actually a very nice person, was under constant pressure to expedite supplier orders caused by changing production plans. In the middle of one of those exasperating incidents, along came Fred from corporate who did not even know what he needed but wanted it now and at a low price. The good news is that several years later, Fred and John both became part of the team implementing a new planning system and procedures that significantly reduced expediting. John's real personality was allowed to emerge.

Buyers can also develop a "got you covered" attitude. They begin to tell you what you want to hear. They are confident that your needs are always changing anyway, so there is no need to overreact to your request. More churn, more firefighting, and no parts or material.

Resisting Change

A railroad engine and car manufacturing company's site Procurement Director's overwhelming personal joy was attending the weekly manufacturing meeting to declare he had "pulled us out of the fire, again" and list the items that would be available that day because of his actions. What he always failed to explain was that he did not use the planning system's schedule because he was too busy chasing shortages. To cover the shortages and persuade suppliers to cooperate with his expedite requests and sometimes simultaneously short other customers, he had been paying premiums or buying larger quantities. Imagine the inventory of parts and material not needed while other materials required expediting. In this case, planning was not the problem; his inability or unwillingness to use the planning system was the real problem, but he loved being a hero.

On one demonstrator project he was getting suppliers to provide their parts for free with the promise of advertising on the sides of the train we were proposing to run in service and demonstrate to customers its potential. A particular, and expensive, component was urgently required, and the only way he could achieve his "free" supply was to buy two of them and get one free. He allocated the free component to the project and put the others in storage. Because the company had an Engineer-to-Order strategy, those components remained in inventory for years. His individualistic approach and his refusal to follow the schedule is an extreme example of behaviors that must be addressed and corrected during planning system implementations. The Business Excellence Planning hierarchy is completely integrated and fails if each step is operated independently by individuals who believe their approaches are better than proven procedures. Procurement, like Sales, deals with important companies and people in those companies. If their representation is unprofessional and undisciplined, expect supplier representatives to exhibit similar undisciplined behaviors. The company-to-company relationship becomes a spiral of disaster. In this example, there were serious cash flow problems resulting in truly urgent material orders being put on hold pending payment. No cash, no payment; no payment, no parts; no parts, no delivery; no delivery, no cash from the customers. A nasty outcome caused by not following new procedures.

While coaching a company that was starting to operate with a Class A culture, we noticed that Procurement was not making any progress. During a coaching session with the Procurement Manager he said, "You are getting the wool pulled over your eyes." Procurement was still getting thousands of MRP expedite messages (move in/reschedule in), which he showed us from the last planning system update. The rule we recommended, and which the President supported, was, "No customer order will be accepted inside lead time without concurrence from Supply (Manufacturing and Procurement) confirming that they have the resources required to produce the product." The President called together his Supply, Sales, and Marketing VPs along with Order Entry, Master Scheduling, Procurement, and Material Requirements Planning managers, in our presence, to reinforce the rule. We suggested maintaining a record of any customer orders accepted inside lead time with the cause and action taken. Two weeks later we met again to review the situation. A total of 23 customer orders had been accepted by Order Entry inside lead time following approval by the affected Supply organizations. Master Scheduling said they rescheduled the same 23. The MRP run produced 28 action messages, one each for the 23 customer orders plus five more related to inventory, bill of material accuracy issues, and scrapped items. The Procurement Manager said his organization was not keeping track of these short lead time orders. Further investigation revealed that Procurement was not even working their action messages. A new Procurement Manager was hired and immediately started working all MRP messages. That represented the President's commitment to change and resulted in better than 95% supplier delivery performance.

Procurement is one of the few functional organizations that demonstrate resistance to these new operating principles. These are not "bad employees" but employees that have learned to survive despite terrible schedules and have been viewed as "heroes" who can make miracles happen. They are initially reluctant to lose that recognition and have their excuses eliminated.

A purchasing material planner in a cosmetics company, when asked if this improved planning process implementation effort was of any value to him, thought for a moment and responded, "I had not thought of that until you just asked. I used to get to my desk at about 6:30 every morning only to find countless yellow sticky notes asking about missing materials or the need for an emergency order for different materials. I spent the entire day scrambling to discover materials that were here but not transacted in the planning system, or begging suppliers for immediate schedule changes. But over the past few months, I have been getting to my desk at 7:30, finding absolutely no yellow sticky notes and spending about half my day working with my suppliers to reduce lead times, inventory, and material costs."

Procurement Importance

Procurement can have a huge impact on business success. The amount of success depends on the amount of outsourcing required, employees' skills, and validity of planning information. With such impact, Procurement must be effectively integrated and recognized as a key team member in a transformation initiative. Gone are the days when you could outsource problems and pass blame on to suppliers. As with Procurement, suppliers must also be recognized as a vital part of your virtual Supply Chain team, even though you do not own them or have 100% control over them. Why? If they fail, you fail, but if they succeed, you are more likely to succeed as well. Perhaps part of your Supply strategy should be to get close to them, create lasting customer-supplier relationships, invest in the relationship to improve quality, reduce costs, reduce inventory, reduce lead times, and increase flexibility for both of you, not just your own. This approach used by a recent client resulted in a supplier's GM participating in the client's final Class A Certification assessment to ensure that we knew just how dramatic his customer's transformation was to his company as well.

Product cost elements confirmed by hundreds of companies include the following breakdown:

Cost of Sales
- Material = 40–60%
- Direct Labor = 5–15%
- Overhead Burden = 55–25%

Sometimes we hear there is more purchased content in some companies' products, and, occasionally, we hear that there is much more purchased content in some companies' products. Regardless, about half or more of product cost is the result of materials purchased from suppliers. Yet management in most companies continues to focus on reducing direct labor cost, which has been the smallest of the three components since the Industrial Revolution! It is well past time to turn attention to working with suppliers to reduce material costs.

Management should help their suppliers be the best they can be by supplying as much information as possible to improve their planning by working with them to improve their processes and by undertaking joint projects to drive waste out of the Supply Chain.

Coaching at a large over-the-road truck engine supplier, on their journey to Class A, the initial assessment revealed some very helpful and important information. From conversations with 10 members of the Procurement Team, including the Director, they all eagerly informed us of the great job they were doing and how they were already meeting all Class A requirements. Their suppliers delivered components every afternoon to support the next day's production. The day before shipment, their suppliers were required to send a notification saying that the required items had been shipped. If the transaction was not received on time, the MRP system automatically sent a message to the Buyer, who immediately contacted the supplier in question. Supplier delivery performance was better than 99% on time in full. "What more," they asked us, "could you ask for?" The answer was simple: "Do you send your suppliers schedules they can trust not only for shipping materials, but also scheduling future production, planning capacity (people and equipment), for planning long lead time materials and capacity changes?" This question was greeted with dead silence. We then asked, "So, how do your suppliers deliver on time without a valid schedule?" The answer, delivered less eagerly, was that their suppliers stocked lots of extra parts because of the constantly changing requirements. We then asked, "Do your suppliers operate efficiently?" The response was even more subdued. They confessed that their approach to suppliers was to beat them up as much as they could without putting them out of business. To their credit, they were encouraged to learn that all the other departments in the facility were working with us as well to improve the validity of their schedules.

Our assistance was asked for by the GM at a large heavy equipment transmission plant, as the rest of the organization was moving forward toward Class A practices, but Procurement was lagging behind. While reviewing their limited progress, the Procurement Manager became visibly angry. It was his belief that we did not know anything about Procurement. He proclaimed, "You have to be very skilled in beating up a supplier on price and know how to expedite effectively." Less than a month later, one of their major casting suppliers closed its doors overnight because they were losing so much money. Wow, talk about churn and expediting! Suddenly, transmission cases had to be welded together from plate steel as an alternative to supplied castings to try and maintain the production rate until another casting supplier could be found and qualified. It was obvious that the Procurement Manager was not close enough to the supplier to know its financial status (apparently the supplier was not good at it either). The continuous expediting and excess inventory the supplier needed to respond to the transmission plant's poor scheduling was clearly a part of the financial problem. This disaster precipitated an important change in the Procurement Manager's behavior; he began sharing MRP requirement information and schedules to help suppliers plan more effectively. You will get far more from a supplier if the supplier recognizes and acts like your partner in the business of satisfying your end customers, thus increasing your (and the supplier's) bottom-line results. The old phrase of being in a "win-win" partnership has too often been interpreted as a "win-lose" partnership by Procurement.

Suppliers and customers all face the same problems and challenges. The better the information they receive from you, the better the job they can do and the more likely it is that they will pass along some of the benefits of good information and predictable schedules. Of course, if you have lousy plans, passing them along will not help the supplier. Conversely, if your plans are reliable but your relationship with the supplier is strained and you are not a trusted partner, neither of you will benefit.

Supplier Schedules

Providing a supplier with a valid supply schedule, as shown in Figure 13.3, is an easy task; the schedule can be updated and distributed daily/weekly directly from the planning system. The schedule can be structured to cover an agreed-on planning horizon and can show the firm zone, often shown by day; the trading zone, often by week; and the open planning zone, often by week for an agreed period and then by month or even quarter in the outer months. Agreements with suppliers should be reached to confirm the agreed duration of each time zone. Obviously, the supplier can only plan with the information it has been given and should use the information with no second guessing. If there is believed to be an error or problem, then this must be discussed and

Item No.	< Firm Zone >				< Trading Zone >				Free Zone	
	24/5	31/5	7/6	14/6	21/6	28/6	5/7	12/7	Next 4 weeks	Next 4 weeks
222	200			200		200	200		400	400
1579	20	20	20	20	20	20	20	20	80	80
2267	300			500			500	400	1600	1600
456		720			680			720	2880	2160
R002	150					300			300	300

Firm = instruction to deliver

FIGURE 13.3 Supplier Schedule

resolved between both parties, not one working in isolation. In general, terms the agreements reach are:

- In the firm zone the supplier may ship and expect payment for scheduled orders in that zone, orders that have not been formally changed, since their production capacity will have been reserved and materials acquired to support that schedule. This is not to say that schedules cannot be changed, although in this zone every effort should be made to avoid changes, but with agreement from the supplier, changes can be made but incur an extra fee negotiated in advance.
- In the trading zone the supplier will be asked to reserve required capacity for scheduled orders. However, there is an understanding with the supplier that the mix of items on the schedule may be modified, and the supplier is expected to have the ability to accept these mix changes with minimal disruption.
- In the free zone it is important for the supplier to understand the potential workload so any improvement plans, or investments, can be made with knowledge of the potential workload. It is agreed with the supplier that this information is provided as information only for their own decisions about capacity improvements and that the schedules in the free zone could change dramatically, which the supplier would be expected to support without issue as long as they do not exceed the maximum capacity negotiated.

Trusting the supplier schedule, suppliers will enter those orders into their plans. This should happen routinely, but the problem is that most customer schedules are inaccurate and not trusted at all. When the schedules are not trustworthy, suppliers should use firm planned orders as described in Chapter 6 MRP. Realizing significant supplier performance and cost improvement requires the customer to clean its own house first. Providing reliable supplier schedules, meeting periodically (quarterly, for example) to review progress, discuss challenges, and conduct two-way performance reviews, and working on joint business improvement projects is transformational in creating strong customer-supplier relationships and in improving bottom-line business results for both parties.

Commodity Manager/"Internet Age" Buyer's Role

The Buyer role of yesterday is gone. No one should simply release purchase orders and seek a supplier's acknowledgment of receipt of that purchase order. That's the reason for the dual title of this section, "Commodity Manager" and "Internet Age Buyer." So, what is a Buyer's job today? There is only one parameter: the need for a valid plan (accurate and achievable). When there is a valid plan and suppliers receive supplier schedules, the need for day-to-day supplier communication is significantly eliminated and, when needed, MRP planners can conduct those communications. This allows today's Buyer to operate more strategically as described below. Today's Buyers lead Customer-Supplier Teams to resolve issues, manage customer requests, and implement improvement initiatives in the following areas:

- **Quality:** Resolve existing quality problems and analyze the processes to ensure that quality is being built into rather than inspected into products.
- **Value Analysis:** Ensure that material designs and supplier manufacturing capabilities are compatible. Value is built into products when designers apply techniques such as Design for Manufacture, Design for Production, Design for Assembly, Design for Packaging, Design for Cost, and so forth.
- **New Technology:** Develop long-term relationships that enable suppliers to implement new technology and capabilities to improve quality and reduce costs.
- **Manufacturing Process Capabilities:** Work with and encourage suppliers to continuously produce quality items at a reasonable cost, and to reduce scrap caused by manufacturing process variation.

- **Planning Improvements:** Encourage suppliers to improve their planning process and effectively use the supplier schedules being provided to them. Know their bottlenecks and how they limit the supply of required materials.
- **Supplier Time Fences:** Negotiate, agree, and comply with the supplier's time fences. Agree on procedures to be followed in the event of an emergency when placing an order inside the time fences would be of benefit, but not without agreement of the supplier.
- **Agreed Supplier Improvements:** Review the progress of agreed improvement projects, offer support when necessary, and make sure projected results still match original objectives.
- **Net Item Quality Variations:** Validate that the specifications for a new material/part are being met and validate the supplier's ability to deliver the materials on time meeting quality requirements. Ensure that their capability is not confirmed on the basis of a single lot that has had quality inspected in.
- **Transportation Time:** Determine if transit time from the supplier is consistent and meets delivery dates consistently. Determine if it makes more sense for the company, rather than the supplier, to arrange and manage transportation.
- **Sourcing and Total Cost of Ownership:** Determine the total cost of ownership (TCO) for each item or service purchased. Agree to join continuous cost improvement initiatives to encourage long-term supplier relationships but be prepared to change suppliers in the event of a supplier's reluctance or failure to pursue continuous improvements.
- **Risk Mitigation:** Identify and prioritize supply-based risks; develop risk mitigation plans for execution in the event a risk materializes. Determine which procured items are single-sourced and develop an alternative in the event of a major outage. Determine which procured items are sole-sourced and make every effort to eliminate the need for that item in the company's products.
- **Supplier Contract Negotiations:** Since accurate future plans have been shared, allowing the supplier to better plan with fewer expedites, there is room for a price reduction reflecting efficiency improvements gained. Request the supplier to separate your pricing, including overhead, from other customers' pricing because of the improved planning information being provided.
- **Monitor Supplier Performance:** Quality, on-time delivery, price, and flexibility should all be part of supplier contracts. Monitor performance and host two-way review and feedback sessions for continuous improvement.

■ **Continuing Performance Issues:** Involves the supplier's Sales Representative when efforts of the MRP Planner to communicate and resolve continuing performance issues are unheeded.

Today's Buyer cannot be expected to be skilled in all these topics. Internal experts should accompany the Buyer in assessing supplier capabilities. The objective in these areas is to create a win-win partnership and long-term relationship.

Supplier collaboration is a key to business success across all functions of a company. This close relationship need not be developed for commodity suppliers or for suppliers who provide minor quantities once or twice per year, but these relationships are critical for major suppliers. The number of major suppliers should be reduced through consolidation and the relationships should become long-term to encourage supplier investments in improving quality and productivity. No supplier will invest in continuous improvement projects if they suspect you will offer their business to a competitor through annual contract negotiations.

Communication between customer and supplier must not be constrained by the need to funnel all company-to-company communications through the Buyer and the supplier's Sales Representative. Figure 13.4 shows how the

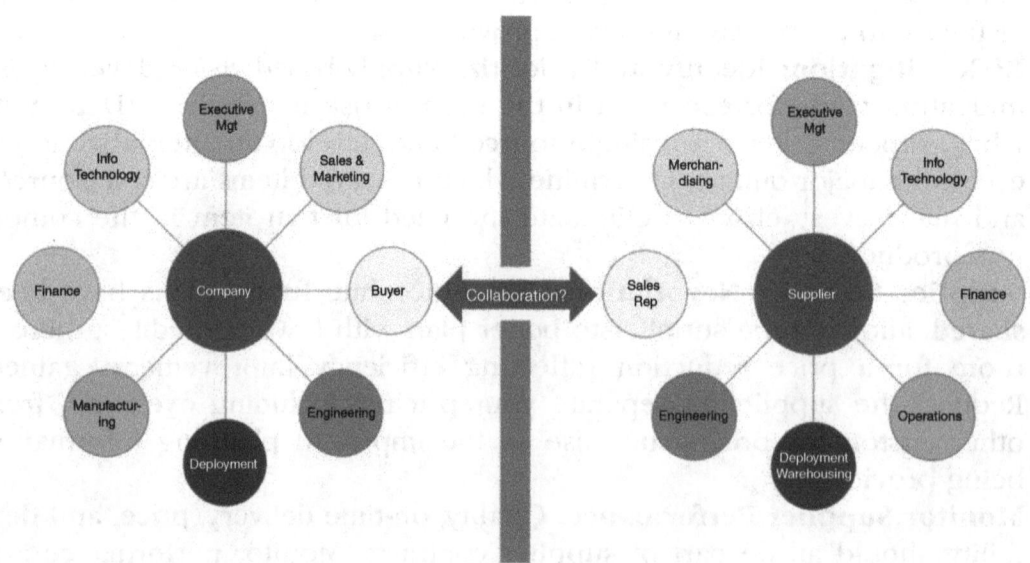

FIGURE 13.4 Typical Mature Relationship, Often Very Contractual

communication works typically and traditionally. This is a very formal and con-tractual relationship, based on legal agreements, not on mutual trust and under-standing. This communication model is slow and error prone since those who know the most about an issue's technical details are not often involved in direct communications with their counterparts in the other company. Issue resolution is often delayed because either the Buyer or Sales Representative is involved in other meetings or traveling to other locations.

Figure 13.5 shows the complete reversal. This model allows the right resources in each company to interact with each other to resolve issues quickly and cost effectively. The Buyer and Sales Representative retain key legal and contractual responsibilities and control, but the best and most appropriate technical resources are authorized to work directly to resolve issues and meet agreed objectives.

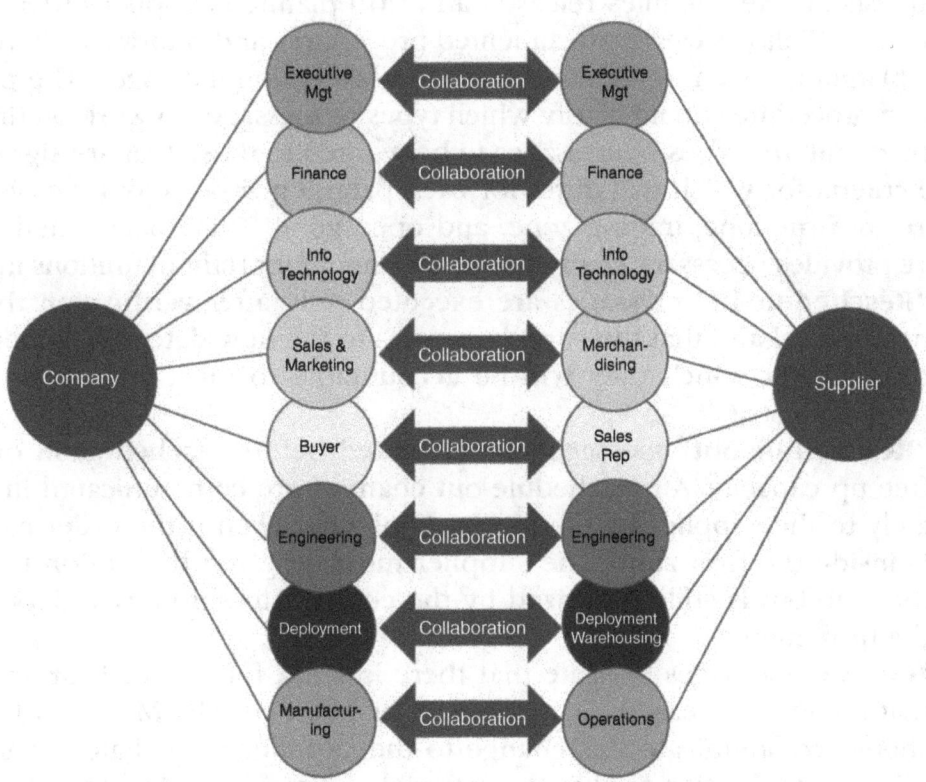

FIGURE 13.5 A Mature and Fully Collaborative Relationship

These two diagrams are often referred to as the "bow tie" and "diamond" approaches. See Chapter 14 for more on collaboration. The first example is the bow tie model in which all communication is between the Buyer and Sales Representative. In the diamond collaborative model, relationships exist in all functions and appropriate levels of both companies. The contract serves as a legal backstop should something unforeseen happen.

MRP Planner's Role

The MRP planner routinely:

- Runs and manages MRP for their assigned items.
- Releases firm planned orders and planned orders after quick review to confirm validity of planning system recommendations.
- Requests and reschedules released and firm planned supplier orders when necessary. Follows clearly documented procedures and priorities for working the planning system reschedule and other exception messages. The prioritization procedure should clarify which types of messages to work on first and should limit the types of messages to be worked to those that are significant, the criteria for which will differ for each planning zone across the planning horizon: firm zone, trading zone, and open zone. This documented procedure provides necessary clarity for the Planner. Important definitions include:
  - **"Reschedule-in"** messages are executed only after verification that the need is real and that the supplier agrees to the new date, which becomes the date for which they will be accountable to meet and to be measured against.
  - **"Reschedule-out"** messages are executed before reschedule-in ones to free up capacity. All reschedule-out changes are communicated immediately to the supplier by the materials planner even if the order changed is inside the firm zone. The supplier must be given the option to move the date but is still authorized by the contract to ship any orders inside the firm zone.
  - **"Cancel"** messages indicate that there is not a future need for an order that could be released, firm planned, or planned. The Materials Planner should communicate this change to the supplier immediately. The supplier has the option to ship the material and receive payment if the order is inside the firm zone.

- Conducts routine communications with the supplier's Master Schedulers and MRP Planners.
- Resolves minor, routine problems.
- Notifies the Buyer of issues that cannot be resolved, performance issues that continue despite the MRP Planner's efforts with the supplier, or regarding requested contract changes.

Buyer/Planner Concept

Some years ago great things were being said about combining the Buyer and MRP Planner roles into a single position called the Buyer/Planner. That combination was to enable one person to do the job of two. The roles of Sam, a client's steel and castings buyer, and Melvin, the client's steel and castings planner, were changed to make Sam the buyer/planner for steel and Melvin the buyer/planner for castings. The change proved to be a terrible mistake. Sam had built incredible rapport with the suppliers but was a less than competent planner. The steel supplier complained on occasion that the company's planning processes had deteriorated. Melvin was a great planner but, as one supplier said, "He has the personality and communications capability of a dead fish." That does not say that the Buyer/Planner position will never work but it requires combining significantly different capabilities into a single role and person and reduces the focus on each of those capabilities.

Expedite Loop

Even in the best Class A companies, things will still go wrong. The difference is not that things can go wrong, but that the frequency with which they go wrong is much lower. In most non-Class A companies, there is a never-ending stream of fires to be extinguished, which has become their norm, but Class A companies' fires are the exception. When things do go wrong, frequently or infrequently, the recovery must be as efficient and effective as possible. Let us follow a traditional expedite loop.

Traditional Expedite Loop
- MRP Planner to Buyer: "We need 100 more of item 1234 next week."
- Buyer to Planner: "Next week?! I will have to call the supplier."

- Buyer to Sales Representative: "Can we get 100 more of item 1234 next week?"
- Sales Representative to Buyer: "Really? Next week?! I do not know; I'll have to call our Master Scheduler."
- Sales Representative to Master Scheduler: "Can we get 100 more of item 1234 to our best customer next week?"
- Master Scheduler to Sales Representative: "Hang on; let me check. [Pause] No, but I can give them 50 next week and another 50 in two weeks. Will that work?"
- Sales Representative to Master Scheduler: "Uh-oh. I do not know. I will have to call their Buyer and see if that works."
- Sales Representative to Buyer: "I cannot give you 100 next week, but I can get you 50 next week and another 50 in two weeks. Will that work?"
- Buyer to Sales Representative: "That's not good news. I do not know; I'll have to talk with our MRP Planner."
- Buyer to MRP Planner: "The supplier cannot get you 100 next week but can get you an extra 50 next week and another 50 in two weeks. Will that work?"
- MRP Planner to Buyer: "Hang on, let me check. [Pause] Yep, I can make that work."
- Buyer to MRP Planner: "Okay, I'll tell them to go ahead and give us the 50 and the second 50 in two weeks."
- Buyer to Sales Representative: "Okay."
- Sales Representative to Master Scheduler: "Okay. Send them 50 next week and the other 50 in two weeks."

And how long did that take? It all depends on whether people are available and the necessary information is at hand when phones ring. In some companies it could be a week. No wonder there are so many shortages.

Direct Approach with Available to Promise

- MRP Planner to Supplier's Order Entry Associate: "Can we get 100 more of item 1234 next week?"
- Order Entry Associate to MRP Planner: "Let me check the Available to Promise (ATP) quantity. [Pause] "Good news. No, but I can give 50 next week and 50 the week after. Will that work?"
- MRP planner to Order Entry Associate: "Yes. Thank you so much."

A one-minute communication; it is done!

Direct Approach without Available to Promise

- MRP Planner to the Supplier's Order Entry Associate: "We have an unplanned order. Can we get 100 more of item 1234 next week?"
- Order Entry Associate to MRP Planner: "I'm not able to get ATP information until we finish implementing our new planning system, but let me check with my Master Scheduler."
- Order Entry Associate to Supplier's Master Scheduler with the Supplier's MRP Planner on the call: "Can we get our best customer 100 more of item 1234 next week?"
- Supplier's Master Scheduler to Supplier's Order Entry Associate and MRP Planner: "Unfortunately, I cannot get 100 next week but can get 50 next week and another 50 in two weeks. Will that work?"
- MRP Planner to Master Scheduler and Supplier's Order Entry Associate: "Hang on a minute; let me check my operating schedule. [Pause] Yep, that works well for us."

A three-minute communication; it is done!

Many company Procurement organizations will say that direct communication with supplier will not work, or that they cannot do things that way. Many Buyers are not confident in the plans being developed or in their operating departments' capabilities to execute those plans, and, beyond that, they resist giving up that responsibility. Therein lies the major problem with many corporate initiatives in changing the culture and procedures being suggested in this book. People resist change; the challenge is in getting them to accept change. Hmmm, seems like we have discussed this before. People, processes, and then, and only then, tool and technology. Provide them education on the new processes; empower a core team of educated personnel to design the new processes; and then put in the technology configured to support those new processes as well as the discipline to follow them. Who should do the design? *Following education*, process owners and leaders design the new processes with coaching from a few outside experts who have personally experienced the transformation and then have experience coaching others on their journey to Class A. Never ask or allow outside resources to complete the designs; those who must follow the new processes will not embrace them, will design their own variations of the processes, and will never be vested in making them work.

Sourcing and Supplier Performance Measures

As in all other chapters, this topic has a variety of useful measures, listed below in order of importance:

- **Quality:** If the product received does not meet quality standards, the product has not been received! Even if the quality defects are caught during incoming inspection, churn begins immediately. Hopefully, you have progressed beyond this maturity level with your suppliers. By the time the supplier replaces the defective materials, there will be a production interruption if you are running Lean as has been suggested. Carrying safety stock at either your site or theirs represents waste. Of course, a worse outcome, at more than 10 times the cost of finding the defects during incoming inspection, is to use the defective materials to build finished products and have those products fail in the field. Meeting all quality standards is a key part of the contract negotiated by the Buyer and is the Buyer's responsibility to enforce, supported by the Quality Department, as discussed earlier. The Quality Department should participate in determining how to measure the suppliers' quality performance.

- **On-Time-In-Full Delivery (OTIFD):** This is a critical measure. A minimum of 95% of all shipments are expected to be received on time at the last agreed due date within time tolerance (could be a day or two early as agreed, but never late), in full within quantity tolerance (as agreed to allow for full pallets or drums, for example) and meeting all quality requirements. Many companies protect against late deliveries by carrying safety stock at their manufacturing sites or at their suppliers' sites. This is an expensive way to mask planning problems and never resolve them. Find the root causes and fix the problems. The same OTIFD measure should be used for suppliers and for production operations (see Managing Internal Manufacturing Priorities, Chapter 11). As performance improves, the measure can be tightened to On-Time-In-Full to Promise (OTIFP) and then tightened again to the most desirable measure, On-Time-In-Full to Request (OTIFR).

- **Unit Landed Cost:** The total unit cost of a supplier's materials is listed as third in this list but is considered by many companies as the most important measure, and, too often, the exclusive criterion for awarding business. Contracting the least expensive materials that have quality problems or do not run efficiently in the production operation can end up increasing product cost. Material cost is impacted by countless factors but can be reduced significantly through application of all the recommendations presented in this chapter.

- **Lead Time:** Reducing supplier lead time will significantly improve MRP and supplier schedule accuracy and take much of the uncertainty out of Demand Planning in the firm and trading zones.
- **Supplier Reaction Time:** Nearly all companies place great value on a supplier's ability to respond to short-notice changes. Suppliers know this and, as a result, often overstate their lead times, potentially making this measure less than meaningful especially early in a relationship with a new supplier. Including key supplier resources as part of the Resource Requirements Planning and Rough-Cut Capacity Planning processes allows capacity constraints to be identified well in advance, enabling a supplier to commit to reserving the required capacity. Another problem difficult to recognize is a reduction of a supplier's response time when the supplier sells more of its capacity to other customers. The Buyer must understand all suppliers' capacity strategies, another good reason for consolidating the number of material suppliers.

Summary

This chapter has described Unparalleled Planning and Execution Practices for Procurement organizations. A summary of the key points follows:

- **Valid Schedules:** Schedules must be accurate and achievable.
- **Buyer Support:** A Buyer cannot be expected to know in detail all the company's functions or scheduling details, so support from those in other functions and departments is essential in assisting the Buyer in discovering and resolve problems that have not been resolved by the Supplier.
- **Supply Chain Streamlining:** Continuously drive waste out of the Supply Chain. A nearly infinitesimal amount of time is spent actually transforming raw and packaging materials into finished products compared to the amount of time between materials being received by the suppliers' suppliers and shipped to the end customers. The rest of that time represents waste. Apply value stream mapping and lean techniques to eliminate all types of waste, such as the expedite loop described earlier. Measure and track progress.
- **Education:** The first step in changing the way people think and behave is process education. That must start internally at the top of the organization (remember that culture change flows downhill) and then move on to the

suppliers. The best people to conduct supplier education are the Buyers and other company process experts who are open, honest, and very knowledgeable. Suppliers always appreciate the attention and information, and they recognize, because of the education, that they are viewed as a valued part of the Supply Chain. Determine which internal roles and which external supplier associates should receive this education and track the percentage of those who have received the education.

- **Measures:** Measures to track performance and identify gaps to plan are essential, but measuring without corrective action is a waste of time. No supplier can change its results instantly any more than a customer can, but if their behaviors do not change and the results do not begin to improve, there must be consequences.

- **Implementation Plan:** Developing the appropriate plan requires an initial assessment of current practices against Unparalleled Business Planning and Execution Practices in order to determine how best to focus change efforts. Make sure the implementation team includes one or more people, or external coaches, who have significant experience and who have personally experienced the transformation on a journey to Class A.

For more information on quality see:

Dr. W. Edwards Deming, *The Essential Deming: Leadership Principles from the Father of Quality* (McGraw-Hill, 2013)

Dr. Joseph M. Juran, *Quality Control Handbook* (McGraw-Hill, 1951, OCLC 1220529)

For additional but more specific reading please visit the Oliver Wight Website and gain access to the extensive library of White Papers.

CHAPTER 14

Supply Chain: Ensuring There Is End-to-End Flow

In the previous chapters, we have discussed how to establish world class planning and execution practices in various Supply Nodes. This enables them to quickly improve to perform individually and sustain that performance

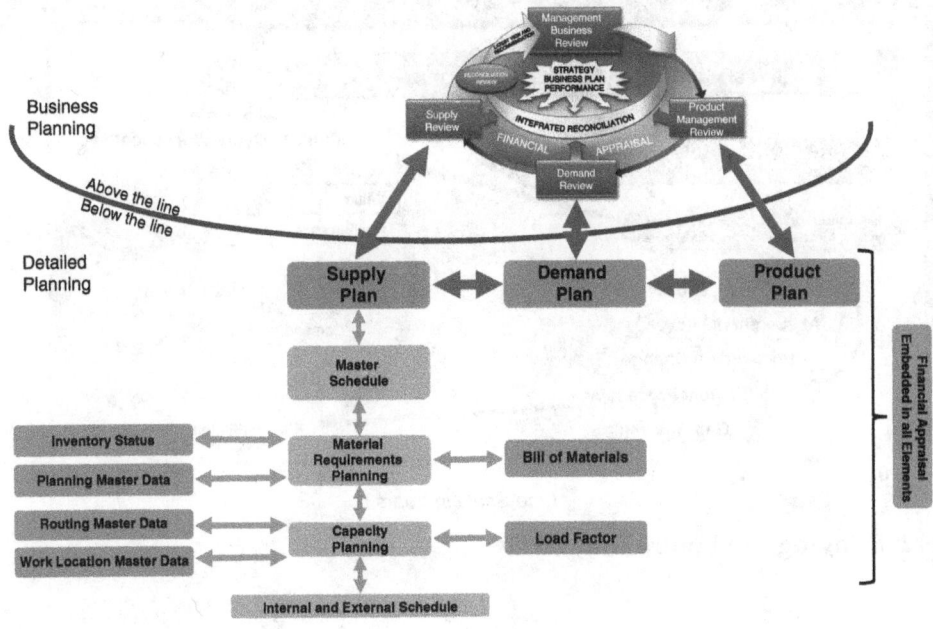

FIGURE 14.1 Business Excellence Planning

at a high level. The focus now is to ensure that these Supply Nodes are not left as independent activities but are built into an integrated Supply Chain that ensures flow is established to deliver or exceed customer requirements. A Supply Chain, therefore, requires all the elements shown in Figure 14.1, Business Excellence Planning, to be fully integrated and requires measurement to identify how yield changes through the Supply Chain can highlight further improvement opportunities.

Strategically Driven

The design of your Supply Chain must be aligned with your overall strategy and must not be built in isolation to ensure that it reflects market and product needs today and in the future. Figure 14.2, Bringing the Future into Today, shows that the 5- or 10-plus-year Strategic Plan must be supported by Driving and Supporting Roadmaps to ensure the right level of granularity is available for planning by all supporting functional organizations.

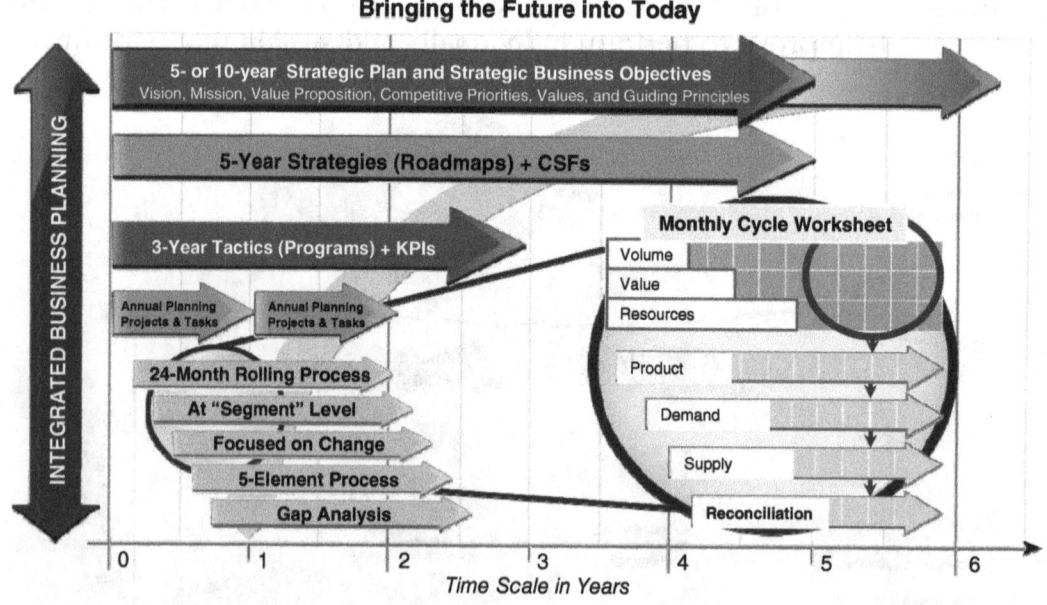

FIGURE 14.2 Bringing the Future into Today

As mentioned in Chapter 9, there are Driving Roadmaps (Sales and Marketing; Product and Portfolio; Supply Chain and Finance) and Supporting Roadmaps (Human Resources; Information Technology; Quality and Legal) that must be developed through a process of one building off the other to ensure complete integration and a common direction.

The Supply Chain Roadmap is built from an understanding of the Sales and Marketing plus Product and Portfolio Roadmaps; taken together, they explain how the market will develop and, as a result, how the company's offerings must change over time. This Roadmap ensures the Supply Team will understand where they are playing, who they are playing with (customers and competitors) and what they are playing with (Products and Services today and in the future) so they can best design the organization structure needed to best supply customers over time. The design details must incorporate global, regional, and local Supply organizations.

Supply Chains require significant time to establish and/or change because of the many resources included. Additionally, a clear understanding is needed of current Business Maturity (see Chapter 1), including:

1. How well defined is the strategy? Is it just a simple Vision and Mission that has been communicated poorly, or is there an Integrated Strategic Plan with Integrated Roadmaps clearly defining the future and Strategic Business Objectives (SBOs) driven by documented Critical Success Factors (CSFs) in the Roadmaps?
2. Your current Business Maturity. Is it:
   a. "Eyes Down and Look In"?
   b. "Eyes Up and Look Out"?
3. Your customer base and how well you will be able to predict their needs now and into the future, and what level of collaboration is possible (see later section).
4. Your competition and its impact on your market or market segments, their level of Supply sophistication, and whether that competition is on price, customer intimacy, or product leadership.
5. How well your product and service offering has been developed. Is it adequately competitive? Does it reflect your customers' needs now and into the future?

Understanding your maturity and the maturity of environment elements and activities that impact your business will enable design of your Supply Chain and how it must evolve over time to remain cost effective, competitive, and attractive to your customer base.

Elements and Activities to Be Considered When Designing a Supply Chain

Figure 14.3 shows the types of elements and activities that must be considered when defining a Supply Chain. Some of these are physical and must be aligned to enable flow from your suppliers through to your customers and/or consumers.

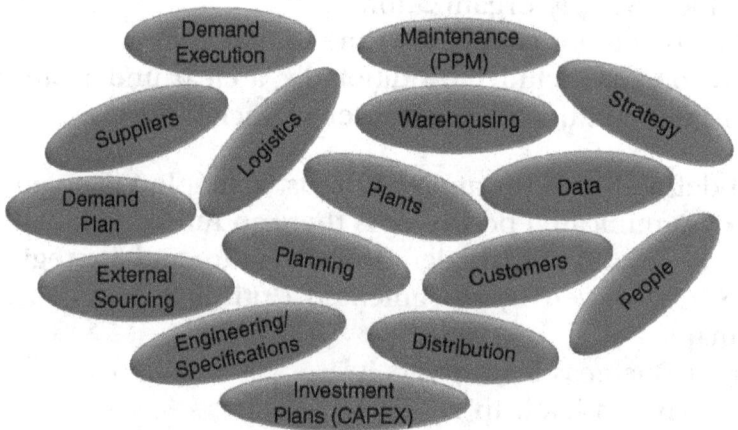

FIGURE 14.3 Activities to Be Considered When Designing a Supply Chain

It goes without saying that a picture like Figure 14.3 will not enable flow and will encourage more independent, rather than integrated, activity. All too often, when visiting companies for the first time, we find a very haphazard and unsynchronized Supply Chain and, in fact, often hear Procurement referred to as the Supply Chain.

Activities shown in Figure 14.3 are often referred to as Nodes/Supply Points, which are the elements included in building a Supply Chain. Figure 14.4 shows the evolution of Supply Chain designs from simple Supply Management to more complex fully integrated Advanced Supply Chain. The Supply Chain and Advanced Supply Chain designs would often be referred to as the Extended Supply Chain or the End-to-End Supply Chain. Both have the aim of enabling flow and integration from the suppliers to the customers.

In addition, there is an incredible amount of waste at each Supply Chain interface, both between Supply Chain partners and at each internal interface inside each Supply Chain partner. It is therefore very important to carefully design a fully integrated Supply Chain from the supplier's suppliers through to customer's customers. The entirety of this book addresses how to make that happen.

Activities identified in Figure 14.3 that are left to operate as independent activities or Nodes/Supply Points are challenged since many of the activities should be integrated to perform more effectively and with flow. This leads to multiple sets of numbers and different agendas and will often lead to firefighting or churn. It is for this reason companies authorize a journey to design and implement a fully integrated End-to-End Supply Chain that enables the flow of information from the customers through all Nodes/Supply Points and back. Doing so enables the flow of Product or Service deliveries from suppliers to the customers/consumers.

Figure 14.4 starts with a very simple supply activity that has been termed Supply Management. In this design, there are just two Nodes/Supply Points, Tier 1 Suppliers and Primary Production, supplied with some very basic Demand Information to initial Planning. In this context the Supply Management aspect is focused on the internal capability of the Node/Supply Point to deliver to its Demand Requirements. Consequently, at this level of maturity not all aspects shown in Figure 14.3 are integrated; they become more relevant as the Supply Chain design expands.

On such a journey, the next level of maturity has been termed Basic Supply Chain, which has an additional Node/Supply Point representing basic integration with the primary customers. This design enables collaboration with the customer and results in a much deeper understanding of the market, not just some incidental demand information. This level of maturity results in "one set of numbers," a shared agenda and performance generally at 95% capability levels. All processes would be mapped and followed, with most improvement activities coming from the formal use of continuous improvement tools and with the occasional application of Lean methodologies.

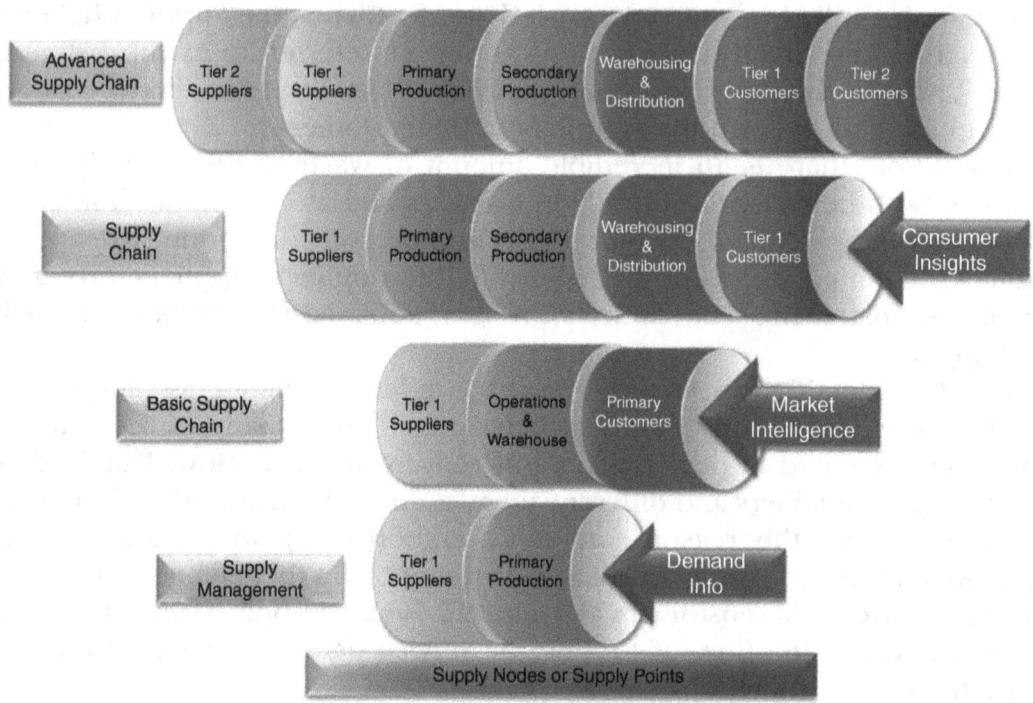

FIGURE 14.4 The Evolution of Supply Chain Models

Source: © Oliver Wight International.

A more fully defined Supply Chain, which is the first step to being an Extended or End-to-End Supply Chain, is next enabled with the introduction of Warehouse and Distribution and the integration of both Primary and Secondary Production organizations. Consumer insights further expand market intelligence and, hence, the ability of all Nodes/Supply Points to understand their market challenges through this information flowing from right to left. A shared understanding of consumer and customer needs enables delivery to then flow from left to right in an integrated response to that improved market intelligence. Clearly, the design complexity is increasing, but the maturity of processes, systems, and people is much higher and, consequently, the organization begins seeking simplification and accelerated response. This level enables a cost-effective response to unexpected demands through the systemic deployment of Lean and Agility methodologies.

The addition of Tier 2 suppliers and customers completes the Advanced Supply Chain design. It fully integrates all the elements identified in Figure 14.3

into a logical End-to-End Flow with each Node/Supply Point working for the respective needs of the next. In this environment, effective communication and information sharing is a given, often enabling even better collaboration (see later). It is fair to say that some examples of this level of collaboration are enabled as well by the previous Supply Chain design. This final design is now a full Extended Supply Chain or End-to-End Supply Chain with all relevant elements and activities fully integrated, enabling both the flow of information and data along with the delivery of products and services.

Why do we recommend that companies embark on establishing a Supply Chain? Because the benefits to be gained include:

1. Improved integration and a move from individually managed functions and departments.
2. Improved collaboration leading to better understanding, shared direction, and shared goals.
3. The uninterrupted flow of information and data and flow of product and services.
4. Improved performance and quality:
   a. On-time delivery.
   b. Significantly reduced scrap rates and rework in all Supply Chain Nodes.
   c. Improved final product quality delivered to the customer.
   d. Customer complaint resolution because of less rework and schedule churn.
   e. Results visibility throughout, for example, Supplier Quality Assessments.
5. Higher efficiency and productivity due to availability of accurate data. Today, more and more is in real time, so efficiencies are even higher.
6. Keeping up with demand and sharing actual customer requirements throughout the Supply Chain, enabling better inventory control across the Supply Chain, and elimination of demand amplification or the "bullwhip" effect.
7. Reduced overhead costs due to reduced inventory, improved flow, better utilization of assets, and suppliers with strategies and investments aligned to the overall goals.
8. Improved risk mitigation since the Supply Chain is proactive as opposed to reactive. Having valid (accurate and achievable) and shared data throughout enables each Supply Chain Node to respond in alignment with the overall strategy and goals.
9. Improved cash flow: The above benefits allow companies to make better decisions, select the right partners, understand the market/customers and

demand changes, and reduce Supply Chain disruptions. All of this means the bottom line will improve – significantly. For example, partnering with more reliable suppliers not only means fewer disruptions and more satisfied customers, but it also improves cash flow by allowing more immediate invoicing.

The descriptions in Figure 14.4 are very high level but provide insight into the opportunities available to companies when they are considering their Supply Chain design and capabilities. However, we must also recognize the need for segmentation of the portfolio and how the Supply Chain can be then viewed with this deeper understanding of the market in mind. Supply Chain design has been mentioned on several occasions; to explore this in a little more depth to further explore Supply Chain design, we must consider the following design considerations.

Supply Chain Design Considerations

Figure 14.5 illustrates that the Supply Chain design must satisfy specific needs of the marketplace it is servicing and how it must differentiate and respond to changes.

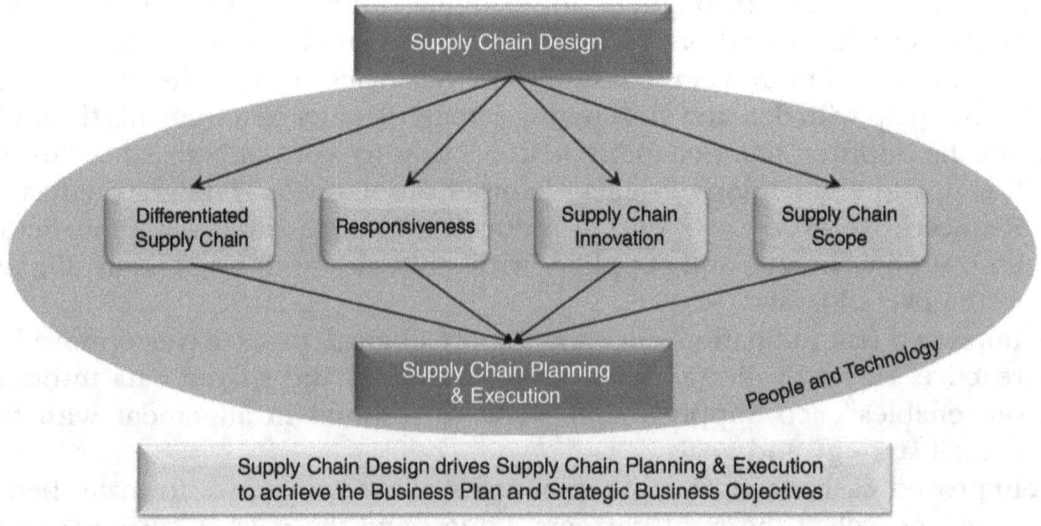

FIGURE 14.5 Supply Chain Design Considerations

Supply Chain Scope: In a way this has already been covered in Figure 14.3 as the activities required to design a successful Supply Chain. The design problems encountered are based on how these activities developed historically within your company and how the managers respond to changes in their reporting lines. The old saying "Turkeys do not vote for Christmas" is similar to responses encountered when moving from disparate activities to fully integrated activities. This kind of defensive response by the managers of different activities is normally more prevalent in organizations with lower levels of maturity, understanding, and knowledge.

When the new Supply Chain scope has been established and agreed, it is then possible to redesign how the included activities/organizations relate and integrate.

Supply Chain Responsiveness: A responsive Supply Chain is, of course, what all customers and companies desire, but the degree of responsiveness must be based on the right reasons and the right investment (cost, capital expenditure [CAPEX], people, etc.). Understanding your market expectations and your current capability is essential when considering the proposed responsiveness. Lower levels of Supply Chain maturity impact the ability to respond and usually result in firefighting because too many customer-requested changes are being received. But is this true? Are the requests really customer-induced or are they the result of poor visibility of their needs?

- **Planning Horizon:** Too near-term to see trends and enable timely decisions.
- **Internal Problems**: The "Eyes Down Look In" scenario in which all of Leadership's attention is focused internally and very near-term. This compresses the organization and limits or even eliminates Leadership's ability to make decisions about future trends.
- **Limited Customer Information:** When a customer always hears "of course" when in truth you do not know how something will get done, they will receive a message that you have infinite capacity and cost-effective agility. The consequence: they do not believe you need a forecast and therefore do not supply one. If they do provide a forecast, they will not worry about its accuracy.
- **Fragmented Supply Chain Design:** As previously mentioned, instead of Nodes and Supply Points working together, they tend to work more independently and may use different demand signals.

▪ **Process Velocity:** Again, with low levels of maturity, processes are often not documented. If they are, they are poorly integrated. Generally, there is a huge "people" dependency on what, when, and how things get done. When processes have not been mapped or correctly integrated it is impossible to Value Stream Map and focus on improving process velocity.

▪ **People, Teamwork, and Capability:** Underpinning everything is the most important asset: your people. If they have not received education and training, how can their individual and team-based capability be expected to improve and provide the right solutions? Processes do not map and improve themselves.

So, to implement the required responsiveness, it is vital that these issues are resolved, and Supply Chain redesign initiated to enable an integrated End-to-End capability approaching the Supply Chain structure shown in Figure 14.4.

To implement a cost-effective response, it is important to understand the relationship between Lean and Agility, which is explained in Chapter 15. Lean is about the elimination of waste to improve process velocity, and Agility is the use of this Lean capability to respond to unexpected/unanticipated customer demands. In addition, Agility may also require assets such as spare capacity (people and equipment), strategically held inventory, equipment that does multiple operations with no set up, and plans with time included for unforeseen issues to deliver the desired response. These are just a few examples of how Agility can be achieved.

Control Towers

Another consideration is the whole organization being associated with the Planning activity; is it best to keep it local or should it be reorganized into Control Towers to maximize the ability to flex between individual facilities, countries, or regions?

A Control Tower is a centralized hub with the appropriate people, processes, and technology to capture, analyze, and use Supply Chain data to provide short, medium-, and long-term information to support decision-making. The need for this End-to-End visibility is being driven by the increased complexity Supply Chains need to handle through increased globalization but with the same pressure to deliver increased revenues and profit. Typically, they are designed to monitor, measure, and manage transport and inventory movements and how these transactions have been planned across the End-to-End Supply Chain.

The use of Control Towers needs to be carefully thought through and should be aligned to the Supply Chain Roadmap to ensure it fully aligns with the overall Strategic Plan, and the Roadmaps developed for Commercial and Product and Portfolio. The considerations are:

1. Where do you sit in the overall End-to-End Supply Chain and what influence do you have?
2. What is your current Business Maturity and readiness of adjacent Nodes/ Supply Points to respond?
3. What flexibility need is required to more cost-effectively deliver, and can the other Nodes/Supply Points support that flex need?
4. How are you structured/should be structured globally, regionally, or locally?
5. Do you have the right level of system integration and use to capitalize on a Planning Tower approach?
6. Do you have the right people available to execute through a Planning Tower, and if not, how can they be obtained? Through recruitment, education and training, or a combination of both?

The use of Control Towers can certainly deliver advantages and need to be carefully thought through to ensure the design implemented meets market and customer needs but also the aspirations of the business based on Strategic Business Objectives (SBOs) and the supporting Critical Success Factors (CSFs).

As Supply Chains become more complex, they are more like global networks rather than an End-to-End linear Supply Chain. Complexity increases as more activities are outsourced to secure better prices to help the drive to improve margins. This introduces more risks and drives the need to make decisions, in all business horizons, quickly. So, one of the main benefits that Control Towers bring is increased visibility of data, which in turn means greater control and improved decision-making capability, which helps to minimize Supply Chain risk.

Implementing Control Towers is not an easy journey, as you need to ensure that information is real time to get the benefits required from quick decisions; this is why you need to carefully think through the previous six considerations.

Supply Chain Innovation: When it comes to Supply Chain innovation, we generally mean improvements in the way that Supply Chains operate, and, more specifically, in the way that products, information, work, and funds flow throughout the Supply Chain.

So, why care about Supply Chain innovation? *To identify a competitive advantage that will differentiate your capabilities from those of your competitors.* Leaders of world-class organizations realize that process differentiation is more sustainable than product differentiation because products are more easily copied and/or reverse engineered.

Supply chain processes that integrate multiple Nodes/Supply Points and focus significantly on the flow of product, information, and finance can be complex and require a collaborative environment to be sustainable and successful. Future-proofed investments provide significant cost savings and improved customer service through the Nodes/Supply Points, as they all drive to support the End-to-End Supply Chain strategy. The benefits of these improvements, once proven to be sustainable, can be passed on to the customers and used to demonstrate your competitive advantage.

How do you drive ideation on this? Ideas are needed to create a pool of opportunities that can then be authorized as innovative projects. To drive ideas, it is essential to gain an understanding of your customers' requirements. Armed with these insights and the implementation of formal integrated processes, the Supply Chain can work as a multifunctional team to realize these improvements and drive cost and delivery improvements.

Supply Chain Differentiation: What is the definition – what does this really mean? Definitions are vital in any company for all aspects of their business, and it is no different for Supply. Supply Chain Differentiation means the execution of an individual (unique) Supply Chain for a specific market segment to ensure that customers within that market segment are provided the service required to meet or exceed their business and strategic needs.

In doing this, the Supply Chain becomes focused on each market segment and the customers that segment includes. The Supply Chain is thereby differentiated from the competition as customer-specific delivery solutions are enabled.

Customers continue to become more and more sophisticated with their demand requirements and are requesting more focused and unique services. Concurrently, technology developments are shortening life cycles, and global reach is restructuring the face of competition. Competing in a highly competitive, knowledgeable, and dynamic environment requires more innovative and tailored business approaches.

The question is how to determine the differentiation required, and then how that differentiation is to be implemented. With an "Eyes Down Look In" maturity, this is more difficult; you do not yet have the capability to truly understand your markets, competition, and customers. Essentially, this reactive approach must be transformed into a more proactive capability, which takes time; the balance of this book identifies how Unparalleled Business Planning and Execution Practices should be deployed to progressively enable sustainable Supply Chain Differentiation, but at the right time.

People: Moving from independently managed Supply Chain activities, such as those shown in Figure 14.3, is a big deal for Leadership, Management, and Employees. The effort required must not be underestimated because Leadership ownership for the new Supply Chain approach is essential for sustainability and success. Chapter 17 covers the people and behavior aspects in more detail, but for a Supply Chain to become truly End-to-End and Integrated, people from many different Nodes or Supply Points must work as an aligned team.

As Chapter 18 explains, there are different people challenges with different levels of maturity. However, for a Supply Chain there may be added complexity in that there may be Nodes or Supply Points working in the same flow but having different maturity levels.

Defining and implementing a strategy to move to a Supply Chain or Advanced Supply Chain design is essential to ensure that all involved understand the intent and the process so that buy-in and ownership can begin.

Leaders, Managers, and Employees must share the same understanding of what is required, which is best achieved through tailored education and application workshops designed to explain the current market and customer challenges and those into the future, and how the business must evolve to enable continued business success.

This new knowledge must be captured in the company's documented policies, processes, and procedures to ensure that it is sustainable, shared, and available for periodic audit and continuous improvement.

If we do not empower our people, how do we expect to improve and maintain a competitive advantage?

Technology: To enable successful Supply Chain management, it is imperative that suitable software is acquired and correctly implemented to ensure all

Supply Chain aspects are integrated and easily controlled. The types of software functionality required include:

1. Customer Requirements Planning (CRM)
2. Purchase Order Processing
3. Sales and Distribution
4. Inventory Management
5. Goods Receipt and Warehouse Management
6. Supplier Management/Procurement (External Sourcing)

Additionally, there is also a requirement to integrate forecasting software to ensure that customer demands are captured and accurately presented for Supply Chain Planning. However, it must be remembered that the software has to reflect the carefully developed Demand Planning processes, explained in Chapter 10, which are used to specify the software functionality.

There is also a requirement for tight integration with finance software, which is generally available with most current Supply Chain Management software packages. This provides complete integration for Accounts Payable, Accounts Receivable, and the General Ledger.

Additionally, there must be consideration for the information requirements of Integrated Business Planning and how all relevant information to support the Supply Review can be made available monthly with minimal manual inputs.

What Are the Key Pitfalls?

It is fair to reflect on the many Supply Chains that we have seen and assessed over the years. Many of them have evolved over time because of poor delivery and performance issues experienced; they have not developed "because of."

By "because of" we mean the following design aspects have not been fully thought through, communicated, and tested prior to embarking on the design:

1. Having a very clear and deployed strategy, supported by a Roadmap.
2. Ensuring that the Operating Model is fit for purpose.
3. Having KPIs that are structured in a Measures Hierarchy to ensure alignment and continuous improvement.
4. Ensuring that the Nodes/Supply Points have the resilience to sustain their performance.

5. Investigating the emerging Supply Network costs to ensure they are acceptable.
6. Understanding customer needs now and into the future.

What Is Required for Supply Chain Excellence?

Figure 14.6 highlights what is required to enable Supply Chain excellence. Consequently, when developing a transformation journey to redesign a Supply Chain, these aspects must be present and designed for the specific needs of your market, customers, and business aspirations. Each of the elements shown must be carefully thought through to ensure that the Supply Chain will create a flow that benefits both the customer and the business; reduced costs benefit all parties. Profitability, like inventory, is a consequence of how well the entire business is integrated and how well these integrated processes perform. So, if inventory and profitability are a consequence, then it is essential to focus on the processes, performances, and improvement opportunities that deliver them.

The elements listed in Figure 14.6 are discussed in more detail in the remaining chapters, but this figure does represent the importance of having a

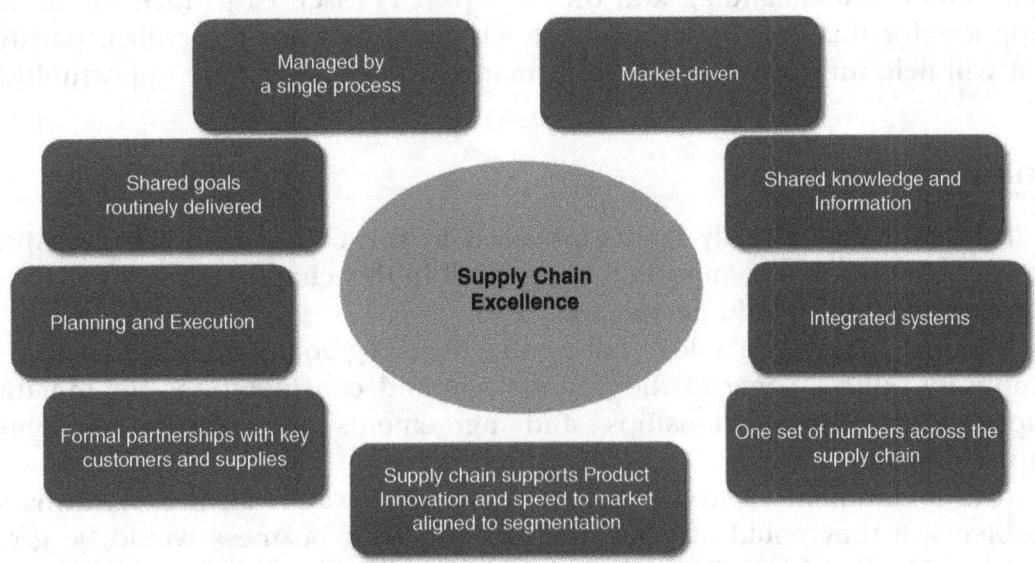

FIGURE 14.6 What Is Required for Supply Chain Excellence?

holistic capability both internally and through the other Nodes/Supply Points within the Supply Chain.

There is a saying that a Supply Chain is only as fast as its slowest part or can only deliver at the output dictated by the weakest element. This introduces the concept of "demonstrated performance" in the Supply Chain and the need to improve those Nodes/Supply Points that reduce its overall performance. Only when this is accomplished can the plan output be increased. In the section on measures, later, "Supply Chain Yield" is introduced as the applicable yield measure for a Supply Chain.

Supply Chain information flow is just as important as Supply Chain product flow. Consequently, development of more beneficial and competitive collaborative agreements is essential in continually improving relationships and resulting benefits for all Supply Chain partners. Collaborative maturity is discussed later in this chapter and identifies the steps required to potentially enable Collaborative Planning and Forecast Replenishment (CPFR).

With improved relationships and better supplier alignment to customers' strategic direction and goals, it becomes easier to implement a Segmented Supply Chain to better service specific markets and the customers therein. To achieve this alignment, there must be a well-communicated, deployed, and believable strategy to which all Supply Chain partners have contributed to ensure their understanding and ownership. It is essential to identify the key suppliers for this collaboration; those suppliers that are the critical partners that will help improve delivery performance and enable future opportunities.

Collaboration

Collaboration has already been discussed in the External Sourcing chapter; however, we think it is important to revisit it in this chapter to view collaboration from a supply chain perspective.

There are many available Collaborative Planning books, so this brief section simply introduces some of the key aspects and considerations for initiating improvements in relationships and agreements throughout the entire Supply Chain.

It is a commonly stated belief that customers cause all the performance problems; if they could just get their act together, business would be great. Honesty is painful but the reality is that you first need to get your own act together before having a realistic opportunity to influence up and down the Supply Chain. But who should be influenced first? Again, there is more to be gained through a focus on key suppliers first, as shown in Figure 14.7 through the spotlight numbered "1st." The light first shines on your own in-house issues and then on those of the suppliers; this is depicted by the light being in two shades of gray.

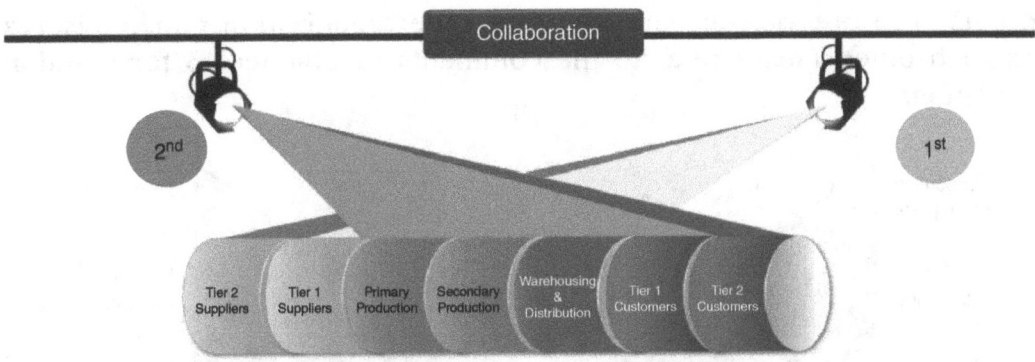

FIGURE 14.7 Where to Focus First to Initiate Collaboration

Having looked back into the Supply Chain it would then be possible to take these demonstrated improvements to the customers, who will now be more likely to listen, and work with them to improve the flow and quality of their information on future requirements. This process of focusing back and then forward continues as the Supply Chain's maturity gradually improves over time.

Collaboration requires a significant investment in time and effort between the Nodes and Supply Points to enable sufficient development of trust and better sharing and use of reliable information. Why is this so important and what will be the benefits? They are potentially significant and must be equally attractive to all parties. So, why invest in collaboration?

1. Improve communication and understanding
2. Agree on performance expectations
3. Improve forecasting
4. Reduce inventories
5. Improve service levels
6. Improve quality
7. Increase trust

Improving the relationship between two organizations is best achieved when more people in each organization are encouraged to communicate and build mutually beneficial working relationships. Traditionally, relationships between Nodes/Supply Points were defined through contracts and follow-on contract management activities. This relationship was limited to contact between a Buyer and a Salesperson, as shown in Figure 14.8. This design is often referred to as a "bow-tie," since the touchpoint for each organization is one person to one person. The balance of the organization remains isolated from each other. Please refer to the comments in Chapter 13 for additional information.

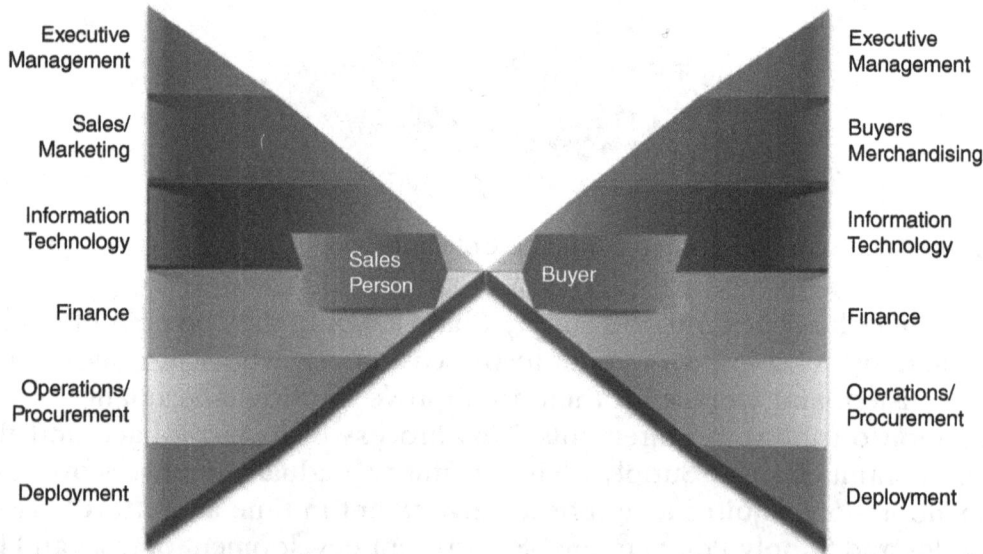

FIGURE 14.8 Bow-Tie Collaboration

To gain better insight, greater understanding, build better relationships, enable the two organizations to build trust, and achieve the benefits of effective collaboration, the above representation must be completely reversed to represent a "diamond" design, as shown in Figure 14.9.

The diamond design enables conversations and information sharing at all organizational levels and in all functions. As we know, we can often receive quite different and conflicting information from the various levels and functions, especially in the early days of a relationship. Hearing those different perspectives is not a bad thing, providing there is a process to highlight and

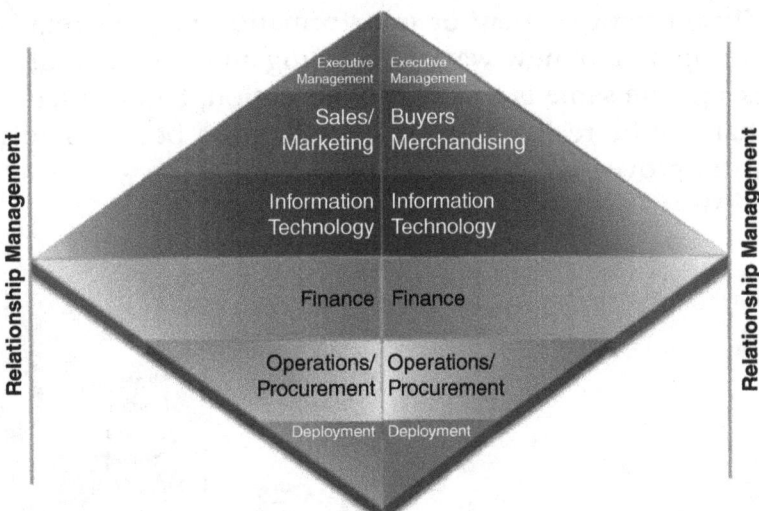

FIGURE 14.9 Diamond Collaboration

resolve them or understand the different perspectives. Quite commonly, the cause is a simple misunderstanding.

The primary objective of the diamond is to establish the required trust between two organizations. This can be more difficult if there has been a history of conflict and mistrust. If that is the case, a third-party facilitator can be very useful in breaking the ice and opening the conversations required to begin building that trust.

To initiate a "collaboration journey," there must be a burning desire between the respective Leadership Teams of adjacent Nodes/Supply Points. Without this drive and understanding, the journey will stall. Leadership must make the decision to commit to building the right relationship to enable a more productive environment, which is typically successful when the collaboration effort is contractual. Required elements of such a contract include:

1. Agreed Values.
2. Realistic Vision, shared and well communicated.
3. Realistic and energizing Strategies and Goals, shared and agreed.
4. Leaders who are skilled in empowering their organizations.
5. Leaders who want to learn and want others to learn, share knowledge and experience.
6. An understanding of desired mutual benefits.

Any significant improvement or transformation process requires a journey to ensure development of new ways of working and sustainability of those new ways of working. The same is true for collaboration; Figure 14.10 identifies the transitions that will be realized as the collaboration between adjacent Nodes/ Supply Points improves.

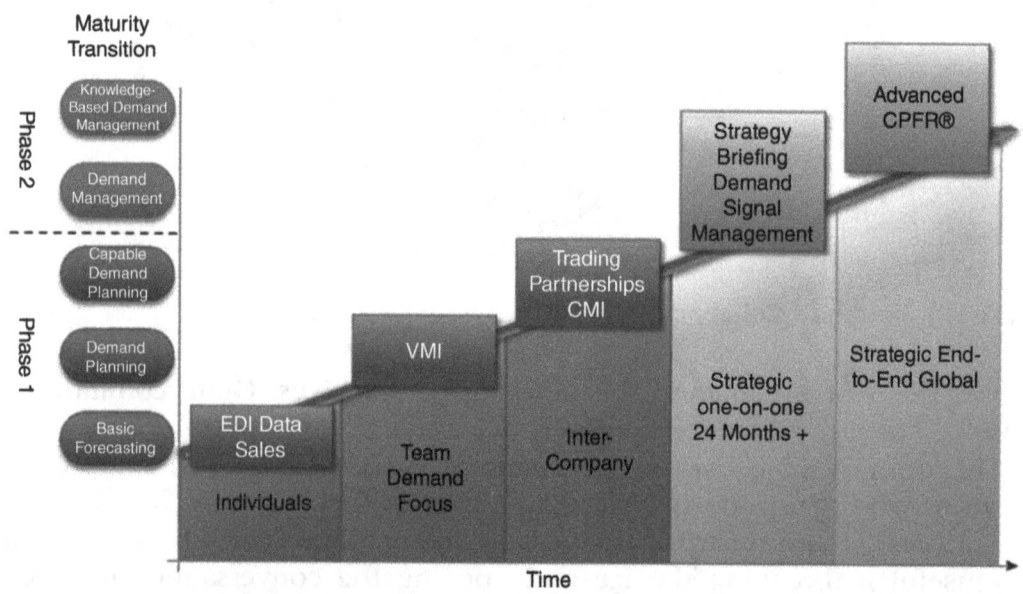

FIGURE 14.10 Collaboration Maturity

EDI Data is a very early form of collaboration between two entities, with the ultimate goal being Collaborative Planning, Forecasting, and Replenishment (CPFR). Getting to this final capability takes time, effort, and two dedicated organizations determined to move from being untrustworthy to trustworthy.

Figure 14.11 identifies the steps required to achieve the desired level of collaboration, which might be different for key suppliers in Tier 1 compared to those in Tier 2.

The real objective of collaboration must be the desire to share information and the resulting benefits. If one of the parties is reluctant to be open and share the results, then trust will be lost, and the collaboration will fail. For that reason, there must be shared investment, shared risk, and shared benefits. Collaboration cannot be a one-way street.

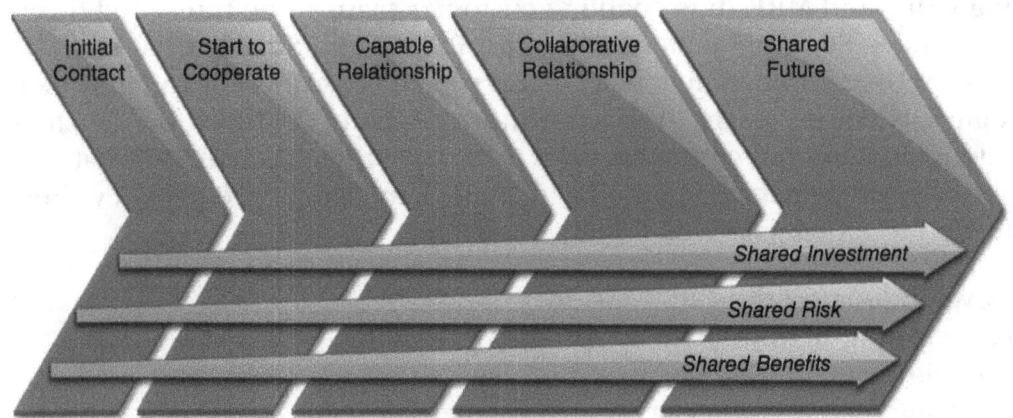

FIGURE 14.11 Steps to Sustainable Collaboration

Figure 14.12 shows the application of collaboration in a Supply Chain between suppliers and the manufacturer and from the manufacturer to the customer. The Supply Chain is enabled through Business Excellence Planning, which develops the agreed and approved future view of the business through Integrated Business Planning and delivers signals to the near-term planners

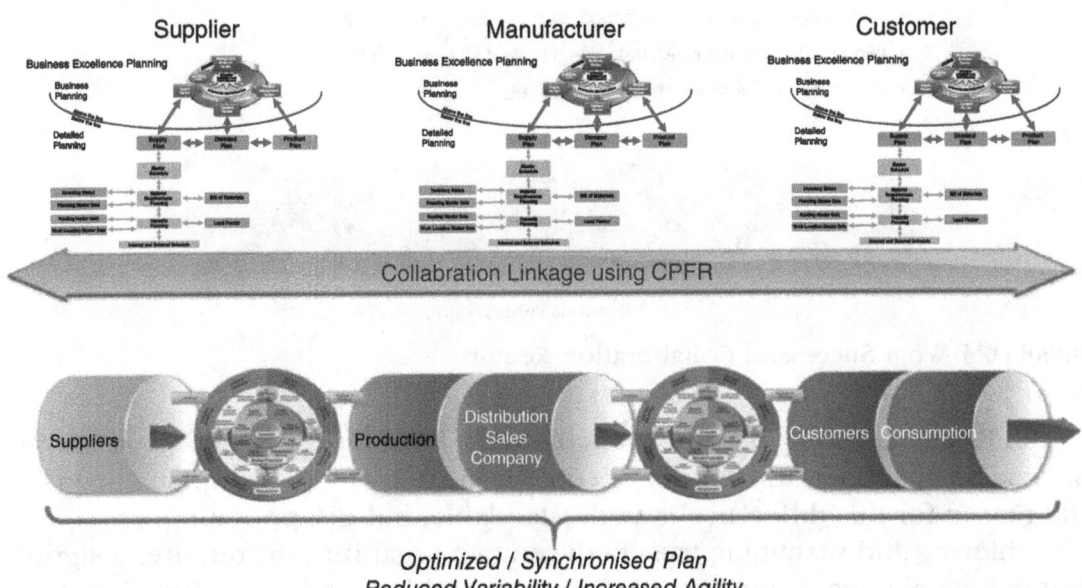

FIGURE 14.12 Extended Supply Chain IBP with CPFR – Move to Market Driven

through MPS and MRP, thus enabling customer plans to be translated throughout the Nodes/Supply Points of the entire End-to-End Supply Chain.

The level of collaboration required in the supplier base must be carefully thought through; it is not necessary to have CPFR everywhere. So, based on the strategic direction, suppliers and customers need to be analyzed to determine what level of collaborative investment is required and an implementation program developed.

Key requirements for this initiative include:

1. Developing a shared CPFR Vision.
2. Participating in joint business planning sessions.
3. Agreeing on common goals and measures to track progress.
4. Agreeing on technology standards for sharing data.
5. Measuring and reporting joint benefits and performance results.

The Agreement, a formal agreement, is key for a successful Supply Chain collaborative partnership.

Ensuring a collaboration journey is successful requires the following, as shown in Figure 14.13.

- Trust – People, Data, Information
- Leadership – Trust, Direction, Drive
- Knowledge – Shared, understood, and applied
- Aligned Organizations – Strategies, Goals, Data
- Documented – Agreement, Processes, etc.

- System Integration
- Plan Do Check Act
- Quality
- DIFOT

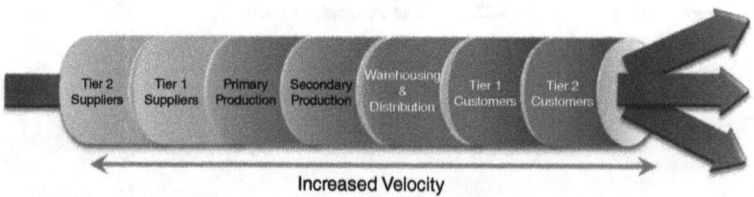

Increased Velocity

FIGURE 14.13 What Successful Collaboration Requires

CPFR and bar coding became available at the same time, in 1995. Interestingly, bar coding has been universally accepted but not of CPFR implementations. The reason for this difference is understandable, but disappointing.

Achieving and sustaining trust between two organizations requires a significant culture change, is not easy to maintain, and is very easy to lose. The time and effort required, particularly with Leadership, often made this quite a laborious initiative that seemed to challenge the effort versus the benefit, especially when the benefits are not fully understood. In addition, when Leaders change in either organization, the dynamics between the organizations can often change and challenge the sustainability of CPFR.

Forecasting, as we all know, is inherently challenging (see Chapter 10). If forecast accuracy is not viewed as improving, the relationship between the two organizations is stressed and trust in the data is undermined.

Because of these and similar cultural challenges in implementing CPFR, its adoption trailed the adoption of bar codes, a "shiny object" that required little culture change. However, for those who have invested in CPFR, benefits have often exceeded expectations in improved customer service, lower inventories, increased sales, reduced logistics costs, and improved replenishment cycles.

Collaboration and its resulting benefits should not be overlooked. If CPFR is not your ultimate goal, there are still significant benefits to be gained from improved collaboration maturity, as shown in Figure 14.10.

Supply Chain Segmentation

In simple terms there are five good reasons why Supply Chain Segmentation, the process of subdividing the Supply Chain to better serve markets and customers with differing needs, should be considered:

1. **Complexity:** Figure 14.14 is a very simple picture designed to illustrate some of the choices, but it also shows how complex Supply Chain relationships can be. Without segmentation this complexity increases significantly and confuses Supply Chain signals and service capabilities.
2. **Flexibility:** Making better use of manufacturing facilities across Supply Chains when standard components can be done by multiple manufacturing sites across the segmented Supply Chains. Clearly, this must have the primary objective of protecting deliveries to be made within the segment. If available capacity remains, it should be used to support other segments. Correct execution will reduce overall product costs.
3. **Product/Service Standardization:** This subject has been talked about for years, but there are many companies that still do not design for manufacturability or design for service. Standardization must first become a business strategy; only then will the advantages of standardization be realized. In

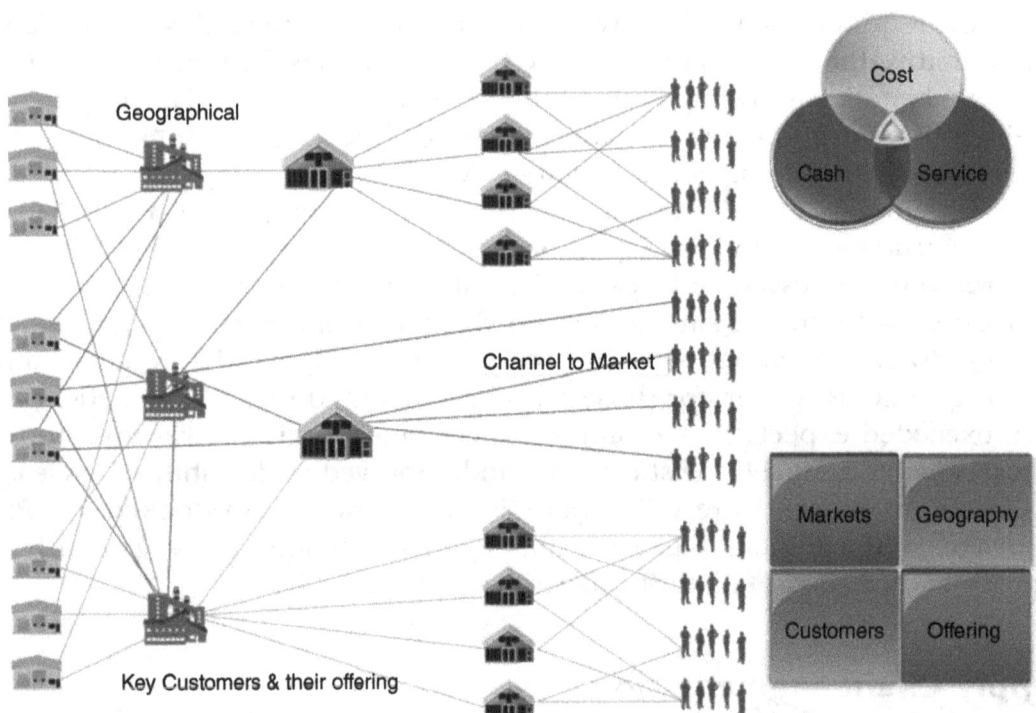

FIGURE 14.14 Supply Chain Segmentation Options

doing this, the flexibility just mentioned would also be realized. Further-more, standardization has the additional benefit of reducing the number of products and parts, which presents the opportunity to reduce inventory.

4. **Integration:** Although there may be multiple segmented Supply Chains in your business, having them informed from one integrated source, specifi-cally Integrated Business Planning, increases visibility and the ability to ex-ploit opportunities that cross all the segmented Supply Chains. Remember, all Supply Chains take their sole requirements signal from the Demand Plan to prepare to deliver products both in the here and now and across the full planning horizon. Keeping the segmented Supply Chains integrated in this way also ensures that capacity investments are prudent.

5. **Customer Satisfaction:** Clearly, a consideration for segmentation has to be the Value Discipline to be used to deliver, which in turn has been based on the Value Proposition. These are communicated to the market and be-come the basis of how customers can expect to benefit from working with a particular segmented Supply Chain. A segmented Supply Chain could be

focused on product leadership, customer intimacy, or a price competitive approach, all of which offer very different options for customers.

a. Product Leadership: Latest technology, fast application of technology to new products, frequent product changes, but results in high prices and low volumes.

b. Customer Intimacy: Extensive portfolio (offerings), tailored solutions, partnership approach, agility, and flexibility.

c. Price Competitive: Few products or services, standardization, high volumes required, low cost, and competitive pricing.

Ensuring that the right Segmented Supply Chain is agreed for each customer ensures that customer expectations are met.

As is shown by Figure 14.14, there are four considerations (geography, markets, offering, and customers) that could influence the above segmentation choice considerations.

Inventory

Is inventory an asset or a liability? This has always been a hot discussion topic. Although inventory levels (finished product, subassemblies, and components) and locations must be planned, fundamentally inventory is a consequence of everything done well or poorly. If there is a reliability problem in any part of Business Excellence Planning, this problem will probably need to be buffered with inventory. As the number of problems is reduced, then the amount of inventory required is also reduced. Looking at this through a Supply Chain from one Nodes/Supply Point to the next we find the scenario shown in Figure 14.15.

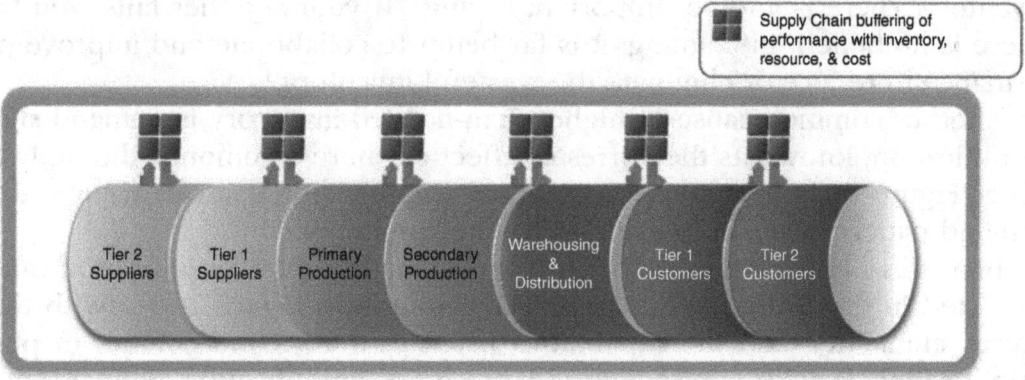

FIGURE 14.15 Inventory Buffers through the Supply Chain

Each receiving Node/Supply Point has the expectation that the supplying Node/Supply Point will deliver 100% of what has been requested, on time and in full. However, the actual deliver could be less, say 95%. In some less mature Supply Chains, the 95% could be much lower; examples have been seen at 50% or less. So, for the receiving Node/Supply Point to successfully deliver its requirements to the next Node, it will need a buffer in place to make up for the 5% loss. Imagine the inventory investment required if the performance of each Node/Supply Point is 50%. It is an enormous investment (and waste), and is not, unfortunately, uncommon.

It is essential that inventory levels be based on a forward view of customer demand and potential marketplace changes. These changes could mean new customers, more competition, or a combination of both. Either way, the forward demand view over the business planning horizon of a rolling 24 months or more is vital to ensure that the investment in inventory is logical and aligned with delivery needs. Inventory held that has a near-term future need is an asset; inventory held with no future need is a liability. It is for this reason that we suggest moving away from recommending "reorder points" to determine inventory replenishment triggers because reorder points are based on historic deliveries, which may have nothing in common with future requirements.

Understanding where inventory is held throughout a Supply Chain is essential for continuous improvement; wherever there is inventory there is an improvement opportunity. The inventory could be by a supplier known to have inefficiencies. In that case it is in the customer's best interest to, potentially, invest in the supplier's capabilities to help improve its performance, reduce the inefficiencies, and thereby reduce or eliminate the need to hold "just-in-case" inventory. There is another important saying, "If your supplier fails, you fail." There is no benefit in blaming; it is far better to collaborate and improve performance to reduce or eliminate the wasteful inventory.

Another common cause of higher-than-needed inventory is demand signal amplification, known as the Forrester effect or, more commonly, the bullwhip effect. Figure 14.16 illustrates the potential amplification that can occur and the demand pattern when amplification has been eliminated.

In Nodes/Supply Points with low levels of maturity, the amplification causes are listed in the "Informal & Supply-Led" column in Figure 14.16. With these causes eliminated and the capabilities listed in the second column in place, amplification is fully controlled, and inventory amplification reduced, often eliminated.

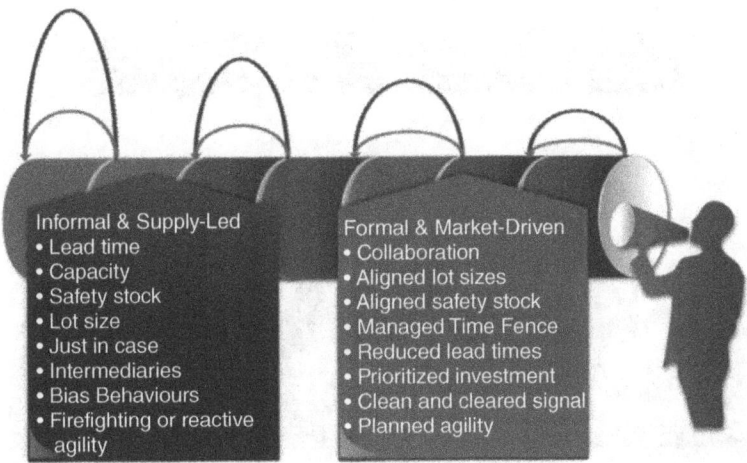

FIGURE 14.16 Amplification through the Supply Chain

Without doubt, inventory in most companies is a huge focus because cash is simply tied up on shelves, in tanks, or in warehouse aisles. If it is the wrong inventory, this inventory is simply wasted money that comes straight off the bottom line. Inventory is a consequence, but visibility of what your inventory profile could be based on future demand and current Supply Chain performance is recommended: if the trend is increasing, that visibility gives you time to look into the cause, make improvements, and ensure that the trend is reversed. Figure 14.17 illustrates a typical inventory profile over time and what contributes to its shape.

- **Cycle Stock:** materials ordered and used in the same month.
- **Safety Stock:** quantity driven by policy designed to protect against unplanned events.
- **Pre-Stock:** for seasonality.
- **Hedging:** between Supply Chains.
- **Lead Time:** materials with a long lead time that must be preordered or held to reduce end item lead time.
- **Footprint:** held between adjacent Nodes/Supply Points.

The final type of inventory in Figure 14.17 is termed "Undesirable" and very often manifests itself as a stock write-off at the end of the year. One thing is for certain, if next year is a repeat of the current year, then the same level of Undesirable write-off will be repeated. The idea with a picture of inventory like

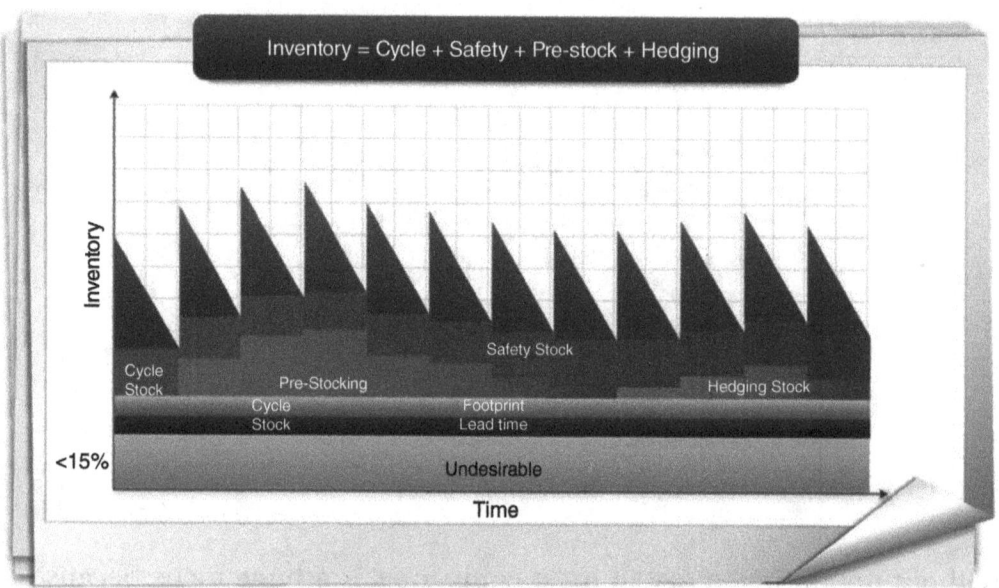

FIGURE 14.17 Inventory Management

this is to then understand the cause/need and, where possible, to seek ways to reduce or eliminate this inventory. One of our clients, for example, with $13 billion in annual revenue was able to reduce its inventory investment by $1 billion while also increasing its customer service performance.

What Causes Inventory

- Long lead times.
- BOM: Errors in the structure, quantities, or times.
- Time fence violations: Numerous changes to plans/volumes.
- Demand Plan errors.
- Capacity: Not planning or not resolving issues.
- Machine breakdowns: Planned Preventative Maintenance is ignored.
- Lack of flexibility.
- Compressed organization: Too focused on near-term requirements.
- Inventory policy: Lack of or poorly communicated.
- Inefficiencies: Buffers are required to cover poor performance.

- Data inaccuracy: simply planning with the wrong information.
- Customers: No forecasts and constantly changing requirements.

Inventory, being a key focus, should be made visible, should be measured, and should be used to drive improvements throughout the Supply Chain.

Measurement

Obviously, measures are required within each Node/Supply Point to measure their own performance and to drive improvement programs.

Similarly, Supply Chain measures are required to gain an understanding of the overall Supply Chain's performance and to highlight where further improvements can be achieved. Figure 14.18 lists typical Supply Chain measures that should be in place.

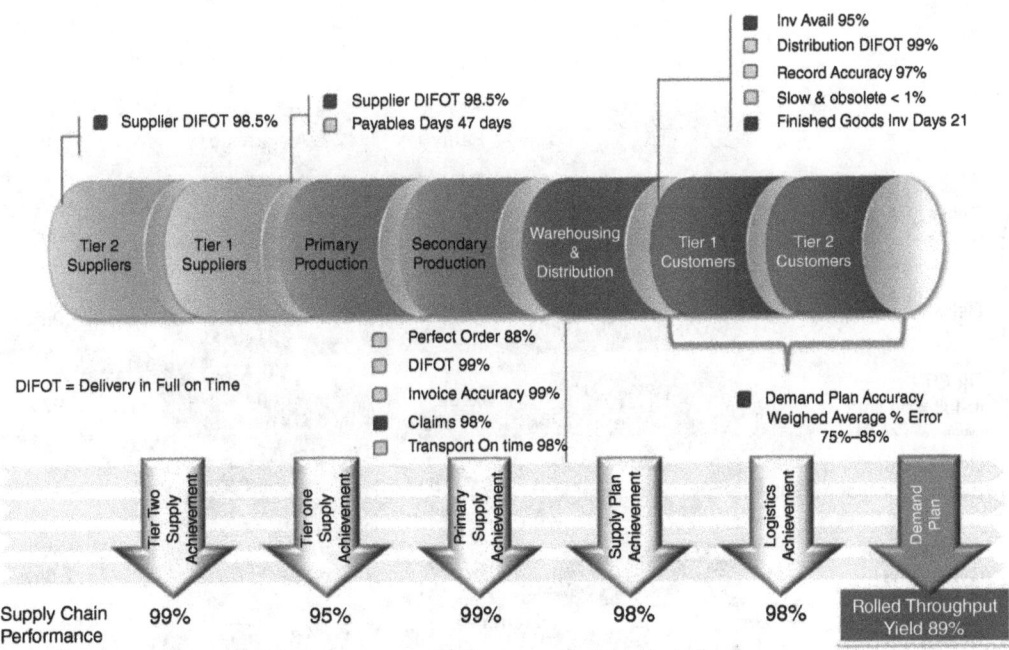

FIGURE 14.18 Examples of Supply Chain Measures

Please note the measure at the bottom of Figure 14.18, the Rolled Throughput Yield, which is calculated by multiplying the performances of each individual Node/Supply Point. This provides the overall Supply Chain Yield and shows the consequence of performance on performance. In this example the calculation is:

$$(0.99 \times 0.95 \times 0.99 \times 0.98 \times 0.98) = 0.89 \text{ or } 89\% \text{ Yield}$$

To better understand whether the performance measured of a Supply Chain indicates that it is a Leading Supply Chain, Lagging Supply Chain, or roughly on a par with other Supply Chains, undertaking a Benchmark study is recommended. A Benchmark study allows a Supply Chain's performance to be compared to a database of Supply Chains in a similar industry or from all industries to see how the performance compares to Best in Class (BIC).

Figure 14.19 shows the actual results of a Supply Chain Benchmark study for a company who also wanted to understand Best in Class (BIC) results, which are shown to the right of the figure.

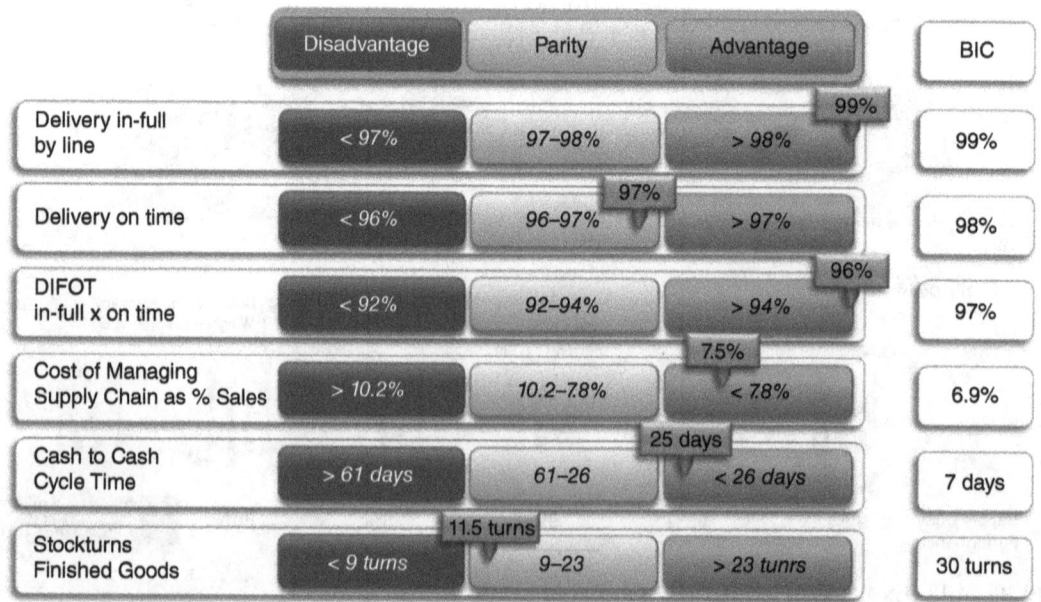

FIGURE 14.19 Benchmark Results for a Sample of Supply Chain Measures

The company's results, against each measure listed (just a sample of the measures), are shown in the rectangular gray box, within which is the actual percentage recorded.

Overall, the Benchmark, for this company, confirmed that it was in a strong position, but gains could still be made by investigating how to improve delivery performance and inventory turns.

So why is it that some companies still do not have a well-managed Supply Chain?

1. Because they do not have their house in order and would be sharing poor information, which would make them look bad.
2. Because organizations often develop as the "result of" rather than "because of" and, consequently, there will be many Leadership roles created that would need to be redefined for an Extended or End-to-End Supply Chain. As mentioned earlier, "Turkeys do not vote for Christmas." These modifications introduce lots of resistance to change. People will see their power reduced and their empires restructured.
3. The time investment is often seen to be excessive; taking key people from their "day jobs" to focus on the design becomes an excuse to avoid doing what is needed.
4. Because you may have too many key suppliers who are as big, if not bigger, than yourself. Having "gorillas" like this in your potential Supply Chain can frustrate the intention.
5. Lack of knowledge and understanding of the benefits and of how to proceed masks the need to embark on a transformation journey.
6. The investment cost and time to implement can often be a limiting factor.
7. Poor strategy and a lack of market and customer knowledge.

Summary

Well-defined Supply Chains are essential for companies to outperform their competitors when servicing markets and customers but will be developed out of necessity either formally or informally from varying levels of Business Maturity depending on the company. The subjects covered in this book provide the foundations required for Nodes or Supply Points to gain control, eliminate churn, and provide a platform to become part of an integrated Supply Chain that can provide significant bottom-line benefits for all parties.

Moving from a conglomeration of disparate activities, individually managed, with potentially many sets of numbers and different agendas, to a design that enables unimpeded and reliable flow from suppliers through to the customers and consumers must be the goal.

It is generally recognized that markets and customer demand changes are accelerating, which, if you are not prepared, will introduce instability and unnecessary change. However, if you are also causing your own internal instability and churn due to broken processes, multiple sets of numbers, different agendas, and employees with varied knowledge levels, then market-driven instability will be magnified exponentially.

Sure, it is less easy to influence customer changes; however, it is made much worse when you are basically focused on internal problems and cannot provide, consistently, the customer service expected. The *first step must be to get your own house in order* and then understand what instability and change is being caused by customers.

Some of the instability will stop due to improved communication and Demand Planning but it is fair to say that even with Unparalleled Business Planning and Execution Practices there will always be the need to deal with short-term surprises. Understanding what these are will enable planned, cost-effective Agility rather than an expensive, reactive response (see Chapter 16).

This summary identifies, depending on the starting maturity and position of your company, a transformation from being disjointed and dysfunctional to one of reliable flow and integration. This does not happen overnight, which is why we support organizations on their journeys to Supply Chain success, (see Chapter 18).

Can you find the 800-pound gorilla in your Supply Chain?

"Optimized supply chains deliver best-in-class service at half the cost"

Recommended Reading

Correll, James, and Kevin Herbert. *Gaining Control: Managing Capacities and Priorities* (John Wiley & Sons).

Crum, Colleen, with George Palmatier. *Demand Management Oliver Wight Best Practices: Process, Principles and Collaboration* (J. Ross Publishing).

Groves, Dennis, Kevin Herbert, and Jim Correll. *Achieving Class A Business Excellence, An Executive's Perspective* (John Wiley & Sons).

Groves, Dennis, Kevin Herbert, and Jim Correll. *An Executive's Guide to Achieving Class A Business Excellence* (Oliver Wight International).

Ireland, Ronald K. *Supply Chain Collaboration – How to Implement CPFR and Other Best Collaborative Practices* (J. Ross Publishing).

For additional but more specific reading please visit the Oliver Wight Website and gain access to the extensive library of White Papers.

CHAPTER 15

Finance, Integrated and Proactive: Top-Down and Bottom-Up

Supply Chain–related functions have only been addressed in passing; now it is time to focus on Finance and Accounting and explain the importance of their full integration, top to bottom, to support gap analysis and

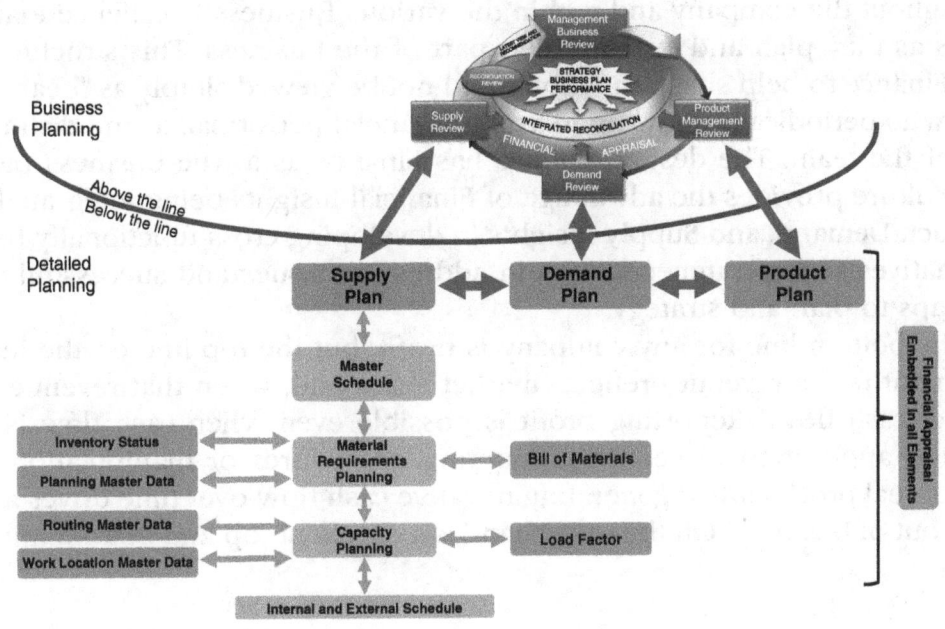

FIGURE 15.1 Business Excellence Planning

decision-making at all levels of the organization. They are embedded in every process described in the previous chapters, and the measures they track influence each area of the business. Financial health improves when the recommendations in this book are followed and suffer when they are not. Financial health is a consequence of everything done by a company, good or bad, and financial measures reflect and report how a company has performed in the past. Many Finance organizations forecast future financials but they are not based on an integrated approach with future demand and supply plans. Class A companies project financials that are fully integrated and developed directly from IBP-approved plans from Demand and Supply and the resulting Master Schedules, MRP, capacity plans, and operating schedules. One set of numbers must be used by the entire business to ensure that trust is established to support decision-making requirements. All decisions made are based upon volume and value, not just volume.

To take advantage of the information provided through Business Excellence Planning, Figure 15.1, a culture change in Finance is required to move from keeping score to a much more proactive role in creating the business's future. When advice from the previous chapters has been followed, accurate data and valid plans are now available. To best understand and use this new, more accurate and valuable information, Finance representatives must be embedded throughout the company and within the various Business Excellence Planning teams as they plan and execute their part of the business. This structure enables Finance to help shape the future and not be viewed simply as "bean counters" who periodically show up to assess financial performance and distract the rest of the team. The desired culture has Finance as a true business partner. This culture provides the advantage of Financial insights being integrated with Product, Demand, and Supply insights in developing cross-functionally holistic alternatives and recommendations in addressing issues and successfully closing gaps to plan and strategy.

The bottom line for any company is profit, but the top line on the income statement (sales revenue) reflects market share and, when that revenue is received, cash flow.[1] Reporting profit is possible even when cash flow is poor through application of certain accounting procedures or manipulations. But lack of real profit and/or generating negative cash flow over time drives a company out of business. On the other hand, an excellent top and bottom line over time results in happy investors and satisfied employees, who have opportunities to grow throughout their careers. Good bottom-line results are wonderful, but could they be better than they are? If your company has any of the following conditions, there is room for considerable improvement!

- High inventories.
- Late customer deliveries.
- High costs.
- End-of-month crunch/end-of-year push.
- Routine expediting.
- A constant "save-the-day" hero culture.
- Surprises in the Management Business Review.
- Financial surprises.
- Funny/unreasonable numbers.

The preceding chapters offer solutions for all these conditions, and, when followed, enable the few issues that do arise to be dealt with quickly and with minimum negative impact. Take the last two, financial surprises and funny/unreasonable numbers. Who bears the burden when those arise? Finance, of course, usually bears the brunt of financial deficiencies even though Finance does not control the numbers. Is the burden properly placed on Finance? Absolutely! Finance and Accounting measures can be counterproductive when they are misunderstood or misapplied. External financial reporting data is rarely appropriate or even useful for making internal (management) decisions. Decisions such as "make or buy" or "lot size" must use incremental cash flow data, not averages of relatively fixed-cost data.

So, what should Finance and Accounting do to avoid bearing the burden of financial surprises and funny numbers? They must ensure that their data is not misunderstood or misused and insist upon accurate reporting from the rest of the company. When business results are trending down, there is very little that can be done to improve those business results quickly and significantly, in the short term. Certainly, one customer can be served well at the expense of a few others, but significantly moving the business results needle is not possible. Therefore, Finance must participate in Integrated Business Planning and other planning and execution teams to develop realistic and reliable future financial projections. These projections must be based on approved Product, Demand, and Supply Plans to provide an integrated future view. These plans enable progress to be highlighted and gaps identified, which must then be closed while there is still time to plan and implement cost-effective gap-closing solutions. There are limited opportunities for this in the short-term horizon.

A young professional woman, the Controller of a division in a company that chose not to begin a journey to Class A, was enjoying a great career because of her financial knowledge, ability, and hard work. She was rewarded with a promotion to become the Controller of the company's largest division. She was often in the office seven days a week for as many as 12 hours a day trying to fix funny numbers and avoid financial surprises. After over a year of trying to straighten out the mess and pushing hard on the other functional areas to report results accurately, she saw some, but not much, improvement. When asked how many of her hours she could free up if the company's inventories, bills of material, routings, and reporting were accurate, and if the planning functions (Integrated Business Planning, Master Scheduling, MRP, and Capacity Planning) produced valid plans, she laughed and said almost all of them. She went on to say that she could not do the work she went to school for – financial analysis. Not long after that conversation, she resigned and went to a completely different industry, flipping houses. Leadership lost a tremendous talent because of its decision not to identify and eliminate the causes of continuous churn and the resulting blame culture.

The Role of Finance in a Business Excellence Planning Environment

The following is a list of Finance responsibilities when operating in a Business Excellence Planning environment:

- **Integrated Business Planning Key Participant**
  Participates in all IBP Reviews and as a partner in the enabling processes.
  The Finance VP (CFO) participates in and is critical in a successful Management Business Review (see earlier reference in this chapter) in ensuring that projected financials are driven directly from the approved MBR Plans.

The CFO ensures the right level of financial support for the Reconciliation process and review to ensure that the presentation deck used in the MBR represents "truth as we know it" both in volume and value projections from a financial perspective.

- **Annual Plan (Budget)**

Ensures that the top line is on budget or that either the gap-closing plans are sufficient to bring the company back in alignment or the plan is adjusted if the gap cannot be closed.

Ensures that the bottom line is on budget or that either the gap-closing plans are sufficient to bring the company back in alignment or the plan is adjusted if the gap cannot be closed.

Tracks and reports the exact status against the budget.

Recommends courses of action developed in the Integrated Reconciliation Review for closing gaps and improving financials.

- **Standard Costs**

Finalizes, at the beginning of the year, the "frozen budget file" against which actual performance throughout the year is measured.

Reviews and validates the operations file used throughout the fiscal year to update and track performance improvements.

- **Financial Commitment Plan Adjustments**

Approves top-line, bottom-line, and cash flow adjustments to the committed numbers. Ensures that the data used to develop the numbers is accurate and the plans valid to minimize the adjustments needed.

- **Budget Variances**

Reviews and validates labor, material, and overhead budget variances and approves action plans to close gaps. Ensures that data used to develop the numbers is accurate and the plans valid to minimize gaps requiring closure.

- **Capital Budgeting**

Reviews and concurs with the timing and accuracy of required capital investments escalated to the MBR for inclusion in approved aggregate plans across the entire planning horizon. An active team member of capital project development.

- **Spending**

Supports the review of spending across all departments to ensure that actual spending is on track with the budget. Ensures that cross-functional gap-closing plans are developed and escalated to the IRR and MBR for approval.

- **Strategic Planning**

  Participates in strategic planning activities ensuring that strategic business objectives are reasonable yet stretching and appropriately link supporting people, process, and technology initiatives required to achieve the objectives. As a key MBR participant, helps to ensure that the strategy is linked through IBP to execution activities.

- **Mergers and Acquisitions**

  With less time required to investigate and eliminate plan and budget variances, finance can support business strategy development and related strategic initiatives, such as mergers and acquisitions, designed to deliver strategic business objectives.

- **Cost Management**

  Enable the monitoring of current costs and projected costs to identify, as early as possible, actions that may be needed to avoid or close developing gaps to committed plans, considering the implications today and in the future.

- **Waste Control**

  Enable the tracking and reporting of sources of waste, such as queue, Work in Process, excess inventory, scrap, production delays, and so forth, that increase product costs. Supports the development of plans to continuously reduce these unnecessary costs.

- **Move Spending Ownership to Operating and Support Departments**

  Holds operating and support organizations accountable for spending and revenue enhancement decisions; supports those organizations in shaping those decisions and in meeting financial commitments.

- **Eliminate the "Mystique"**

  Makes Finance accessible, transparent, and understandable.

- **Future Projections**

  Supports development of volume and value projections based upon approved IBP aggregate and detailed plans and schedules.

- **Scenarios and Modeling Exercises**

  Ensures that all scenarios and models for projecting future volumes and value are created with accurate financial information.

Financial Planning and Projections Supported by Trusted Planning Submissions

- **Financial Integration:** Time-phased financial projections across the planning horizon based upon approved aggregate and detailed plans and schedules enable improved decisions. Information needed for internal, tactical decisions is very different from the information Finance needs for external reporting; excellent integrated planning processes provide that information.

- **One Set of Numbers:** Facilitates Managerial Accounting and decision-making:

  One set of volume and value numbers used by all functions eliminates the fog of functional numbers and accelerates development of gap-closing action plans.

  Accurate operational data supports accurate costing.

  Provides different functional views of the same set of numbers and supports useful risk and opportunity analysis.

- **Planning System Consolidates and Integrates Plans:** The planning system performs countless accurate calculations, when the data being fed to the system is accurate. No spreadsheets are required for planning but can be used for, when appropriate, analytical purposes. The results of such analysis should be presented graphically with identified targets to enable quick identification of trends and gaps to be closed.

- **Instant Inventory Projections:** Supply, not Finance, is responsible for inventory reduction efforts such as reducing lead time, reducing lot sizes through setup reduction, removing safety stock for anything except forecasted items, removing safety stock to cover for late supplier deliveries, utilizing master schedule overplanning rather than safety stock for end items and options, and so forth. It should be noted that inventory is a consequence of everything that happens, good or bad, in a business, so Product (in terms of New Product Introduction and End of Life projects) and Demand also have a responsibility to support inventory reduction targets. Finance can use the planning system to track future inventory levels and ask operating departments when and by how much they plan to reduce inventory levels when gap-closing is required. They then use the planning system to track progress against inventory reduction plans. That is holding the right people accountable, the people who actually control the inventory rather than the Finance organization.

- **Accurate Information:** When data integrity accountability is clear, change control procedures are followed, and data integrity measures are maintained at Class A accuracy levels, Finance can confidently use planning system information to project future financials based upon accurate:

  Inventories

  Bills of Material

Routings

Reporting

- **Valid Material Plans and Capacity Plans:** Developed with accurate planning data and future demand that represents "truth as we know it," Finance can confidently develop product costs directly from the planning system.
- **Confident Standard Costing for Pricing Existing and New Products:** Standard costs can be used to establish base prices but allow consideration of increased pricing for perceived value.

When faced with bad data and poor results, very bad decisions can be, and often are, made. For instance, when inventory is too high at the end of the year, some companies stop supplier deliveries to reduce inventory. Unfortunately, this usually increases operational churn and, in turn, production inefficiencies and can even disrupt customer shipments, which will drive inventory even higher. The best way to reduce inventory and increase cash flow, or at least receivables, is to ship product to customers on time. If for some reason your company can turn off supplier deliveries and customer shipments are not affected, there is something seriously wrong with your planning and execution processes. Look for poor planning procedures, inflated planning parameters, or a combination of the two. There is an opportunity for significant bottom-line improvement in short order!

As mentioned earlier, inventory level is a clear indicator of what is being done well or poorly in planning and executing those plans. Inventory is a consequence of Product, Demand, and Supply Planning. If it is too high, find and eliminate the root cause, and inventory will come down. Usually, excessive inventory is the result of multiple poor practices, not just one specific cause. In many companies, inventory is literally created to absorb fixed costs and becomes an asset (Work in Process or Finished Goods) whose costs are not recognized until the item is sold (identified as cost of goods sold). This is called the "matching principle" in full absorption accounting. If inventory is not unnecessarily created, fixed costs would have to be reported in the period incurred or recognized, thus reducing profit in that time period. Does a company's bonus calculation reward inventory reduction or reported profits? Telling people how their performance is measured and how bonuses are awarded will determine actual outcomes in nearly every case. Everyone in the company becomes part of the problem and must become part of the solution.

At another company, Finance refused to allow the MRP system to refresh and update inventory balances following a physical wall-to-wall or cycle inventory count. The counts would always reflect an increase in the total on hand inventory value (increased investment means reduced ROI), which would put the Finance VP in a very uncomfortable spotlight. As a result, their planning system would calculate and recommend plans based on understated balances and create planned orders for materials when those materials were not needed, or it would not create orders when the system inventory was actually overstated. The result, more and more churn and firefighting. Not smart, but beyond not being smart, the company was knowingly falsifying financial results, potentially a criminal offense.

Selling the Improvements

The past 14 chapters have provided countless pointers on improving top- and bottom-line results. But the pointers need to be put into action, which requires support from Leadership and Management, often a challenge. As a reminder, this is a significant culture change, and culture changes must be driven from the very top of the company – the President, CEO, Managing Director, or General Manager. The challenge is getting their attention, interest, and commitment to drive the required changes. An important lever is that Leadership speak the language of money. Show them how these improvements increase the top line, bottom line, and cash flow results and they will understand. Figure 15.2 shows a cost/benefit analysis chart that we have used successfully with many companies.

A commonly used method of introducing companies to the benefits has been to include the investment approach in a workshop with Leadership. At the beginning of the workshop we simply ask attendees representing each area of the business to state their major concerns and document their responses on a flipchart. When asking the questions, we keep the chart, Figure 15.2, in the back of our minds knowing we will use the information at the end of the workshop.

The Leadership Workshop consists of explaining the Unparalleled Business Planning and Execution Practices (basically this book). As the class concludes, we go back to the flipchart and ask what improvement percentage they would expect to see if the Unparalleled Business Planning and Execution Practices were

Financial Benefits

Example Company	Company Profile	Expected Improvements	Tangible Benefits
Sales ⬆	$1 Billion	10%	$10 Million***
Cash Flow ⬆	$200 Million	20%	$3.2 Million**
Productivity ⬆	$80 Million	20%	$16 Million
Purchasing Spend ⬇	$250 Million	13%	$32.5 Million
Inventory ⬇	$175 Million	30%*	$10.5 Million
Total Tangible Benefits Each Year			$109 Million

* 20% Inventory Carrying Cost
** 8% Cost of Capital Savings
*** Includes Margin Calculation

FIGURE 15.2 Financial Benefits Summary Chart

implemented. As each response is given, we record their comments and percentages.

For example, Sales and Marketing VPs would often say that on-time delivery was the biggest concern. We would then ask how improving delivery performance to above 95% would impact sales. The number the VP provides is usually staggering. Similarly, when asking the Supply Chain VP how much improvement in Supply performance would be possible if they received a more accurate demand forecast, the response often requires a good deal of time. The process continues with each area.

Next, we display a chart like Figure 15.2 but without the improvement categories or percentages. We then go back to the flipchart and show the activities and percent improvements captured at the beginning of the workshop. Figure 15.2 shows a very typical company's chart and profile. What is recorded is in their company's terms, so it is very understandable to them. Simple math is used to calculate the benefits. The tricky one is inventory, but it is easy enough to get the Finance VP to talk about the math.

The tangible benefits in this example may appear high, but they are low compared to those recorded in some workshops and those experienced by Class A Certified companies. The expected improvement percentages are conservative based on our observations and surveys completed by companies that have implemented Unparalleled Business Planning and Execution Practices. Also, this list does not include typical benefits, often quite large, in other areas. These other typical cost reduction opportunities include, for example:

- **Obsolescence:** With accurate bills of material and effective use of planning tools, obsolescence can be reduced significantly. The Materials Manager of a heavy equipment company, after implementing Unparalleled Business Planning and Execution Practices, was asked by the VP responsible for all manufacturing plants what the obsolescence value would be for a new product just being introduced. The company measured obsolescence by the value of a truck. New to the job, but with a thorough understanding of the techniques to control obsolescence, the Materials Manager replied, "one truck" (the cost of one truck). The VP looked amazed and commented that would be good. After the meeting, the Materials Manager met with her boss, the facility GM. He shook his head and told her statements like that should not be made without research because the typical number for new product introduction was 20 trucks. He told her that she and her team would be held accountable for meeting the one truck number. The final obsolescence number came in at one-half of a truck without any special attention required. Was she held accountable? Given a raise? Not in this case. We have seen these kinds of results again and again with client companies we have coached.

- **Transportation Costs:** An acquaintance shared that the auto industry electronics manufacturing company for which he worked leased a Boeing 747 and used it to fly parts every day from one of its plants to its customer's assembly plants because they were unable to deliver on time without it. Seems like a significant, unnecessary increase to product cost. Do you fly parts to customers? Do you ever use couriers to hand-deliver parts? These costs are avoidable.

- **Overtime:** Using overtime is not always improper, and, in fact, from a financial perspective it can at times be very cost effective. But those times must be determined based upon formal capacity planning (see Chapter 11) and, applied properly, not just used to cover poor planning. Overtime used regularly becomes an expected part of employees' earnings and begins to undermine the culture.

- **Indirect Payroll:** Planning and execution improvements eliminate the need for headcount increase and/or overtime to deal with churn and firefighting caused by poor planning.

- **Product Quality:** While there is no direct correlation between excellent planning and quality, poor planning results in churn, rework, errors, excessive overtime, and, on occasion, running at maximum capacity, which leads to increased quality defects and safety issues. A brand-new Machine Shop Manager was expediting an order that required an elaborate setup for the first operation. He stood watching the operator as the supervisor went to the downstream machines to start other setups when the operator turned to the Machine Shop Manager and asked if there wasn't something else he could be doing. Of course, there was, but he understood the company's "make it happen" culture. His reply was, "No! These parts are needed tomorrow morning. I am here to make sure nothing gets in your way." The operator replied, "You are making me nervous, and I have already put the wrong tool in the machine. Could you at least stand across the aisle?" How many times does rushing to finish orders cause mistakes? It is all too common, and expensive.

- **Movement:** Moving a product from one work location to another is a non-value-added activity; value cannot be added to a product or assembly when it is being moved. In assembling large vehicles, one facility calculated that about 33% of its weekly operating time was lost moving the vehicles from one station to another. Simply rearranging the assembly line to minimize movement to around 5% increased the facility's productivity by over 60%.

- **Quality of Work Life:** Far too many people, both operators and managers, who work in End-to-End Supply Chains express to us displeasure with their jobs. They leave at the end of the day feeling dejected by their inability to do what they know they should be doing because of churn and firefighting. A Supply Chain VP kept track of her time and told us that she was spending 80% of each day reworking plans, schedules, and projects that had missed commitments. Following the recommendations in this book makes a huge difference. Recall the executive who had never attended one of his son's Little League baseball games, but after achieving Class A certification, was able to begin coaching his son's team. Quality of work life is not directly relatable to improved costs except that people are able to use the recovered time working on business improvements, advancing their careers, and are less likely to look for work elsewhere.

When these benefits are presented, it is surprising how much buy-in there is. It is common and very encouraging that executives in companies that have been through the Class A transformation are willing to share their experience with others considering initiating a similar journey to Class A.

Investments

The investment required in a journey to Class A is critical in deciding whether to go forward. These investments include using the right tools and technology to enable the Business Excellence Planning processes explained in these chapters. Software and hardware requirements will vary from company to company, but our experience is that a planning system currently available in a company is likely to be completely capable of doing the job. Little or no investment might be required. We advise against replacing software until a diagnostic assessment has determined that it does not have the required base functionality. One client owned an ancient DOS screen planning system from the 1980s. It was no longer supported, and all operating manuals had been destroyed. All planning activities were performed using Excel spreadsheets, no two of which were alike or contained the same data across the company. A creative project team member decided to print every help screen from the software package and trained the planners, all of whom were hired after the software package was no longer in use in the planning system's use. Within about two months, all planning was being done in that ancient software package, taking advantage of the improved data integrity and planning processes implemented in the previous year. Remember that almost all business results improvements come from accurate data, clear accountabilities, valid plans, and improved business processes, all supported by proper operation of the planning system.

People, processes, and then, and only then, technology and tools. Keep in mind that the tools and technology, in our experience, are the least impactful contributor in achieving improved results, but they are still needed. Finance leadership in a global consumer goods company studied the results of their company's journey to Class A and reported that, while their new planning system was required to support the new business processes, of the total top- and bottom-line benefits, they attributed 90% to education and process improvements and 10% to the planning system software, although the investment in software dwarfed the investment in education, process redesign, and coaching. More important than the capabilities of tools and technology is learning to use their available capabilities effectively. This requires investment in education, training, and coaching of the user base. Companies that follow the recommendations in this book realize high levels of success. The bad news about this kind of success is that companies tend to relax after they achieve their goals, and their people move on to higher-paying jobs. New people arrive to take those jobs without going through onboarding sessions to understand the policies, procedures, measures, roles, responsibilities and effective use of the planning system. Personal preferences and old behaviors creep back in. Without fail, everyone moving into one of these planning and execution roles must have the benefit of formal onboarding and periodic education and training opportunities.

The chart shown in Figure 15.3 displays an example of initial and ongoing software, education, and coaching investments for a mid-sized company or a division of a large company. Education and coaching investments are typical; the software investment varies the most, sometimes very significantly, from company to company. In fact, we know several large companies that have spent as much as $1 billion on software.

Investments

| Category | Example Company | |
	One-Time	Ongoing
Software / Hardware Upgrades	$4 Million	$1 Million
Education	$1 Million	$0.25 Million
Coaching	$1 Million	$0.25 Million
Totals	$6 Million	$1.5 Million

FIGURE 15.3 Investment Summary Example

Return on Investment

Knowing the annual benefits, cost of implementation, and ongoing expenses for this example company enables an important calculation to determine the return on investment (ROI) using the simple formula shown in Figure 15.4. There is no need to be precise with this calculation since the ROI is always staggeringly large; more precision adds nothing.

$$\text{Company Return on Investment} = \frac{\text{Annual Benefits} - \text{Ongoing Expenses}}{\text{One-Time Cost of Implementation}}$$

$$\text{Example Company Return on Investment} = \frac{\$109 \text{ Million} - \$1.5 \text{ Million}}{\$6 \text{ Million}} = 1{,}792\%$$

FIGURE 15.4 Example Return on Investment Calculation

The ROI in this example of more than 1,700% is typical, but an ROI over 2,500% is not unusual. When presented with this typical ROI, Finance normally and immediately resists; they do not believe the number. However, we have seen many Finance VPs/CFOs not only believing the number but championing implementation of Unparalleled Business Planning and Execution Practices. Those individuals have been almost uniformly open-minded going into the education and engaged throughout the Leadership education workshop. The real question is not whether the benefits are achievable but whether people will be held accountable for adopting the required behavior changes that deliver the benefits. That responsibility ultimately falls in the hands of the President.

Cost of Delay

When the return on investment has been agreed, most Leadership Teams agree that they should go forward. The problem in moving forward is bureaucracy; it takes over and excuses and delays begin. The sense of urgency fades quickly as people think about the coming changes and the work required to effect those changes. In those cases, and really for all implementations, a simple calculation of the cost of delay can establish and/or restore that sense of urgency. While the transformation's total benefits may seem a somewhat academic number, the cost of delaying some of the transformational work required, for reasons often not all that compelling, reinforces the need and advantage of moving the implementation forward expeditiously regardless of any reasons to delay that work. Finance sees the benefit of money to the bottom line; Sales and Marketing, the top-line revenue and market share growth; Supply Chain the increase in productivity and reduction of product costs. The calculation is quite simple: subtracting ongoing expenses from annual benefits and dividing that number by 12 yields the savings per month (see Figure 15.5). Delaying the implementation at any time reduces the bottom line by that amount. It is always a number that cannot be ignored, a number that overwhelms any other project

$$\frac{\text{Company}}{\text{Cost of Delay}} = \frac{\text{Annual Benefits} - \text{Ongoing Expenses}}{12 \text{ Months}}$$

$$\frac{\text{Example Company}}{\text{Cost of Delay}} = \frac{\$109 \text{ Million} - \$1.5 \text{ Million}}{12 \text{ Months}} = \$8.9 \text{ Million per month}$$

FIGURE 15.5 Example Cost of Delay Calculation

or reason to delay the required work. Rarely, if ever, have we come across a company with a project that provided a greater ROI than that of a Class A implementation.

There are very few, if any, examples of a good reason to ignore a bottom-line increase of $8.9 million per month. This implementation will not generate that return until some of the processes are implemented successfully. It is not uncommon for companies to lose its sense of urgency in implementing Business Excellence Planning projects because of a number of reasons, like the chaos of daily firefighting required to meet customer orders, but the monthly cost of delay cannot be ignored by Leadership and it keeps the project on schedule. The cost of delay calculated recently in a client's workshop using their numbers exceeded $1 million per day. Yes, per day!

That is a staggering number even if for a year or a month. Any President, if they believe the numbers they provided for the calculation, would most certainly ask, "What is it we have to do, and how soon can we get these bottom-line results?" The answer, which has been presented throughout this book, is summarized in the following section. While Leadership speaks the language of money, they must understand what is required to realize the benefits and know what questions to ask when tracking progress. Remember that commitment without understanding is a liability!

The answer the Leadership is looking for is briefly summarized next. It is a quick review of each element of Business Excellence Planning, Figure 15.6. Step-by-step implementation details and complete explanations are included in previous chapters.

Business Excellence Planning Elements

- **Inventory Accuracy:** Processes must be in place to achieve and maintain extremely high levels of inventory accuracy, minimum 95% initially by location, including all required planning system data elements.

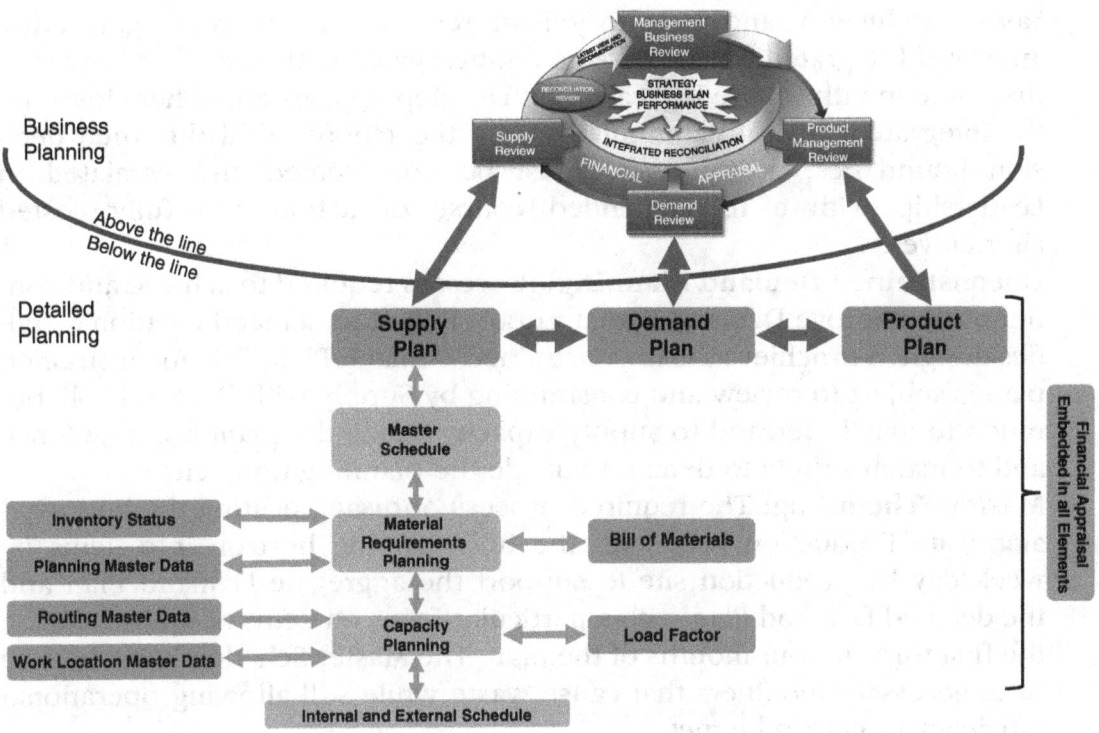

FIGURE 15.6 Business Excellence Planning

- **Bill of Material Accuracy:** Processes required to achieve and maintain extremely high levels of bill of material accuracy, minimum 98% initially, must be in place so that planned material usage and consumption match reality. In some industries the bill of material could be called a Recipe, Formula, or Specification.
- **Routing and Work Location Accuracy:** Processes must be implemented to achieve and maintain extremely high levels of routing and work location accuracy, minimum 95% initially, to ensure that planned workloads are aligned with what can actually be processed by those individual resources.
- **Integrated Business Planning:** An aggregate planning process (Sales, Production and Inventory Plans by families, categories, and segments) by month over a rolling minimum 18–24 months is required to validate plans that support Strategic Business Objectives and business and annual plans.
- **Integrated Tactical Planning:** A series of weekly Demand and Supply Team meetings led by the Demand and Supply Managers to monitor actual

Sales, Production, and Inventory Plan results and progress against the approved Integrated Business Plans disaggregated to the item level over the first three months of the IBP calendar. Developing gaps are either closed by the Integrated Tactical Planning Teams, if the actions fall within their decision boundaries, or the issue must be documented and escalated to Leadership with a recommended course of action and fully costed alternatives.

- **Unconstrained Demand Planning:** Processes required to achieve and continuously improve Demand Plan accuracy linked to demand creation activities designed to achieve the unconstrained Demand Plan. The unconstrained plan is subject to review and constraining by Supply with Demand collaboration to match demand to supply capacity inside the planning time fence and to match supply to demand outside the planning time fence.

- **Master Scheduling:** The required process of disaggregating the approved aggregate Production Plan over the full planning horizon into items by week/day by production site to support the aggregate Demand Plan and the detailed Demand Plan with a particular focus on items or options inside the first three to four months of the plan. The Master Schedule must be free of unnecessary modifiers that cause waste while still allowing operational efficiency targets to be met.

- **Material Requirements Planning and Item Master Accuracy:** The process that must be in place for planning receipt of the right quantity of materials at the right time; it requires excellent inventory accuracy, item master accuracy, bill of material accuracy, a valid Master Schedule, and correct behaviors to ensure that materials plans are executable while maintaining minimum inventory levels by working all system-generated action messages daily. As with the Master Schedule, MRP must be free of unnecessary modifiers that cause waste while still achieving targeted levels of operational efficiency.

- **Capacity Planning and Validation:** The process that must be performed for all planning levels (IBP—RRP; Master Schedule—RCP and MRP; Internal and External Supply—Detail Capacity Planning) to ensure capacity is available when needed, and, if it isn't, the Capacity Planner and Supervisor provide options to the Master Scheduler and Production Manager to support the plan.

- **Internal Priorities:** Breaking down order due dates into due dates for each required operation that enables tracking of order progress through Internal Scheduling and increasing the likelihood of meeting the order due date by a factor of 10.

- **Demand Control/Execution:** The process managed by Supply Planning and Demand (often Customer Service) using Available-to-Promise, Forecast Roll, and Forecast Consumption to ensure that valid customer promises are made when customers request an order delivery date. Demand Control provides near-term insights regarding actual customer orders, which, if different from the MBR-approved Demand Plan, must be investigated for action and may require changing the forecast, which will then eliminate the firefighting for that issue.
- **External Sourcing:** The process of enabling Buyers, given reduced need to expedite orders, to work closely with suppliers to improve quality, on-time in full delivery performance, reducing product costs and shortening lead times, facilitated by collaborative two-way sharing of valid plans across the full, agreed MRP planning horizon.
- **Finance:** Rather than keeping score and independently developing revenue, profit, and cash flow projections, Finance must be integrated into the planning processes so that projections are developed from the same set of numbers used by other functions and that scenarios, risks, and opportunities contribute to better decision-making and improving company performance.

The biggest challenge for most companies' leadership in realizing the benefits of the processes recommended in this book is changing behaviors and changing a company's culture. Those changes require understanding and commitment from Leadership. Culture change does not flow uphill!

Principles

There are relatively few principles that must be followed in changing the culture. The underlying and supporting behaviors must be lived by Leadership, who must hold themselves and everyone else accountable for living these principles.

- **Tell the Truth:** Truth eventually becomes self-evident and cannot be avoided. It is astounding how much bad news is covered up to make a department look good. Covering up bad news prevents a company from identifying and eliminating the root causes of the bad news. When sharing that bad news finally becomes unavoidable, it is often very expensive and even too late to recover. The principle that must be followed is delivering both bad news and good news as early as possible. An important corollary to this principle for Leadership is not to "kill the messenger" who delivers the bad news. Killing the messenger even once or twice will ensure that bad news is never delivered until it is too late to recover.

- **Silence Is Approval:** When a flawed plan is distributed, whoever recognizes a flaw that will prevent successful execution of that plan is responsible for speaking up immediately. People are expected to tell the truth not only when asked, but also even if not asked. If there is a flaw that prevents someone from successfully executing a plan, and that person does not speak up, he or she becomes accountable for executing that plan as distributed!
- **Workforce Education:** People in an organization and those joining the organization, even those in executive positions, must be formally educated in the related business processes, measures, roles, responsibilities, and expected behaviors.
- **Culture:** Each individual must do what they are expected to do and what they say they will do. There should never be a need to follow up or chase people to do their jobs.
- **Accountability:** Individuals receive timely feedback (positive and negative), are held accountable for carrying out their roles, and are rewarded for doing their job.
- **Valid Plans:** Plans at all planning levels are valid, that is, accurate and achievable. Any plan with a date that is past due is not valid.
- **Planning with Demonstrated/Planned Capacities:** All plans are based upon work location output achieved over the past few months modified with planned capacity changes. Desired output levels are never used for planning until demonstrated.
- **Valid Delivery Dates:** Any order not shipped as planned must be rescheduled with a valid delivery date.
- **Documented Processes:** All processes must be formally documented and periodically reviewed to ensure they are being followed or are being modified to reflect process improvements. The organization cannot be people-dependent, meaning reliant upon people just knowing what to do, having had that information passed down informally from other people.
- **Business Focus and Teamwork:** Business Objectives take precedence over functional objectives. Cross-functional teamwork is essential in closing gaps to strategy and annual plans.
- **Strategic Business Objectives and Goals:** Strategic Business objectives and goals are understood across all functional organizations. Accountability for achieving those strategic business objectives and goals is shared by the Leadership Team and across all areas of the business.

■ **Shared and Integrated KPIs:** While each function has specific measures that allow all areas to optimize its resources, the primary KPIs should relate to business results supported by those functional KPIs. KPIs should be used to ensure "we are doing what we said we would do" and as the basis for continuous improvement. If there are KPIs that do not serve these objectives and are not being used to drive improvement, they should no longer be tracked and reported.

Summary

This chapter has focused on the Finance organization, even though it does not appear in Business Excellence Planning, Figure 15.1. Finance is embedded in every process shown in the Business Excellence Planning figure. When Finance becomes a partner and not a scorekeeper by integrating the financials into all processes, the result is one set of numbers for planning the entire business. All decisions made are based upon value and volume, not just volume.

For additional but more specific reading please visit the Oliver Wight Website and gain access to the extensive library of White Papers.

Note

1. Cash flow is not revenue, but the succession collection of that revenue through the accounts receivable process is cash flow.

CHAPTER 16

Business Improvement:
Being Lean and Agile

This chapter is not an in-depth discussion of Lean or Agile. Many books already cover those techniques well. Rather, this chapter addresses how Lean and Agile can contribute to excellence in Business Planning and Execution

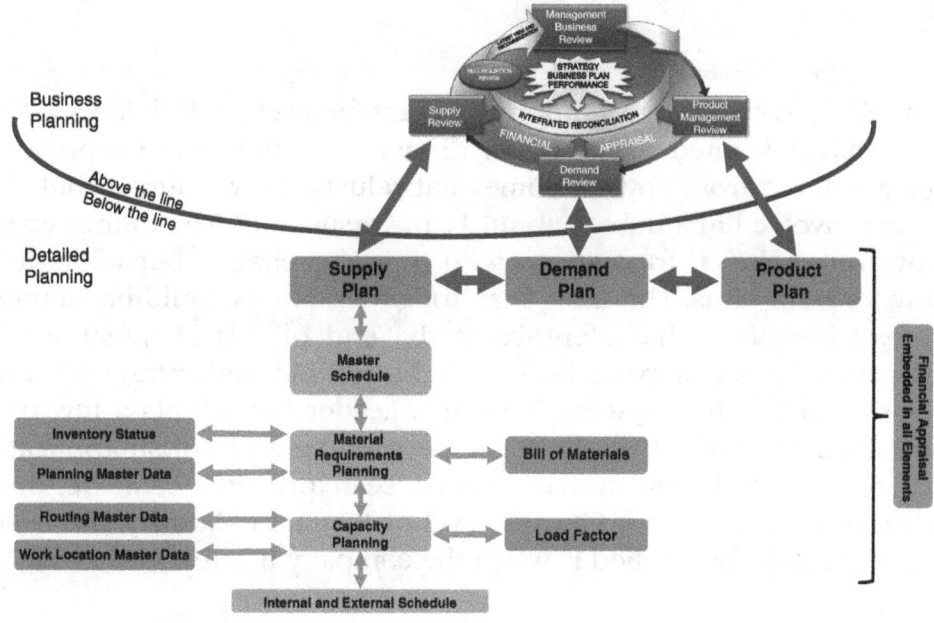

FIGURE 16.1 Business Excellence Planning

and, consequently, improve the overall performance of Business Excellence Planning:

Let us be clear, Lean is not about headcount reduction; it is about improving process velocity through the elimination of waste. One way to measure Lean progress is cash-to-cash cycle time.[1] All too often, senior executives say their companies are very Lean because they have reduced headcount, but this is not the purpose of Lean. If headcount is reduced to save cost or satisfy shareholders, then who in the future will want to improve business results? Who will be motivated to work on improvements if improvements mean elimination of their, or their colleagues', jobs?

Additionally, with improved process velocity, the business should be able to do more. In this example, fewer people are needed to operate high-velocity processes rather than many people to operate broken processes having lots of embedded waste. People who are freed up should then be trained to support other parts of the growing business. In order to do this the business must have an improvement strategy based on delivering its Strategic Business Objectives.

Lean and Agile are very closely related. That relationship is described in this chapter.

Lean

While working with a large equipment manufacturer in Belgium, a Class A Project Manager wanted us to go to dinner with the new Corporate Lean Director just hired from Toyota. Somewhat reluctantly we agreed but did not want to get involved in a debate about Lean versus MRP. The dinner conversation, however, included frustrations with trying to change behaviors inside a company for both of us. The Lean Director's frustrations could be summed up by Jeffery Liker's (see the reference at the end of this chapter) statement, ". . .companies have embraced Lean tools but do not understand what makes them work together in a system. Typically, Leadership adopts a few of these technical tools and then struggles to go beyond the amateurish application of them to create a technical system." While Lean principles can be, and are, applied in companies with a Phase 1 level of Business Maturity, the best time for the principles to be applied is when the company has reached Phase 2 with a focus on end-to-end processes. Why? Because end-to-end processes have eliminated the traditional gaps between functions and departments, and the waste that exists between them is ready to be identified and eliminated.

Our conversation started a long-standing relationship because we discovered we were in complete alignment. Working together in Belgium, we were able to break down the barriers between Lean and Business Excellence Planning. The Director invited us to continue working with them in their biggest US plant.

He asked us to read *The Toyota Way* (Liker 2004), which highlighted and reinforced the many similarities between the Unparalleled Business Planning and Execution Practices implementation approach and Toyota's improvement approach. Liker states, "Toyota is a true learning organization that has been evolving and learning for over a century. This investment in its employees should frighten those traditional companies . . . that merely focus on making parts and counting quarterly dollars. . ." That is the same starting point for us: people, processes, and then, and only then, technology and tools. After people have been educated and trained in Business Excellence Planning, they must then be empowered to improve those processes.

Take away the waste in and between processes and you do not need the time or energy to manage it. So, with a Lean implementation, make sure you involve Sales and Marketing to win more business in order to utilize the resulting increased capacity. "Lean and Mean" does not mean fewer people.

Kanban

The Director's biggest frustration was with his new company's singular focus on Kanban.[2] He was in total agreement with Liker, who wrote in his book *The Toyota Way*, "Yet TPS [Toyota Production System] experts get very impatient and even irritated when they hear people rave and focus on *Kanban* as if it is the Toyota Production System. *Kanban* is a fascinating concept and it is fun to watch" (Liker 2004, p. 110). Toyota didn't have computers at that time to do the scheduling, so they had to communicate schedules by developing manual systems. They used a two-bin system but understood that two-bin systems don't work well with erratic schedules and long lead times. With that in mind, they reduced options to provide more schedule stability. At the same time, they shortened lead times by implementing one-piece flows and reducing setup times. With those changes, their two-bin system had a chance of working. Liker does take exception to Kanban with this remarkable statement: "Remember: the *Kanban* is an organized system of inventory buffers and, according to Ohno, inventory is waste . . . So, *Kanban* is something you strive to get rid of, not be proud of" (Liker 2004, p. 110).

We are a big proponent of Kanban when used in the right place at the right time. However, the effort to replace Business Excellence Planning with Kanban has gone overboard. The Corporate Planning VP, at the same heavy equipment manufacturer, asked us to visit with him at a couple of his sites that were doing extraordinary things with Kanban. The first site was a division making pads or shoes for the vehicle tracks. They first set up Kanbans for the pads, which quadrupled the inventory, not only because of the spares required, but also because of the varying demand of production parts. While on the shop floor reviewing the process, the Pad Lean Team explained a new process, just implemented, that reduced the required inventory to support the Kanban. The tracks were assembled by a local supplier. The Pad Lean Team said they got the schedule from the supplier that assembled the tracks, which represented 90% of the total demand since the pads were mounted to the supplier's tracks. By having that schedule they could eliminate all of the Kanbans for the pads used in production because they knew, with 90% certainty, what the demand would be. When we asked where the supplier got that schedule, the Lean group said they didn't know, but their own Master Scheduler for the division, who was standing off to the side, said that the supplier's schedule came directly from his Master Schedule. (We had previously worked with this site on their processes to create "valid schedules.") So all the effort that went into developing Kanbans for the pads used in production and all the inventory held in Kanbans was a complete waste. The VP said nothing but was obviously upset at all the waste.

The next site we visited was an assembly plant that was using Kanbans to build the frames for one of the assembly lines. They had cleared a very large area where Kanbans were set up for each style of frame. The major difference between most of the frames was the location of welded studs. They were working overtime to fill all the Kanbans and the inventory (which skyrocketed) but were very proud that they had figured out how to use Kanbans to support the line. The foreman of the welding area, with whom we had previously worked, grumbled to us that this was the "stupidest" thing he had ever seen and that the line schedule tells them exactly what frame to make without the need of all the Kanban inventory. The VP walked away shaking his head. In the car on the way back to his office, we asked him what he would do about what we had just learned. He said, sadly, there was nothing he could do because Leadership was convinced that Kanban was the reason for Toyota's success.

A little knowledge and commitment without understanding can be very dangerous, and often leads to a "flavor of the month" approach, which means when Leadership hears of a new "thing," it gains a superficial understanding of it and then makes the decision to implement it everywhere. It is much better to have detailed knowledge of all options and then implement the right one where it is needed – "horses for the right courses."

Scheduling

As Liker says, "There are many examples of scheduling throughout Toyota" (Liker 2004, p. 110). We need to stop here and refer back to statements in previous chapters. It is not just a schedule that's needed but a valid schedule, one that is accurate and achievable. The Toyota culture would not permit anything other than a valid schedule. Here is another interesting thought from Liker: "When Toyota managers do schedule they are preoccupied with timeliness. In other words, the schedule is not simply a guideline that you should do your best to make, more or less. It is a deadline, and you move heaven and earth to make the deadline." Starting with a valid schedule, this very same aspect of the culture must be inherent across a company for schedules to be successfully executed, but this passion is missing in 90% of the companies we visit. When a schedule is not valid, it is impossible to meet. Where is the ownership if people don't believe their schedules?

Another excellent Liker quote is, "People Do the Work, Computers Move the Information" (Liker 2004, p. 161). A culture that emphasizes continuous improvement is essential for the processes explained in previous chapters to be successful.

Key Lean Improvements

Key Lean improvements used to drive waste out of a production process include:

- **BOM level reduction:** Engineering design often needs multiple levels in their bills of material, but the manufacturing process does not always need as many. Simple planning system coding allows design engineering levels to exist but makes them invisible for planning and execution purposes. A BOM with fewer levels enables shorter lead times; this is waste reduction and is part of a Lean approach.

- **Single piece flow:** Every time a single-piece flow is established (see Chapter 11), one or more operations can be eliminated. Continue creating single-piece flows and eventually there will be only one operation. Combine that operation with the parent item assembly and a BOM level is eliminated. What does that mean for planning? Fewer items to plan and manage – a win/win.
- **Lead-time Reduction:** Every time an operation in a BOM level is eliminated, lead time is reduced, inventory is reduced, cost is reduced, and so forth.
- **Setup Reduction:** Setup time is the cost of changing over from producing one item to another; it is pure waste. An order quantity of one (see Managing MRP, Chapter 6) is always the best because that means there will be no unneeded parts sitting in inventory (another form of waste). Unfortunately, setup times normally prohibit a lot size of one. In those situations, the best option is a fixed order quantity developed using an economic order quantity formula. A common formula used is:

$$\text{Economic order quantity} = \frac{\sqrt{2 \times \text{Setup time} \times \text{Annual usage}}}{\text{Carrying cost}}$$

Using Lean techniques to reduce a work location's setup time, especially for a constrained work location, will ultimately reduce setup time to zero, resulting in an economic order quantity of zero. Only what is needed at the moment need be produced.

The objective of Lean is elimination of waste through understanding what is truly value add compared to what is non-value add or essential but non-value add (customer inspection, for example). Waste examples include:

- **Overproduction:** Too much, too early, just-in-case.
- **Waiting:** The enemy of smooth flow (materials, money, information).
- **Transporting and moving:** Directly proportional to damage and scrap, which delays the revenue stream.
- **Inappropriate processes:** Using a hammer to crack the nut.

- **Unnecessary inventory or work in progress:** Masks problems that lie hidden and creates additional waste.
- **Unnecessary motion:** Indicates the need for application of workplace ergonomics
- **Defects:** The waste of internal and external failure.
- **Untapped human potential:** Failure to create a culture of inclusion and teamwork; wasting human resources on firefighting.
- **Energy:** As simple as leaving unneeded lights turned on or machines running when not required.

Velocity

Velocity is a simple calculation shown in Figure 16.2 that enables you to understand the percentage of time value that is being added to a product out of the total time in residence from the time component parts are received from suppliers to the time the finished product is shipped to customers, and then, following improvement, recalculating the velocity to see how well the process has improved. It is a type of benchmarking approach to measure and visualize improvements. It should be noted that the velocity equation can be applied to any Business Process either end-to-end or in part. Additionally, this is a formula that can be applied to any process in any part of the business; it is not just for Supply Chain.

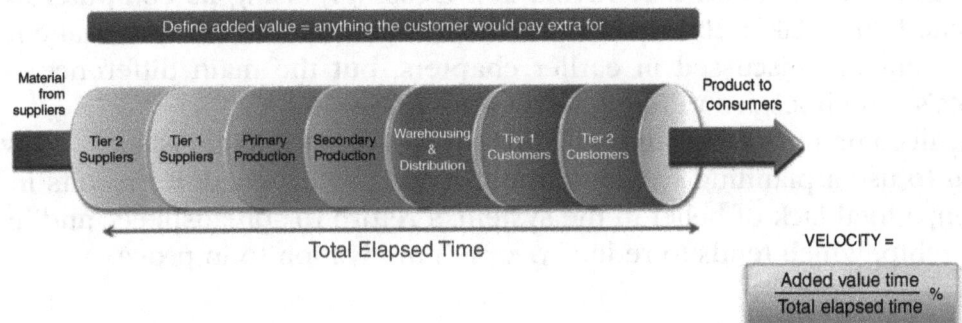

FIGURE 16.2 The Velocity Equation

When process maps have been converted to value stream maps, the more difficult task is to get people to think of value-add differently. Traditional wastes, such as those listed earlier, are relatively easy to eliminate; the trick is to ensure that the process focuses on value-adding steps. A good way to change thinking would be to get people to think of value as something a customer would pay for.

What Comes First?

There could be a long debate regarding what comes first, implementing or upgrading a planning system or Lean? The answer lies in the company's current situation and level of Business Maturity. Typically, companies today have a planning system that is being poorly utilized, and, at the same time, they have initiated some Lean. Unfortunately, these are often in conflict and neither delivers its full potential, usually because processes are broken, not well integrated, and often very people dependent (the true process is in the memory of the person and not documented in the process). The focus must first and foremost be aligned to the strategic business objectives, not on a random or loosely associated sub-element of the business or on the efforts of well-meaning individuals; these will not sustainably improve bottom-line business results. However, the primary effort must be on creating valid schedules, which eliminates the need for Kanbans that must be maintained as schedules change.

Schedules

Liker states in his book that Toyota is increasingly using its computer system for scheduling (Liker 2004, p. 159). This sounds a bit like the "just make it happen" mentality discussed in earlier chapters, but the main difference is that Toyota's schedules are valid, and everyone knows it.

In all companies with valid schedules, this same attitude must exist. However, trying to use a planning system without having valid schedules results in frustration, a total lack of belief in the system, a return to spreadsheets, and limited ownership, which tends to reduce people's motivation to improve.

Agile

Agile has been around for many years with lots of papers written and many seminars attended. Rather than compile that information in this book, Wikipedia provides the following definition:

"Agility is a term applied to an organization that has created the processes, tools, and training to enable it to respond quickly to customer needs and market changes while still controlling costs, quality and maintaining issued schedules. An enabling factor in becoming agile has been the development of support technology that allows all resource managers (like the marketers, the designers and the supply chain personnel) to share a common database of parts and products, to share data on production capacities and problems. This is particularly important where small initial problems may have larger downstream effects. The cost of correcting quality increases as the problem moves downstream. It is easier and cheaper to correct problems at source."

Agility must not be confused with Flexibility; they are very different and must be understood correctly. Compared to the definition for Agility, Flexibility is investment in people, tools, and systems to enable them to quickly and cost-effectively move, activity to activity, without any loss of time, quality, or focus.

Many will advocate that Agile is just an extension of Lean while others look to technology to provide the answer. For instance, one client company eliminated setup time totally by purchasing an array of machines, each of which could produce any part with zero setup. This reduced inventory, allowed them to be more Agile, and improved cash flow since raw material and in-process inventories decreased. Just load the fixture and produce what is on the Priority Schedule (dispatch list) explained in Chapter 11, Internal Priorities.

The debate between Lean and Agile is unnecessary because both improve results. What is clear, however, for Agile to be most effective is "development of support technology that allows all the functional resource managers (the marketers, the designers and the supply chain personnel) to share a common database of parts and products, to share data on production capacities and problems. . .," as stated in the Wikipedia definition. The planning system described throughout this book provides the foundation for successful agility.

The relationship between Lean and Agile and their application is shown in Figure 16.3.

Lean, Agile, and Required Behaviors

It is fair to say that successful implementation of Lean (not a tool to be simply dropped into a business because it's a different way of doing business) in a business requires a significant shift in employee and management mindset/behavior. Through elimination of waste, Lean progressively and systematically

Agile & Lean – They work together

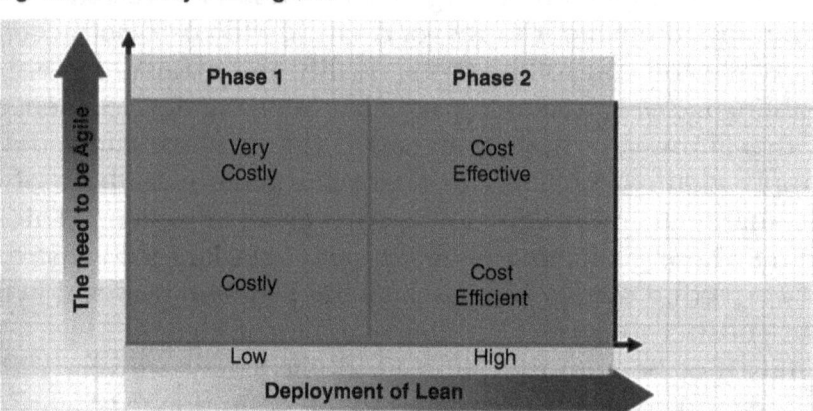

FIGURE 16.3 Relationship between Lean and Agile

eliminates traditional excuses and enables an environment in which people feel supported and at ease to report bad news early. The business will benefit from Lean only if problems and issues are surfaced quickly.

Business Maturity must be relatively high to gain the full benefits of Agile capability. Agile requires faster (high velocity), streamlined, and integrated processes driven through effective teamwork and shared/aligned goals and measures.

At the top of Phase 1 in Figure 16.3, processes should be fully mapped and available for conversion to Value Stream Maps for elimination of waste. At this point in development, processes should no longer be dependent upon people or personalities, and adjacent processes should be more easily integrated with each other.

Providing customers cost-effective Agility requires a planned response to potential issues and risks. If these do not exist for at least the most likely issues and risks, responses are not Agile, but reactive and costly, in essence a firefighting environment. More about people and behaviors can be found in Chapter 18.

Figure 16.4 shows the relationship between the various available Business Improvement options and Business Maturity. If Lean is deployed in a Phase 1 environment it tends to deliver benefits by function or department rather than

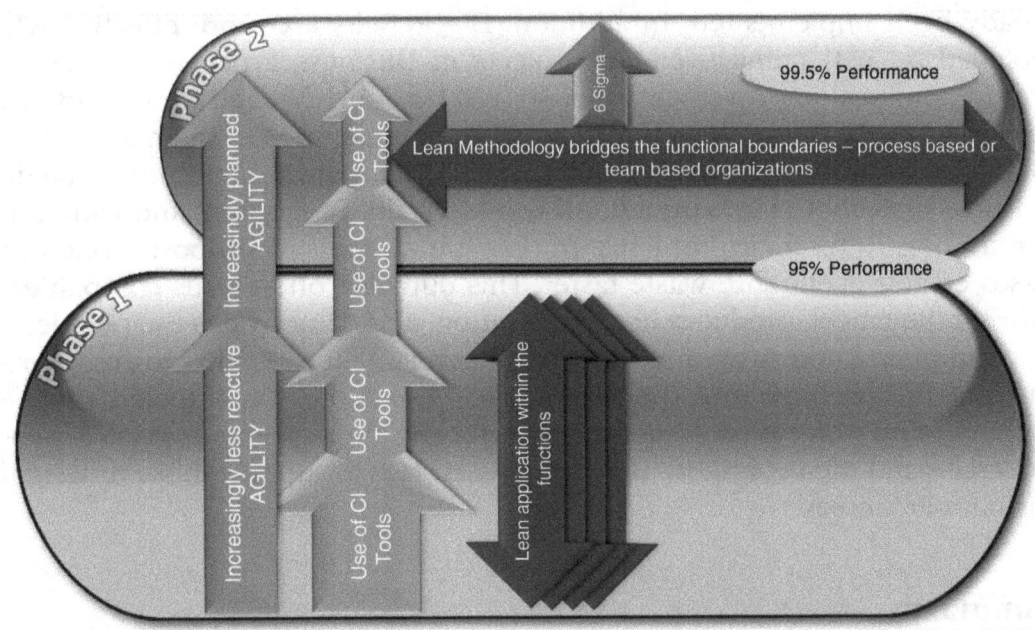

FIGURE 16.4 Maturity and Business Improvement Techniques

the benefits that would be gained in a Phase 2 deployment in which you would apply the principles to End-to-End Business Processes.

Figure 16.4 also shows how agility moves from being reactive (more like firefighting or churn) in Phase 1 to planned in Phase 2. This is more cost effective when the business is more in control and approaching the boundary between Phase 1 and Phase 2.

In addition, the arrows showing the use of Continuous Improvement (CI) Tools (fishbone diagrams, 5 Why's, Pareto's, etc.) are shown in Phase 1 where their use is more urgently required. The opportunity for their use is greater the lower the Business Maturity level. Their use should be encouraged since enabling people to implement their own improvements increases ownership, and it changes paradigms. So, the added advantage of using CI tools is the culture change it begins to enable.

Finally, Six Sigma is clearly shown building on the implementation of Lean in Business Processes since its methodology works on the belief that Lean has already been implemented. In addition, Black Belts are more effective when deployed on major improvement projects in Business Processes rather than working on local improvements that should be done through local teams with simpler CI tools. Before beginning any Lean or Agile project there should be a good understanding of Unparalleled Business Planning and Execution Practices and how they should be applied. All too often this is ignored, and companies turn to tools to fix their problems. Implementing tools to support broken processes creates even more waste faster. This outcome often leads companies to reinvent the wheel, produces huge frustration, and demotivates the people, not to mention is a poor use of an expensive investment. It is vital to fix the root cause of the problem, not the symptoms. Ensure the Unparalleled Business Planning and Execution Practices have been incorporated into Business Processes, and then configure the planning system to support those redesigned Business Processes.

Summary

There should be no conflict between Lean, Agile, and Business Excellence Planning! Companies must understand how each of these will help them improve performance and provide competitive advantage. Properly integrated into Business Excellence Planning, Figure 16.5, these techniques can make a company invincible in the eyes of its competitors.

Liker, Jeffrey K. 2004. *The Toyota Way: 14 Management Principles from the World's Greatest Manufactures*. McGraw-Hill.

For additional but more specific reading please visit the Oliver Wight Website and gain access to the extensive library of White Papers.

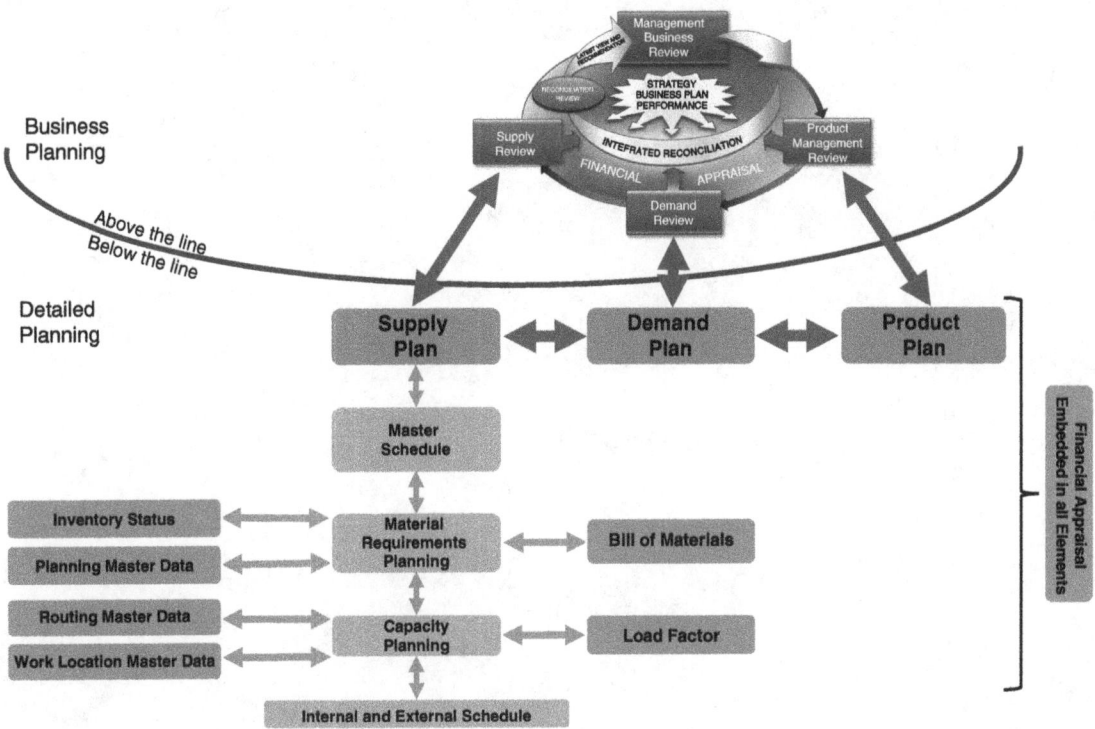

FIGURE 16.5 Business Excellence Planning

Notes

1. The APICS/ASCM Dictionary defines "cash-to-cash cycle time" as an indicator of how efficiently a company manages its assets to improve cash flow. Cash-to-cash cycle time is calculated as inventory days plus accounts receivable days minus accounts payable days.

2. A method of production scheduling that uses standard containers or lot sizes with a single card attached to each. It is a system in which work centers signal with a card that they wish to withdraw parts from feeding operations or suppliers. The Japanese word *Kanban*, loosely translated, means card, billboard, or sign, but other signaling devices such as colored golf balls have also been used.

CHAPTER 17

Technology Enhancements: What You Need and Not Just Following a Market Trend

This chapter provides a few examples of enhancements made to current planning system technology and future enhancements. These are only a

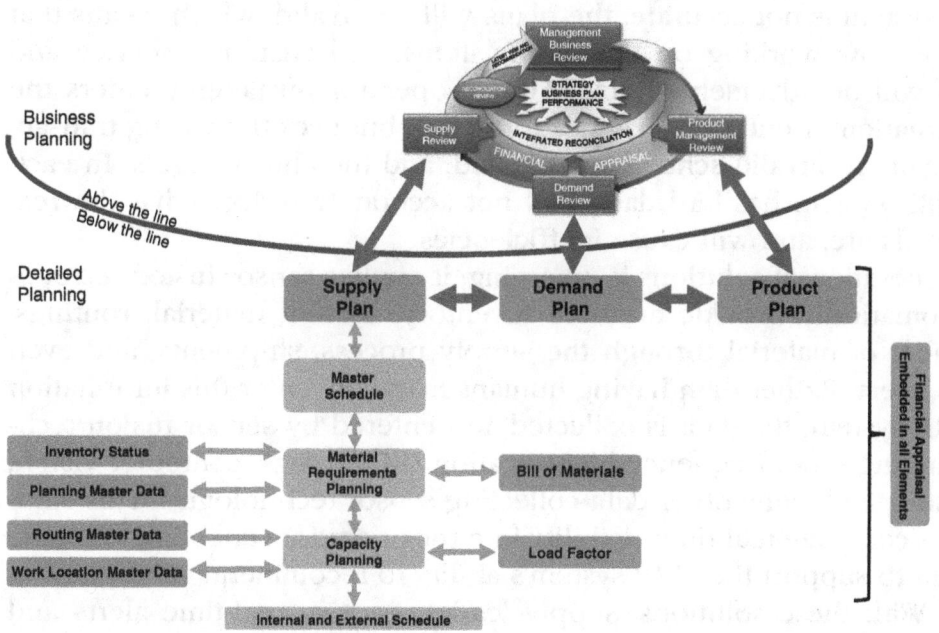

FIGURE 17.1 Business Excellence Planning

select few, but they provide a starting point. From the day this book is published, this information will be outdated given today's rate of technological change.

All described enhancements are applicable to Business Excellence Planning, Figure 17.1. Will the model change? Probably, but, as technology improvements come along, the basics will always remain.

Data Accuracy

Historically, Materials Requirements Planning (MRP I) and Manufacturing Resource Planning (MRP II) solutions have been very high touch, requiring workers to manually enter information regarding inventory, bills of material, routings, work orders, and shipments. Workers had to enter almost everything they did to provide accurate information to the planning and execution systems to assure that a valid plan (accurate and achievable) was in place. As described in previous chapters, those plans provide operational direction to meet customer requirements in the most economical way possible and at the same time provide visibility to cross-functional leaders. The manual entry of this data can create latency and accuracy issues in the MRP system. If the data in the MRP system is not accurate, the plans will be invalid, which means that Operations is now working on the wrong items, and customer service and profitability will be adversely affected. If the operator mistakenly enters the wrong information or enters the right information but uses the wrong transaction type, again an invalid schedule is created, and the churn begins. In each case, the MRP system has bad data, will not accurately reflect what the real customer needs are, and will cause inefficiencies.

A new generation of solutions is emerging; it applies sensor fusion technology[1] to automatically provide accurate inventory, bills of material, routings, and movement of material through the supply process, shipments, and even customer delivery. Rather than having humans manually enter this information into the MRP system, the data is collected and entered by sensor fusion technology, including radio-frequency identification (RFID) tags, computer vision, weight sensors, and many other data-collecting sensor technologies. This solution provides complete real-time visibility into the operation, enabling real-time accurate data to support the MRP system's ability to recommend valid plans at a low cost. With these solutions, supply leaders receive real-time alerts and notifications indicating when the plan is out of balance (not valid) so proper corrective action can be taken. Now there is confidence in the plan and people can focus on plan execution.

Sensor fusion technology can help in the following areas to significantly improve data accuracy and provide information needed for a valid plan (accurate and achievable):

- **Inventory Accuracy**
  - **Receiving into the Facility:** Raw materials and inventory are tagged and on-boarded into the system, enabling them to be tracked throughout their lifecycle. With RFID tags applied at the supplier, on-time shipment and transportation can also be tracked automatically.
  - **Receiving into a Specific Location:** After the product is received into a receiving location, it then goes into a specific storage location such as 12-6-B-A (aisle 12; rack 6; level B; slot A), which is used to quickly find the product.
  - **Stock-to-Stock Transfers:** When stock is moved to a different location, the new location is automatically updated in the planning system.
  - **Issuing from a Specific Location to a Work Order:** When the product is moved from its storage location for production, it is issued to a work order in the MRP system.
  - **Back Flushing:** Back flushing at each station on the production line instead of the end of the line is done quickly and efficiently.
  - **Scrapped Items on a Work Order** – When a work order is released to manufacturing, losses can occur because some of the product may be scrapped due to defects or line damage. That loss should be reported in the system but often is not. When the product is moved to the next operation, a signal is sent to the planning system indicating that the quantity is not correct. This allows the work order quantity to be adjusted and immediate corrective action can be taken.
- **Bill of Material Accuracy**
  - **Issued to Work Order:** When material for a work order is pulled from its storage location, the material is automatically scanned and checked against the bill of material to ensure that all required components and correct quantities have been issued. With sensor fusion technology, automatic issuing can be transacted with a deficiency report generated

and sent to the material planner for action to resolve the issue now and prevent future problems.

- **Completed Work Order:** When an order/assembly is completed, scanning the item will determine if everything according to the bill of material is present or if anything additional is present. This assures product conformance and allows the planner to immediately investigate discrepancies.

- **Routing Accuracy**
  - **Work Location Correct:** This compares the work location scanned to the work location on the Routing. One company GM was pushing to increase productivity when, through an audit, he discovered that jobs were being run frequently on alternate machines, which lowered productivity. Productivity increased by 9% when detail capacity planning was put in place and permission to run on an alternate machine was required from Industrial Engineering. A more significant result of this change was an on-time delivery increase from 31% to 97%.
  - **Setup/Run Time Correct:** Was the setup time reported within a preestablished tolerance? Reported to a cell phone, the supervisors can immediately see if the time was within tolerance, giving them an opportunity to talk to the operator to identify and eliminate the root cause of the problem.
  - **Sequence Correct:** Did the sequence of the work completed match the Routing? This information provides a great opportunity to improve the quality of the work. Often the sequence is changed on the shop floor because it delivers a higher-quality product, but no one takes time to change the Routing.

- **Work Order Tracking by Operation**
  - **Scrap:** Was the scrap reported the same as the actual scrap produced? This information gives the planner the opportunity to see problems developing. The planner can then release another order at lead time to avoid shortages resulting from scrapped materials.
  - **Rework:** Was the rework reported the same as the actual count? When rework is identified, the planner can schedule production to satisfy demand.
  - **On-Time Release:** Was the order released on time? If Manufacturing and Purchasing are to meet due dates, a minimum of 95% of orders must be released on time. If on-time release performance is below 95%, the root cause must be identified and eliminated.
  - **On-Time Operation Started/Completed:** Was the operation started/completed on time? This information gives the supervisor the real-time information needed to resolve potential missed order due dates.

- **On-Time Order Completion:** Was the order completed on time? On-time order completion is what MRP relies on and must be above 95% to achieve on-time order completion dates.
- **Time Constraint Alert:** If there is a time constraint on an operation an alert is sent to notify that the operation time constraint is in jeopardy of being missed.
- **Planning Data**
  - **Scrap Percentage:** What was the scrap percentage on the order compared to the scrap percentage included in the planning system? Including scrap factors in the MRP system addresses the reality of scrap in the supply chain, but, if not monitored and updated regularly, system material recommendations will become invalid. If scrap levels are reduced, the reduction must be updated in the system. This system capability results in messages being sent to the planner each time an order is run with analysis of the scrap factor.
  - **Rework Percentage:** What was the percentage of rework? Like scrap, rework must be analyzed to ensure plans are valid.
  - **Lead Time:** What was the actual lead time compared to the planned lead time in MRP? The two are not expected to be identical because from the time the order is released to the time it is completed, the timing could be changed based upon MRP system expedite or de-expedite messages but they should be close. If the variation is large, or if the variation is consistent, the differences must be investigated and corrected in the planning system.[2]

Blockchain for Supply Chain

Blockchain technology[3] is another potential driver of data accuracy across the supply chain, including upstream to suppliers and downstream to the end consumer. This technology is most widely known for its use with cryptocurrencies, such as Bitcoin. The strength of the technology is due to its base nature; it is essentially a distributed data ledger. Real benefits within the supply chain include:

- **Transparency:** All partners across the supply chain have a common picture of the current situation.
- **Truth:** By its distributed nature, there is only one set of numbers since every transaction must pass stringent approvals established by the participants.

- **Traceability:** Supply chains requiring lot and batch traceability benefit by recording the full history of every transaction, from raw material at the origin country and supplier of origin through finished goods at the end consumer.
- **Real-Time Monitoring:** Partners can monitor the real-time status of goods moving through the supply chain to address issues faster and sooner when there are still multiple courses of action available to resolve the issues.
- **Insights:** Availability of information from the end of the supply chain, like changes in demand, can be leveraged immediately at the beginning of the supply chain to better balance demand and supply.

At the time of this publishing, data standards are still being developed to support use of this technology within the supply chain, but the benefits appear to be incredibly promising.

Artificial Intelligence

Artificial intelligence (AI) exists in several forms. For over 30 years, capacity planning systems have attempted to solve capacity overload and underload problems. This is a form of artificial intelligence. Most of these systems used if/then logic, also called rules-based logic. For example, *if* required capacity exceeds planned capacity, *then* first look at using overtime (within the constraints of some rules, like no more than 10%, no more than two weekends in the summer, and so on). *If* that does not solve the problem, *then* look to see if the work can be done on an alternate work center with available capacity or reschedule the work. Those systems were generally called finite loaders. The biggest problem with finite loading occurred during rescheduling when the system needed to move the load out into the future or pull it in. If pulled in it could make operations past due and if pushed out it could push the order past the need date.

While participating in an APICS testing committee, we had a disagreement with a committee member who worked for a company that used and sold infinite loading software. We said infinite loading did not work; he said it was great. To help resolve the different positions, the next test committee meeting was scheduled in a location where a finite loader was being used. On tour, we listened to the foreman rave about how good the system was. If the foreman missed the operation due date, the system automatically pushed the order out, resulting in no late orders. As this staged demonstration continued, we saw some executives talking farther down the aisle. Never shy, we moved closer to listen in. One person was very unhappy, and another person was trying to calm him down. We asked someone listening what was going on. She said it was the Sales VP trying to understand why Operations kept missing customer delivery dates and explaining that the customers were very unhappy. She said they had already lost customers because the system kept automatically rescheduling orders out into the future, and missing customer due dates.

As an aside, one solution to the problem of missing operation dates is compressing the queue between operations. When that happens, the system back schedules the remaining operations, resulting in some operations being past due. This must be done only with agreement of Production, who must have a plan to meet the order due date.

A newer form of artificial intelligence (AI) includes neural nets, deep learning, and machine learning. These types of AI work quite differently from if/then rules-based logic. Basically, they work more similarly to how human brains work. This means they need a good deal of "training" or "learning." For simplicity, these forms will be referred to as neural net AI with its training/learning in two forms: supervised and unsupervised.

With unsupervised learning, the AI algorithm learns on its own. This works, for example, when an AI algorithm learns to play a game such as Go[4] or Risk. Once the rules of the game are put into the algorithm, the machine tries a move and, using the rules of the game, the machine determines on its own whether what it tried was successful or not. Doing this over and over gradually trains the algorithm, and computers are capable doing this type of learning millions or billions of times.

Supervised learning requires outside help. For example, an image recognition AI algorithm needs to know if the picture is, for example, a tiger or not a tiger. It cannot learn this on its own. Instead, it needs to be fed labeled pictures of tigers and labeled pictures that are not tigers. After being fed millions of pictures of tigers and not tigers, the algorithm is capable of determining whether or not a picture is a tiger. This tiger example is a simple illustration intended to explain the concept; actual image recognition AI algorithms are more general and are not restricted to one type of image.

With that as background, will neural net AI provide significant benefits to planning systems? Possibly, but some fairly serious limitations exist at the current time. One concern is the massive amount of data required for learning.

Consider, for example, a neural net AI algorithm designed to automatically handle exception messages recommending that an order should be rescheduled to an earlier date. If the item is a manufactured item, how many remaining operations must be completed; how long will they take; can the work be done on other equipment; is there available capacity at an earlier date; is there move and queue time that can be compressed (as explained earlier); are there other orders also having their move and queue time compressed; are there limitations in skilled operators; and so on?

The number of combinations of all these variables becomes extremely large. For the algorithm to learn what to do, it would have to be exposed to many of these different combinations of variables. At any one company, there just may not be enough learning data available.

So, the question is, can we use learning/training data from many companies to train this exception AI algorithm? Possibly, but the situations in the various companies would need to be similar. For example, one company might operate with small margins and be willing to make a customer wait rather than incur a large cost to reschedule an order to an earlier date. A second company that produces low-volume, high-margin products may be willing to incur higher costs to reschedule an order to an earlier date to deliver a finished item to a customer earlier. We would not want to confuse this exception AI algorithm with this type of inconsistent training data.

If, at some point in the future, these neural net AI algorithms are capable of learning from much smaller training data sets, then it might be feasible for an algorithm to be trained on a single company's data, assuming the company does not have too many different types of products (as in the example), some high-margin products, some low-margin products, and so on. It also assumes that the business has not changed significantly so that what a planner would do to handle a situation in the past is also how that situation would be handled in the future. For example, if a business has been disrupted by a new technology, such as electric cars, then the way someone dealt with a planning situation in the past may not be appropriate in the future. In such a case, it would be necessary to train the AI algorithm on the new business realities to prevent the algorithm from blindly taking actions that would be appropriate for internal combustion–powered cars but not appropriate for electric cars.

The basic issue is that judgment and creativity are things people apply reasonably, and computers do not, at least currently. So, if there is a significant amount of judgment and/or creativity required in a situation, and there is not a huge amount of training data, then that situation is probably not a good opportunity to use a neural net AI algorithm.

A more reasonable case could be made for categorizing abnormal demands using a neural net AI algorithm. Looking at a pattern of sales and identifying outliers is something that could possibly be similar across many companies and for many products. Image recognition is a skill which deep learning neural nets have been proven to do well, and a sales pattern is a type of image. If/then rules-based logic has been used for years to identify outliers, and so it would be interesting to see if an AI algorithm trained across many companies and many products would give better results.

A second basic issue with neural net AI algorithms is accountability, also an issue with if/then rules-based artificial intelligence. If it is not clear how an artificial intelligence algorithm came up with an action or recommendation, then it is difficult to hold someone accountable for any resulting problems. Remember, when something goes wrong, you cannot tell your boss, "The computer made me do it!"

In some of the capacity planning and scheduling systems that used if/then rules-based logic, the resulting plans were displayed in a Gantt chart. Someone could look at the chart and decide whether or not the plan looked good. While the logic used to come up with the plan was not visible on the chart, the plan itself was visible in a way that it could either be approved or modified.

Accountability is limiting the use of neural net AI algorithms in several situations. For example, an AI algorithm recommending parole for prisoners was accused of racial basis. The parolee's lawyer demanded to know how the algorithm came up with the parole ruling, insisting it was biased against his client. Since the logic is not visible within the algorithm, the parole board was unable to defend against the claim of bias.

Similarly, an artificial intelligence algorithm that recommends purchasing material, scheduling overtime, subcontracting work, and other expenditures of the company's money will need to enable some way to justify the expense. As mentioned before, many of these decisions involve elements of judgment and/or creativity, and so, because the algorithm is not infallible in these situations, some method of maintaining accountability will need to be developed.

All this means is that using AI algorithms to manage a planning system is mostly in the future. However, progress has been rapid recently, so there may be some breakthroughs. The general view within the AI community is that current AI capabilities are narrow and require a large amount of training data.

These algorithms are quite effective in uses like image recognition, natural language processing (including sentiment analysis), and general pattern recognition such as what other items may interest a buyer, what other movies may be good recommendations for a viewer, what time of day to increase electrical power production, and so forth. So, it is likely that these fairly narrow situations will dominate AI use in the near term.

One obvious type of pattern analysis is forecasting. There is a pattern of sales activity and a number of factors, some or all of which may have an effect on sales. For example, what is the effect of price, different types of advertising, time of year, competitive prices and advertising, other products that cannibalize sales, and so on? If enough training data were available, a neural net AI algorithm should be able to make predictions accounting for all these different factors. As mentioned earlier in the explanation of using a neural net AI algorithm to handle exception messages, the question is whether a company has enough suitable data for training (amount of data and data that is consistent and not confusing, such as grouping items that behave differently into the same training set), and if the results are visible enough to hold someone accountable if they choose to accept the AI forecast. It is important to note that such a forecast assumes the future will be like the past, and in any forecast it's necessary to also consider how the future would be different from the past and apply these assumptions to the AI-generated forecast.

EY's Evolving Thinking with "Lights-Out Planning"

With all that said about AI it certainly does not mean that companies are not moving forward. Companies, with support from EY, are still in the very early stages, but progress is building, and good results are being realized on the way to that goal. There is a handful of organizations, those with more mature business planning and execution processes, that are making excellent progress, based on their specific needs. Work on this journey continues as these organizations pioneer, with EY, the application of technology to modify traditional planning into a capability where human intervention is less and less likely based on their systems capability to utilize captured knowledge – a truly non-people-dependent environment.

EY has identified five core pillars on the journey to lights-out planning. They are not intended to represent a maturity journey, but the sequential implementation of sustainable "pillars of capability" that must be established to enable superior technology performance and the redirection of planning roles:

1. **IBP:** See Chapter 8. Required to ensure a stable foundation, good decision-making, integrated processes, and a team-based culture and environment.
2. **Planning Service Centers:** A constant focus on data accuracy and its speed of availability and use.
3. **Segmentation and Synchronization:** When considering a more technology-based future, what is the best way to segment your business to maximize the delivered value and what synchronization will be enabled when implementing this approach?
4. **Optimization:** In order to take advantage of the increasing speed of data availability, and its analysis, through improved system architecture has the organization been structured to enable resources to perform more effectively and service markets with greater and more cost effective agility?
5. **Automation:** At this point it would then be possible to initiate a complete lights-out planning approach.

These five pillars are designed to ensure that the right things are in place to enable a planner less capability. There will always need to be people involved but not as traditional planners. As these five steps build, the capability introduced allows real value stream management, ownership of the End-to-End, and progressively eliminates the need to be hands-on. From this, EY has identified a new role, the SC Engineer, a specialist who helps tune the "engine," an ongoing activity from refining data, setups, algorithms, and so forth.

The first two steps are essential to ensure good control, eliminated (nearly) firefighting, and so forth. The Planning Service Center is all about building data accuracy, managing the data, and ensuring real-time availability. Trust in the data is essential for this journey.

Step 3 is to ensure the right structure to segmentation, ensuring they have been synchronized to deliver value back to the customers. If steps 1, 2, and 3 have issues, you are not ready for optimization and automation. In steps 1, 2, and 3 you are moving from people-dependent processes to non-people-dependent ones; in other words, the processes run independent of human intervention because they accurately reflect what needs to be done and have been accurately replicated by the system. The non-people-dependent phase is capturing the decision-making tree to enable the system to quickly replicate that element of traditional planning.

The expected results are:

- Reduced, possibly eliminated, need for Traditional Planners.
- Reduced dependency on inventory to buffer the traditional waste in processes and systems.
- System-executed real-time decision making; with less people involvement there is less human error.
- Improved business performance, due to increased speed and efficiency.
- Improved competitive advantage; leaders are interested in driving system efficiency to move the business forward and beat the competition.

EY has found that there is an evolution from high touch, high intervention to real human-machine symbiosis. As a result, some parts of planning become fully autonomous and others involve high touch where this is value add.

The planners who remain are also keen to understand the influence of market disruptors and the impact they may have on the business, now and in the future. How will these disruptive influences adjust the data and what does this mean – how quickly can this new data be structured to enable the systems to take over? So, initial human intervention is needed to set up the decision-making trees, the machine learning, and so on, and then the system self helps.

In terms of demand, early adopters have been using this capability to work with demands that are not too volatile, have a more stable history, and hence can be more easily predicted and the data available used to build decision-making trees and so forth.

Consider an ice-capped mountain with lights-out planning being the pinnacle. Currently, there are a handful of companies at the pinnacle, frozen in the ice trying to develop their approach with optimization and automation. Today the ice is not yet melting so there is limited influence by those companies, from their melt water, to the next level, the early adopters. In the foothills and plains, however, there are still a melee of companies who just live in a world of firefighting and churn rather than starting a journey to climb the mountain of opportunity. A transformation message to support companies on their journey up the mountain is essential, with the eventual destination possibly being different for different businesses and their markets. Pioneers in the ice cap are few; nevertheless, the capabilities being developed need to be understood so decisions to adopt or not can be made. Different companies and their markets will demand different levels of investment. Doing the Unparalleled Business Planning and Execution Practices explained in this book will position your company to climb the mountain of opportunity quickly and make possible the journey to lights-out planning should that be required.

For additional reading on lights-out planning, please see EY's white paper "Lights-out planning the wave of the Supply Chain future?"

Integrating the Supply Chain

In retail, a completely integrated supply chain would extend from point-of-sale at stores or ecommerce fulfillment centers back through the distribution network, supply chain plants, and raw material suppliers.

This is accomplished using Distribution Resource Planning (DRP) at the store level and integrating with DRP at the retailer's distribution centers, manufacturer's distribution centers, Master Scheduling and MRP at supply chain plants, and suppliers.

Experience from working with retailers and suppliers has shown this works well, improving customer service, reducing inventory, and increasing productivity. These improvements materialize not only for the retailer but also for supply since the supply chain no longer guesses what the retailer is planning to buy from them.

One of the major obstacles to this integration has been the enormous SKU count and number of transactions through customer checkout at the retail store level. For example, a small retailer might have several million SKUs and a large retailer can have several hundred million SKUs.

To effectively manage these data volumes, software must be designed to reduce the labor hours per SKU and the computer processing cost per SKU. The good news is that software that has been tested and proven in both areas does exist. Labor hours to run the system are at levels equal to or below the labor needed to run the prior generation of reorder point systems, and the computer processing costs are economical and on a scale similar to the cost to run the prior generation of reorder point systems. However, it is worth mentioning that some retailers have attempted to use software designed for manufacturing distribution centers at store level. The results have been mixed since this software was not designed for store-level data volumes and the resulting labor hours and the computer hardware costs are high.

Summary

In this chapter we have explored a few current planning system technology enhancements and future enhancements. As you were reading this chapter you probably had more technology enhancements pop into your mind. If you can describe them we would love to hear from you.

For additional but more specific reading please visit the Oliver Wight Website and gain access to the extensive library of White Papers.

Notes

1. From Wikipedia: Sensor fusion is the combining of sensory data or data derived from disparate sources such that the resulting information has less uncertainty than would be possible when these sources were used individually. The term uncertainty reduction in this case can mean more accurate, more complete, or more dependable, or refer to the result of an emerging view, such as stereoscopic vision (calculation of depth information by combining two-dimensional images from two cameras at slightly different viewpoints).

    The data sources for a fusion process are not specified to originate from identical sensors. One can distinguish direct fusion, indirect fusion, and fusion of the outputs of the former two. Direct fusion is the fusion of sensor data from a set of heterogeneous or homogeneous sensors, soft sensors, and history values of sensor data, while indirect fusion uses information sources like a priori knowledge about the environment and human input. Sensor fusion is also known as (multi-sensor) data fusion and is a subset of information fusion.

2. Special thanks to Rich Rogers (rich.rogers@xemelgo.com) for his help with this section.

3. From Wikipedia: Originally block chain, a blockchain is a growing list of records, called *blocks*, that are linked using cryptography. Each block contains a cryptographic hash of the previous block, a timestamp, and transaction data (generally represented as a Merkle tree). By design, a blockchain is resistant to modification of the data. It is "an open, distributed ledger that can record transactions between two parties efficiently and in a verifiable and permanent way." For use as a distributed ledger, a blockchain is typically managed by a peer-to-peer network collectively adhering to a protocol for internode communication and validating new blocks. Once recorded, the data in any given block cannot be altered retroactively without alteration of all subsequent blocks, which requires consensus of the network majority. Although blockchain records are not unalterable, blockchains may

be considered secure by design and exemplify a distributed computing system with high Byzantine fault tolerance. Decentralized consensus has therefore been claimed with a blockchain. Blockchain was invented by a person (or group of people) using the name Satoshi Nakamoto in 2008 to serve as the public transaction ledger of the cryptocurrency bitcoin. The identity of Satoshi Nakamoto is unknown. The invention of the blockchain for bitcoin made it the first digital currency to solve the double-spending problem without the need of a trusted authority or central server. The bitcoin design has inspired other applications, and blockchains that are readable by the public are widely used by cryptocurrencies. Blockchain is considered a type of payment rail. Private blockchains have been proposed for business use. Sources such as *Computerworld* called the marketing of such blockchains without a proper security model "snake oil."

4. From Wikipedia: Go is an abstract strategy board game for two players, in which the aim is to surround more territory than the opponent. The game was invented in China more than 2,500 years ago and is believed to be the oldest board game continuously played to the present day. A 2016 survey by the International Go Federation's 75 member nations found that there are over 46 million people worldwide who know how to play Go and over 20 million current players, the majority of whom live in East Asia.

CHAPTER 18

People and Behaviors: Get the Team Behind You and Plans Will Be Delivered

I t is not enough to have all planning processes correctly defined, documented, and integrated. Leadership and Management must demonstrate the required

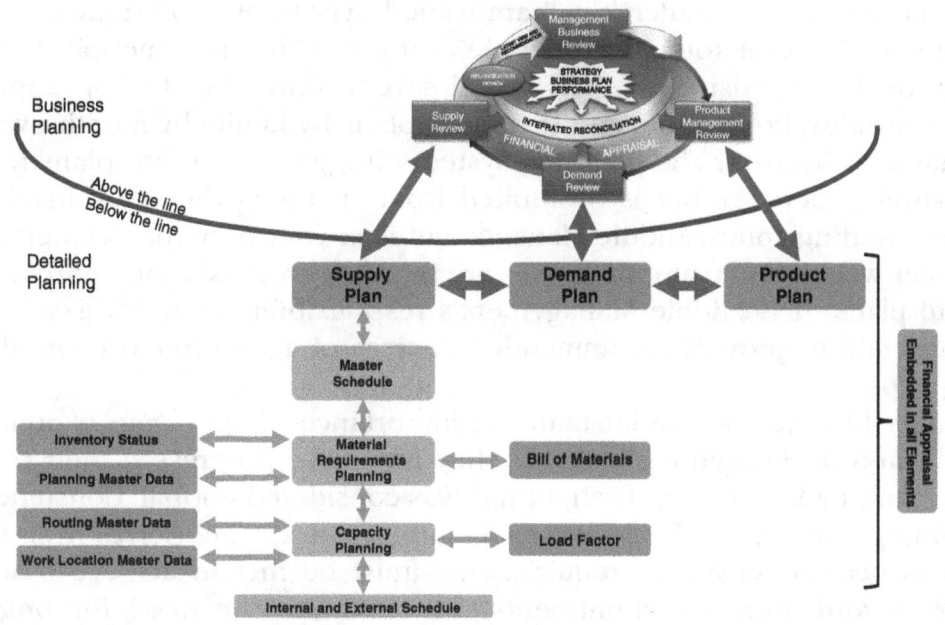

FIGURE 18.1 Business Excellence Planning

behaviors, create a culture that supports the approved processes, and hold people accountable for following the new ways of working.

As with culture change, the expected behavior change starts with Leadership, ensuring they set the expectations for others. People must be educated, comfortable, confident, and empowered in working with new processes before they will fully align.

Without question, the most often observed behavior that undermines Business Excellence Planning is the failure to distinguish between aggregate and detailed planning and the different management approaches required for each. All too often, Leadership becomes distracted with problems associated with execution details, in the firm and trading zones (usually months 0–3), the zones in which Middle Management should be leading. The near term is where the aggregate plans, previously approved by Leadership, are converted into the detail required for successful planning and scheduling. When Leadership and Middle Management are both focused on the near term, described as a compressed organization, Leadership takes its eye off months 4–24, guaranteeing they will remain trapped in the near term with both Leadership and Middle Management doing the same work.

A colleague of ours was in a board meeting for a company in exactly this situation. One of the Leadership Team leaned over to our colleague and said, "You know, if I ever found two people doing exactly the same job, I would get rid of the expensive one!" As stated several times, Leadership approves aggregate Sales, Production, and Inventory plans by family by month over the full planning horizon. The planning system disaggregates these plans for the full planning horizon, but is prohibited from changing the detail inside the firm and trading zones. Middle Management is in control of the detailed plans and meet weekly to ensure deliveries are trending to satisfy the approved aggregate plans. It is Middle Management's responsibility to notify Leadership of issues and to provide recommended courses of action to close any developing gaps.

Leadership may not understand the importance of aggregate planning to avoid near-term firefighting because, they may have progressed their careers in companies where churn (firefighting) was considered normal. Consumed by firefighting, it is then difficult for Leadership to extract themselves from those activities because customer requirements must be met to achieve monthly, quarterly, and annual commitments. To eliminate the need for ongoing firefighting, Leadership must understand what is disrupting the organization's capability to execute plans. A compressed organization is present when the Leadership Team spends an enormous amount of time (one client VP estimated more than 80% of her time) churn/firefighting. In truth, they should be empowering others, so what are the most common causes of a compressed organization? They include:

- Broken Integrated Tactical Planning processes (see Chapter 8, Integrated Business Planning) in the execution horizon, typically months 0 to 3.
- Inaccurate data and poor data management.
- Lack of good management information for decision-making.
- Poorly deployed/communicated strategy, forcing people to develop their own, which leads to multiple agendas and objectives.
- Leadership mistrusts their people and/or data and uses these excuses to take over.
- Middle managers, who should be managing the near term, do not trust that Leadership will support them.
- Leadership has not provided adequate near-term capacity.
- Lack of Middle Management empowerment by Leadership.
- Lack of a management process to identify future gaps, document issues, and enable the development of fully costed recommendations, including possible alternatives, to avoid or resolve any gaps.
- A poor business culture that, for example, relies on the knowledge and capabilities of individuals rather than on formally documented procedures and expectations.
- Leadership that:
  - **Blames**, rather than rewards, "bad news early."
  - **Considers** firefighting to be an effective management technique.
  - **Rewards** individual and functional success over business success.
  - **Allows** conflicting goals, prefers top-down decisions rather than empowerment, and so forth.
- Poor cost control and cash flow management.
- Allowing Sales representatives and customers to request product directly from Leadership or from their plant contacts that cause changes inside the firm zone. Bypassing the formal planning process may satisfy one customer but this is probably at the expense of other customers.

- Poor supplier delivery performance resulting from:
  - **Changes:** frequent changes inside the agreed firm zone.
  - **Poor direction:** lack of clear direction that the supplier can use and trust.
  - **Renegotiation of contract:** being subjected to contract renegotiation due to enormous amounts of change.
  - **Blame:** being blamed for poor performance when the cause was change inside the agreed lead time, and so forth.

This list is not intended to describe your company but may include a few familiar issues. Having Leadership recognize some of these issues is the first step; gaining their full commitment to resolve them is often more difficult. It is true to say that when the environment described here exists and is recognized but is then accepted, the rest of the organization has ready-made excuses for their poor results. Nevertheless, motivating Leadership and people to embark on a transformation journey is the key to unlocking underutilized human potential at all organization levels.

As the journey begins, signs of improvement must be recognized and celebrated through a companywide communication, encouraging Leadership to expand the improvement activities and empower others to execute them. This enables leaders to monitor progress and progressively step further away from involvement in day-to-day details. One leader, in a client company, estimated that this change alone freed up, for him, 9–13 hours per week. When a company establishes a maturity level that we describe as being "in control," the organization is well on the way to being decompressed and more than half of the listed causes will have been eliminated. Building upon this foundation, and as maturity develops to a business process focus managed by multifunctional teams, it becomes fully decompressed with all the key Strategic Planning, Business Planning, and Execution horizons given the right level of focus and attention by the right teams.

Start at the Top

Leadership cannot delegate culture change or this type of transformation initiative. Their involvement and commitment to demonstrating the new ways of working must be seen regularly throughout the company. For Business Excellence Planning to work consistently, cost-effectively, and accurately, Leadership must create a positive culture of engagement, ownership, support, and teamwork. The good news is that there is a roadmap for transitioning to the maturity level that enables people to take ownership, drive improvement, take initiative, make decisions, and actively support the development of teamwork.

There are generally four phases of Business Maturity. This chapter focuses on Phases 1 and 2, shown in Figure 18.2.

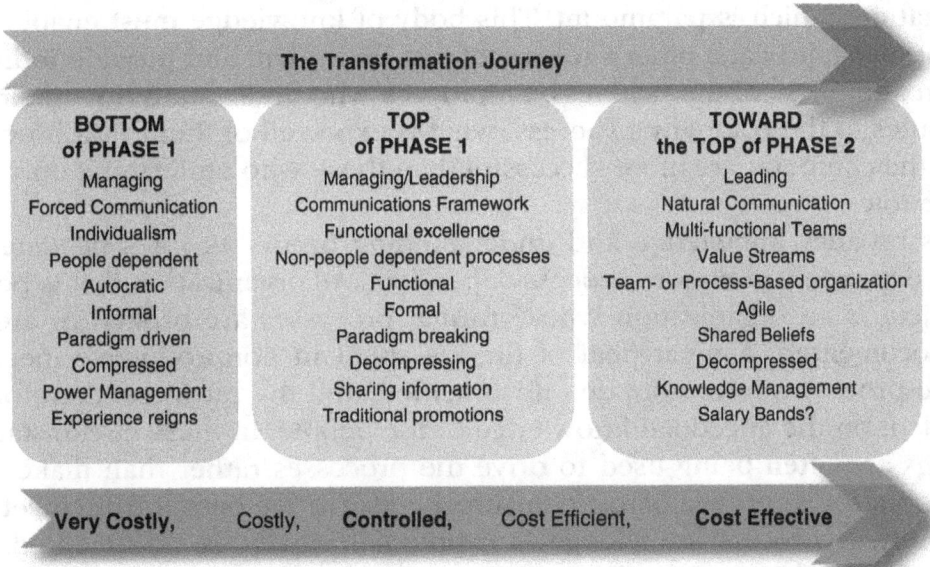

FIGURE 18.2 The Transformation Journey Focusing on Behavior Change

Education and Training

People who have been in an organization for 20 or 30 years and have not been exposed to alternative methods, processes, or ways of working may have difficulty challenging or being challenged. If they lack experience or exposure, then they cannot – or will not – challenge their current ways of working. After all, they have been successful for 20 or 30 years, have they not? They may have the misconception that what they have been doing during their careers is what everyone in similar jobs has been doing. They simply "do not know what they do not know" if they have not been exposed to alternatives through education and training. This is frequently the result of limited education and training opportunities, which is symptomatic of a Phase 1 organization. What is worse is that when new people join the company, especially coming from a more mature organization, they are told very quickly by the people already there to forget those new ideas because that is not the way things are done here. The body of knowledge that exists and is used within a company is key to transitioning to a higher maturity level. Education and training can build and maintain a body of knowledge, but it is the knowledge itself, at all levels of the organization, which is paramount. This body of knowledge must enable people to understand each other's roles, not just their own, and provide individuals a broader view of the business. Employees who understand how their role contributes to the company's success, what is expected of them, and how they fit into the company, are more successful than those who understand only their specific role.

This broader knowledge and understanding occurs as roles become less people dependent and more process dependent. An organization that is people dependent is an organization whose formal processes are broken or are not even documented. A great deal of time is spent in nonproductive meetings because processes have not been documented, and the business, therefore, is dependent on the anecdotal knowledge of the people. In these circumstances, meetings are often being used to drive the processes rather than make decisions about the approved plans to ensure a constructive output from meetings. Conversely, if process knowledge is captured formally, is documented, and approved, those processes will work as expected irrespective of the individuals involved. Consequently, this formality enables companies to create effective education and training programs for onboarding new people and enabling job rotation, developing capable people who can perform multiple roles and manage multiple processes. This approach builds deep understanding of the business within the workforce. An effective technique, in assessing behavior change progress, is to review process documentation. Ask for examples of how process and outcome requirements are applied daily and look for evidence that required actions were taken when the process results had failed to meet minimum requirements.

For organizations at the bottom of Phase 1, processes are people dependent. The first objective of these organizations is to move quickly toward becoming process-focused and decompressed, as shown at the top of Phase 1.

A Little Knowledge Can Be Dangerous

Knowledge motivates people to change behaviors, which is why it is crucial to formally educate employees as they onboard or change jobs. Formal education is even more important in this digital age since "knowledge" can inadvertently seep into a process based solely on the specific interests of individuals browsing on the Internet. Knowledge seeping into the processes, informally, is not always valid, is almost never cohesive or consistent and will certainly not be shared. Individuals who obtain knowledge independently, even when they read the same information, will interpret the information differently, which results in confusion. A topic will be discussed on the assumption that everyone involved shares the same knowledge which is rarely the case.

Especially important is providing education to those on the Transformation Team (more on the organization for transformation is presented in Chapter 19, Implementation) involved in redesigning business processes before beginning redesign activities. Education on the concepts and principles covered in this book is essential to ensure they are incorporated into the new ways of working.

Business processes must be formally documented and have rigorous change control procedures. These formal documents become the basis for educating teams and guiding the teams in using the approved procedures in running the business. This shared knowledge empowers employees and is the basis for accountability.

Pain before Gain

On the other hand, some organizations implement IBP and Detail Planning in parallel, because they see the need for both. Understanding and being honest about the current situation allows organizations to take a step back and decide objectively what to address first. For some, this will be implementing a program to bring some semblance of order to the day-to-day business. It might be as simple as improving inventory record accuracy, reassessing demonstrated capacities, or improving weekly Integrated Tactical Planning (ITP) meetings. This assessment and understanding are an essential first step for organizations with broken near-term (as well as long-term) processes. It does not matter how well planned the future is; if near-term processes are not functioning, organizations will compress to deal with the resulting near-term problems. Often, through improving the near-term management processes, Leadership's confidence in Middle Management's ability to manage the near term increases, hence freeing them to focus on IBP's full planning horizon. Some companies prioritize improving IBP first to force Leadership out of the near term. In doing this Leadership can then manage the future and make longer-term decisions to resolve issues and gaps before they become a near-term fire. Yet other organizations choose to implement IBP and Detail Planning processes in parallel because they see the need for both, and because the implementation teams are made up of, for the most part, different people.

A transformation start point and implementation plan depend on the results of the initial assessment and availability of low-hanging fruit to deliver early gains, which can be communicated to help build momentum for the change initiative. Whatever the starting point and sequence of initiatives, the steps required to achieve decompression will undoubtedly produce some pain before there is any gain.

One of the most important decisions during a transformation is determining when to put a "stake in the ground," a declaration of when the new ways of working will become effective. It can be tempting to revert to churn/firefighting (people revert to type, as shown in Figure 18.3) when the new processes are still in their infancy and not functioning optimally. For this reason, it is important to declare, "From this day forward, the business will operate with these procedures. If there are problems with the new procedures, those problems

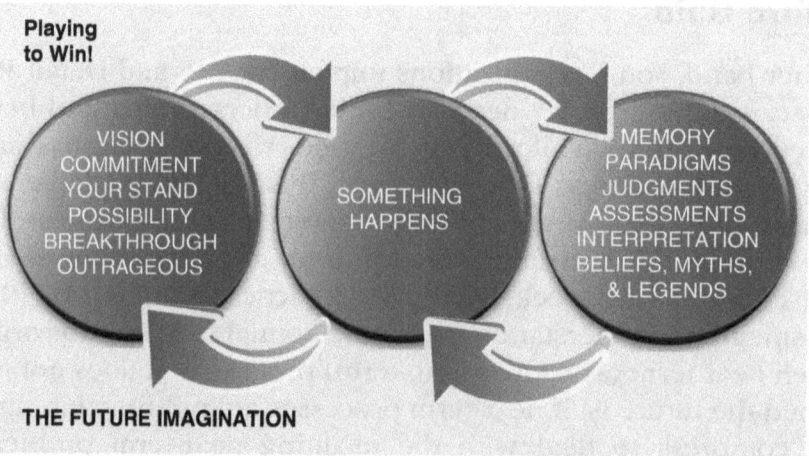

FIGURE 18.3 The Virtuous Circle

will be resolved immediately." Organizations must utilize the weeks before start-up of the new ways of working to ensure adequately educated and trained staff are in place to manage and drive the redesigned processes and procedures. This may challenge the capacity of staff in some areas to prepare activities for the "go live" date. This means that for a short period of time managing the near term may be even more painful than it already is.

Sometimes, things will get worse before they get better.

Organizations must develop the right processes and capabilities rather than trying anything for a quick fix. Too often, organizations muddle along with a series of quick fixes, moving daily from one to the next. This approach creates a false and ever more confusing bridge across a vast pit of problems. It hides the real issues because quick fixes are designed to quickly alleviate symptoms rather than identifying and eliminating the root cause of all those problems. Often repeated, this approach fatigues everyone in the organization. However, if the root cause is identified and eliminated and the Band-Aids are no longer required, then order begins to replace the culture of churn and firefighting.

To begin, organizations must develop plans and schedules using their demonstrated performance and capacities rather than using planning data that is based on what they believe the President wants to hear. When this happens, the time normally spent firefighting can be redirected to continuously improve demonstrated capacities, eliminate waste, increase productivity, and increase quality. Sustaining these results allows people to spend even more of their time on achieving even higher performance levels.

Trust

Very often in a compressed organization, and with Leadership drawn in to managing the day-to-day details, the cause is a pervading lack of trust throughout the organization. If the President does not trust the Leadership Team with IBP, and, in turn the Leadership Team does not trust Middle Management's ability to execute the approved aggregate IBP plans, then there will be an inevitable collapse of focus into the near-term details. Of course, trust is mutual. Employees must trust Middle Management and the President just as much as the President, Leadership, and Middle Management Teams must have confidence in the employees. Lack of this mutual trust leads to an internal disconnect and a demotivated workforce.

The Trust Equation

If employees believe they are not trusted to do their job and/or are being unnecessarily managed too closely, it prevents them from fulfilling their potential and dissuades them from taking ownership and responsibility. Of course, Management must stay close enough to ensure the new ways of working are being followed, which can be accomplished through "managing by walking around," reviewing team boards, and through careful listening. Management must address quickly any evidence of failure to follow the new procedures. These approaches will not erode workforce empowerment and may even reinforce empowerment, but constantly looking over employees' shoulders and second-guessing the smallest of details will. The Trust Equation, shown in Figure 18.4, provides an honest way, although very subjective, of assessing your own circumstances and those of your company. What does this tell you?

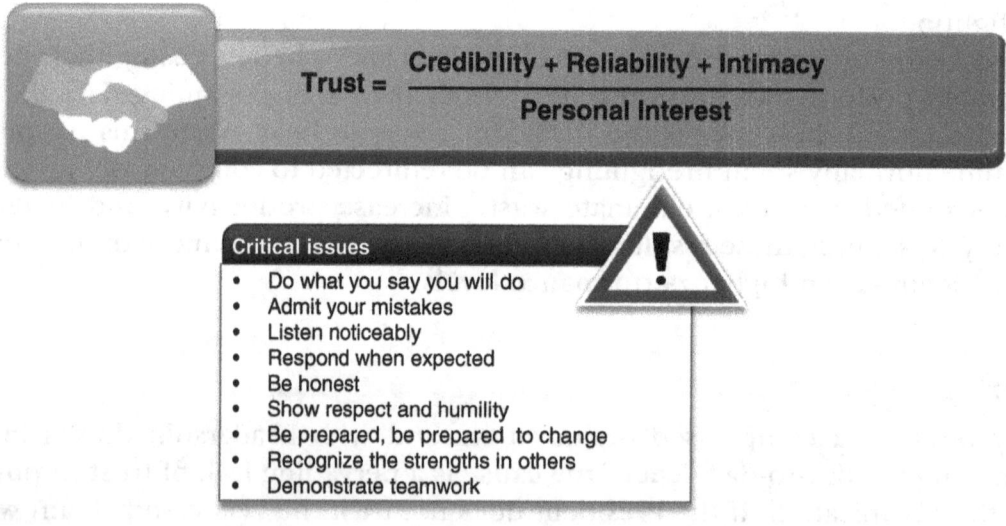

$$Trust = \frac{Credibility + Reliability + Intimacy}{Personal\ Interest}$$

Critical issues
- Do what you say you will do
- Admit your mistakes
- Listen noticeably
- Respond when expected
- Be honest
- Show respect and humility
- Be prepared, be prepared to change
- Recognize the strengths in others
- Demonstrate teamwork

FIGURE 18.4 The Trust Equation

In successful companies, empowered people at the lowest possible organizational level take the initiative and make decisions. If the boss is constantly peering over their shoulder or second-guessing them, that contradicts the communicated expectation of empowered decision-making. The reaction will be, "Oh well, the boss is here, so he/she should make the decisions." Leadership Team actions must match their words. The workforce quite rightly expects those at the top to "walk the walk" in return for their reciprocated trust.

Conversely, there are companies in which the President and Leadership Team are so divorced from near-term problems that those managing and working in that time frame will avoid making decisions for fear of being second-guessed.

It is vital to communicate and demonstrate the right balance of control so that all people have the same understanding of decision boundaries, leadership expectations, the strategic direction, and that mechanisms are in place to escalate issues appropriately.

One way to enable all parties to understand the current situation, in each area of the business, is through the use of "Visual Management," which ensures that everyone will engage in positive communication and share, with others, what they are doing.

Visual Management: Use of Team Boards/Displays

Introducing Team Boards/Displays can often be a challenge initially because some teams do not understand their value. They may see them as threatening. Leadership must "walk the talk" and use these Team Boards/Displays to engage in positive, supportive conversations, praising the team on their successes and asking where management can support their improvement projects.

Effective team displays include:

- Team members and individual information such as skills, interests, main tasks, etc.
- A list of improvement projects underway and planned.
- Current performance graphs such as the ones described in this book.
- Team issues being addressed.
- Team achievements related to past improvement projects/tasks.
- Team-building activities such as charities, sponsored events, team games, etc.

With this information, management can relate better to the team, get to know the team members, understand how the team is supporting the business, engage in knowledgeable conversations, and be supportive, but at the same time challenging. Team Boards/Displays enable Leadership to walk the talk and enables the team to experience management walking the talk.

An example of a Team Board/Display is shown in Figure 18.5. In this example the Team Board/Display was owned by the team, and it was their responsibility to keep the information current.

FIGURE 18.5 An Example of a Team Board/Display

Please note that Team Board/Displays are equally effective in factories, production areas, and in office areas. If used uniformly throughout a company, Team Board/Displays begin to eliminate the only too often present culture of "us versus them." Importantly, displays such as these enable teams to get credit for their successes. Can you imagine watching a sporting event without a scoreboard? Interest would be lost very quickly!

Establish ownership of the displays by allowing the teams to design and develop their own, with some guidance to include specific information that enhances cross-team understanding and value.

Effecting Desired Behavior Changes

The following steps have been proven to facilitate sustained behavior change and to develop a business culture that will lead to success:

1. Using so-called hard management tools,[1] which should be used to support culture change and influence the development of the desired behaviors:

    a. **Roles and Responsibilities:** Clearly defined roles and responsibilities are essential to ensure that people understand they should now focus their attention on processes and no longer on traditional functions and departments. Roles and responsibilities must describe how individual roles interface and integrate with others. People involved in Business Excellence Planning must have documented roles and responsibilities, equally those not directly involved in the formal meetings such as the Demand Review, IRR, MBR, and ITP, but participate in preparing for these meetings must also have clearly documented roles and responsibilities to sustain these processes. Roles and responsibilities must clearly define decision-making boundaries; additionally, the expectations of each role in becoming part of a team and contributing toward team building and team effectiveness must also be included.

    b. **Process Maps:** The overall process design must be captured in a process map to ensure its logic and sustainability. The map should show integration with parallel processes *and* with previous and succeeding processes in the end-to-end supply chain. If processes do not identify these relationships, they remain isolated; people working those processes will also, almost by definition, remain isolated and fail to develop into a supply chain team.

    c. **KPIs:** Measures should be clearly defined and understood throughout the organization. Since what gets measured gets done, the issue is about selecting the key measures needed to achieve performance objectives and organization alignment. These need to be the key few to ensure we are not flooding the organization with unrelated and meaningless tasks. Without adequate understanding and acceptance of the importance of those key measures, people will take them personally and bend the measurements to make themselves look good. Do not overload people with so many measures that they are inclined to cherry-pick the measures that align with management's flavor of the month. Balance the number of measures throughout all organization levels and areas: if one area is heavily measured and another is not, that will result in an us-versus-them scenario – one area feels micromanaged while the other feels free, as they simply do not have the same number of performance objectives. Finally, measures must be used to improve results and not be used to place blame. Measures have been discussed in every chapter, but the focus in this chapter is the use of measures to influence behavior.

2. **Ensuring Accountability and Consequences:** It is important to recognize and praise the new ways of working in a transformation initiative. It is equally important to recognize and correct (not discipline, at least initially) failure to follow the new ways. There are always skeptics in organizations who hear Leadership establish new expectations and then believe it is their responsibility to test Leadership's resolve by pushing the new boundaries. There is another segment of the population that will observe this testing and, if the testing is not challenged by Leadership, follow the lower bar set by the skeptics and erode the new ways of working across the entire organization. When behaviors not in compliance with the new requirements are observed, Leadership must openly challenge the individual or team by politely asking them to explain why they have done or said something different from what has been communicated. Others will observe this interaction and realize the new Leadership position is required – a great example of walking the talk.

3. **Walk the Talk (Be a Role Model):** Leadership and Management must demonstrate its commitment to the new environment, performance requirements, teamwork, and so forth, to ensure transformation success. If employees struggle with the new ways of working, Leadership and Management must demonstrate their support and help rather than blame and ridicule. Others observe this Leadership behavior and are encouraged to comply. See Chapter 3, Inventory, for an example.

4. **Eliminate the Old:** In a transformation, it is just as important to eliminate remnants of the old ways of working as it is to implement the new. Old, redundant meetings will continue if they are not formally ended and seem to be part of the new programs; old habits are difficult to break. No meetings outside the Business Excellence Planning (BEP) process should be conducted; all meetings should have been analyzed for inclusion or eliminated before the new processes begin. The rule of thumb is that old meetings must be either absorbed into the new or eliminated.

5. **Uninvite Redundant People from Required Meetings:** It is common for companies to allow uncontrolled growth in the number of meeting attendees. Too many people in a meeting is a sign of other serious problems. Misunderstanding of the meeting's purpose, lack of communication channels to share information, or, as a recent client stated, "Asking them not to attend will make those people feel unimportant" are all common causes of uncontrolled growth in the number of attendees. Attendance of everyone in every meeting must be reviewed and challenged as appropriate. Important information can be provided in other ways. Attendees must be limited to those who are required to make or escalate decisions and to commit to executing the decisions made or recommended. No others should participate, except for someone required to provide information about an issue on the agenda during the time that agenda item is addressed. Reducing the number of people frees time for those people to carry out their own organizational responsibilities.

   For example, an IBP Review should include 3 core team members (Chairperson/Owner, Facilitator, and Finance partner) and *up to* 7 to 9 other attendees, not 20 or more, who are required to make decisions and commit to executing the decisions made or recommended. An inflated number of attendees will limit open, and honest, discussion of sensitive issues because some of the attendees will not be at the right level in the organization to be exposed to those types of issue. This undermines the Review and wastes the time of all attendees because the right issues cannot be discussed.

6. **Eliminate Unnecessary Reports:** All previously required reports must be reviewed to understand their purpose and to determine whether their need has been superseded or eliminated by new reports designed to support Business Excellence Planning. Reports often proliferate to meet the desires of specific people. For example, an individual receives a system report in a landscape format. The individual prefers the report in portrait format, so downloads the data into Excel to create the preferred report format. This is wasteful behavior that should be ended. Modifying planning software configuration to support personal interests is even more wasteful and is often carried out without understanding the impact to the ongoing software use and support. One client, for example, did not understand the purpose or value of a planning time fence that controlled the ability of the system to change an order inside that time fence. The stated reason for the software change was to ensure that up-to-the-minute changes in requirements were

made visible. The client was also unaware of the purpose and value of action/exception messages. The net result was a reinforcement of a culture of chaos and firefighting, and complete rejection of the planning system by the planners. Commitment to change without understanding is a liability. Determining what meetings are required, who should attend, and what reports are essential is a time-consuming exercise, but it is essential in supporting transformation to the new ways of working.

7. **Shortcuts:** If a new process is too cumbersome or time consuming, creative employees will develop shortcuts that, when discovered, indicate the need to review and streamline the new process. If not addressed, the shortcut will be repeated, probably differently each time, and displace the new process. It is imperative in the transformation initiative to quickly end the need for shortcuts or the transformation will become just another failed management initiative.

8. **Launching Initiatives Prematurely:** Initiatives must be prioritized and scheduled according to resource availability and business need. When leaders and senior managers act unilaterally, not as part of their team, there is significant risk that initiatives will be launched prematurely, before completion of education and training and before a requisite level of understanding and buy-in has been established. Communication, repeated communication, is essential for success. It is not acceptable for people to say they did not know. Ensuring that information is available must be a priority. When a launch plan has been formally authorized (through IBP) and communicated, it must be followed as scheduled unless a recommendation for change has been submitted through IBP and approved in the MBR.

9. **Consistency:** Leadership and all others must be consistent, insistent, resistant, and persistent in following the new ways of working and resistant to informal, unauthorized changes.

People Tools

The use of what some call "people tools" is quite varied from company to company. However, one commonality is that companies that have used some of these tools generally apply them as a one-off. In truth their use is often by one person in the organization rather than it being a companywide approach. Nevertheless, this more individual use of the tools does highlight to Leadership and Managers how the workforce could be managed, motivated, and supported more effectively. They enable Managers and Employees to better understand each other and, over time, enable employees to be managed for who they are, not who others think they are. Some of these tools are very easily learned and deployed by teams, following some level of training. The education and training required is dependent on the tool selected for use. Some may require the support of specially educated and trained internal coaches. The following is a list to example some of the available tools, there are many:

- Myers-Briggs Type Indicator
- Personal Style
- Change Loop (Bereavement Curve)
- Hill Tops
- Belbin (Team Selection)
- Good meetings (they are not a natural event)
- Consequences (mentioned earlier)
- And many others

If a decision is made to employ one or more of these tools, there must be a strategy in place to ensure their regular and consistent use across the company. The more these tools are used, the more they become part of the culture and the more they are understood. A primary use of the tools selected is elimination of false perceptions about individuals; false perceptions become reality if not corrected.

Right People in the Right Jobs

The question is, "If the newly transformed management structure is decompressed, do the employees and managers, appointed to manage the near-term, have the right skills and capabilities"? It is essential that Leadership trust them to drive the processes and make the right decisions. Likewise, those managing in the near term need to trust that Leadership will support and trust them also.

An organization that has been compressed over a long period of time can be imprisoned by the status quo. In this context, people have grown accustomed to decisions being made by Leadership. If those remaining abdicate responsibility, their reaction will inevitably be, "What am I supposed to do now?" Handing people the reins without the appropriate education, training, and understanding will significantly undermine the desire to decompress and keep pulling leadership back into the near term. That will slow, if not end, the transformation initiative.

An essential part of this transformation is moving people into the right roles. In some cases, this requires external recruitment, but not often; roles can be filled internally through structured education and aligning roles and responsibilities to the requirements of the business; this is the place to start. For example, it is often the case that the role of the Demand Manager (a crucial role in Business Excellence Planning) does not actually exist within an organization. The solution could be to identify the person in an existing job that is most similar, for the sake of argument, 60% of the Demand Management role, and then educate and train that individual to meet the other 40%.

We worked with one pump and turbine manufacturer who, as part of its Business Excellence Planning process, created several new roles such as a Demand Manager and Supply Chain Manager. Not only were they recruited from within the business, but both employees were originally in administrative roles, proof that change generates opportunities for existing staff who are truly engaged and invested in decompression and advancing their careers.

Staffing decisions should not be based solely on headcount. It is fundamental to recognize which processes need management attention in the near term to ensure the right people are appointed – people willing to be educated and empowered and who are willing to accept decision-making responsibilities. The selection/recruitment process needs to ensure the right people have been selected for the right roles.

Communication

Communication, in the context of running a business, is not about the glossy magazine. It is about regularly providing quality and relevant information to enable people to understand the business and make good decisions but without the need to attend information-sharing meetings. This is a huge culture change for many companies.

Leadership must allocate adequate time to enable a good communications program, to ensure there is clear ownership and to develop a clear "Communications Framework" to be followed. Figure 18.6 is one approach. The transformation team must determine what communication program is most appropriate prior to launching the new ways of working.

In addition, ensure that there are effective Notice Boards, a further example of Visual Management, and that these notice boards are positioned to ensure all people have access to them and the information they provide. It must be

Communications Framework

Frequency	Briefer	To Whom	Subject	Venue	Time
Annual	Chief Exec	All Employees	Company Results	Canteen	1hr?
Quarterly	Director	All Employees	Company Results and Prospects	Canteen	1hr?
Monthly	Manager	All Their Own Employees	Site and Own Area	Conference Rooms	½hr?
Weekly	Manager	Their Team Leaders	Short Term	Office	½hr?
Daily	Team Leaders	Their Teams	Yesterday Today	Workplace	5mins

Note 1: Communications must be two-way: Need for Feedback: Measure

Note 2: These Briefing events are mandatory: They must never be skipped

FIGURE 18.6 An Example of a Communications Framework

remembered that not everybody in an organization has regular access to computers or laptops and hence the communications structure needs to ensure their regular involvement.

The need to communicate in a structured and meaningful way has been covered; however, often missed is the need to also ensure that all involved listen and accurately receive the messages intended. To address this, it is recommended that communication is measured; in doing this, people generally pay more attention because, as mentioned earlier, what gets measured gets done. Another trick is to communicate that leadership will randomly contact people at various levels in the organization to check what they have heard. This tends to ensure that people listen more carefully and will also help Leadership understand the effectiveness of their communications. Good communication is a real investment in Leadership's time and therefore it is essential to ensure that it is effective; you must also remove the habit some people have of claiming they never heard about something.

Summary

Ultimately, creating the right environment for all employees, up and down the organization, is the main aim of any transformation initiative. Having world-class processes is of limited use if there is weak ownership and employee support, at all levels, to work in teams and deliver integrated results based on accepted Strategic Business Objectives.

Clearly, it is Leadership's responsibility to initiate a transformation initiative. The new culture will take shape based upon how they agree to work and behave. So, transformation must begin at the top and progressively influence all to work with the new ways of working and team-based/integrated business processes rather than with the traditional functions and department focus.

This chapter highlights some of the key behavior changes required for successful and sustained transformation. However, behavior and culture change take a lot longer than the education and process redesign phases. Companies often miss this aspect of transformation because it requires a more long-term view and the benefits take a little longer to be realized. Do not be put off by this; benefits are being generated throughout a transformation, and that includes the benefits of behavior change. It simply takes more time for the employees in the lower organization levels to buy in and develop trust.

For additional but more specific reading please visit the Oliver Wight Website and gain access to the extensive library of White Papers.

Note

1. This is a reference to the use of measures, processes, procedures, and so forth, often called "hard management tools." Hard because they are used to drive people without necessarily knowing who the people are and what makes them tick. On the other hand, there are soft management tools like the use of situational Leadership, Myers-Briggs, Belbin, and so forth, that enable Leaders and Managers to manage people for who they are and hence not just as a commodity. Ultimately, the Soft stuff becomes recognized as the Hard stuff because changing behavior is the hardest thing to do.

CHAPTER 19

Implementation: Where to Start

The easy answer is, everywhere. This is not as absurd as it might sound. In most cases the resources to create the fundamentals of Business Excellence Planning are different by department and even within a department, so there

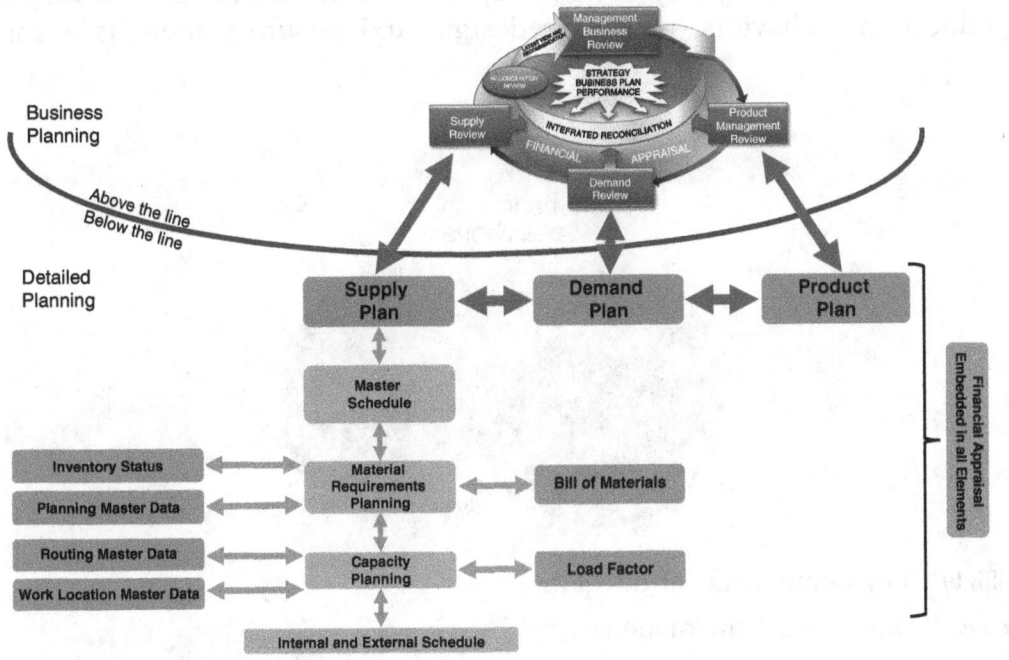

FIGURE 19.1 Business Excellence Planning

would not be a drain on any specific resource. The people who would work on achieving inventory accuracy are different from those who would work on achieving accuracy of Bills of material (BOMs), Routings, MRP item masters, work location item masters, Demand Planning, Master Scheduling, IBP, Material Requirements Planning, Product Planning, and so forth. So many of these can progress concurrently; for all the required elements, see Figure 19.1. To guide implementation and creation of the required structured planning, Oliver Wight developed, over the past 50 years, the Proven Path, a transformation process described later in this chapter.

Integration of People, Processes, and Tools

The success of Business Excellence Planning depends on people having the right behaviors, business processes, and tools integrated to support the new ways of working. Figure 19.2 shows this integration with their overlap, the amount of integration, increasing as maturity develops. Focusing on any one and ignoring the others is a guaranteed roadmap to failure. Over the years an enormous amount of money has been spent on software (tools) but very little on education, behaviors, process redesign, and ensuring there is a shared

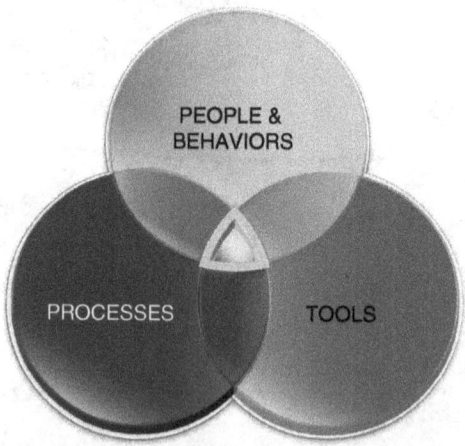

FIGURE 19.2 Key Components of Integration
Source: © Oliver Wight International.

understanding of the redesigned and integrated business processes. It is little wonder that many planners continue to rely on spreadsheets and then feed that information into the planning system rather than having the planning system feed that information to them.

By way of an example, a client company with 18 divisions was implementing new software and at the same time pursuing an OW Class A certification. The company spent large sums training employees to use the software and similar amounts on consultants to configure and change the software to represent the way the company did business. Of the 18 divisions, 14 sent people for software training to corporate Information Systems and started implementing that software immediately. The balance of four divisions, all component suppliers, approached it differently. The Oliver Wight Proven Path approach (see the section later in this chapter) provided this group of four with education, training, and coaching. Note again, there was a provision for education, not just training. Education was provided to explain "why" a Class A company needs to operate differently; training provides the "how" to use the tool (software) to enable the processes. The effort with people, processes, and tools (software) was to enable these four divisions to integrate all three, maximizing the overlap and building the sweet spot, which continues to grow over time, ensuring that all three are working together; this is integration. The four component divisions were the last to implement the software, but the first, by far, to achieve Class A certification because of their focus on people and processes. In the meantime, the other divisions were claiming that Class A was not possible with the new software!

Business processes are information dependent; however, they need to reflect how the business should be managed through integrated and high-performing processes. New process designs will determine the data requirements used to generate the information and clearly identify what the software must support and enable. Designing processes first, and ones that reflect the actual business needs, enables the software needs to be better specified. Consequently, when new software is being procured you can then hold more informed discussions with any software provider. If any tradeoffs are required because of software limitations, better decisions can be reached when the tradeoff discussion is steered by the company, not the software provider.

Start with People

Major process implementations will transform your organization. The foundation for this transformation is aligned behavior from the very top to the very bottom of the organization.

Chapter 18 described in some detail the way cultures develop and some of the challenges culture change poses for any organization. However, with the implementation of a process structure, such as Business Excellence Planning, it is necessary to understand both the current culture and the desired end state culture. Figure 19.3 represents the "normal" distribution of people and types of response that should be expected in a transformation initiative.

Many of the elements in Figure 19.3 are intended to deliver a very strong message about Leadership's need to be engaged, open, aligned and, most of all, to demonstrate their complete support and ownership of the transformation communicated.

Expectations: With a transformation of this magnitude, Leadership must be in complete alignment and then communicate their expectations repeatedly. Additionally, they must demonstrate, regularly, their alignment to these expectations through taking the lead and "walking the talk." If expectations are not clearly communicated, it is very difficult for others to understand the changes

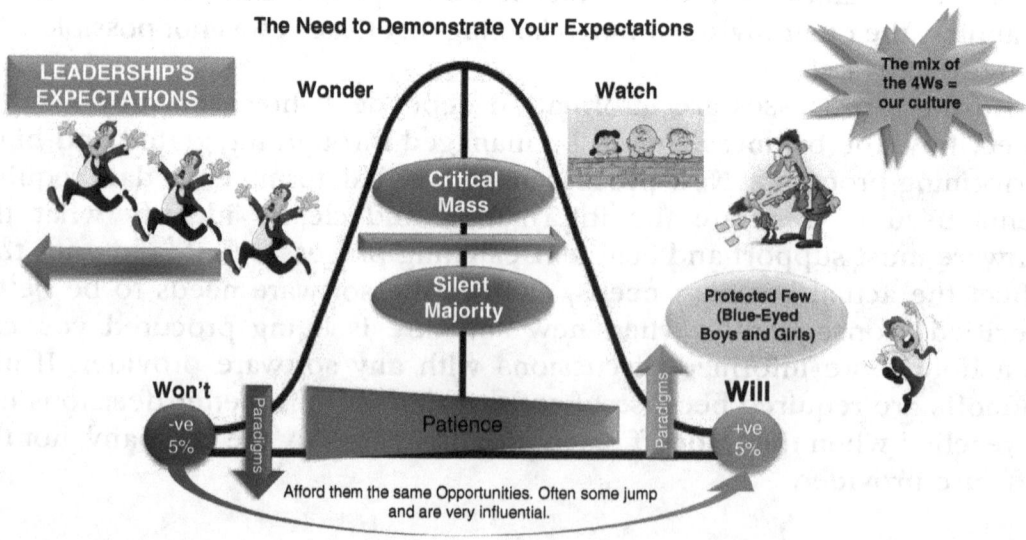

FIGURE 19.3 The Need to Demonstrate Your Expectations

required. Consequently, this will undermine their engagement and ability to align with Leadership's vision for the future.

Normal Distribution: The bell curve in Figure 19.3 represents the normal distribution of behaviors in an organization, in this case a distribution of 50/50 around the median. However, depending on the starting culture and effectiveness of activities leading up to the beginning of the transformation, the median could be either further to the left (less positive) or further to the right (more positive).

At the base of the bell curve are the two extremes, the negative 5% and the positive 5%, each of which present challenges:

- **The positive 5%** generally need to hear only part of the message and they are off implementing like mad. These are great people to have in your corner, cheerleaders for the transformation, but they must be reined in a bit so they can influence others.
- **The negative 5%**, even with one-to-one communication, will resist and may never align. These individuals, although negative, can often be very influential. An effective approach, to ensure they do not openly undermine the transformation (a case for disciplinary action), is to afford them all the same opportunities and involve them in designing the new ways of working. In doing this some of them will become less negative and become more positive and in so doing influence other skeptics to support the transformation.

The Transformation Challenge: With transformation the objective therefore is to move the "Silent Majority" or "Critical Mass" more to the right and hence have a more positive culture.

The 4 Ws: In a transformation initiative it is important to identify individuals in the 4 Ws:

- Those who Will
- Those who Watch
- Those who Wonder
- Those who Won't

As the star in the top right corner of Figure 19.3 indicates, this 4W analysis provides a view of the mix at present and hence a view of the current culture.

Those Who Will – Often seen as "The Protected Few"! It is fair to say that most organizations have a group of employees often referred to as the "the protected few." No matter what changes are made, whether successful or not, these individuals are always seen to be supported and valued by leadership. It is also true that those in the Watch, Wonder, and Won't categories observe this leadership support, which aligns with the communicated expectations. It must, therefore, be remembered that these individuals will have heard leadership say the following:

- You can expect that from now on you will be supported when taking the initiative to advance the transformation.
- You are empowered and are expected to make decisions.
- As Leaders we are here to help. Be open so it is clear when Leadership involvement may be needed.
- Blame and power management are a thing of the past; the new culture must be free of fear.

With these statements Leadership is encouraging others outside the protected few to step up, embrace empowerment, take initiative, make decisions, and so on.

Those Who Watch: Having heard Leadership's expectations and observed support for those who Will, some of the Watchers will adopt a more positive attitude, take the initiative, and make decisions, moving from looking over the protective wall to taking part in the transformation. This is exactly what Leadership needs. Should an initiative or a decision made by somebody in the Watch category turn out to be incorrect, yet they are still seen as being supported by Management, then those who are in the Wonder category will also be encouraged to begin moving to the positive side of the normal distribution curve. But should the response to that incorrect initiative or decisions be observed as blame, the balance of those who Watch, Wonder, and Won't will lean further to the negative side and become even more entrenched. Observations such as these that take place early in the transformation are crucial and have a lasting effect.

Those Who Wonder: Although they have heard Leadership's expectations, those who Wonder, because of past experiences and disappointments, do not easily align. They do Wonder what will happen if some of the Watchers become more positive. If they observe traditional Leadership behaviors and reactions and see that Leadership are not walking the talk, they will become even more deeply disappointed and negative, a situation that makes recovery even more difficult. Leaders must be fully cognizant of the impact of their behaviors and responses and ensure they remain committed and supportive.

Those Who Won't: No matter how positive the culture, there will always be a percentage of the employees that thrives on being more negative than positive. Leadership's objective over time is to minimize the number of individuals in the Won't group as much as possible. You may recognize typical comments from this group when Leadership expectations fail to be achieved:

- I told you so.
- Just another Leadership fad.
- It was never going to work; Leadership just does not understand.

Patience: People change at different rates and cannot be expected to jump on the transformation train all at the same time. Transformation, as a result, requires Leadership patience. No one hears everything the first time; one presentation about the transformation and why it is needed is not enough. People need to hear it again and again, need time to think about what they have heard, and need to see for themselves signs that the new ways of working are beginning to happen.

Patience is also required to allow more time for those on the negative side of the normal curve to come around and embrace the changes.

Push too hard too soon and people, especially those in the Won't group, will move further to the negative side. Continuing and repeating communications is essential. If this is thought to be boring for leadership, then communicate it again 10 more times. Communication during a transformation initiative is essential; it must be top down, bottom up, honest, relevant, continuous, consistent, and motivating.

An Example of Positive Support

Some years ago, a Supply Chain VP explained that during the formative years of his career he was promoted to a line manager for the first time and, in so doing, inherited the previous line manager's team and processes. Very soon into his new role, he had to tell his direct boss about a major problem that had cost his company about $500,000. Before talking with his boss, he analyzed and eliminated the root cause of the loss but could not recover the financial loss incurred.

Meeting with his boss he explained what had occurred, the solution he implemented, and then handed in his letter of resignation. His boss listened carefully, understood the situation and, although unhappy about the financial loss, controlled his annoyance and asked why the manager wrote the letter of resignation.

The line manager explained that he did not want to have a sacking on his record so felt it better to resign. His boss could not have responded more appropriately. He said, "If you think I am going to invest $500,000 in your education just to let you go, you have it all wrong. Thanks for the openness and the solution."

Oliver Wight Proven Path

The Proven Path, shown in Figure 19.4, was developed by and refined by Oliver Wight over the past 50 years to help companies navigate the complex and daunting job of implementing business processes such as Business Excellence Planning. While the Proven Path has been refined through the years,

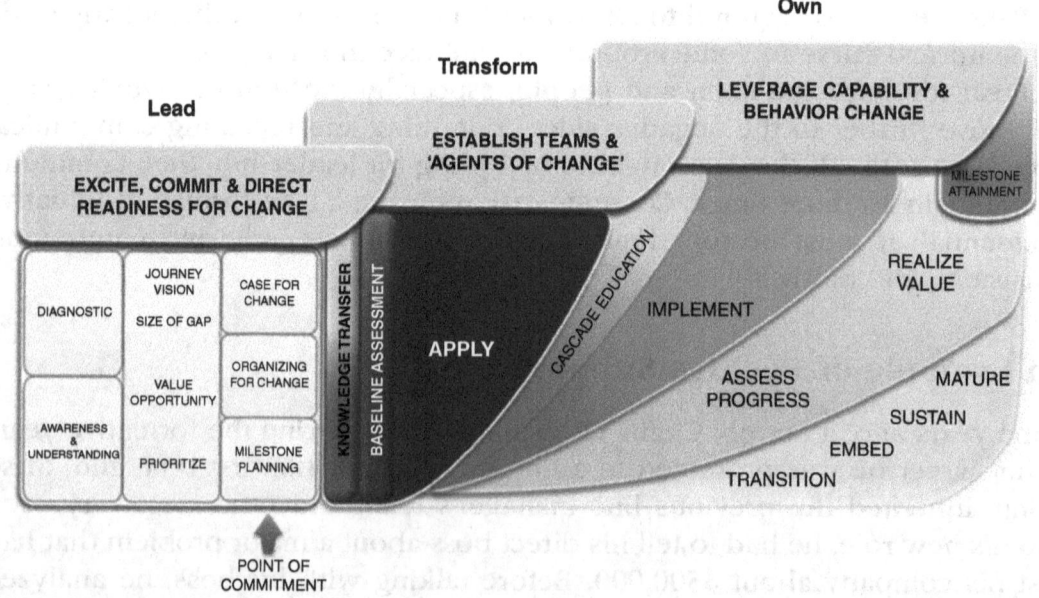

FIGURE 19.4 The Proven Path

Source: © Oliver Wight International.

its fundamentals remain the same, ensuring successful transformations every time it is followed.

The Proven Path is a high-level plan that fits every situation, but every project is as different as the people involved. Divisions of the same large company, right down the street from each other, have required subtly different applications of the Proven Path. Using the Proven Path as the foundation for a transformation initiative enables project teams to develop executable plans for successfully implementing every aspect of Business Excellence Planning.

Leadership (knowledge and commitment) from the top remains a prerequisite for success. Then people, processes, and tools must be developed and implemented following the Proven Path. Finding software is not a problem today because there are hundreds of packages that can get the job done, but only as the third element of the transformation initiative. First, people must receive education in the new ways of working. Then those who have been educated must be empowered to appropriately redesign the current processes. Then, and only then, the software must be correctly configured to support the redesigned processes. Redesigning business processes is challenging but can be accomplished quickly and efficiently by following the concepts and principles described in this book and with coaching to gain the benefit and experience from those who have personally experienced similar transformations.

Other supporting Oliver Wight books and papers are also available; they have been listed at the end of each chapter for easy reference.

Proven Path Explained

The Oliver Wight Proven Path has three distinct phases, as shown in Figure 19.5.

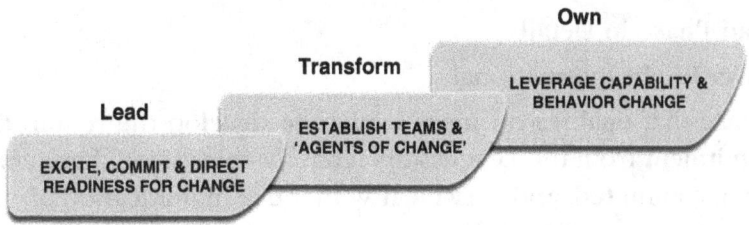

FIGURE 19.5 The Three Phases of the Proven Path
Source: © Oliver Wight International.

1. **Lead:** Executive understanding, commitment, support, and direction is essential for success (see Figure 19.6). If this is not clearly demonstrated and observed in the Lead phase, there is no reason to move into the next two phases.

2. **Transform:** Transformation cannot be outsourced; it must be accomplished internally using outside resources only for education and coaching. Hiring outside resources to do the work of transformation may be enticing, but it will lead to failure.

   - **First**, it is very expensive.
   - **Second**, the resources will likely be recent college graduates with little to no experience in industry and are learning on your time.
   - **Third**, and by far the most important issue with this approach, is lack of ownership.

This kind of culture change requires leadership by your own Leadership Team and the participation of your key personnel. If outside people design

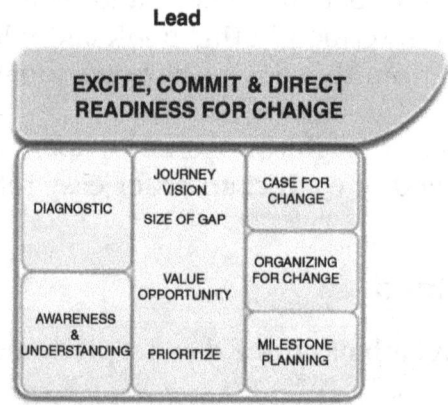

FIGURE 19.6 Lead Phase in Detail

Source: © Oliver Wight International.

This is the phase that enables business leaders to develop the required level of support and commitment from the Leadership Team for this major change initiative. They must be excited, committed, and very clear with the communication of, and realization of, the strategic business objectives supported by this initiative. It is important that Leadership understand what they are getting themselves into, otherwise they will not remain committed for the duration of the transformation.

and implement the new business processes, those documents will be put on a shelf and the behaviors will disappear as soon as the outside implementation team leaves. We strongly recommend limiting outside involvement to education and coaching by people who have experienced such a transformation. Like any sports team the experienced coach will not go out and play the game but will enable the players to be successful. This Transform phase includes education, process redesign, and the development of internal change agents (see Figure 19.7).

3. **Own:** In this phase the new ways of working are implemented throughout the organization by internal experts and teams of change agents. Progress is tracked to ensure the new ways of working are being used, that modifications are made quickly when issues arise, and that the transformation objectives are met (see Figure 19.8).

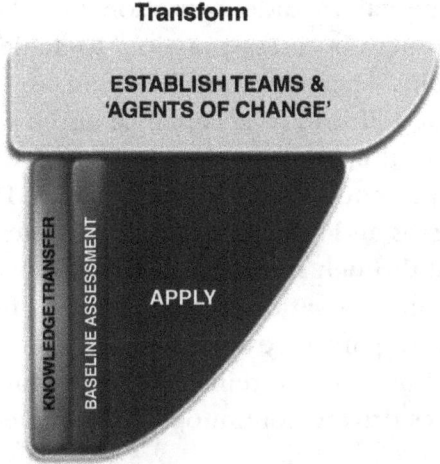

FIGURE 19.7 Transform Phase in Detail

Source: © Oliver Wight International.

This is the education and design phase, undertaken by a critical mass of the client's key influencers, operating through cross-functional teams with leadership sponsors. It is this group, along with selected key influencers, who are empowered to become experts in the new ways of working and therefore be agents of change. It is imperative that the client's people, not the consultants, become the experts, otherwise the transformation will not be sustainable.

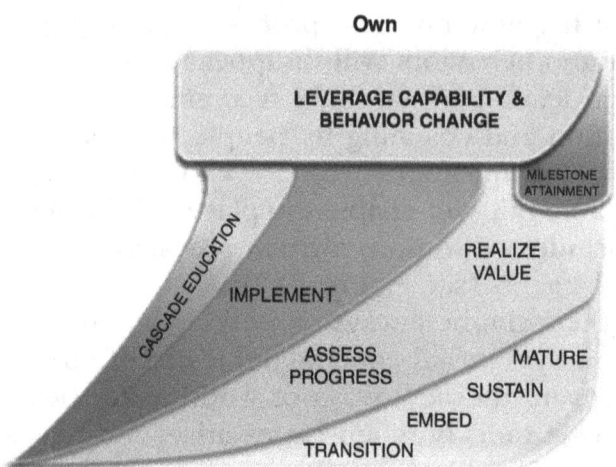

FIGURE 19.8 Own Phase in Detail

Source: © Oliver Wight International.

Through a program of internal cascade education (see later), *all employees* must understand and follow the new business practices to achieve the expected benefits and strengthen sustainability. The education program, in digestible portions, must provide the knowledge that will lead to acceptance and ownership. There must be a broad understanding of how the company currently operates and will operate in the future based on process and required *behavioral* change. These changes need to be tied back to specific processes and roles associated with each team. Progress is driven by effective leadership and through early signs of performance improvements which are communicated to maintain motivation. Systems training follows. The authors firmly believe that all employees require investment through easily digestible knowledge transfer to ensure buy-in. This must be reinforced and supported by Leadership and the use of integrated metrics driving continuous improvement.

"Lead" Phase Descriptions: Excite, Commit, and Direct Readiness for Change Descriptions

Diagnostic, Awareness, and Understanding

The purpose of the diagnostic is to quickly assess the maturity of the current culture through examination of all Business Excellence Planning elements. The diagnostic enables development of a recommended course of action defined by an accurate and practical project plan. It also enables development of a tailored leadership education package helping to justify the initiative (addressed later in this chapter) and enable understanding of the design/redesign process. An effective approach is first to conduct the diagnostic, which will require introductory education of those participating in the diagnostic, and then to report the diagnostic results to leadership. The results feedback is best achieved through a two-day workshop that provides information and time to internalize the value of the "to be" processes, clearly demonstrating the opportunities available from transforming the as is. This feedback must be done well and include an impressive case for change, allowing Leadership to commit to moving forward with the required resources.

Journey Vision

Every successful implementation begins with a vision of the end state. As Stephen Covey says, "Begin with the end in mind." The vision's level of detail can vary, but the clarity of the vision correlates directly with the number of people at all levels who will buy in. One of the best examples of a simple, clear vision that motivated countless people was John F. Kennedy's vision, ". . . before this decade is out, we will land a man on the moon and return him safely to earth." High-level visions are essential in aligning the entire company, but each area inside the company can develop its own supportive vision, such as "We will have accurate available-to-promise (ATP) information (Chapter 7) by the end of the year." This vision would align master schedulers, order entry personnel, and Sales, and would motivate them, because it would simplify their jobs and improve customer service at the same time.

Size of the Gap

Depersonalizing the size of the gap is enabled by the diagnostic. Some Business Excellence Planning elements may be close to meeting Unparalleled Business Planning and Execution Practices while others might reflect a significant gap. Each gap must be analyzed to determine the sequence in which they should be attacked along with the time and resources required to close those gaps.

Value Opportunity

There are many facets of value opportunity that result from a transformation initiative. The benefits driven to the bottom line, the value to the customer that will increase both top and bottom line, and, no less important, the value to the employees in terms of quality of work life (i.e., how much less stressful the work becomes with time freed up to further improve the business). Each element of Business Excellence Planning can be represented by a value statement. Each of those can then be added up to create the business case.

Prioritize

The priority of each individual improvement opportunity must be established in terms of business impact, financial benefit, time to realize the benefit, and resources required. An individual element's priority might be higher than or less than that of the entire project. The bottom line is that the overall business case will determine the priority of the entire project. If an individual improvement element has a priority that delays implementation of other elements of the Business Excellence Planning initiative, its priority must be raised to the level that allows that project to move forward without delaying the remainder of the implementation.

The Case for Change

The case for change is the critical step in the Lead phase, and in the entire Proven Path. We have seen company Presidents/Managing Directors stand up and give the direction to launch the transformation initiative without a business case for moving forward. Initially, this is very encouraging; the project gets off the ground quickly with clear Leadership direction right from the top. A serious, perhaps even fatal, disadvantage is that the cost of delay (see Chapter 11) is not understood by Leadership. Unnecessary and very expensive delays are caused by other less important issues without the necessary level of urgency to resolve them and get back to the transformation initiative and its benefits, which far outweigh the impact of the minor issues causing the delay. Leadership must determine, and keep in front of them, the case for change.

More often, however, most advocates of Business Excellence Planning do not have the support of a committed leadership team, at least initially. The processes outlined in previous chapters are proven and will improve your company's performance. The first question that comes into the minds of most who contemplate the daunting implementation of Business Excellence Planning is how to get Leadership on board. We have heard the question thousands of times when delivering workshops, a very appropriate question. The whole leadership team must support the transformation, and it must be driven from the very top – the President. The challenge is getting Leadership not only interested but committed (recall the pig and chicken story) to lead the transformation. To do this it is recommended to show them how these improvements affect the bottom line and coach them in developing the specific benefits for their business. Chapter 15, Finance, Integrated and Proactive, presented a cost/benefit analysis used with many companies. The return on investment of 1,000–2,000% always gets Leadership's attention. At a large equipment manufacturing division, there was resistance to implementing Business Excellence Planning. The cost of delay absolutely captured leadership's attention and commitment. During a workshop, their cost of delay was developed with rough numbers, which was over $1 million per workday. That, in addition to their increased understanding of how they could realize the benefits of Business Excellence Planning, resulted in rapid agreement to begin implementing Unparalleled Business Planning and Execution Practices. The key to a compelling cost of delay is the use of the company's numbers developed by the company with coaching on the process. Recall the difference between coaching and consulting?

Organization for Change

Figure 19.9 represents a proven implementation structure. No surprise: it all starts with the leadership Champion and Steering Team made up of direct reports. Often a Champion agrees to that role, but that is not enough. The Champion must demonstrate ownership by ensuring that each Steering Team member is accountable for successful implementation in their assigned areas.

The Transformation Leader reports to the Champion, participates and facilitates the Steering Team meetings, and leads the Transformation Team activities and meetings. The Integration Team is made up of leaders of each transformation task team. These task team leaders are accountable for the transformation activities, including due dates, in their assigned transformation processes, such as IBP, Capacity Planning, Master Scheduling, and so forth. The task teams, made up of representatives from each area accountable for redesigning the processes assigned and for closing gaps identified in the diagnostic, can create temporary spin-off task teams to recommend solutions for specific problems within their areas of accountability.

Integration Team member selection is extremely important. Start with the best people since they will be designing the processes used to run the company for the next 20 years or even longer. Individuals selected indicate how serious

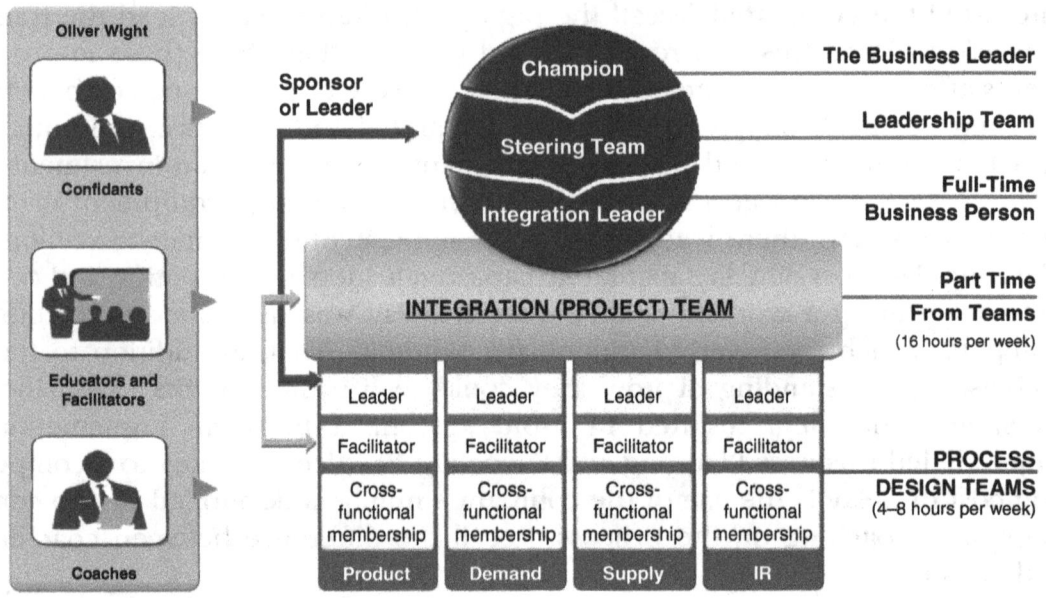

FIGURE 19.9 Organization for Transformational Change

Source: © Oliver Wight International.

Leadership is about successful transformation; no one wants to give up their best people for the average time commitments indicated in Figure 19.9. The owners of each process needs to ask themselves who they absolutely can't do without for populating the Transformation Team and also for the associated task teams. The individual most difficult to give up is the best Transformation Team representative. This is the person who is going to redesign the processes and disciplines that will deliver significant gains in the way the company operates.

While the average times required of individuals during the transformation are shown in Figure 19.9, their responsibilities are not necessarily part-time. If this work is added to these key employees' responsibilities, they must still do their day-to-day job but now are expected to spend a few more hours every day on the transformation initiative. That, in our experience, can be disastrous. These employees are typically working longer than a normal day just to get their work done in a culture of churn and firefighting. Asking them to then take on more work just doesn't compute. Despite their level of commitment and excitement about the project, they will fall short of meeting their project responsibilities, other team members will be resentful, and the transformation will fall behind schedule. A more successful approach is to define what is needed from these individuals and have them work full time until those responsibilities have been completed. Treat them as if there were going on vacation, and fill in behind them until their project work is completed. The cost of delay should make this an easy decision. As one company President used to say, *"Speed kills the competition!"*

When an organization is complex, identified gaps are quite large and the processes will require more time for redesign and implementation; backfilling for team members as if the person were on vacation may not be a viable approach. Resource requirements in these situations will increase for a period before falling back to original requirements or even lower. An approach to backfilling in these situations can be to replace that person with the next-best person and continue that through all organization levels. To replace the people at the lowest organization levels, hire temporary employees until the resource requirements decline. The reasons for this approach are numerous, and there are variations of this approach.

- **New Processes:** People typically resist change. Who better to design and implement the change than the person who is going to be responsible for it in the future? That person is typically the boss. If it is not, then you had better not put the old boss back in charge because there is little chance the change will be successful. The boss going forward is the best person to ensure involvement/commitment and success.
- **Additional Staffing:** If the additional staffing exceeds what can be absorbed immediately, start sequentially with the processes that have the largest gaps and/or the greatest bottom-line benefit.
- **Temporary Promotions:** Promotions, even temporary promotions, encourage those promoted to spring to life trying to demonstrate their capabilities.
- **Temporary Assignments:** Those moved to temporary Transformation Team assignments to design and implement new processes and disciplines (especially the bosses) are motivated to get the job done quickly and get back to their regular jobs.
- **Excitement:** All seeing the leadership commitment and focus to make these organization changes and seeing the improvements and resulting growth of the company become excited and continue the shift of the population from resistant to supportive.

Milestone Planning

Based upon diagnostic findings, elements of the Business Excellence Planning, called Milestones, are arranged in an improvement sequence based upon size of gap, bottom-line impact, time to benefit, and resource availability. With nearly every client, attacking the entire Class A Standard at the same time is neither possible nor necessary. Rather, a company can focus its transformation on specific Milestones, sequentially, on its journey to Class A. The content of each Milestone is defined in an Oliver Wight Class A Milestone Workbook, Figure 19.12, which clearly defines the Unparalleled Business Planning and Execution Practices that must be achieved to maximize the transformation benefits of that Milestone. A gap-closing project plan is then developed by the assigned Transformation Task Team and approved by the Steering Team. Milestone-related measures become important in tracking Milestone achievements and progress. No matter the perception of improvements achieved, if the targeted measures, as described in this book, are not achieved, the transformation is not complete, and the Milestone has not been achieved. If the measurement targets have not been met, the Transformation Team's project plan must be modified or, if the issue is process discipline, compliance must be enforced. Each Milestone Transformation Team must include a specifically named leader, an executive owner to ensure accountability, and a completion date if there is to be accountability.

"Transform" Phase Descriptions: Establish Teams and Agents for Change

Knowledge Transfer

To differentiate between Business Excellence Planning education and training:

- **Education** is about learning the Unparalleled Business Planning and Execution Practices based upon documented successes with client companies and how those Unparalleled Business Planning and Execution Practices can be applied in your company.
- **Training** is about the tactical procedures used to support Unparalleled Business Planning and Execution Practices, such as the specific transactions required in your planning system.

One global client's Finance organization attributed 90% of the significant total bottom-line reoccurring benefits to be the result of education on the new ways of working and the redesigned business processes. They only afforded 10% to the planning system software; although the software is essential, it is the education presented in the Transform phase that:

- **Enables** the participants to redesign, implement, and operate following Unparalleled Business Planning and Execution Practices.
- **Clarifies** the real transformation benefits.
- **Builds** confidence and enthusiasm.
- **Establishes** a new vision of integrated business processes.

Education must provide knowledge but, much more importantly, must also establish the requirement for behavior change. Too often, people attend education to improve the way they operate but fall right back into their old behaviors. The half-life of unsupported education is very, very short. To facilitate change, at the end of each section of an education workshop, there must be time allocated for the team to list action items, dates, and accountabilities for achieving the required change.

Baseline Assessment

On occasion, a company's Leadership Team requires only a simple diagnostic to be conducted during the Lead phase. But to tailor education materials to enable a relevant Application Workshops, a more detailed "Baseline Assessment" is required. While the Lead phase diagnostic is conducted through a series of interviews, with a review of recent results, the Baseline Milestone Assessment is conducted with a specific focus on the business area identified as an opportunity during the Lead Phase Diagnostic, asking more detailed and focused but from a much broader cross-section of the employees. These discussions provide much more detailed information:

- **Knowledge** about the current education level.
- **Insights** about information-sharing effectiveness.
- **A view** of the current culture.
- **Examples** of the current Leadership style.
- **Information** about the current processes, their performance levels, and their integration.

- **Understanding** of the current performance scorecards and their use.
- **Accountability** for meeting performance objectives and project due dates.
- **And** much more related to the Milestone definitions.

With this information, a more informed business maturity level can be determined, from which the Application Workshops required to support the selected implementation can be designed and used.

As the implementation progresses, clients are encouraged to conduct periodic self-assessments against the Milestones. This enables the Teams to focus time and resources on the lower-scoring elements, to more quickly elevate the overall Milestone score.

Apply

With the Education and Baseline Assessment completed, Transformation Task Teams can apply their new knowledge in a series of Application Workshops, carefully tailored to the company's most pressing business needs. Transformation Workshops utilize multifunctional teams that are carefully selected to involve representatives capable of working with all the Milestone topics to ensure the implementation of valid designs that are understood and have clear ownership. To sign off these new ways of working, a detailed review is scheduled to enable approval by the Team's Process Owner, Steering Team, and Leadership.

"Own" Phase Descriptions: Leverage Capability and Behavior Change

Cascade Education

With process redesigns completed, the next major challenge is transferring knowledge from the Transformation Team down through the entire organization. Done well, this ensures transformation success. No surprise that it starts with education. First there must be high-level education for everyone involved with Business Excellence Planning and how all the pieces fit together. This is followed by more detailed and focused education and training in the new ways of working for each area, and who will ultimately own and work the new processes, systems, and behavioral needs. This part of the Proven Path is referred to as "Cascade Education" designed to inform and involve the entire company.

Cascade Education is conducted through a series of workshops with the following objectives:

- **Understand** the vision and benefits of the new ways of working.
- **Learn** the new processes, disciplines, and how they apply to areas of the business.
- **Create** safe environments allowing issues to be raised.
- **Resolve** misunderstanding and issues.
- **Capture** and document all decisions that have been made.
- **Generate** action plans to carry out the implementation.
- **Follow up**, tracking action plans to ensure issues are resolved.

People appointed to lead these Cascade Education Workshops should be:

- **Enthusiastic** about the transformation.
- **Prepared** to lead effective meetings.
- **Knowledgeable** about the area of the business represented by the participants.
- **Experienced** with the maturity of current processes and challenges to be overcome.
- **Familiar** with the attendees.
- **Empowered** to make changes and hold people accountable for the new processes.

Recognizing that this is a tall order, people who might be considered to lead the Cascade Education Workshops could be from the:

- **Training Department:** While these individuals could be enthusiastic about the transformation and could be coached to prepare them, people from the training department fail all the remaining criteria.
- **Outside:** Engaging external experts who possess the required knowledge and are enthusiastic about the transformation because they have personally experienced the benefits and are more than prepared, but, as with training department personnel, fail all other criteria.
- **Inside:** This person could be an authority on the processes, such as a Transformation Team Leader. But even though they work in the area, they might not have the required knowledge of specific, detailed business

processes or the people in the meeting and may not have the authority to hold people accountable.

- **Team Leader or Supervisor:** These individuals meet all the criteria except, perhaps, enthusiasm and preparation. The Transformation Team must build their enthusiasm and prepare those selected to lead the Business Meetings. If this is not possible a critical problem has been identified well in advance and must be addressed quickly.

Remember that Cascade Education Workshop effectiveness is a leading indicator of implementation success or failure. Selection of effective deliverers is critical. To ensure sustainable change, these deliverers must be from within the company. Difficulty in identifying or freeing up these individuals represents a serious issue that must be escalated to the Steering Team with recommendations for resolution.

Implement

To transfer the new business processes, procedures, measures, roles, and responsibilities to be used in running the business to the body of the organization, the schedule for Cascade Education, explained above, runs in parallel with Implementation to ensure all employees learn about the new ways of working immediately prior to having to own and follow them. How much detail the Cascade Education provides depends upon the areas fit into the organization, complexity of the new procedures in those areas, and upon the individuals' authority level.

There are many barriers to change that normally arise during implementation; these must be systematically addressed through the use and full deployment of the Proven Path. These barriers can encompass:

- **Attitudes:** Past experiences in conflict with the new ways of working.
- **Feelings:** Hidden agendas that might relate to not being selected for the Transformation Team.
- **History:** "We have always done it this way, and I'm not about to change now."
- **Fears:** Being frightened about not being able to learn the new skills required.
- **Excuses:** Concern that the new, more formal processes will eliminate excuses for poor performance.
- **Failures:** "We tried this years ago and it was a failure, as we told Leadership it would."

- **Change:** "Why should I bother? Leadership will change their minds in a few years!"
- **Commitment:** Lack of commitment to the new ways of working. "Let's just wait and see what happens!"
- **Paradigms:** "I tried to support changes last time and was ridiculed then. Never again!"

Cascade Education provides broad knowledge of the new ways of working to the entire company, thus providing an opportunity to counter these barriers to change. To reinforce Leadership's commitment to change, it is important to eliminate old meetings, processes, measures, and so forth, to make certain people do not continue using them. Leave them in place and they will undermine the success of the new.

Assess Progress and Realize Value

As implementation is completed area by area and Milestone by Milestone, the Steering Team, Transformation Leader, and Transformation Teams' work continues to drive progress against transformation objectives, behavior change. So, measures and benefits must be tracked to ensure that the redesigned processes are delivering the expected value. Results against objectives will identify gaps and then gap-closing plans must be developed for review with the Steering Team. It may be that the new business processes must be adjusted, more education provided, or behaviors not in compliance with the new ways of working confronted. The end objective is to realize or even exceed (a very common outcome) the expected value of the transformation initiative. Over time, the Transformation Team and Leader roles are eliminated; maintenance and continuous improvement responsibilities of each Milestone fall to the respective Process Owner and Process Leader.

Milestone Assessment

Most of our clients elect to have us provide a formal review of their progress against Milestone requirements resulting in awarding of an Oliver Wight Class A certification – a great recognition for all who contributed to the transformation. This assessment includes a review of the documentation (policies, procedures, measures, roles, etc.), and a review of actions taken when results were out of agreed tolerance. Process leaders describe the changes made and the benefits achieved. A final assessment is normally preceded by a preassessment a few months before the scheduled final assessment to allow any remaining gaps to be identified and closed. The final assessment is nearly always successful when the recommendations in this book are followed and implementation coaches periodically visit during the transformation. Outside business partners, such as suppliers or customers, are sometimes invited to share how the work has improved their planning and bottom-line results. Ultimately, the Milestone Assessment results in a formal celebration of the great work accomplished and improved results delivered.

Transition, Embed, Sustain, and Mature

The transformation is complete, and the output from all the work is captured in the company's formal documentation, as indicated by Figure 19.10, which makes it more sustainable; however, the work continues. Process Owners and Leaders who are involved in the new ways of working must continue to improve results, simplify the business processes, educate those joining the organization, sustain the gains made, reach for higher maturity levels, and take on additional Milestones. The transformation work has freed up resources from the need to continuously fight fires, so these continuous improvement activities require no additional staffing. Those who enjoy an improved quality of work life now have time they can dedicate to improving quality, reducing costs, increasing productivity, and conducting joint improvement projects with customers and suppliers. There will be new products, new territories, new customers, and

FIGURE 19.10 Business Process Redesign – The Deliverables
Source: © Oliver Wight International.

new suppliers that can now be integrated into the business with much less disruption.

Achieving Oliver Wight Class A

An important guide to support the implementation of Business Excellence Planning is *The Oliver Wight Class A Standard for Business Excellence*, Figure 19.11. This Standard contains an excellent compilation of definitions, descriptions, roles, behaviors, and measures that are used in assessing the maturity of current processes, allowing the identification of gaps that must be closed to achieve the benefits of Class A. The Standard's content can also be used by the Transformation Team in developing new processes and ways of working.

Why Class A? Results have shown, again and again, that Oliver Wight Class A Processes and Behaviors result in significant improvement in customer service and bottom-line results at a lower cost. As stated earlier in this chapter,

FIGURE 19.11 The Oliver Wight Class A Standard for Business Excellence

formal recognition of having achieved the Oliver Wight Class A Standard for the selected Milestones results in a great deal of recognition and pride associated with achieving this award.

There is a strong relationship between Oliver Wight Class A and business maturity. The concept of business maturity has been around since the early 1990s when the Oliver Wight Company was invited by Harvard Business School to commercialize a theoretical study they had completed on Beretta, the Italian gun company that had received an order to supply the American Army with guns in preference to the American company, Smith & Wesson, headquartered in Springfield, Massachusetts.

This study resulted in the Business Maturity Map, and over the years the Oliver Wight messages have evolved to focus on the first two phases, which is the capability most companies operate with today. Progressing through the first two phases results in overall KPI performance approaching percentile perfection near the top of Phase 2. For more detail see Chapter 1.

From the early 1970s clients consistently asked, "How well are we doing?," which was the catalyst for Oliver Wight himself to develop the first Oliver Wight Checklist. That first version of the Checklist was a single piece of paper listing 20 questions to be answered either yes or no. If the response to all questions was yes, then clients were confirmed as being in "Good Shape."

Since then there have been six further versions of the Checklist, the latest now titled *The Oliver Wight Class A Standard for Business Excellence, Seventh Edition.*

Comparing the first 20-question Checklist to the Seventh Edition Standard, there are now nine chapters with approximately 750 individual definitions of business maturity reflecting requirements at the top of Phase 2.

As *The Oliver Wight Class A Standard for Business Excellence* is positioned at the top of Phase 2 Business Maturity, a huge leap for nearly every company, Oliver Wight developed a series of Milestone Workbooks to support a journey to Class A. They recognize that the beginning for different companies may be at a lower level of business maturity. The Milestones Workbooks (see Figure 19.12) are made available to support companies on their journey through Phase 1, with a separate suite of Milestone Workbooks to support a journey through Phase 2.

These Milestone Workbooks are designed to focus specifically on those definitions from the *Standard* that would enable Class A processes for the business process in focus, including definitions from each of the other nine

FIGURE 19.12 Oliver Wight Milestone Workbooks

chapters. The Workbooks are deliberately designed to extract definitions from the other chapters to drive the integration of other disciplines because implementations cannot be successful just focusing on one chapter on its own. This compilation of definitions is essential to ensure integration across all Business Excellence Planning processes. For a more in-depth discussion, see *An Executive's Guide to Achieving Class A Business Excellence* (Figure 19.13), an Oliver Wight publication available through the Oliver Wight website.

Ongoing Staffing Levels

Throughout this book we have highlighted the need to do a significantly better job of planning and execution, which results in enormous bottom-line benefits. As a consequence of these improvements fewer people will be needed when plans are valid and executed at 95% efficiency, when the need for firefighting is dramatically reduced, if not eliminated entirely. A large electronics client embarked on an initiative to move all divisions to Class A. Some of its divisions were successful. The transformation freed up 2,000 people. The question is, what you do with the people freed up? There are many alternatives, but by far the best one is for the people freed up to be retrained in other disciplines to support increased demand generated by improved customer service and reduced prices. The entire transformation initiative must be approached with

FIGURE 19.13 *An Executive's Guide to Achieving Class A Business Excellence*

that end in mind so that employees do not feel threatened but become excited about new opportunities ahead of them.

A Message from Our History, Still Relevant Today – The ABCs of Integration

Oliver Wight, when teaching and coaching clients, constantly referenced the ABCs of Business Integration (see Figure 19.14). He said, "All three are needed, but their impact is very different." A is very high, B is high, and C is important as follows:

- **A – People are the A item.** People, based upon Unparalleled Business Planning and Execution Practices, redesign their business processes, educate others, implement the redesigned processes, and provide the discipline to follow them. They not only select the software but decide which software capabilities to use to best support the processes. To select the software or develop the Unparalleled Business Planning and Execution

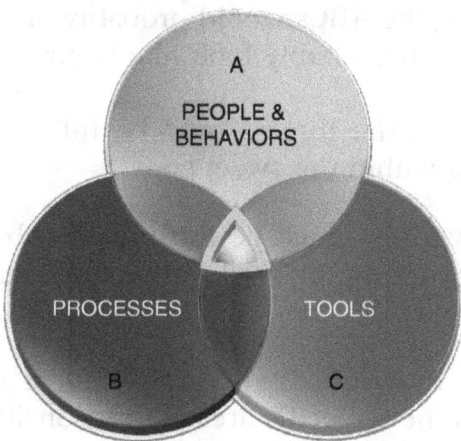

FIGURE 19.14 Key Components of Integration Linked Back to an Original OW Message
Source: © Oliver Wight International.

Practices they must receive education on those Unparalleled Business Planning and Execution Practices. That education must be cascaded down through the workforce, so everyone understands their roles and responsibilities and how they contribute to their company's success.

- **B – The processes.** Improved processes separate excellent companies from all the others. Most of this book is about the processes that we consistently call Unparalleled Business Planning and Execution Practices. They are all tried and proven and are continuously improved, as confirmed by the current Class A Standard, now in its Seventh Edition, over the past 50 years.
- **C – The tools and software.** No, you cannot operate Business Excellence Planning without the tools, but there are many great options. It is like selecting a car to get to work. Everyone has a preferred vehicle, but most get the job done. The basic tool requirements have been discussed each chapter.

The importance of integrating these ABCs was discussed early in this chapter, highlighting the need to maximize their overlap (integration) to operate in the ever-growing sweet spot. Linking this integration to business maturity:

- At the bottom of Phase 1, the ABCs would stand alone with no overlap and, hence, no sweet spot. In fact, C would displace A as the most important category.

▪ At the top of Phase 1, the ABCs would probably have been integrated, and their relationship would probably look like Figure 19.14 with a very small sweet spot.

▪ At the top of Phase 2, the three would be fully overlapping, with most operations occurring within the sweet spot.

As stated repeatedly, users must be the people who redesign and implement the new ways of working. User education and training must enable participants to:

▪ Understand how the redesigned processes work, at a high level overall and at a detailed level in their specific areas of responsibility.

▪ Understand other peoples' roles, responsibilities, and information needs. Some areas will require significant change and new responsibilities while the transformation will have a lesser impact on others. Education and training must be tailored with that in mind.

▪ Take ownership for their parts of the redesigned business processes. Each area will have its own performance measures; employees in those areas must understand how they contribute to those results and be able to take pride in their performance.

▪ Be accountable for:
  ▪ Education – Only the participant can fully understand what needs to happen in their area; that knowledge must be passed down from the Steering and Transformation Teams to the end users through Cascade Education.
  ▪ Implementation – End users must implement the new ways of working or they cannot be held accountable for the results; a less than perfect process will operate far better when ownership is established and accepted than a perfect one where there is no ownership.
  ▪ Results – End users must understand the targeted business results, measures to track and support those results, reasons for the measures, and how they impact the results.

▪ Understand their accountability for data accuracy – This includes practically everyone in the entire company.

▪ Be self-sufficient – *Employees redesign processes, implement them, and drive the transformation*, with coaching from those who have personally experienced such a transformation.

- Make deliberate haste – Delays in implementing the new ways of working can never be justified given the cost of delay; when barriers arise, resources must be redirected to overcome those barriers as quickly as possible.
- Accept nothing less than achieving Class A – While achieving Class A certification requires a very insignificant increase in investment, it significantly improves performance and bottom-line benefits and allows a company to formally recognize its employees for their accomplishment with Class A awards. As a coach there is nothing more rewarding that to see a client achieve all the benefits and then to see senior managers recognize their employees' accomplishments by conducting a Class A celebration. One client's General Manager went so far as having a high school band come to the facility and parade through the facility picking up the employees as they headed to the site of the celebration.

Summary

This book has provided not only a vision of what a great company is, how a transformation can be achieved with significant top- and bottom-line benefits and how it can improve quality of work life, but it has also provided insight into the details of the requirements and guidance on implementation. Hopefully, the book has provided an understanding of the importance of educating, training, empowering, and coaching people to enable and lead the transformation from a low Phase 1 maturity company to the top of Phase 2.

We wish you the same success each of us has experienced over the years, initially in our own companies and then with our clients.

If you would like to contact us, please feel free to do so. We would love to hear from you.

Jim Correll (jamesg.correll@gmail.com)
Lloyd Snowden (lloyd.snowden@oliverwight.com)
Jim Bentzley (bentzleyj@gmail.com)

For additional but more specific reading please visit the Oliver Wight Website and gain access to the extensive library of White Papers.

Glossary

This is not a traditional Glossary. We have defined all the terms as we wrote the book and have provided an index to make it easy to find the definitions without repeating them here. Nevertheless, we decided to create this Glossary of terms that are often used differently across countries, companies, and industries.

Demand Manager – Sometimes referred to as the Demand Planner, this person reports to the Sales and Marketing VP, or, in some organizations, the Commercial VP, and is responsible for Demand Planning covering the aggregate Demand Plan over the full planning horizon and Demand Control for execution of the near-term detailed plans in execution of the aggregate Demand Plan approved in the Management Business Review.

Family – Often a product family is referred to as a category, a segment, or an aggregate product level. This is the highest and most appropriate level company Leadership considers when viewing aggregate plans over the business planning horizon, a minimum of 24 to 36 months rolling with the Leadership focus on months 4 and beyond. Generally, the number of product families for a business should range between 5 and 15, with the families comprised of items that are similarly marketed and sold in order to keep the focus on engaging the commercial side of the business.

Finance – Finance is a part of every single box in the Business Excellence Planning models and must be committed and not involved.

Leadership – Deciding what to call the senior management level of a company was a challenge. Often this is the President and the direct report Vice Presidents, but Leadership, or Leadership Team, is a more current term used by many companies.

President – Rather than name the top level of an organization such as CEO, Managing Director, General Manager, and so on, again and again, we settled on the term President since this term is well understood. Your senior executive may have a different title, but if that person has the responsibilities described in the book, we are talking about the same person.

Product Manager – Sometimes referred to as the Product Planner or Initiative Master Planner, this person reports to the executive accountable for the content of the product/service portfolio and is responsible for ensuring product launch and product rationalization plans are updated at the beginning of each IBP cycle in support of the business strategy and to ensure portfolio changes are visible to Demand and Supply Planners and Finance.

Supply Manager – Sometimes referred to as the Supply Planner, this person reports to the Manufacturing or Supply Chain VP and is responsible for Supply Planning, both the aggregate Production Plan and aggregate Inventory Plan over the full planning horizon in support of the Demand Plan and the near-term Detailed Supply Plan for executing the Supply Plan approved in the Management Business Review.

Acronyms

ATO	Assemble-to-Order
ATP	Available-to-Promise
B2B	Business-to-Business
BEP	Business Excellence Planning
BET	Break-Even Time
BIC	Best in Class
BOM	Bill of Materials
CAPEX	Capital Expenditure
CEO	Chief Executive Officer
CFO	Chief Financial Officer
CLT	Cumulative Lead Time (Identified by the Cumulative or Planning Time Fence)
CMI	Co-Managed Inventory
COO	Chief Operating Officer
COGS	Cost of Goods Sold
CPFR	Collaborative Planning and Forecast Replenishment
CRM	Customer Requirements Management
CSF	Critical Success Factor
DC	Demand Control
DCP	Detailed Capacity Planning
DE	Demand Execution
DIFOT	Delivered in Full on Time

Dist	Distribution
DP	Demand Plan
DR	Demand Review (sometimes DMR, meaning Demand Management Review)
DTO	Design-to-Order
EBP	Enterprise Business Planning
EDI	Electronic Data Interchange
EMT	Emergency Time Fence (identified by the Firm Time Fence)
EOQ	Economic Order Quantity
ERP	Enterprise Resource Planning
ETF	Emergency Time Fence
ETO	Engineer to Order
FDA	Food and Drug Administration
FG	Finished Goods
FTF	Firm Time Fence
GM	General Manager
GMROI	Gross Margin Return on Investment
HR	Human Resources
IBP	Integrated Business Planning
IRA	Inventory Record Accuracy
IRR	Integrated Reconciliation Review
IT	Information Technology
ITP	Integrated Tactical Planning
KPI	Key Performance Indicator
LT	Lead Time
MAPE	Mean Absolute Percentage Error
MBR	Management Business Review
MD	Managing Director
MPDS	Master Product Development Schedule
MRP	Material Requirements Plan
MS	Master Schedule (sometimes MPS, meaning Master Production Schedule; sometimes MSS, meaning Master Supply Schedule)
MTO	Make-to-Order
MTS	Make-to-Stock
NPD	New Product Development
NPMP	New Product Master Plan
NPI	New Product Introduction
OH	On Hand

OPEC	Organization of the Petroleum Exporting Countries
OTIF	On Time in Full
OTIFD	On Time in Full Delivered
OTIFP	On Time in Full to Promise
OTIFR	On Time in Full to Request
OQ	Order Quantity
PAB	Projected Available Balance
P&L	Profit and Loss
P&PM	Product and Portfolio Management
PEST	Political, Environmental, Social, Technological
PMO	Project Management Office
PPD	Perfect Project Delivery
PPM	Planned Preventative Maintenance
PR	Product Review (sometimes PMR, meaning Product Management Review)
PGR	Projected Gross Requirements
QA	Quality Assurance
R&D	Research and Design or Research and Development
RCCP	Rough Cut Capacity Planning
RFID	Radio Frequency Identification
ROI	Return on Investment
RRP	Resource Requirements Planning
S&OP	Sales and Operations Planning
SBO	Strategic Business Objective
SC	Supply Chain
SKU	Stock-Keeping Unit or End Item (the item to be delivered to a customer)
SR	Supply Review (sometimes SCR, meaning Supply Chain Review)
SS	Safety Stock
SWOT	Successes, Weaknesses, Opportunities, Threats
TCO	Total Cost of Ownership
TY	Total Year
UCP	Unconstrained Demand Plan
USD	United States Dollar
VMI	Vendor-Managed Inventory
VP	Vice President
WAPE	Weighted Absolute Percentage Error
WIP	Work in Process or Work in Progress
WMAPE	Weighted Mean Absolute Percentage Error
YTD	Year to Date

About the Authors

James G. Correll

Jim Correll, a retired principal of Oliver Wight who started in 1984, served eight years as chairman of Oliver Wight Americas and co-chairman of Oliver Wight International. As a consultant, he has assisted more than 32 companies attaining Class A performance. These companies include numerous Caterpillar divisions, US Army Material Command and the four supporting Commands, Imperial Tobacco, General Dynamics Land Systems, Martin Marietta Astronautics, Boeing Portland, and Tektronix, Inc.

Jim gained his Class A experience as an employee of Hyster Company; Wagner Mining Equipment, a division of PACCAR; and Tektronix. At Tektronix he served as the Class A implementation manager for the component division. In that capacity, he developed a new organizational structure, implemented new software, and designed and delivered an effective educational training program for both the new software and the behavior changes required to obtain bottom-line results. Jim was the driving force behind the achievement of Class A in the Metal Products Division in less than one year.

A certified Fellow of APICS, Jim has served on the board of the Portland chapter and has spoken at APICS chapter meetings and international conferences, as well as at numerous other professional organizations. Jim is co-author of *An Executive's Guide to Achieving Class A Business Excellence*. He also co-authored *Achieving Class A Business Excellence: An Executive's Perspective* and *Gaining Control: Managing Capacity and Priorities*, third edition, and has written many articles that have appeared in professional periodicals. Jim earned a BS in Industrial Technology from Southern Illinois University.

Lloyd C. Snowden

Before joining Oliver Wight, Lloyd had over 20 years' experience in industry, during which he drove many company reorganizations from the strategic management process through all business processes to enable better delivery and customer satisfaction. Joining the Oliver Wight Team has enabled Lloyd to use all this experience to facilitate Class A programs in a broad cross-section of industries and using his own knowledge help develop the Oliver Wight messages. Using this material Lloyd has successfully supported a variety of organizations achieve Class A Certification and also Advanced Class A Certification.

At Oliver Wight

As an Oliver Wight Associate, Lloyd deploys his hands-on change management experience to drive improvements through Strategic Planning, Integrated Business Planning, Product and Portfolio Optimization, Supply Chain Optimization, and Behavior Change. With this particular people focus, Lloyd helps organizations harness the power of their employees to drive change that will be sustained through the implementation of non-people dependent processes.

Since 2003 Lloyd has been intimately involved with the development of the Oliver Wight Class A Checklist driving both the sixth and seventh edition publications, which saw the Checklist develop into a Standard supported by specific Checklists (the Milestone Workbooks) for all major Business Processes.

As part of the OW EAME Team, Lloyd served on the Management Team and as a result was selected for a two-year term on the Oliver Wight International Board.

Background

Lloyd's career started in Manufacturing, eventually broadening out to manage the End-to-End Supply Chain. These experiences enabled Lloyd to broaden his skill set, which created the opportunity to move into General Management and to his final role, of Managing Director, before joining Oliver Wight.

Lloyd graduated as a Mechanical Engineer in 1982, became a Chartered Engineer, and later a Fellow of the Institution of Mechanical Engineers (IMechE).

James Bentzley

Jim Bentzley has more than 20 years of executive leadership experience in supply chain, strategy planning, and operations management, having held leadership positions in the consumer, electronics, and medical products industries in both the branded and business-to-business landscapes at companies like Medtronic, Becton Dickinson, Kraft-Heinz Foods, TE Connectivity, and Acumed. He has implemented and run monthly Integrated Business Planning (IBP/Advanced S&OP) processes achieving multiple Class A performances and had responsibility for long-range product pipeline planning, sales forecasting and demand planning, sales team linkage with marketing plans, supply planning including inventory investment and capacity planning, and financial planning with scenario generation and trade-off analysis. Along the way he mentored dozens of executive leadership teams on IBP process implementation and leadership of the monthly executive business reviews. His efforts aided these teams in delivering significant revenue growth and unprecedented cost savings.

Jim has spoken at numerous APICS/ASCM chapters regarding IBP and has been a thought leader authoring articles on demand management ("The Overlooked Forecasting Flaw"), strategic planning ("The TAO of Strategic Planning") and change management ("Leveraging a 'No-Man' As Part of Change Management"). Jim earned an MS in Management from Troy University, a BS in Finance from Saint Joseph's University, and an Executive Leadership Certificate from Cornell University.

About Oliver Wight

Oliver Wight was a pioneer in planning processes. Ollie recognized the problems faced by companies and had a clear understanding of their needs. He was always looking to the future and finding ways to improve things.

Oliver Wight had two great gifts. He could take complicated subjects, unravel them, and make them simple.

More important, he had a sensitivity to people that broke down barriers. He had innovative ideas and could communicate them in a way that gained acceptance, commitment, and enthusiasm.

Somehow, in the early years of the computer revolution, the role of people was misplaced. Ollie made it his personal mission to put people back where they belong and to give them the understanding they need to use their new tools. Among his many enduring tenets is, "Computers are not the key to success, people are." This remains a core philosophy of The Oliver Wight Companies.

Oliver Wight used his gifts to build an enduring legacy in business processes. Nearly every company using planning processes and Ollie's philosophies, passed on through teaching, writing, and consulting, experienced significant increases in productivity, inventory turnover, customer service, and growth.

His emphasis on the people side of business solutions earned him a reputation as a leading thinker in business education.

Ollie once said, quite modestly, "I've left some footprints." Those who have chosen to follow them are better off both personally and professionally.

Oliver Wight was 53 years old when he passed away in 1983.

Books by Oliver Wight

1. *Achieving Class A Business Excellence: An Executive's Perspective* by Dennis Groves, Kevin Herbert, and Jim Correll
2. *An Executive's Guide to Achieving Class A Business Excellence* by Dennis Groves, Kevin Herbert, and Jim Correll
3. *Demand Management Best Practices: Process, Principles and Collaboration* by Colleen Crum with George E. Palmatier
4. *Distribution Resource Planning: The Gateway to True Quick Response and Continuous Replenishment* by André J. Martin
5. *Enterprise Sales and Operations Planning: Synchronizing Demand, Supply and Resources for Peak Performance* by George E. Palmatier with Colleen Crum
6. *Gaining Control: Managing Capacity and Priorities* by James G. Correll and Kevin Herbert
7. *Inventory Record Accuracy: Unleashing the Power of Cycle Counting* by Roger B. Brooks and Larry W. Wilson
8. *Master Scheduling: A Practical Guide to Competitive Manufacturing* by John F. Proud
9. *The Oliver Wight Class A Standard for Business Excellence, Seventh Edition*
10. *Purchasing in the 21st Century: A Guide to State-of-the-Art Techniques and Strategies* by John E. Shorr
11. *Supply Chain Collaboration: How to Implement CPFR® and Other Best Collaborative Practices* by Ronald Ireland with Colleen Crum
12. *The Transition from Sales and Operations Planning to Integrated Business Planning* by George E. Palmatier with Colleen Crum
13. *World Class Production and Inventory Management*, by Darryl V. Landvater

Index

NOTE: Page references in *italics* refer to figures.